PSYCHC ISSUES

VOL. VIII, No. 3   MONOGRAPH 31

ELSE FRENKEL-BRUNSWIK: SELECTED PAPERS

Edited by

NANETTE HEIMAN and JOAN GRANT

INTERNATIONAL UNIVERSITIES PRESS, INC.
239 Park Avenue South • New York, N. Y. 10003

Copyright © 1974, International Universities Press, Inc.

All rights reserved. No part of this book may be reproduced by any means, nor translated into a machine language, without the written permission of the publisher.

Library of Congress Cataloging in Publication Data

Brunswik, Else (Frenkel)
    Else Frenkel-Brunswik: selected papers.

    (Psychological issues, v. 8, no. 3. Monograph 31)
    Bibliography: p.
    1. Psychology—Addresses, essays, lectures.
2. Brunswik, Else (Frenkel) I. Series.
BF149.B75   155.2'08   73-8079
ISBN 0-8236-1645-2

Manufactured in the United States of America

PSYCHOLOGICAL ISSUES

HERBERT J. SCHLESINGER, *Editor*

Editorial Board

MARGARET BRENMAN   PHILIP S. HOLZMAN

ERIK H. ERIKSON   GARDNER LINDZEY

SIBYLLE ESCALONA   LESTER LUBORSKY

CHARLES FISHER   HARRY RAND

MERTON M. GILL   ROY SCHAFER

ROBERT R. HOLT   HERBERT J. SCHLESINGER

ROBERT S. WALLERSTEIN

SUZETTE H. ANNIN, *Editorial Assistant*

Subscription per Volume, $20.00
Single Copies of This Number $7.50

CONTENTS

Foreword
    by GARDNER MURPHY   1

Introduction
    by NANETTE HEIMAN AND JOAN GRANT   3

1 PSYCHOANALYSIS AND PERSONALITY RESEARCH   36

2 INTOLERANCE OF AMBIGUITY AS AN EMOTIONAL AND PERCEPTUAL PERSONALITY VARIABLE   58

3 PERSONALITY THEORY AND PERCEPTION   92

4 PSYCHOANALYSIS AND THE UNITY OF SCIENCE   161

5 INTERACTION OF PSYCHOLOGICAL AND SOCIOLOGICAL FACTORS IN POLITICAL BEHAVIOR   232

6 ENVIRONMENTAL CONTROLS AND THE IMPOVERISHMENT OF THOUGHT   261

7 SOME THEORETICAL AND EMPIRICAL ASPECTS OF THE PROBLEM OF VALUES   292

References   311

Else Frenkel-Brunswik: Descriptive Bibliography   319

Index   327

About the Editors   335

FOREWORD

GARDNER MURPHY

Else Frenkel-Brunswik was a person intensely loved by those who knew her, and reverently admired by thousands who knew her work. I shall add nothing here to the devoted labors of the editors in presenting an outline of her basic contributions. Rather, I will attempt to say briefly a word about her place in the psychology of the mid-twentieth century.

First, she was a vital and vigorous expression of the cultural science tradition of the German-speaking world as known since the eighteenth century, richly expressive of the belief that there is a kind of science that is truly science, which is concerned with thought and aspiration as well as with the movements of bodies in space. Her writings on psychoanalysis move easily and naturally into writings on politics and value systems, for she is at home in them all. She belonged to the Vienna that harbored and nourished these writings to an extraordinary development in the period between the two world wars, and she brought valuable seedlings to our American intellectual soil.

Second, she was profoundly concerned with bringing this powerful scientific tool, in which child development, psychoanalysis, history, and the social sciences all played their part, into contact with the great social illnesses of the day that are related to the irrationalities and hatreds characteristic of our time. She will probably be best known for her role in the study of the authoritarian personality. The fact remains, however, that this was merely one expression of an overriding intellectual, personal, and moral concern which lived in her all the years of her Viennese, and especially all the years of her Berkeley existence.

Third, it is impossible to say anything at all about Else Frenkel-Brunswik without reference to the depth of tragedy and the magnificence of her manner of transcending it. When we saw her in Berkeley in the summer of 1938, with her new husband, Egon, she was discovering all that was richest and most beautiful in the great world of eucalyptus and redwoods, freedom and aspiration, all seeming to her a kind of paradise which could not last. Of course it did not last. Of course there was suffering intrinsic in the situation and at times evident in the mortal illness and early death of Egon and of herself. Just the same, it was not only her intellectual work that was magnificent; it was herself.

INTRODUCTION

Midstream and immersed as we are, it is hard to realize the extent to which our work reflects the social and scientific issues of our times. It is only somewhat easier with time and distance. We see in the 28-year span of Else Frenkel-Brunswik's professional life—from 1930 to 1958—a reflection of a number of important developments in psychology, some of which are so taken for granted today that it is easy to forget that they have an only recent history. We are referring here to the impact of psychoanalysis and clinical data on psychology; the establishment of personality as a field of scientific inquiry; its attempt at convergence with other fields and methods within psychology, such as learning, perception, and social psychology; the trend toward interdisciplinary work linking psychology with such fields as anthropology, sociology, and political science; the impact of operationism; and the shift in psychology from the laboratory to the marketplace.

Frenkel-Brunswik was actively involved in these developments. She was among the first who argued for attention to the insights of psychoanalysis and then demonstrated ways of applying them in psychological study. She was part of a group that called attention to the role of personality in the development of social attitudes, and part of another group that was concerned with the relations between personality and cognitive functioning. She dealt with the problem of quantifying clinical material, and she studied distortions in the perception of self and others. She cut across disciplines to consider the role of personality in the functioning of social institutions. She devoted time to considerations of the scientific status of psychology in terms of a philosophy of science. She was concerned with the study of values.

For Frenkel-Brunswik, personality was not limited to motivational facts but included all aspects of the behavior of man in his social setting. She believed that all behavior is the province of the psychologist and that his ultimate responsibility is to integrate its many aspects into a coherent picture of the person. From this point of view she was critical of both the academic psychologist and the clinician. To the former she stated that psychology was being limited in its understanding of human behavior by its refusal to take account of aspects of it that were well-known in the clinic but difficult to verify experimentally. To the latter she maintained that surface behavior is as much a part of personality as is underlying motivation, and that the diagnosis of internal conflicts is important only as it helps in the understanding of behavioral achievements. She insisted on not being bound by an overrigid operationism; she demanded theoretical clarifications from herself and from others; she consistently attempted to deal with the full complexity of human behavior.

In some sectors of psychology, the battles in which Frenkel-Brunswik fought are almost over now: personality today is an acknowledged field of psychological inquiry; it has assimilated from psychoanalysis what it can use at present; psychology has extended the range of its subject matter to include many more aspects of man as well as his transactions with his social environment; it is broadening its concept of operationism.

But if the specific issues in which Frenkel-Brunswik was involved are no longer of central concern to psychologists, we are far from having achieved the integration for which she was working. Psychology continues to be faced with what perhaps may always be a basic dichotomy in its ranks—a conflict between those who seek to establish psychology as unquestionably scientific and those who are willing to yield scientific rigor for the sake of dealing with the totality of human behavior. Throughout the years this division has appeared in one guise or another. Though divisions may be inherent in the dialectic nature of scientific development, we hope for a day when James's tough- and tender-minded types are blended into a truly scientific humanism and we can advance to a new and more fruitful antinomy.

The seven papers selected for this publication emphasize Frenkel-Brunswik's theoretical contributions. Though her major empirical studies have been omitted, they are liberally quoted in the papers included here. The following biographical material is intended to put these papers into some historical perspective, both in terms of her own development and in terms of the developments in psychology during the time in which she wrote.[1]

Professional Biography

Else Frenkel was born in Lemberg, Austria, in 1908. She received a Ph.D. in psychology at the University of Vienna under the direction of Karl Bühler in 1930. One of the great intellectual centers of the world, Vienna in the 1930s offered her contact with the innovators of logical positivism and psychoanalysis as well as with the major figures in the controversy between the latter-day representatives of associationism and Gestalt psychology.

From 1931 to 1938 Frenkel was lecturer and research associate in the Psychological Institute of the University of Vienna, where she worked with Charlotte Bühler.

She fled Austria shortly after the German invasion in 1938 and came to this country. Here she married Egon Brunswik, who had also been on the Psychological Institute staff. Brunswik had met and worked with Edward Tolman during the latter's visit at the University of Vienna in 1933, and it was Tolman who was in great part responsible for inviting Brunswik to the University of California in 1937. Brunswik remained a professor in the psychology department there until his untimely death in 1955. Frenkel-Brunswik took a position as a research psychologist in the university's Institute of Child Welfare,[2] then under the direction of Harold E. Jones, and remained on its staff, part- or full-time, until her death in 1958. At the Institute she worked first on the Adolescent Study directed by Jones and later on the Guidance Study under the direction of Jean Walker MacFarlane.

In 1942 she received a Social Science Research Council fellowship which allowed her to pursue her interests in anthropology, sociology, and psychoanalysis. She spent part of that year in Chicago attending classes and seminars in these fields; the last three months of the fellowship year were spent working with schizophrenics at the then new Langley Porter Neuropsychiatric Insti-

---

[1] For a complete list of Frenkel-Brunswik's publications, see Descriptive Bibliography, p. 319.
[2] Now the Institute of Human Development.

tute in San Francisco and in studying with Alfred Kroeber at the University of California's anthropology department.

Shortly after her fellowship year, Frenkel-Brunswik was appointed lecturer in the psychology department at the University of California. There she gave a series of joint seminars in perception and personality with David Krech and later with Richard Crutchfield.

From 1944 to 1947 Frenkel-Brunswik was a senior staff member of the Berkeley Public Opinion Study, the group which in collaboration with the Institute of Social Research produced *The Authoritarian Personality* (Adorno et al., 1950). The same year that she began her work with Theodor Adorno, Daniel Levinson, and Nevitt Sanford on the adult authoritarian personality, she began an independent study on racial discrimination in children at the Institute of Child Welfare. In 1947 she became a research psychologist and psychotherapist at Cowell Memorial Hospital in Berkeley, the university's student health service.

In 1950 Frenkel-Brunswik received a Rockefeller Foundation traveling grant for the purpose of reporting on the status of European psychology and psychologists. While in Europe she lectured and was consultant to the staff of the Institute of Social Research at the University of Oslo, where she was later to return for a year as a Fulbright research scholar. January and February of 1952 were spent at the Department of Philosophy at the University of Michigan in discussions and seminars on the topic of language and symbolism.

In 1953 she began a study on adjustments to aging at the University of California's Institute of Industrial Relations, and she was working on this study at the time of her death. The study, which was conceived and directed by Frenkel-Brunswik, was ultimately published by her co-workers, Suzanne Reichard, Florine Livson, and Paul G. Petersen (1962), under the title of *Aging and Personality*.

From 1954 to 1955 Frenkel-Brunswik was a Fellow at the Center for Advanced Study at Stanford, California; others participating that year were Harold Lasswell, Clyde Kluckhohn, Paul Lazarsfeld, Ludwig von Bertalanffy, Franz Alexander, and Eugene Burdick.

The year 1955 turned out to be a tragic one for Frenkel-Brunswik; it was toward the end of her time at the Center that her husband, Egon Brunswik, died.

Frenkel-Brunswik accepted a Fulbright research fellowship at the University of Oslo for the academic year 1956-1957. There she gave seminars at the Institute of Philosophy, the Institute of Sociology, the Institute of Psychology, and the Institute of Social Research.

Frenkel-Brunswik's broadness of commitments is expressed in her memberships in the American Psychological Association, the American Sociological Association, The American Philosophical Association, the American Anthropological Association, and the San Francisco Psychoanalytic Society. In the American Psychological Association, she was a diplomate in clinical psychology, a member of the Division of Developmental Psychology, council-member-elect in the Society for the Psychological Study of Social Issues (1953-1959), and president-elect of the Division of Personality and Social Psychology (1957-1958).

Frenkel-Brunswik died in the spring of 1958, before her fiftieth birthday.

Vienna: 1931-1938

Frenkel's first publication, "Atomismus und Mechanismus in der Assoziationspsychologie" (1931a), was her dissertation at the University of Vienna. This paper, in the tradition of early twentieth-century German psychology, drew heavily on the history of ideas as it related to psychology. In it, Frenkel—already influenced by logical positivism—attempted a logical analysis of association psychology, particularly its basic principle of contiguity. In a letter of October 13, 1953, to a colleague, Paul Lazarsfeld, she sums up the intention of this work as follows:

> As you know, Karl Bühler in his book on the crisis in psychology deplored the fact that at that time more modern movements such as Gestalt psychology had turned too radically against the older forms of psychology, and he advocated a synthesis between the older and the newer movements. In this spirit my doctor's dissertation tried to re-establish the validity of some of the older principles, at the same time showing that the total rejection of association psychology was partly due to a misunderstanding and distorted view of that school.

Frenkel's interest in theory, her search for theoretical clarifications, and her tendency to synthesize and integrate differing points of view were to remain primary concerns throughout her work.

After receiving her degree, Frenkel took a position as lecturer and research associate at the University of Vienna's Psychological Institute and there devoted herself to a study of biographical psychology. This project was carried out under the direction of one of the early workers in the field of developmental psychology, Charlotte Bühler. Bühler was interested in general principles of development. She was looking for psychological laws which were as potent as the biological laws of development, and she thought that the psychological ones would closely follow the biological ones. The purpose of the biographical studies was to lay an empirical base for the phases of psychological development in the life span.

Frenkel's contribution to this work was reported in three articles: "Lebenslauf, Leistung, und Erfolg" (1931b), "Studies in Biographical Psychology" (1936),[3] and "Wunsch und Pflicht im Aufbau des Menschlichen Lebens" (Frenkel and Weisskopf, 1937).[4]

These papers are based upon a study in which the biographies of 400 persons, living and dead, are individually analyzed and compared with one another.[5] In the phenomenological tradition, the investigators used what the subjects had to say about themselves, culling information from diaries, letters, and, where possible, interviews. For each subject this information was broken down into three groupings: his actual behavior or activities; his reported subjective experiences; and his accomplishments and productions. A life-span profile on each of the three areas was derived for each subject, and the subjects were then compared on each of the three profiles. In addition, a typology based upon the combined profiles for each subject was derived, and the subjects were compared on these too.

Results indicate five rather sharply demarcated phases through which every person passes in the course of life.[6] These phases lag

---

[3] This article was translated from the German and published in this country.

[4] This monograph is summarized and reported in two articles published in this country (Frenkel-Brunswik, 1950, 1952a).

[5] In a psychology gone sedate, it is refreshing to note that the subjects included such colorful notables as Queen Victoria, Liszt, Andrew Carnegie, John D. Rockefeller, Casanova, Beau Brummell, Jenny Lind, Verdi, Tolstoy, Bismarck, Leibniz, Kant, Hegel, Bruckner, Mozart, Caruso, Goethe, and Goethe's mother.

[6] The results are not unlike an antique version of Erikson's (1950) eight stages of psychosocial development.

somewhat behind the biological phases from growth to decline, a result that suggested to the investigators the presence of some factors in psychological development which account for the lag and which are independent of biological functioning. It is suggested that the factors which modify biological phases include such things as experience, training, interests, attitudes toward life, life goals, and achievements.[7]

These three papers introduce what was to become an abiding interest of Frenkel's: the study of personality from a developmental point of view. Though her later approach to personality is radically different from the approach in the biographical studies, many of the building stones of her new psychology can be found in them: a healthy respect for phenomenological and behavioral data; concern with achievements and adjustments; the use of a wide variety of information in the exploration of personality.

It was in the last of the three papers on biographical study that Frenkel's doubts about taking conscious phenomena and verbalizations at their face value were first expressed. Interestingly enough, these appeared in small print in the chapter on justification of the method. It was to this point that her following two studies addressed themselves. Of the two, "Ichideal und Selbstbeurteilung in Objektiver Kontrolle" (1938) and "Mechanisms of Self-Deception" (1939), the second is by far the more comprehensive.[8] This study aimed at an experimental investigation of illusions about oneself and also sought to discover formal criteria that might be used for diagnosing such illusions. It was based upon a comparison between observations of the actual conduct of a group of students and various statements made by these students about their own behavior. It seems likely that this study expressed her growing dissatisfaction with an approach that limited itself to surface phenomena taken at face value.

---

[7]In suggesting some applications of their results the investigators raised the possibility of a "psychological quotient" or maturity measure based upon a comparison of chronological age with "psychological age." More extravagant was their suggestion that their results might be used to predict length of life. They had found that, in some cases, persons who died relatively young had achieved "psychological ages" much beyond their chronological age. By comparing such cases with those who died late, they thought they might be able to come up with some measures that could differentiate the two groups, and thus predict longevity.

[8]This study is reported rather fully in the present volume in Chapter 3, "Personality Theory and Perception."

In this study Frenkel attempted to demonstrate that self-report is subject to distortion and that it is subject to distortion in specific ways. Mechanisms of self-deception included such things as overemphasis, distortion into the opposite, omission, and diminishing and justifying defects. One can see in this paper the seeds of later emphasis upon formal characteristics of personality (as opposed to content) and, perhaps of greater importance, an early reference to a concept which was to become central to her conceptualizations about personality, i.e., distortion into the opposite, a concept which when reworked and understood within a psychoanalytic framework became "closeness of opposites."

Though written and published in America, most of the work on "Mechanisms of Self-Deception" was done in Vienna. It was interrupted in 1938 when Frenkel fled the Nazi Anschluss of Austria.

PSYCHOANALYSIS AND PSYCHOLOGY: 1940

The first paper in this collection, "Psychoanalysis and Personality Research," was written for a "Symposium on Psychoanalysis by Analyzed Experimental Psychologists." The symposium was edited by Gordon Allport and first appeared in the *Journal of Abnormal and Social Psychology* in 1940, along with contributions by Edwin Boring, Carney Landis, J. F. Brown, Raymond R. Willoughby, Percival M. Symonds, Henry Murray, and David Shakow, and with comments by two psychoanalysts, Hans Sachs and Franz Alexander.

It was Freud's death the year before that gave impetus to attempts such as this to evaluate psychoanalysis as a branch of scientific psychology. Not that psychoanalysis was new to psychology. By 1940, American psychology had had more than 35 years of exposure to psychoanalysis. Articles on psychoanalysis had been appearing in the psychology journals as early as 1906. In 1909 Freud's official recognition by American psychology came in the form of an invitation by G. Stanley Hall to participate in the twentieth anniversary celebration of Clark University. At those meetings Freud, Jung, Ferenczi, and Jones met and exchanged ideas with James, Titchener, Cattell, and Boas. In the years that followed, journal articles gave testimony to an increased interest in the form of experimental attempts to verify psychoanalytic concepts.[9] Later, as European ana-

---

[9] For a review of some of these studies see Sears (1943) and, in this volume, Chapter 4, "Psychoanalysis and the Unity of Science."

lysts fled their Hitler-dominated countries to America, psychologists had an opportunity to experiment with personal analyses.

The biggest impetus for interest in psychoanalysis, however, had come with the establishment of the field of personality within psychology. The publication of a series of books in the mid-1930s marked the unofficial recognition of personality psychology as a field of scientific inquiry. Kurt Lewin (1935) was one of the first psychologists to present a systematic view of personality. Not long after, Stagner (1937) published his *Psychology of Personality,* followed shortly by Allport (1937) and Murray (1938).

Psychology had not, of course, ignored personality before this time. There had been a good deal of speculative writing on needs and instincts, going back to the early part of the century. Discussions of "emotion" were found in most psychology texts of the 1920s and early 1930s, but were submerged in the study of physiological or social psychology. The problem of the over-all organization of personality, however, had not been tackled by the academician, and was left largely to the intuition of the clinician. The most psychology had to offer this group was a few paper-and-pencil tests on adjustment and such isolated personality variables as introversion-extraversion.

While psychology was moving toward motivational concerns, psychoanalysis was moving toward ego concerns. The publication of Anna Freud's book, *The Ego and the Mechanisms of Defence* (1936), marks for psychoanalysis the beginning of a long journey away from instinctual emphasis to areas in which psychology had long been working, i.e., mastery of reality and adaptation. Ego psychology, more programmatic than real, nevertheless helped open the theoretical door between the two fields.[10]

Much of the history of the affiliation between psychoanalysis and academic psychology is contained in the 1940 symposium. The ways in which psychologists became interested in psychoanalysis, the criteria they used to evaluate it, the use to which they put it—or did not put it—were as numerous as the contributors themselves. But for all of them one thing is clear: that the highly subjective, depth-oriented approach of psychoanalysis was not

---

[10]The shifts of interest within the two fields toward the subject matter of the other was one example of the intellectual climate of the 1930s. It was for psychology a period of convergence, a period in which psychologists were attempting to unify theories and schools of psychology, i.e., Anglo-American traditions of empiricism with Continental stress on complexity and scope. The outcome of this period was to establish psychology as a single and unified science. See Brunswik (1952), Boring (1950), and Murphy (1949).

readily assimilated by academic psychology. For the American psychologist, it was the thoroughgoing, objective approach based upon a functionalistic, behavioristic model that made the merger difficult. For Frenkel-Brunswik the problem of integration was somewhat different. As an Austrian psychologist, more familiar with and accepting of a subjective psychology in the form of phenomenology, the problem was to apply that phenomenology to the central layer of personality. When Frenkel-Brunswik says in her contribution that the development of her own interest in psychoanalysis parallels what seems to her the impact of psychoanalysis on academic psychology, she is clearly speaking as a Viennese psychologist. When she says that for her it was the shift within psychoanalysis toward greater emphasis upon ego functions and the shift within academic psychology toward motivational concerns that helped pave the way toward her own resolution of the problem, she is speaking for the American psychologist as well.

Frenkel-Brunswik's contribution to the symposium was written a year and a half after she came to this country from Austria, and not only marks a turning point in her thinking but also lays the foundation for all her future work. She states in her paper that the three major influences on her intellectual life in Vienna were her academic training at the University of Vienna under Karl and Charlotte Bühler, the "Vienna Circle" of logical positivism (Schlick, Carnap, Neurath), and psychoanalysis. Her 1940 paper is the first in which the impact of psychoanalysis is clearly seen.

Her contribution to the 1940 symposium is divided into two parts. In the first section she deals with theoretical issues in psychology and psychoanalysis, and in the second she speaks more personally of her own professional development as it relates to her experiences with psychoanalysis. First she attempts to lay the theoretical foundation of a motivational psychology by establishing the nature of events and of relationships about which an integrated psychology should—and should not—concern itself; by so doing, she is building the bridge over which she, as a phenomenologically oriented psychologist, can travel to avail herself of psychoanalysis.

For her discussion Frenkel-Brunswik chooses the relationship between theory and observation, and begins by defining both the observable and unobservable regions in which psychological events occur. For this purpose she refines concepts used by Henry Murray (1938) in his *Explorations in Personality* (central and peripheral regions of the organism) and draws upon Gestalt psychology for the concepts of proximal and distal effects. There are four regions of events with which psychology should concern itself, she says. Two of these regions, the peripheral and central, refer to the organism; the other two, proximal and distal, refer to manifestations of the organism's activity within the environment, that is, the end results of behavior or adjustment. All regions with the exception of the central one are response variables; the central region alone is considered to be explanatory in nature.[11]

The peripheral region refers to events at "the level of overt reaction, which can be observed directly by looking at the individual in question without making any guesses or interpretations which go below the surface." The immediate effect of a peripheral behavior in the environment is called proximal. It is in a sense an interpretation of the short-term effect of behavior and to that extent it is removed from direct observation. A peripheral behavior might be the statement, "I hate Jews and Blacks"; a proximal effect would be a prejudiced or ethnocentric attitude. Distal effects are abstractive descriptions based upon patterns of proximal behavior. These effects refer to the more remote or long-term results of a person's activities in the environment. Thus ethnocentrism, political-economic conservatism, antidemocratic tendencies, etc., might be abstracted to the distal effect of the "authoritarian." The central region of the organism refers to hypothetical internal processes which are explanatory in nature (an example from psychoanalytic theory would be the unconscious). This region is not directly observable. Though it is independent of the peripheral and proximal regions of the organism, it may be understood by extrapolations from them. Frenkel-Brunswik, in fact, believes that the data of motivational psychology reside in the peripheral and proximal regions and that these regions are "the basis of observation for the hypothetical extrapolation of the central and the abstractive description of the distal." The subject matter of motivational psychology, she says, is

---

[11] In this sense (and perhaps more theoretically than practically) Frenkel-Brunswik has thrown out the old stimulus-response model and has replaced it with an organismic-response model. In her later writings, especially those dealing with political behavior, she incorporates the stimulus into the model and ends up with what might be called an S-O-R design, similar to what Egon Brunswik has called "representational design" (for further discussion of the issues involved, see Egon Brunswik, 1947).

the understanding of the relationship between the central and distal regions. Using this criterion, she attacks those psychologies which have limited themselves to the relationship between the peripheral and proximal regions as not dealing with relevant or essential aspects of personality.[12]

She also points out the danger of confusing the central with the distal and warns against psychologies that label as central face-value descriptions of either proximal or distal effects (e.g., in Murray's scheme, "the need to ask or to answer general questions" is considered "need understanding"; McDougall's theory of instincts). These approaches, she feels, simply duplicate and confuse one region with another. The central region must be independently assessed, a task she sets for herself in "Motivation and Behavior" (1942). She criticizes early psychoanalysis for its exclusive interest in the central layer and its neglect of distal variables, that is, the question of what a person makes of his complexes. She saw the increasing interest in the ego in psychoanalysis as correcting this lopsided approach. In her paper, Frenkel-Brunswik summarizes this point of view as follows:

> Both the central and distal aspects are necessary for a full description of personality. It is their interrelationship, rather than the peripheral-proximal relationships chiefly emphasized up to now, which should be studied. Whereas psychoanalysis has been asking, "Which drive?" and general psychology has been asking, "Which effect?" a unified psychology should ask, "Which effect out of which drive?" [p. 57].

Directing this formulation toward psychoanalysis, she summarizes:

> The ego should remain the subject matter of psychology, and extrapolations should be used chiefly in order to throw light

---

[12]Frenkel-Brunswik is here aiming her remarks toward the behavioristic model of personality. An excellent example of this point of view is found in Lawrence Cole's then current textbook (1939): "When we have measured the intelligence of an individual, studied his interests and strivings, noted the situations which provoke emotional responses and described his method of expressing these same emotions, observed the ways in which he meets his problems (and frustrations), and in particular when we have studied his reactions to other people (his family, the larger social group with its standards and demands), we do not then go on to look for a 'plus something,' a personality which lies behind the phenomena we have studied and which somehow pervades, unifies, and directs the whole. Our study of this totality of the behavior of the individual *is* the study of personality" (p. 624).

INTRODUCTION 15

back upon the surface phenomena of behavior and achievement. In thus returning ultimately to the surface region, we will have attempted a deep psychology of the surface *(tiefe Oberflächenpsychologie)*, rather than indulged in a superficial psychology of the depth *(oberflächliche Tiefenpsychologie)* [p. 57].

In the second part of her paper Frenkel-Brunswik gives a biographical sketch of her professional life. It is in this section that she acknowledges her debt to her teacher, Charlotte Bühler, and then makes an all-important break from her. She now criticizes the phenomenologically oriented biographical study on which she worked with Bühler as one that bypassed the central layer of personality. In terms of the regions she discussed in the first part of her paper, she sees it as a study in which peripheral and proximal behavior is taken at face value and is related to distal adaptations; she evaluates it as a study of the surface, descriptive rather than explanatory. But as is typical of Frenkel-Brunswik, the break is not a renunciation. It comes in the form of an attempt to broaden the base of Bühler's psychology by including the central processes (as expounded by psychoanalysis). The surface behavior, she says, can be used for making extrapolations to the central layers rather than as an end in itself; and the central layers should be related to distal adaptations.

Frenkel-Brunswik goes on to relate the impact of her personal analysis on her thinking in psychology and ends with suggestions for studies that demonstrate the feasibility of including the central region in the scientific study of personality. Among these she includes some of the work done on a monograph that was published two years later under the title of "Motivation and Behavior" (1942). Much of Frenkel-Brunswik's work, in fact, was directed toward the end of formulating and developing a motivational psychology which could stand up under scientific scrutiny, a psychology in which motivation and behavior could be linked in a meaningful and fruitful way.

In 1952, in a letter to Fillmore Sanford, then secretary of the American Psychological Association, concerning the reprinting of the "Symposium on Psychoanalysis as Seen by Analyzed Experimental Psychologists," Frenkel-Brunswik wrote:

> ... in my own case my symposium article represents not only a summary of my previous orientations but, even more, it was for

me a blueprint for future work which I have been following more closely than I had been aware. After I got your letter, I reread my symposium contribution and though, of course, today I would have to expand and sharpen many points, it still represents in many respects my basic outlook. If the plan should materialize [the reprinting of the symposium with comments by the participants], I should like in my comments to make more explicit some of the points which were made only implicitly, especially in reference to designating more sharply and more theoretically the aspects of psychology for which psychoanalysis has proved fruitful and to emphasize even more strongly those aspects of academic psychology which psychoanalysis has neglected and which constitute an essential complementary approach for comprehension of the total personality.

MOTIVATION AND BEHAVIOR: 1942

In "Psychoanalysis and Personality Research" Frenkel-Brunswik argued that the intuitive interpretations necessary to make statements about central variables have as much validity and are to be taken as seriously as the more readily quantifiable peripheral and proximal data. Her work on the Adolescent Study gave her an opportunity to demonstrate this and to show how reference to the central layer could help in the understanding of surface behavior.

When Frenkel-Brunswik began work at the Institute of Child Welfare, two longitudinal studies were in progress. One, the Adolescent Growth Study,[13] had collected a variety of measures on its subjects over a period of several years, including self-reports, projective material, and ratings by adult observers of the subjects' behavior in social situations. Previous work had shown that correlations between an adjustment questionnaire (the self-reports) and the behavior ratings were uniformly low, and the validity of the self-reports had been called in question. Frenkel-Brunswik had just completed work on her study in self-deception in which the self-reports of university students were compared with behavior ratings made by staff observers. In this study discrepancies between the two sets of data had been explained in terms of the subjects' defenses against awareness of their own shortcomings. She now suggested that the self-reports of the Ado-

---

[13]For a description of this study, see Jones (1939).

lescent Study subjects might become more meaningful if they were viewed in terms of the subjects' inner motivational state rather than in terms of their external behavior.

The assessment of motivation, she points out, poses several difficulties. Motivation is inferred from behavior, but the relationship between the two is complex. The same motivational tendency may be expressed in a variety of behaviors and the same behavior may reflect more than one motivational tendency. In fact, the great explanatory power of motivational concepts is that they reduce a wide variety of often unrelated or inconsistent behaviors into smaller conceptual units. This means that extrapolations of motivation from isolated segments of behavior may be wrong as often as right. To make inferences about motivation, one needs as wide a sampling of behaviors as possible. However, motivational inferences cannot be made simply by summing up separate behavior items or by abstracting common factors from them; the possibility of their alternative manifestations must be recognized.[14] Further, motivation is often disguised rather than directly expressed in behavior. The behaviors relevant to a given motivational state are not equally accessible to observation. It is thus necessary to use "minimal" as well as obvious behavior cues.[15]

These assumptions are the working hypotheses of the clinician, whose intuitive judgments are based on a variety of behaviors (or statements about behavior, as in interviews) and who is alert to the voice, gestures, and other expressive movements of his patient as well as to what he says and does not say. In this way the clinician takes account of the concepts of alternative manifestations of motivational states and the use of minimal cues in making inferences. He is seldom concerned, however, with the questions of replicating his judgments or of relating them to future behavior.

Frenkel-Brunswik set herself the problem of duplicating clinician behavior in a way that could be replicated and that would have predictive value. Her solution was to use judges who were familiar with the adolescent subjects over a long period of time and in a

[14] Frenkel-Brunswik compares the use of the concept of alternative manifestations in grouping behavior in terms of its underlying cause, as is done in psychoanalysis, with the use of the concept of vicarious functioning in grouping behavior in terms of its common effects, as is done in learning theory (see 1942, p. 130; also this volume, Chapter 4, "Psychoanalysis and the Unity of Science").

[15] She suggests that it is important to measure distal effects as well as central states, and that this involves similar processes of extrapolation (this volume, Chapter 1).

variety of situations. The judges were asked to make intuitive ratings of drives (such as abasement, aggression, and succorance) without trying to tie these to specific behaviors. This procedure permitted the judges to function as clinicians, but under conditions that allowed some quantification of their judgments. It also permitted an approach to the problem of interrater reliability.

The drive ratings were related to both the social behavior ratings and to the subjects' self-reports. It was shown that the low correlations previously found between these two sets of data could be understood by reference to the drive ratings, and the drive ratings in turn were found to have some predictive value in relation to the subjects' behavior.

One aspect of this study is worth noting here because it represents an early attempt to specify the characteristics of the perceiver and the way these are related to his judgments of others, thus antedating much of the later work on person perception. Frenkel-Brunswik looked at the differing conceptions of the drives held by the raters, as shown by the pattern of intercorrelations among their drive ratings; the relationship between their expressed like or dislike of the subjects and the ratings they gave them; the extent to which a judge's possession of a given motivational tendency influenced her rating of that tendency in others; and the relation between a judge's insight into her own personality and her ability to rate subjects in conformity with the consensus of other judges.

This study was reported in the monograph "Motivation and Behavior" (1942). Its length has precluded its inclusion in this book, but its findings are summarized in some detail in Chapter 3, "Personality Theory and Perception."[16]

THE AUTHORITARIAN PERSONALITY: 1944-1950

Also not included because of its length is what is perhaps Frenkel-Brunswik's best-known work, her contribution to *The Authoritarian Personality* (Adorno et al., 1950). This book, authored jointly by Adorno, Frenkel-Brunswik, Levinson, and Sanford, is a

---

[16]See pp. 97-102 for a discussion of the relationships between drive and behavior ratings; pp. 118-130 for illustrative case studies (previously unpublished); and pp. 130-133 for a description of the study of clinician bias.

report of one of a series of studies in prejudice sponsored by the American Jewish Committee. It was addressed to the problem of what personality characteristics predispose people to prejudiced behavior. Beginning with anti-Semitism, the study quickly expanded to a consideration of minority group prejudice in general and then to a study of the relation of prejudice to patterns of sociopolitical ideology. It was unique from two points of view: the application of psychoanalytic theory and clinical methods to the study of social attitudes, and the linking of ideology to the over-all pattern of personality organization.

The Authoritarian Personality ranks as one of the most important contributions of social science. After reviewing a prepublication draft, Gardner Murphy expressed his reaction in a letter to the American Jewish Committee (November, 1948):

> The study is monumental. There is no other study known to me which deals so systematically, maturely, and competently with the problem of ethnic prejudice and its relations to socioeconomic, political, and other attitude dimensions. Over and above this highly significant achievement is the pioneer deep-level study of the relations of personality structure to all of these interrelated attitude syndromes, making use of ingenious hypotheses, well supported by quantitative material from tests, and with ingenious interview and projective material. . . . This highly important investigation . . . [is] full of profound implications for democratic living and for the basic understanding of personality in action.

Since its publication in 1950 it has stimulated a vast amount of research, though relatively little has been in the tradition of the original investigation.[17] It has also received considerable criticism, concerning both the authors' theory and their methods. They are

---

[17]It would be instructive to count the number of variables that have been correlated with the F (fascist) scale, a measure of "implicit prefascist tendencies" or "antidemocratic potential" (Adorno et al., 1950, p. 224), and the variety of groups to which the scale has been given. Most of these studies, however, have not dealt with the "total person" in the way the authors of *The Authoritarian Personality* attempted to link personality structure and ideology. In this connection, it is interesting to note that Frenkel-Brunswik, discussing possible trends in future research on the relations between personality and perception, predicted "a period in which every imaginable perceptual experiment would be related to every imaginable personality variable." Such are the "pitfalls which endanger undertakings in every field of research which becomes fashionable" (Chapter 3, p. 160).

said to have been politically naïve in their contrast of "fascists"[18] and "democrats," to have claimed that political behavior is a function of personality structure, and to have ignored the importance of institutional roles in social adaptation. They are further criticized for having failed to take account of the relationship between socioeconomic status and attitudes and for treating lightly such sociological variables as group membership; for overgeneralizing their findings; for letting their own biases show in interpreting their data; and for failing to make their underlying theory explicit. Frenkel-Brunswik devoted a good deal of her later writings to answering some of these criticisms and to clarifying her own position on the relations between personality and social structure.[19]

This study took Frenkel-Brunswik into the field of social psychology. It meant a shift from purely clinical concerns to a wider conception of personality and the beginning of a concern with social issues that characterizes much of her later work.

Although she shared with the other authors in all phases of the project, her major responsibility was the formulation of personality variables and their assessment through clinical interviews. This presented some of the same measurement problems posed in the Adolescent Study, with the added difficulty that verbal reports elicited in a single interview are probably more subject to both conscious and unconscious distortion than is observed social behavior. Interview material has the advantage, however, of being "long-range, condensed, and encompassing a wider range of the crucial situations an individual has to face in a lifetime. For this reason it may be considered a legitimate basis of dynamic interpretation . . . under the provision that proper allowance is made for mechanisms of distortion."

As in "Motivation and Behavior," she used generalized motivational categories for assessing personality characteristics. In addition, formal categories—more cognitive than motivational—were introduced for the first time. For these Frenkel-Brunswik drew

---

[18]The work was begun in 1944, in the closing months of World War II. At that time anti-Semitism was an important part of fascist ideology and the concern of the authors was with the rise of German and Italian fascism and its acceptance by the people of those countries. In the early years of the study, the authors talked of the "fascist personality," but in the course of their work the concept became generalized as the "antidemocratic" and later the "authoritarian" personality. The terms are actually used interchangeably throughout the book and in most of Frenkel-Brunswik's writings.

[19]See this volume, Chapters 5 and 6; also (1954b) and (1954d).

upon her previous study of self-deception as well as upon clinical observation. The formal categories included such variables as rigidity and tolerance of ambiguity.

The interview sample was composed of adults selected to represent the two extremes of response on tests of ethnocentrism. Raters were asked to make a series of intuitive judgments on the interview as a whole. The ratings were used to develop composite portraits of the personality patterns of the two extreme groups—the authoritarian and the democratic personality—and thus to test hypotheses about the relations between personality and ideology.[20]

While work on *The Authoritarian Personality* was in progress, Frenkel-Brunswik undertook an independent but similar study with children and young adolescents. The Child Study, as it will be referred to here, is distinguished from the better-known study with adults by two features: interviews with the parents of its subjects, which permitted a direct approach to the problem of what makes a person develop authoritarian characteristics, and the introduction of cognitive and perceptual experiments to verify independently some of the assumptions about authoritarianism and motivation.

The Child Study has never been completely published, but various reports on its findings were made over the next few years. Both adult and child studies are discussed extensively in four of the papers presented here.[21] These studies furnished much of the data on which Frenkel-Brunswik based her later writings, particularly those concerning the relationship between personality and perception.

---

[20]Various syndromes within each of the two major types were identified in this study. Thus, within the group scoring high on ethnocentrism, five subtypes were described: the conventional person, the authoritarian, the psychopath, the crank, and the manipulator; five subtypes of low scorers were also described, characterized as rigid, protesting, impulsive, easygoing, and genuinely liberal. In his chapter on "Types and Syndromes" Adorno defended the use of typologies in these words: "The construction of psychological types does not merely imply an arbitrary, compulsive attempt to bring some 'order' into the confusing diversity of human personality. It represents a means of 'conceptualizing' this diversity, according to its own structure, of achieving closer understanding. The radical renunciation of all generalizations beyond those pertaining to the most obvious findings would not result in true empathy into human individuals but rather in an opaque, dull description of psychological 'facts': every step which goes beyond the factual and aims at psychological meaning . . . inevitably involves generalizations transcending the supposedly unique 'case,' and it happens that these generalizations more frequently than not imply the existence of certain regularly recurring *nuclei* or syndromes which come rather close to the idea of 'types' " (Adorno et al., 1950, pp. 747-748).

[21]Findings from the Child Study are presented in Chapters 2 and 3; see also Frenkel-Brunswik (1948c, 1951a, 1954b, 1955a), Frenkel-Brunswik and Havel (1953). Descriptions of the two extreme types, based on findings from both studies, appear in Chapters 5 and 6.

Personality and Perception: 1949-1951

When personality developed as a field in its own right in the late 1930s, it did so without seriously disturbing the rest of psychology. Elementary texts added a separate chapter on personality to the traditional chapters on learning, thinking, perception, and so on, but though they stressed that personality was the study of the "whole person," the personality traits that constituted data about whole persons were rarely integrated with findings from these other fields.

The situation began to change during and after World War II. The rapid growth of both personality psychology and social psychology reflected psychologists' growing concern with clinical and social problems. At the same time experimental psychologists were beginning to think of individual differences as something more than error variance and to look to motivational and situational variables for their explanation. These two trends converged in the study of perception as a rapidly growing number of studies demonstrated that both needs and the nature of the experimental situation can influence percepts. This shift in focus from the normative to the projective aspects of perception, dubbed by Krech (1949) the "New Look," represented an attempt to break through the compartmentalization of both data and theory in psychology and to take another look at "whole man." This was the culmination of a period of convergence that had actually begun in the mid-1930s. Frenkel-Brunswik's 1940 paper, "Psychoanalysis and Personality Research," was an early contribution to this movement.

The theoretical issues represented by the convergence period were brought together in the 1949 *Journal of Personality* in a "Symposium on Interrelationships between Perception and Personality." Following this same trend, the University of Texas devoted its 1949-1950 Clinical Psychology Symposium to a series of invited papers on perception as "a basic approach to an understanding of personality and interpersonal relations." The latter were published the following year as *Perception: An Approach to Personality* (Blake and Ramsey, 1951). Frenkel-Brunswik contributed papers to each of these symposia. The two papers, "Intolerance of Ambiguity as an Emotional and Perceptual Personality Variable" and "Personality Theory and Perception," are reprinted in this volume (see Chapters 2 and 3).

While most psychologists were concerned with bringing data from personality into perception, Frenkel-Brunswik approached the convergence of the two fields by a different route. In "Psychoanalysis and Personality Research" (this volume, Chapter 1) and again in "Motivation and Behavior" (1942) she had been concerned with the organizing value of central concepts (drives) as a way of understanding behavior. By behavior she referred not to experimental conditions but to the phenomenon of the person in his life situation. In *The Authoritarian Personality* the life situation was expanded to include the data of social psychology, but the central variables used were still centered on the concept of drive. It was in this study that she began to think in terms of formal ways of characterizing personality organization.[22] The study of prejudiced persons had led her "to expect prejudice to be associated with perceptual rigidity, inability to change set, and tendencies to primitive and rigid structuring of ambiguous perceptual fields." She asked, "Can basic formal attitudes such as subjectivity, rigidity, fear of ambivalence and of ambiguity, etc., be taken as unified traits of the organism, or are we to find a more differential distribution, varying from one area to another?" (this volume, p. 62). This question had been posed by the German typologists as one of unity of style. Her concern in the articles reprinted here is to demonstrate that this unity does exist and that it can be described in terms of such formal variables as tolerance versus intolerance of ambiguity.

She is not explicit about the conceptual relationship between such variables and the drive variables used heretofore. Much of the time, and particularly when discussing specific cases, she seems to be using them as the formal expression of ways of handling drives, that is, of defenses and character traits. Intolerance of ambiguity, in this sense, is seen as "somewhat related" to the concept of perceptual defense. At other times, however, she talks of intolerance of ambiguity as an "emotional-cognitive personality variable," its emotional and cognitive forms being but different aspects of the same personality characteristic. She emphasizes that such variables have

---

[22]She had first used formal concepts as a way of describing behavior in "Mechanisms of Self-Deception" (1939). At that time these concepts were seen as representing defenses against conscious awareness of one's own defects rather than, as she came to consider them later, dimensions of personality organization.

an adaptive rather than a purely defensive function. The individual's pattern of adaptation depends upon a variety of factors. As a clinician, she appears most impressed with the conditions of emotional learning through interaction with parents, and particularly with the fate of aggressive impulses. She also suggests that these emotional-cognitive variables show developmental changes and can be expected to vary with age (she finds here a link to the work of Heinz Werner) and that they may be related to constitutional differences, either as special areas of weakness or sensitivity or as special patterns of ability.[23] In her later papers she goes beyond the relation of the individual to his immediate environment to consider the effect of the culture as a whole on individual adaptation patterns. This effect can come about in two ways: indirectly, through parental mediation of cultural values, or directly, through the impact of society on the individual, as in institutional pressures for conformity.

For Frenkel-Brunswik, data on perceptual or cognitive functioning were seen as a way of learning more about the total functioning of the person rather than as a way of learning more about the nature of perceiving or knowing. As she had earlier pointed to opposing behaviors as sometimes expressing the same drive state (as alternative manifestations of the drive), she now points to opposing modes of perceiving or cognizing as expressions of the same personality characteristic. In terms of intolerance of ambiguity, undue rigidity of behavior may be shown by the same person who shows unusual flexibility, and overconcrete interpretations of sense data occur in persons who at other times tend toward overgeneralizing; in each case, both extremes represent alternative ways of handling ambiguity. These kinds of relationships are seen as examples of "closeness of opposites," which she considers a basic principle of personality organization. Her concern then is with individual styles of feeling-cognizing-perceiving, that is, with individual patterns of adaptation.

---

[23]Work on the Child Study indicated that children were in some respects more like authoritarian than democratic adults (1948c, p. 305). This led Frenkel-Brunswik to suggest that some aspects of authoritarianism might arise in part as ways of handling developmental problems and could thus be considered as measures of the adaptive capacities of the individual. In "Psychoanalysis and Personality Research" she emphasized the importance of the function of adaptation in understanding personality and suggested the complicated developmental interactions among drives, abilities, and environment. Neither here nor in her later work were these ideas fully developed.

... a great variety of perceptual and cognitive processes may be considered as formal approaches to reality which may be very revealing of a person's style of life. The establishment of the relationship of these formal aspects to content is an important task of psychology. The question may be raised as to what are the consistencies and positive correlations, and what are the compensations in terms of behavior [this volume, p. 70].

In this way she stands outside the general stream of literature on this topic which, though with important exceptions,[24] has been more concerned with establishing general laws of the relationships between dimensions of personality and perceptual functioning.

Frenkel-Brunswik's work in this area was confined to the single variable of tolerance of ambiguity. Unlike Klein (1958), who has suggested the possibility of a variety of adaptive patterns, all of which may work equally well, she placed tolerance versus intolerance of ambiguity on a continuum of good-to-bad reality adaptation. By arguing for good, that is, for flexible adaptation, she is able to argue also that the pattern of personality organization characterized by tolerance for ambiguities is, in the long run, the better-adjusted one. She thus answers an argument that was raised first in connection with the conception of the "authoritarian personality" and that appears again in her discussions of personality and sociopolitical behavior and of the role of the social sciences in problems of value.

Psychoanalysis and Science: 1954

In a footnote to "Psychoanalysis and the Unity of Science" (this volume, Chapter 4), Frenkel-Brunswik states that this work, an attempt to clarify the standing of psychoanalysis in the framework of the unity of science movement, is a return to an assignment suggested to her some 20 years before by her teacher, Otto Neurath. Frenkel-Brunswik had studied with Neurath, Schlick, Carnap, and others of the "Vienna Circle" and she, like many other psychologists, had been strongly influenced by it.

The unity of science movement, a philosophical movement which directed itself to the logical and methodological analyses of scientific procedures and theories, was inaugurated in Vienna to-

[24]The work of Klein is notable here; see especially (1951).

ward the end of the 1920s and within a short time became, both here and in Europe, an influential tool in the methodological armamentarium of the sciences, particularly mathematics, physics, and behavioral psychology.

Herbert Feigl, who later named the movement logical positivism (or logical empiricism), found William James's term "tough-minded" an apt one to describe the logical positivist and his philosopher ancestors—those worldly (as opposed to otherworldly) philosophers for whom logic and experience were the arbiters of judgment.

With regard to factual confirmation, logical positivism states that all factual knowledge depends for its validity upon confirmation by observation (experiential, operational, or experimental). Among the tougher of the tough-minded logical positivists are those who urge a narrow positivism which views science as dealing with descriptive facts and with their regularities as formulated in empirical laws; for them, only direct and complete verification (in the sense of truth or falsity) is factually meaningful. This extreme view (radical positivism) is opposed by a somewhat less tough-minded view which takes the position that confirmation rather than verification is the aim of science, that theoretical formulations are acceptable, and that not every concept in a formal system need be interpreted in terms of observables; for them, indirect and incomplete testing can yield confirmation of factual knowledge. It is essentially the radical positivist seen in the guise of the experimental psychologist toward whom Frenkel-Brunswik—a less tough-minded positivist—directs her arguments in "Psychoanalysis and the Unity of Science":

> Many of the objections against psychoanalysis have their origin in an overnarrow interpretation of the version of scientific empiricism commonly known as operationism with its stress on the rooting of all concepts in concrete manipulations and observations, and generally in a vaguely antitheoretical attitude, rather than in a legitimate criticism of psychoanalytic theory [this volume, p. 162].

Frenkel-Brunswik takes the position that radical positivism, taken over by the experimental psychologist, was long ago discarded by the logical positivists themselves. Narrow operationism, referring to the demand that all abstract terms of science be interpreted in terms of sense observations, has now been replaced, she says, by a broadened operationism which requires only that "enough propositions of the conceptual system be firmly enough connected with sensory experiences"—a statement made by Einstein, who thus justifies the existence of the unobservable atom in the science of physics.

Though she sees Freud's turning away from the directly observable as too radical a departure to suit the requirement that scientific theory be anchored to observation, she interprets recent developments in ego psychology as correcting this objection. Methodologically speaking, Frenkel-Brunswik places psychoanalytic theory in the same category as atomic theory, and takes the position that the criterion of indirect and incomplete evidence enables psychoanalysis to take its place among the community of scientific theories.

In taking up further the question of confirmation of psychoanalytic theory, that is, the issues involved in indirect evidence for the theory, Frenkel-Brunswik discusses MacCorquodale and Meehl's (1948) now famous paper, "On the Distinction between Hypothetical Constructs and Intervening Variables." While she welcomes their distinction as being in the spirit of a broadened operationism, i.e., their emphasis on differences in the degree of indirectness of evidence, she feels that MacCorquodale and Meehl's distinction between intervening variables and hypothetical constructs is too strict and overdifferentiated. Contrary to their position, Frenkel-Brunswik argues that intervening variables are not reducible to all possible meanings, that they, like hypothetical constructs, contain surplus meaning; and since confirmation, not verification, constitutes the criterion for testability, exhaustibility of statements by observables is not necessary anyway. By thus diminishing the degree of difference between hypothetical constructs and intervening variables, she attempts to liberalize the requirements for the translation of concepts into operations, and thus liberalize too the requirements for the confirmation of theory.

Frenkel-Brunswik summed up this paper and its intent as follows:

I undertook to compare theory construction in psychoanalysis with theory construction in other sciences, including physics. In doing so I applied the current revisions of operationism, which have taken place within logical positivism itself, to an evaluation of psychoanalytic theories. Initial steps were taken toward a logical analysis of some of the basic psychoanalytic concepts, such as that of the unconscious and of instinct; the question as to how far these theoretical constructs are introduced by postulates or else are in the nature of dispositional concepts connected with the empirical data through reduction sentences was also raised. This discussion further led into the general problem of concept formation in the social sciences and into that of the relation between explanation and description; the specific explanatory value of psychoanalytic concepts was thus examined and an attempt made to point out what phenomena psychoanalytic theory may be able to explain and what phenomena must be left to concepts not focally contained in psychoanalytic theory but present in behavior psychology and in the social sciences. Attempts at experimental verification of psychoanalytic hypotheses were examined and some major misunderstandings which have befallen many of them were pointed out. Most of these misunderstandings stem from ignoring the fact that psychoanalytic theory is inferential in nature and thus must lengthen the chains which connect the principles with the observational protocols. Thus greater ingenuity is needed for its confirmation [1954e].

The "Unity of Science" paper, in preparation for at least four years, and published in 1954, is a reworking and summary of her thoughts on issues that she had been writing on for 14 years. In this sense, it represents the culmination of that phase of her work which deals with the integration of academic psychology and psychoanalysis. The convergence period was drawing to a close in psychology too, and psychologists were turning their attention elsewhere.

Personality and Society: 1952-1954

For Frenkel-Brunswik, the shift was to consideration of the role of individual personality and the family unit in the development of personal ideologies, and their expression in social movements. She had touched on this issue briefly in her psychological writings on the authoritarian character, but had not fully developed it. Invitations to present papers to two groups of nonpsychologists gave her an opportunity to present her views in more systematic form.

The earlier of the two papers included here, "Interaction of Psychological and Sociological Factors in Political Behavior" (Chapter 5), was prepared for a Symposium on Sociological and Psychological Problems Involved in the Study of Social Stratification and Politics at the 1951 meeting of the American Political Science Association. As a psychologist, she takes up the question of the relative explanatory power of psychological and sociological concepts in dealing with social behavior. She takes a position midway between those concerned exclusively with the determining effects of personality and those concerned only with social structure. Sociology and psychology, she says, represent "different levels of organization and abstraction"; both are needed for a full understanding of behavior. Aside from the work of the cultural anthropologists, there have been few attempts at linking the two fields (Lasswell, Fromm, and Erikson are notable exceptions). Psychologists and sociologists rarely consider data from outside their own field, while psychoanalysts have limited their view of the problem to the way in which instincts are transformed under socially transmitted pressures, and have ignored the adaptive aspects of social institutions.

Since she is talking to a group more familiar with sociological than psychological concepts, her concern in this paper is to demonstrate that an understanding of the relationship of such sociological variables as group membership or economic status to behavior can be increased by reference to psychological concepts. She suggests that we can improve our ability to predict behavior by a consideration of both—not in an additive fashion, but in terms of the interaction between the two. In making this point she is not asking sociologists to become part psychologists, or vice versa. On the contrary, she has several times defended the right of the single investigator *not* to deal systematically with all relevant variables. Rather, she is asking sociologists and political scientists to avoid the error of assuming that the same stimulus evokes the same response in all people and that behavior always "means" the same thing. In a sense this is the same as the plea for the recognition of individual differences in a psychology given to the discovery of general laws of behavior characterizing all people.

She illustrates the blend of the two disciplines through the history of her own use of the concept of marginality.[25] In the Child Study she began with the notion that loss of socioeconomic status might help explain why some families tended to produce authoritarian children and others did not. Her data forced her to the conclusion that status loss (a sociological concept) was meaningful only when considered in terms of what the loss meant to the person in terms of his status aspirations (a psychological concept). She revised her hypothesis, linking authoritarian attitudes not to objective status loss but to perceived or felt loss.

"Environmental Controls and the Impoverishment of Thought" (Chapter 6) deals more explicitly with the origin and function of ideologies. It was prepared for an interdisciplinary conference on totalitarianism held under the auspices of the American Academy of Arts and Sciences in 1953 and was presented as part of a conference section on the psychological aspects of totalitarianism. In this paper Frenkel-Brunswik maintains that adherence to social and political beliefs cannot be understood solely in terms of the manifest content of the belief and the self-interest of the individual. Totalitarianism, she suggests, was able to maintain its hold on its many adherents in the absence of reinforcement of the promises it made because its appeal lay not in the content of its ideology but in the approval it gave to certain irrational forces within the individual. She points to parallels between the development of an individual's perception of the world and the development of sociopolitical ideologies. A key issue is the handling of authority and discipline by parents, with its consequences for moral learning and for emotional and cognitive development. A set of moral principles imposed arbitrarily on a child before he is able to comprehend reasons for them produces an adult who may submit to a given authority but whose underlying resentment makes him quick to shift allegiance from one authority to another, whose outward conformity cannot be relied upon. Such discipline reduces receptiveness to social-psychological views of the world and leads

---

[25]This does not represent her first interest in the effect of social variables on personality development. In "Mechanisms of Self-Deception" she had suggested that the negative character of the guiding principles expressed by the students might have been related to their facing professional life "in a small and impoverished country of central Europe" with consequent "cultural negativism and skepticism" (1939, p. 417). In "Motivation and Behavior" she attempted to relate drive ratings of the adolescent subjects to the social mobility of their parents (1942, p. 259).

to an oversimplified and hence distorted view of it. An authoritarian home impoverishes its citizens.

Frenkel-Brunswik suggests that Western culture is now experiencing "an eruption of the irrational and ... a skepticism concerning reason and science." In the face of this trend, she asks, how can we impart the complexity of democratic values to people who want certain answers and black-and-white presentations of reality? Social science—and specifically psychology—has a contribution to make in answering such questions. Moreover, she claims, they cannot be answered without reference to psychology, that is, to considerations of the nature of man, and of individual men.

Aging

Frenkel-Brunswik's last major empirical study, uncompleted at her death, brought her into touch with another social problem, the role of the aging in an industrial society. Using methods similar to those used in the authoritarianism studies—both clinical interviews and a variety of cognitive, perceptual, and perceptual-motor tasks—she sought to study the relationship between personality and adjustment to aging. Personality, she assumed, is related to the kind of adaptation the person makes to growing old, and growing old in itself is but one stage in the development of personality. This stage brings its own unique changes. Frenkel-Brunswik saw these changes as having implications not only for individual adaptation but for social organization as well. Suggesting, for example, in an early description of the study, that aging might be accompanied by a decrease in such qualities as flexibility, tolerance of ambiguity, and ability to restructure the cognitive field, she wrote:

> Actually, in our civilization there may be more room than meets the eye for the constructive use of the increased rigidity under which the features just mentioned may be subsumed. Such specific utilization of the labor force after age 65 may prevent the development of feelings of marginality and of being uprooted, feelings which in turn have in another context been found to be one of the most potent factors determining the susceptibility of a group to demagoguery of various kinds and to fantastic promises of relief from all ills. The social and ethical

outlook of our subjects is being analyzed with an eye on the aspects just mentioned, and the relations of their value systems to underlying personality dynamics, on the one hand, and to social factors, on the other, are being investigated [1954e].

From this study Frenkel-Brunswik began to move toward an empirical study of values, an issue which was becoming her dominant concern.

Values: 1955

The study of values, once the exclusive province of religion, philosophy, art, and poetry, was beginning to take a place in the subject matter of the social sciences.

Within psychology, it was the shift from the thoroughly objective study of the subsystems of man—his sensations, perceptions, thought—to a less rigorously objective interest in the whole man—his needs, achievements, social and political attitudes—which established the possibility of the empirical study of man's value systems. Psychologists, like others of this generation, were pressed to the search for stable values by a complex of social forces, prominent among which were the new social mobilities and their accompanying uncertainties that had been created by political and technological revolutions of this century. Compelling, too, was the fact that the eighteenth- and nineteenth-century conception of man as a rational being had been challenged by psychological theories such as psychoanalysis. This conception was also severely tested by World War II with its unleashing of powerful destructive forces expressed in the rise—and near success—of fascism and in the construction of nuclear weapons capable of annihilating the human race. The question of how man could resolve the conflict between rational and irrational forces within himself and in society became an imperative one to solve. Frenkel-Brunswik put the issue forcefully in a letter (December, 1954) to philosopher Philip Rice:

> It seems to me of utmost importance that philosophers devote some thought on work in the field of political and social philosophy in times when basic values which have been taken for granted are questioned; thought-out philosophical and scientific considerations of basic orientation are then especially called for, otherwise irrational forces will take over. In times of anxieties

and uncertainties, there is always a search for certainty and some systematic outlook on life. If philosophers don't undertake a concerted effort to promote a *Weltanschauung* based on the knowledge available in philosophic political theory and social sciences, prejudgments based on dogma and convention will prevail.

The search for conditions—both psychological and social—under which man could survive and flourish was taken up by many, both outside and within the sciences. Psychologists approached this problem in many ways: through the study of decision making, conflict resolution, power structures, clinical behavior. Some turned to the issue of values.

Of those who believe that the study of values lies within the subject matter of the social sciences, two major groups seem to have emerged with regard to the logical status of the problem. On the one hand is a group of scientists who believe that ethics is a branch of the natural sciences; that statements about values are reducible to facts, and that they are open to verification in the same way that scientific statements are. Another group, represented by Frenkel-Brunswik's writings, believes that there can be disagreement in ethical judgments even where there is agreement about the facts, and that while genuine ethical statements necessitate knowledge verified by empirical study, they cannot be completely reduced to empirical statements. Although she feels that science cannot provide a thoroughly empirical system of values, she does believe that the social scientist has an important contribution to make[26]:

> Although the social scientist, as a scientist, cannot make the ultimate choice for mankind, his function is to throw as much light as possible on the implications involved in existing value systems, and to make explicit all the ramifications inherent in the options [this volume, p. 310].

"Some Theoretical and Empirical Aspects of the Problem of Values" (Chapter 7) was written in 1955 while Frenkel-Brunswik was a Fellow at the Center for Advanced Study in Stanford, California, and was presented at the University of California Social Science Faculty Colloquium on Value Theory in the Social Sci-

---

[26] For an excellent discussion of some of these same ideas, see Hobbs (1959).

ences in 1955 along with papers by Clyde Kluckhohn, Kenneth Boulding, and others. It is published here for the first time.

Frenkel-Brunswik's interest in values arose a number of years before she wrote this paper. Her earliest concern with this subject revolved around the issue of the experimenter's bias in scientific work, a matter she discussed in rebutting attacks of investigators' bias against the authoritarian personality and in relation to the Nazi psychologist Jaensch, with whom she was in factual agreement but with whom she disagreed in the interpretation of the facts.[27] Also to be found scattered throughout her earlier writings are other issues she takes up in this paper—the logical status of value systems, the influence of values upon the development of the physical and social sciences, the constructive use of values in the social sciences, the ethical implications of theoretical systems, the social and psychological determiners of value systems, the role of the social scientist in contributing to the choice between alternative value systems. Rethought and integrated, these topics are brought together in this paper as various aspects of the problem of values. The paper appears to be a kind of ground-clearing effort, preparatory to further thinking and empirical work in this area. At the time of writing this paper, Frenkel-Brunswik was planning a book on values, and it is possible that the areas she outlines would have been elaborated and included in such a book.

While other commitments kept her from starting her book, her 1956-1957 Fulbright year at the University of Oslo—and especially her contact there with the Norwegian philosopher, Aarn Naess—again stirred up the desire to begin work on it. In 1957 she wrote to Harold Lasswell, with whom she was already working on a study on the value systems of psychotherapists:

> During my stay in Europe I have increasingly realized that the problem of values is now my major interest. My theoretical and scientific preoccupations have been converging toward this topic for a long time. In fact, I have a book in mind which should cover ideally the philosophical aspects of the problem as well as the conclusions to which we can arrive on the basis of the accumulated knowledge in social sciences. . . . The whole book would also include the analysis of major value systems

---

[27] These issues are taken up systematically in her article "Social Research and the Problem of Values: A Reply" (1954d).

and their analyses from a philosophical and empirical point of view. . . . Over and above the collection of data from psychiatrists and psychoanalysts, I started to interview individuals who are involved in problems of personal value reorientation, and who consider themselves at crossroads and confronted with a choice between alternative ethical outlooks.

In the same year she wrote to friends in Berkeley about the therapists' interviews she had collected in Europe:

My findings . . . clearly indicate that cultural and social factors influence the therapists' notions about goal of therapy, normalcy, rationality, reality principle, etc. While the Norwegian therapists are all oriented toward releasing affect, the Viennese and Swiss psychiatrists are concerned with the problems of the meaning of life and are strongly under the influence of Existentialism.

Frenkel-Brunswik's death in the spring of 1958 prevented the completion of these projects.

1

PSYCHOANALYSIS AND PERSONALITY RESEARCH

More than any other period in the history of psychology, the present seems to be one of convergence of previously heterogeneous trends. The task set in this symposium, to evaluate personal experiences with psychoanalysis in their general significance to psychology, seems to the author best fulfilled by discussing first, in a systematic fashion, some basic concepts suggested by a comparison of the general psychology of personality with psychoanalysis (part I) and then to refer to the development of her own scientific interests and orientations with particular emphasis on her personal experience with psychoanalysis (part II). This development exemplifies to her what seems typically to happen, on a large scale, to academic psychology under the impact of psychoanalytic ideas.

I

In studying personality, emphasis may be laid on different kinds of events. Closest at hand is the level of overt reaction, which can be observed directly by looking at the individual in question, without making any guesses or interpretations which go below the surface. In this sense it also offers the greatest possibilities for being "exact," at least if exactitude is taken in its customary meaning. One has only "to notice what one sees"; one may even be able to measure the events observed. In accordance with the customary terminology, this layer may be called "peripheral."

In contrast to studies focused upon the peripheral region there are attempts to discover the inner forces guiding human conduct.

First published in *The Journal of Abnormal and Social Psychology*, 35:176-197, 1940.

The region in question is called "central." Though recognized as the more essential part of personality, study of this layer has been handicapped by the difficulty of getting access to it. The direct physiological approach has, for many reasons, its definite limitations. Thus overt behavior has been utilized as a basis for extrapolation into the central region. In such cases behavior is taken not at its face value but merely as a cue to be interpreted in terms of more underlying dynamic causes.

At present, much emphasis is put on this distinction between the peripheral and central approaches to personality. Yet some further distinctions have to be introduced for greater clarification. Let us see what Murray (1938), to whom much of the credit for emphasizing this distinction should go, understands by peripheral and central:

> In summary, it may be said that the peripheralists are apt to emphasize the physical patterns of overt behavior, the combination of simple reflexes to form complex configurations, the influence of the tangible environment, sensations and their compounds, intellections, social attitudes, traits, and vocational pursuits. The centralists, on the other hand, stress the directions or ends of behavior, underlying instinctual forces, inherited dispositions, maturation and inner transformations, distortions of perception by wish and fantasy, emotion, irrational or semi-conscious mental processes, repressed sentiments and the objects of erotic interest [p. 10].

In going over this list, we find that too great a variety is comprehended under peripheral as well as under central. Thus the items headed under peripheral include not only simple reflexes and other events observable at the surface of the organism, but also social attitudes, traits, and vocational pursuits. The defining criterion in these latter cases contains reference to the environmental terms of the activity in question, by the use of such adjectives as "social" or "vocational." In the same way the central items refer not only to hypothetical internal events such as underlying instinctual forces or repressed sentiments, but also to ends of behavior, objects of interest, or such terms as "maturation," which seems to point toward the degree of adjustment to the environment.

In order to facilitate a sharper differentiation between properly inferred central forces and actually achieved observable results, it seems that a second distinction symmetrical to that made between peripheral and central must also be made between the immediate and remote manifestations of organismic activity within the environment. The immediate effects of peripheral behavior in the environment may be called "proximal," and the more remote results of the individual's activities may be labeled "distal." This distinction, introduced by Gestalt psychology,[1] found a major systematic expression in the research on perceptual thing-constancy by Egon Brunswik (1934, 1939a) and has also been applied to the action side of the organism. In the present paper the attempt is made to apply these concepts to the larger units of adjustment which are studied in the psychology of personality. Thus certain features which otherwise would be considered distal (e.g., the performance on a minor task) appear in the present connection grouped with the proximal.

A distinction somewhat similar to that between proximal and distal is also made by Murray (1938, p. 55), when he differentiates between "actones" (referring to the bodily movements as such) and the "effects" which have been produced by the patterns of actones—without, however, differentiating sharply between the two pairs of concepts, peripheral and central on the one hand, and proximal and distal on the other.

In the list by Murray quoted above as exemplifying the objectives of the psychology of personality, we call reflexes and related physiological changes peripheral, because they can be studied by observing the surface of the organism without considering its relationship to the environment. Items such as social traits and vocational interests, on the other hand, may be called proximal, because they signify a relationship to the environment which in most cases is defined by short-term observation. For example, if sociability is defined by criteria such as the "number of contacts made within a certain period of time," we do not yet know whether or not the person in question is ultimately sociable, that is, whether or not a many-sided and prolonged observation would reveal the attainment of real social ends.

Since both the peripheral and the proximal refer to "molecular" observations only, they were sometimes grouped together. Yet it was an essential step forward when personality research

---

[1] Koffka (1935). Special emphasis is given to this distinction by Heider (1939).

went beyond the study of peripheral bodily events to include proximal behavioral traits.

On the other side, we have also to differentiate between observable distal results of behavior and central dynamic causes assumed hypothetically within the individual. Indeed, problems of adjustment and of distal achievement *(Leistung)* in general have often been treated in the psychology of personality without a sufficient consideration of the underlying inner forces. Examples may be found in the beginnings of clinical psychology as influenced by Kraepelin. It will thus be seen that concentration of scientific effort upon the central was not truly attempted before psychoanalysis. Correspondingly, psychoanalysis has, especially in its beginnings, comparatively neglected the distal results and achievements of behavior. Thus the specific contribution made by psychoanalysis to the psychology of personality cannot be properly appreciated without keeping in mind the two distinctions suggested above.

Among the reasons why, nevertheless, these distinctions have not been made consistently, the following is of greatest importance. As was emphasized by many authors, the peripheral and the proximal are alike in that they both play, in many cases, the role of the changeable link between stable poles. They thus connect, but in a rather unspecific fashion, the central causes and the distal results. The following is an example from the field of personality. A fundamentally egotistic central attitude may in the proximal layer be represented either by withdrawal or by a great number of superficial contacts, neither of which leads to the establishment of good social relations. The comparative irrelevance of the actones is strongly emphasized by Murray (1938, p. 57), who concludes that since "certain effects are more fundamental to life and occur more regularly than any observed action patterns," one should classify in terms of effects rather than in terms of actones.

Even though we accept this comparatively unessential character of the peripheral-proximal region, taken in and by itself, we still have to recognize it, when not taken at its face value, as a cardinal basis of observation for the hypothetical extrapolation of the central and the abstractive description of the distal. This latter pair of layers, the central and the distal, now seems to emerge as constituting the essential aspects of life. Murray's distinction between peripheral and central may, in fact, ultimately point to nothing else than a distinction between the unessential and the essential.

The fact, however, that both the central causes and the distal results are essential and actually linked together in many instances does not in itself justify their being thrown together. Is there really a specific central need corresponding to every distal effect, and a specific kind of distal effect to every central need? It seems to me that Murray (1938) sometimes answers this question in the affirmative, by choosing to define a need as "the force within the organism which determines a certain trend, or major effect" (p. 61), though in other passages the difference of structure between observed results and hypothetical needs is clearly stated. " 'Need' or 'drive' does not denote an observable fact—the direction of activity for example. For this, we have the terms 'behavioral trend' or 'behavioral effect' " (p. 72). But in looking through Murray's stimulating and important list of needs we get the impression that in some instances the description, at its face value, of a certain overt and essentially distal pattern in the process of mastering reality is simply introjected, in the sense of casting a duplicate copy into the central region, by just adding in front of the item the phrase "need for." For example:

> Under the need for Understanding we have classed: the tendency to ask or to answer general questions; interest in theory; the inclination to analyze events and generalize; discussion and argument; emphasis on logic and reason; self-correction and criticism; the habit of stating opinion precisely; insistent attempts to make thought correspond to fact; disinterested speculation; deep interest in abstract formulations: science, mathematics, philosophy [p. 225].

Most of the defining criteria in this list are behavioral or distal, such as "habit of stating opinion" and "abstract formulation." From a point of view more distinctly limited to the central aspect, intellectualization is, however, but one of a series of possible mechanisms of defense symptomatic of an instinctual danger. This fact was pointed out by Anna Freud (1936) in a discussion of problems of adolescence and will be discussed later.

A further example of a so-called dynamic theory in psychology, based upon introjection of a face-value description of manifest patterns, is McDougall's theory of instincts, though he apparently starts from the emotions accompanying the basic effects in life.

A *reductio ad absurdum* of the procedure of introjection is represented by the fictitious examples discussed by Stagner (1937, p. 225) and by Murray, (1938, p. 127), in which, for every concrete activity or habit such as "sitting down on that couch" or "reading the newspaper," a separate central drive or need would have to be assumed. Even if the recognized criteria for "behavior"—persistence and variability of activity relative to some end—should be fulfilled, it would not mean that this behavior unit had to be located, as such, somewhere else than in the more superficial layers of the personality. The result in any event would be an endless list of forces, of little use for the purposes of explanation and parsimonious reduction.

In comparison, let us consider an example of the analysis of motivational background as performed by the more interpretative methods of psychoanalysis. In discussing the case of a criminal, Alexander and Healy (1935a; see also 1935b) arrive at the following conclusions about the unconscious causes of his becoming a thief. The more detailed argument may be found in the orginal essay itself.

> First, the patient's stealing, his apparent daringness and aggressive masculinity, is an overcompensation for a feeling of inferiority. This feeling of inferiority is a reaction to a strong wish for dependency which expresses itself in the desire to receive things without working for them. Two sources of this receptive attitude are distinguished in the patient, a parasitic, oral-receptive fixation toward the mother and an intense admiration for a stronger brother to whom he has developed a passive-feminine attitude. Secondly, his stealing is a means to get rid of guilt feelings toward the brother. He helps his brother in any way he can, exposing himself to danger and even going to jail for him. Thirdly, the patient's stealing represents defiance toward the mother by whom he feels himself neglected in favor of the brother and of other men. He wants to show that he can "take" somewhere else what he thinks is denied to him by her. Fourthly, the authors assume the further motive (revealing itself in a number of dreams) to use crime as a means to an infantile, vegetative and parasitic existence behind prison bars [1935a, p. 199].

The point to be made here concerns not the truth or falsity of the specific conclusions arrived at by Alexander and Healy, but rather the differences in the method of approach between the procedure of duplicating introjection of the effects into the central, on the one hand, and the interpretative method of real extrapolation of the central, on the other. In terms of a purely distal approach, criminal involvement would have to be accounted for by reference to such tendencies as acquisitiveness or offensiveness. Introjecting the distal results into the central thus would ultimately consist in nothing but abstracting the most conspicuous distally relevant gross features of behavior. By doing so, however, one would still be taking effects at their face value. The contrary is true in the case of our example from Alexander and Healy, where the gross behavioral feature of overdaring, aggressive masculinity was interpreted as revealing a basically insecure, passive attitude.

Aside from the psychoanalytic procedure, assumptions about central factors have often been made deductively by contemplation of the biological necessities of an organism or species, and by assuming corresponding central needs as the causes of survival and propagation or of other biologically relevant results. This procedure is, from a formal point of view, no different from the examples given above to illustrate a duplicating introjection into the central of distal results observed in the process of keeping alive. The difference lies chiefly in the fact that the number of independent drives is further reduced by this speculative procedure. Tacitly assuming that biologically relevant distal results are always due to the corresponding drive, it even implies that central causes directed toward such distal results will never lead to other effects. The sources of disturbance of the central-distal correlation are, however, so great that this ideal state is far from being realized. There are too many central causes leading into side tracks (such as maladjustment) and blind alleys (such as compulsion symptoms), and too many distal results not due to central causes explicitly directed toward them. The only way out is to investigate the distal and the central independently of each other. Only such a separation will enable us to check one against the other and thus to reveal their true relationship in an empirical fashion.

It should be added that psychoanalytic extrapolation and biological constructions do not cover entirely the same ground within the central region. Psychoanalysis considers secondary effects superimposed upon the basic biological needs, such as complex entanglements of the sex drive. The relation of the two is somewhat similar to that stated by Tolman (1937, 1938) in his differentiation of the intervening from the independent variables. As far as psychology is concerned, the intervening variables describing the actual pattern of demands are of much greater interest.

Considering the basis of extrapolation, psychoanalysis is by no means limited to the distal region. The bulk of evidence, on the contrary, is proximal (such as social mannerisms) and peripheral (such as associations or dreams). Thus psychoanalysis is an attempt at an access to the central, which will be independent of distal introjections not only in its formal procedure but also in the material from which its inferences are drawn. Interpretative extrapolation into the central region is what should be called depth psychology, in contrast to surface psychology, which is focused upon the directly accessible gross features of peripheral, proximal, and distal phenomena at their face values.

The exclusive interest in the central region of the personality as displayed by psychoanalysis, at least in its beginnings, actually proved itself to be too narrow to catch all the essentials of personality. As long as psychoanalysis concentrated its efforts upon the "id"—that is, the unorganized, primitive, pleasure-seeking system of instinctual drives—the reduction left too little space for further differentiation in distal terms. Taking the shortest possible way to the "id," which is conceived as "timeless," an adult could be of interest only insofar as he revealed in his behavior a dynamic pattern stamped in him as a little child.

There was relatively little interest in the question of what that person has "made out of" his complex—in other words, whether a drive pattern like that discussed by Alexander and Healy has, in spite of conflict, been successfully worked out to great achievement, as in art, or whether it has led to a highly unsuccessful adjustment. And, indeed, it is of far-reaching importance to have discovered that in both cases "similar" drive patterns could have been at work as the underlying central forces, differing from each other only in shades at the most. On the other hand, we understand the objection made by Allport (1937) that "needs are disembodied and depersonalized to a greater degree than is justified in elements that are to serve as the radicals of personality" (p. 241). Restriction of interest to the "id" actually means a depreciation of the functions directed toward the mastery of reality (the ego) to mere diagnostic means. It also means that the environment as a stimulus is chiefly emphasized only insofar as it permits a repetition of childhood reactions to father, mother, or other persons in the past social environment of the child.

It cannot be denied that within certain limits the procedure of introjection may be justified. But, unless supported by special investigations of the central layer by a different set of criteria, the procedure is not much more than an admission of ignorance, or else an undue duplication of the structure found in one layer by carrying it over to the other. Before such an additional investigation is made, we are entitled to suspect that a central psychology based upon concepts read from distal observation is in fact not central but distal psychology.

One of the chief services psychoanalysis can render a behavioristic psychology of personality is to contribute toward the forging of an additonal instrument which can be utilized as an independent probe into the nucleus of personality. Generally speaking, no process of interpretation, proceeding through extrapolation in the sense of the formation of hypotheses about the history and the actual character of the central pattern of demands, takes surface phenomena at their face value. It rests, rather, on "minimal cues." It embraces a wide variety of circumstantial evidence—as furnished, for instance, by the techniques of psychoanalysis (free association and transference). A motive is considered central only after it has been recognized in a large number of behaviorally, or distally, diverse or even opposing features revealed in succession (such as an alternation between aggression and overprotectiveness)—if only these features have in common the same symbolic value empirically established by generalized evidence of the genetic or other type. Quite aside from the question of the material correctness or incorrectness of the extrapolations into central dynamics made by psychoanalysis, one has to recognize that it actually has shown a great resolving power in conceptually bringing together an apparently chaotic variety of behavioral features relevant to life. It was in the service of this process of reduction that such important mechanisms as repression, denial, reaction formation, sublimation, projection, and displacement were discovered.

It has, however, to be emphasized that psychoanalysis seems to be undergoing a change in this respect, thus rendering irrelevant many of the older objections.

Somehow or other, many analysts had conceived the idea that, in analysis, the value of the scientific and therapeutic work done was in direct proportion to the depth of the psychic strata upon which attention was focussed. Whenever interest was transferred from the deeper to the more superficial psychic strata—whenever, that is to say, research was deflected from the id to the ego—it was felt that here was a beginning of apostasy from psycho-analysis as a whole. The view held was that the term *psycho-analysis* should be reserved for the new discoveries relating to the unconscious psychic life, i.e. the study of repressed instinctual impulses, affects and phantasies. With problems such as that of the adjustment of children or adults to the outside world, with concepts of value such as those of health and disease, virtue and vice, psycho-analysis was not properly concerned. It should confine its investigations exclusively to infantile phantasies carried on into adult life, imaginary gratifications and the punishments apprehended in retribution for these [A. Freud, 1936, pp. 3-4].

Thus Anna Freud herself seems to consider the early stages of psychoanalysis as limited to the central, emphasizing at the same time the shift toward the ego, which is defined, in psychoanalysis, as the instance governing the relationship of the individual to actual reality and responsible for the obtained results:

When the writings of Freud, beginning with *Group Psychology and the Analysis of the Ego* and *Beyond the Pleasure Principle,* took a fresh direction, the odium of analytical unorthodoxy no longer attached to the study of the ego and interest was definitely focussed on the ego-institutions. Since then the term "depth-psychology" certainly does not cover the whole field of psycho-analytical research [p. 4].[2]

In the same way Hartmann (1939) recently pointed to the fact that psychoanalysis seems increasingly concerned with the total

---

[2] See also Bernfeld (1931b).

personality, going beyond its traditional emphasis upon conflict by including the viewpoint of achievement *(Leistung)* per se. The expansion into environmental adjustment, if the program is carried out in detailed work, will indeed be of basic importance. It was chiefly achievement and adjustment which differentiated our fictitious example of the thief from the artist and which also would differentiate a person, also referred to above, who through an instinctual danger became intellectualized from the person who out of a "similar" inner situation became restricted and stupid. It is not only the drive, in short, which determines the fate of ability but also ability which determines the fate of drive. Only recently has psychoanalysis considered achievement directly, of itself, rather than merely as it is indirectly touched upon in dealing with central causes.

The concern with distal events such as war led Freud to the assumption of a destructive instinct, thus widening his conception of instincts. We may expect that a further inclusion of the distal events and their interrelations, and of all other surface phenomena—in short, of "facts" as known to academic psychology—will further enlarge the scope of psychoanalysis. On the other hand, all surface research will become more intelligible when viewed in terms of a genuinely central interpretation.

Before concluding our general remarks on psychoanalysis, it should be said that the animistic language used in psychoanalysis and adopted in part in this article may easily be translated into a language which looks less harmful. The disadvantages of the animistic language, the rigidity of its hypostases, is compensated for by the stimulations which may result from empathy.

A good example of the concrete influence exerted by the "central" science of psychoanalysis upon the experimental psychology of the overt behavior of personality is found in "projective methods." These methods have in common with psychoanalysis the desire to "gain insight into the individual's *private world* of meanings, significances, patterns, and feelings.... We find a wide variety of techniques and materials being employed for the same general purpose, to obtain from the subject, 'what he cannot or will not say,' frequently because he does not know himself and is not aware what he is revealing about himself through his projections" (L. K. Frank, 1939, pp. 402, 404).

The way of approaching this aim is also similar to that of psychoanalysis, since any kind of surface event, whether peripheral (conscious or verbal), proximal (handling of material), or distal (mastery of a segment of reality), may be utilized, if only it is not taken at its face value but interpreted as a projection of the person's own pattern of personal drives into the environment. Everything is considered in relation to its significance, direct or symbolic, for the internal situation of the person. And again, the most minute differences in surface events may become emphasized as minimal cues for the central, whereas most conspicuous surface differences may be overlooked entirely. Generally it will be suspected that interest in subtleties and shades, connected with a disregard of large differences, paves the way for a shift of the researcher's chief interest toward a deeper layer which he is not directly observing or seemingly dealing with.

Being deeply infiltrated by psychoanalytic attitudes, the projective methods nevertheless possess important differences from psychoanalytic procedure. The subject's inner life is in most cases not as intimately known to the observer as that of a patient to the analyst. On the other hand, the subject is observed under a set of carefully controlled stimuli which are applied to a number of other subjects as well, thus making possible a comparison with others by means of the statistical techniques developed in the study of individual differences. The well-known examples of such common stimulus situations are the Rorschach inkblots, the William Stern cloud pictures, and the Murray pictures, play situations, etc. For the purposes of interpreting the results obtained under fulfillment of the conditions of a psychological experiment, one may resort to some of the generalized knowledge of psychoanalysis. On the other hand, the minute knowledge of objective facts about the subjects' lives as collected in clinical studies may also imply the possibility of checking back some of the psychoanalytic assumptions.

Besides the content of perceptions, associations, and manipulations, language itself can be utilized as a projection screen for central factors. In a recent study the author has found that certain formal characteristics of speech—e.g., overemphasis (exemplified by phrases such as "at any cost")—when used by a subject in referring to some favorable character trait ascribed to himself (such as benevolence or sincerity) indicate a lack of the trait in question rather than its presence (Frenkel-Brunswik, 1939).

II

The author now wishes to refer to her own scientific development and the influence of psychoanalysis; and, at the same time, to illustrate further the influence psychoanalysis might exert upon the empirical study of personality.

The author had her academic training at the University of Vienna under Karl and Charlotte Bühler. She was connected with the Department of Psychology from 1928 to 1938. Besides psychology, her main interest while a student was in systematic and logical problems of science as represented by the "Viennese Circle" of logical positivism (Schlick, Carnap). Both of these backgrounds resulted in a skeptical attitude toward psychoanalysis, because of its not being sufficiently proved and conceptually worked out. And yet, as a psychologist living in the center of psychoanalysis, the author found that both theoretical interest and an expectation of developing her personality were sufficiently aroused to suggest an actual experience with this discipline. In 1932 she went through a psychoanalysis, which after eight months was interrupted by a protracted bodily illness. Psychoanalysis at that time had not yet exerted much influence upon the author's scientific work, which was still predominantly of a theoretical and systematic character. Analysis was, therefore, not resumed until early in 1937. It was terminated by the political changes in Austria in the spring of 1938. In this second period of analysis the infiltration of psychoanalytic experiences and ideas made itself strongly felt in the author's whole scientific outlook. This influence of psychoanalysis is also connected with the fact that, except at the beginning, the chief research interest of the author has been personality, especially from the developmental point of view. For both periods, the analysts were highly recognized members of the strictly Freudian group; the second was especially known for his contributions to psychoanalytic theory.

The author had the privilege of working for a number of years with Charlotte Bühler in the field of biographical psychology (see C. Bühler, 1933; also Frenkel, 1936). This approach was, by definition, limited in scope to surface phenomena taken at their face value. Among these phenomena were peripheral ones, as represented by introspective statements collected from letters or autobiographies, and proximal ones, as represented by reports on the external activities of the individuals studied. Furthermore, a characteristic feature of Charlotte Bühler's approach was the introduction, on a large scale including statistics, of what Karl Bühler (1927) has called the *Werkaspekt.* In our terminology, this represents the distal layer of the individual's activity, embracing such items as creative products in science, art, or business, and other more or less permanent and detached results of life, such as the founding of a home and fortune, the bringing up of children, etc. In the same line lies Charlotte Bühler's (1931) distinction between "function" (representing the peripheral and especially the proximal) and "achievement" *(Leistung und Werk,* representing the distal) which had become all-important in her biographical as well as in her child-psychological work. The universal theoretical signficance to psychology of the distinction between proximal and distal became evident to the author by the strong emphasis which Egon Brunswik had given to the distal objects as contrasted to the mediating proximal stimuli in studying the achievements of perceptual thing-constancy.

Charlotte Bühler paid, however, relatively little attention to the central layer. She considered her topic to be the description, not the explanation, of the essential phenomena in life history. An objective for which an individual was found overtly to strive all through life was accepted as the goal of life in a straightforward fashion rather than interpreted as standing in some indirect (e.g., symbolic) relationship to an underlying drive. In this sense Charlotte Bühler's approach always remained within the realm of surface phenomena though it did cover a wide variety of such phenomena and brought them into interrelationship with each other.

By thus restricting oneself to "phenotypes" one develops an attitude of self-restraint sharply contrasting to the inclination (often found in clinical psychology as influenced by psychoanalysis) toward short-cut attempts at explanation without careful previous analysis of the material at its face value. Having gone through the first steps of taking down the inventory, and still sticking to "phenomenology," one is forced into a more abstract "formal" analysis. It is through such an attitude that there develops a feeling for subtleties which furnishes the proper basis for a true extrapolation into other layers. Only after a thorough classification of surface phenomena, including all possible angles, can we hope to find an adequate explanatory system.

Even before being explicitly influenced by psychoanalysis, the author found that by applying criteria of the formal type one may get hints for extrapolation. For instance, she found (Frenkel and Weisskopf, 1937) that certain objectives which a younger adult would be inclined to list under his "feelings of duty" rather than under his "wishes" would appear in older adults under the latter heading. This "internalization" of duties which occurs during the course of life is comparable to what Freud has described as the amalgamation of cultural values with the dynamic factors within the personality in the formation of the superego. The two procedures, the psychoanalytic as well as the formal analysis of surface phenomena, have led independently, in this instance, to similar statements.

Another example from the same study is the following. In comparing the number of wishes and of feelings of duty directed toward one and the same objective, the greatest discrepancy was found in the case of utterances by the subject concerning himself. Here the wishes far outnumbered the duties. The number of wishes and duties was most nearly balanced in statements about family and work. From a quite different angle, the importance of work is also emphasized by Freud (1930, p. 80, fn.; see also Bernfeld, 1931a). Work brings us close to reality and to society and at the same time takes care of a large number of libidinal components. The purely phenomenological convergence of wishes and duties under the aspect of work thus may have some dynamic significance.

We may also refer again to the author's above-mentioned publication on the formal analysis of certain features of verbal expression. Phenomenological subtleties such as overemphasis, which on a statistical basis were found to indicate traits contrary to the content of the statements made by the subject, are widely used in psychoanalysis in a similar role. Where there is lack of cause and effect, in the sense of an exaggerated reaction, analysts will suspect the presence of a drive to the contrary (such as cannibalistic tendencies in the case of vegetarianism, or aggression in the case of overprotectiveness).

As far as the author's direct experience with psychoanalysis is concerned, the following might be said. Having learned to concentrate upon surface phenomena in their pure appearance, she became impressed with the difference she found between these layers and the central layer, as aimed at by psychoanalysis with greater directness and concentration than by any other discipline. As a result, she felt the necessity of distinguishing between these two, a necessity which might be less urgent if one had become acquainted with neither or with only one example of these opposing extremes. Having just gone through a period of emphasis upon effects in studying the histories of human lives, the author was surprised at the way in which her own seemingly diverse reactions, in a wide variety of life situations, became reorganized theoretically under the aspect of unifying psychoanalytic experiences. So she discovered that, in situations which distally, proximally, or peripherally seemed very different from, and often openly contrasting to, each other, she was guided by but one single motive—of which, as such, she had never before been conscious. Situations characterized by herself as "extremely boring," for example, turned out to be ones of extreme interest, only disguised by defense mechanisms. By means of comparable interpretations, her insight was increased in relation to many other reactions.

In the process of analysis the whole manifest material is thoroughly discussed, working toward extrapolations, though technical terms are seldom mentioned explicitly by the analyst. The concrete procedure of analysis is often more convincing than the theory. It has been the author's experience that certain interpretations thus arrived at by herself or offered to her by the analyst on the basis of the evidence available—in specific terms coined to cover the particular case—have proved to be fruitful in making understandable not only the material already known, but also data which at that time were not yet known.

An example is the following. From the reports given by the author about her behavior, and from associations concerning her two sisters, the analyst had interpreted what he called a "Cordelia motive." He suggested to her that she was displaying in her life the role of Cordelia, the youngest daughter of King Lear. To her answer that she had read most of Shakespeare's dramas but not *King Lear,* the analyst replied that Cordelia was the best and most generous daughter of King Lear, who nevertheless preferred his other two daughters because of their flattering attitude. Such an interpretation was at that time refused by the author rather emotionally. Later it was received somewhat more favorably. But it was still very surprising to her when, much later, she discovered, in looking through old notes, that at the age of about 15 she had copied the entire role of Cordelia. Thus she must have been very much concerned at that age with the fate of Cordelia, with whom she probably had identified herself, later repressing not only this identification but also all other memories of the play.

Generally it seems to the author that the most plausible interpretations made in psychoanalysis are those concerning the persistence of certain inner situations and roles, and the resulting attitudes and mechanisms determining the whole course of life. Interpretations of her dreams were also highly plausible.

In comparing her two divergent backgrounds, it became clear to the author that a full understanding of an individual's personality could be gained only by an approach in which the central and the distal aspects were interlocked with each other. The reduction should be attempted from both sides with mutual determination.

A concrete example of the possibilities of such a cooperation out of the writer's present work is the following. In studying the reactions of children to the set of pictures designed by Murray for diagnostic purposes, two lines of possible approach can be distinguished. One, especially emphasized by Murray and his collaborators, can be characterized as the "contentual." In this procedure the types of action read into the picture by the child are classified according to certain more generalized "needs," which are then assumed to underlie the child's interpretations of the picture. For example, a mention of killing would be taken as a concrete instance revealing the need for aggression.

The second possibility can be characterized, in connection with our previous discussion, as the "formal" approach. We can take the stories told by the children at their face value, namely as the mastering of a task or, more specifically, as a literary achievement. They could then be analyzed according to the usual standards of evaluation of artistic productions, that is, in a formal way. We could, for instance, determine whether the presentation is dramatic or epic, tragic or comic, logically coherent or incoherent, realistic (in the sense of being practically possible) or fantastic. We could look also for parallels with motives found in the literature, or we could analyze the particularities of the sequence of motives, etc.

Both the contentual and the formal approach could be carried out independently of each other. In fact, they represent, respectively, a psychoanalytic type of interest in the central and an interest in achievement, in the sense in which the two concepts have been distinguished above. Correlations between items of the two sets of data could be computed—as between the amount of aggression revealed (defined by the number of aggressive acts mentioned) and the degree of realism (defined by the degree to which impracticable solutions are avoided); or between the amount of tension and conflict (existing, for example, between ambition and passivity) and the degree of logical consistency. Such investigations might answer some centro-distal problems. One might discover, for instance, which specific subtleties of a conflict situation are likely to lead to a climax of logicality and which are likely to destroy logicality. In this way we might learn something about the possibility, discussed earlier, that instinctual conflicts may lead either to an increase or to a decrease of intelligence. On the other hand, one might also discover which specific types of logicality would be likely to go with certain gross differences in the central drive pattern.

Another example of the way in which general psychology and psychoanalysis might converge is the following. Working with some of the material of the Adolescent Study at the University of California, the author first tried to look for certain relationships between the adjustment questionnaire (self-ratings) and the observations, made by classmates and adults, of the subjects' external behavior. Her aim was not primarily to add to the evidence already collected concerning the "agreement" between the subjective and objective data, as by comparing self-rating on the item "popular" with the corresponding observations made by adults in play situations. Such correlations were already known from other publications to be rather low. The chief interest was, instead, to see whether the subjects might indirectly give themselves away, thus revealing the true "meaning" of their self-ratings. In that case one might expect some correlations between items not explicitly synonymous with each other, perhaps between popularity as observed by adult raters and the subjective statements about the degree to which games were enjoyed by the subjects. These indirect correlations were also low, however, save for a few interesting exceptions which will be discussed in another publication. This fact may be due to the lack of psychological significance of the type of self-reports requested (that is, to the yes-no form of the question, leaving too little free play for self-expression), or rather to the fact that external behavior is not a true focus determining personality. Pointing toward the consistency of these self-reports, Vernon (1938), however, concludes "that the self-rating tests do measure something, though not perhaps what the authors of tests generally assume." There is still the possibility that self-ratings in their entirety may depend on the inner status of the person, as defined by drives and attitudes, more than on external behavior. Thus an attempt to focus observation upon this inner motivational pattern would seem to be worthwhile.

Such observations are contained in abundance in the "comments" made by the staff purporting to characterize, in a free fashion, the subjects over and above the standardized adult ratings. In going through some of these comments and comparing them with the rest of the material, it has occurred to the author that some of the items of self-rating might be associated with certain inner features. For example, it might be that self-ratings asserting a lack of social adjustment are determined by the subjective demand to belong to a group (the "need for affiliation") rather than by real popularity (that is, the external status in the group) or by real adjustment. Thus some subjects who characterized themselves as socially not adjusted were characterized in the comments either in terms such as "He has prestige, though he does not strive for it," or else by "He has no prestige but is not bitter about it (has no desire to be part of the group)." In these two cases, although the social effects are different, the central situations are similar. This example, of course, represents only one of the many possibilities which can be put to test by rating inner demands independently of the self-ratings and other projective tests, and then correlating the former with the latter.

It was psychoanalysis which first emphasized the fact that external success itself is not the basic datum from which to start, but rather the meaning which the idea of success has acquired for the subject, that is, the relationship between the objective and the subjective. We may also refer in this connection to the contrast between the type of neurotic who is not enjoying his success, since his desire is insatiable and he depreciates his achievements, and the well-balanced person to whom much less is enough. It was through her own psychoanalysis that the author was struck by a realization of how much less important the external data of life are compared to the role which demands play in life.

The conclusion to be drawn from such considerations must stress the importance of an access to the subject's inner demands. Besides rating for proximal popularity, one may also attempt to rate children for their central demands for social ties and recognition. Such ratings will necessarily have to be interpretive, though based upon material somewhat different from that of psychoanalysis. They will have to rest on minimal cues and will as a rule require that the raters be closely acquainted with the subjects over a long period of time. Both from everyday experience and from looking through the free comments about the children of the Adolescent Study, the author feels that such interpretive ratings ought to be possible. In a recent study, in fact, Murray and Wolf (Murray, 1938, pp. 243 ff.) have shown that interpretive ratings are not less reliable, as far as the agreement among different judges goes, than ratings of directly palpable features of behavior.

Independently of the central, the effects should also be rated on their own status. In some cases, such as in studying detached products, distal results might be as measurable as peripheral and proximal phenomena. In other cases, however, such as in questions about how a subject faces failure, the distal success will have to be abstracted from a wide variety of observations in a rather synoptic fashion comparable to the approach to the central.

Rating lists thus might be set up which would catch in a standardized fashion the private subjective opinions of the judges about the ultimate demands and the ultimate success of the subjects, with the two categories mentioned kept sharply apart. Thus the desire for recognition would have to be rated separately from established prestige. Correlations then might be computed within each category and also between items of one category and items of the other (e.g., aspiration level with the manner in which failure is met). Especially one might also correlate central as well as distal estimates with peripheral and proximal events (for instance, self-ratings or behavioral reactions in an experimental situation) in order to widen the diagnostic basis.

It goes without saying that in this connection the term "rating" stands for any kind of possible access to the layers in question, some of which might be more reliable than is rating in the technical sense of the word. The point to be made here is that because of the interpretive character of the approach, especially to the central layer, more than one of a series of mutually independent instruments of access should be utilized.

Let me add a few words about the interpretive procedure as such. Objections have been raised against it for the reason that the standards of intersubjective observation and communication, in short, of exactitude in the sense of physics, are violated. This difficulty has been especially emphasized for the case in which interpretation is of the intuitive rather than of the rational type. The objection is often made in the name of positivism. Yet for positivism any kind of statement is acceptable if only the operation leading up to it is kept in mind or can be "rationally reconstructed" and thus traced back to facts from which a certain interpretive datum, such as a demand, has been inferred. It would be in line with a properly understood positivistic ideology if intuitive interpretations were not eliminated but, on the contrary, were taken quite as seriously as surface data; if, in other words, the usual procedure of empirical treatment, such as statistics, were applied to them.

It seems that in many investigators a silent belief has grown that one can be exact only about less important things, namely, the peripheral and the proximal aspects. The more important things, on the other hand, have for intrinsic reasons to remain within the private. In this sense, the search for laws became restricted, and often failed of results. Aspects most relevant for the study of personality were banished from the nomothetic into the idiographic realm, by being limited to case histories. The escape into uniqueness was thus in fact an escape from the limitations of the merely peripheral-proximal approach. But the sacrifices involved are not at all necessary. We merely have to start from the right kinds of interpretive units, to the selection of which comments and case histories can give us the most valuable hints, and then try to apply statistics to them. Thus properly focused, this type of statistics may well reveal important laws, or at least yield higher correlations than those found within the peripheral-proximal region alone. This kind of approach has not yet been sufficiently tested. The decision about its fruitfulness can safely be left to a posteriori decisions of statistics, such as the above-quoted study by Murray and Wolf.

One might also remember that physics, too, started in its beginnings from data not sharp in character, the further fate of which could be decided only after they had been brought in relation to other data. In the same way, psychological intuitions and interpretations have to be checked back to the mass of surface data. Unless this is done, the data remain without empirical meaning. All the more does this statement hold true for psychoanalysis. The ego should remain the subject matter of psychology, and extrapolations should be used chiefly in order to throw light back upon the surface phenomena of behavior and achievement. In thus returning ultimately to the surface region, we will have attempted a deep psychology of the surface *(tiefe Oberflächenpsychologie)*, rather than indulged in a superficial psychology of the depth *(oberflächliche Tiefenpsychologie)*.

In conclusion, we can say that most psychological attempts to approach the "central" have been found not central, but rather "distal" (environmental) in character, with the major exception of psychoanalysis. Both the central and distal aspects are necessary for a full description of personality. It is their interrelationship, rather than the peripheral-proximal relationships chiefly emphasized up to now, which should be studied. Whereas psychoanalysis has been asking, "Which drive?" and general psychology has been asking, "Which effect?" a unified psychology should ask, "Which effect out of which drive?"

2

INTOLERANCE OF AMBIGUITY AS AN EMOTIONAL AND PERCEPTUAL PERSONALITY VARIABLE

Introduction

In recent years there have been an increasing number of attempts to integrate the field of perception with that of motivation and of personality. These attempts may take either of two opposite directions. One is characterized by a basic dependence on the outlook, the problems, and the techniques developed in the general psychology of perception. This approach may be further subdivided in the following manner. The motivational angle is either, first, superimposed upon this nucleus of general problems of perception as an additional element or factor, or second, derived from it by an expansion of concepts or principles originating in the field of perception. Both these subdivisions may be characterized as perception centered.

The opposite direction is taken by a third group of investigations. These are organized about major patterns of findings originating in some area of personality research; problems or findings of perception psychology are brought into the picture by way of analogy as convenient means in the testing of hypotheses, or in some other secondary role. This may be called the personality-centered approach.

This is not to say that with the first two cases the primary interest is always in perception, and with the third always in personality. On the contrary, the decisive slant may in each case be given by the new element of thought injected, rather than by the core to which this new element is added.

First published in *Journal of Personality*, 18:108-143, 1949. © 1949 by Duke University Press.

In the present paper the third, personality-centered, approach is applied to concepts and findings originating in the sphere of emotional ambivalence and to their expansion into experiments on perceptual ambiguity proper and on related subjects which had been treated under different aspects so long as they were left within the framework of the psychology of perception.

Perception-Centered Studies in Motivation and Personality

Examples of the first subvariety of the perception-dependent approach, that in which motivation is superimposed upon a problem rooted in the tradition of the general psychology of cognition, are given by Murray's (1933) investigation of the influence of fear on perception, Sherif's (1936) work on the need for conformity, and Bruner and Goodman's (1947) experiment on values as determining perception in the poor as contrasted with the well-to-do. Emphasis is in each case on temporary or otherwise relatively personality-alien factors, defining a single motivational force in relative isolation. Characteristically, the experimental task itself is one borrowed from the inventory of routine perceptual problems. It may involve the traditional problem of geometrical "illusion," or it may be a problem of aesthetic appreciation previously limited to a more formal approach. Want, fear, or social influences are now added as further determinants to complete the existing list of interferences already known. And while the motivational factor is superimposed upon a well-structured cognitive core, it remains unrelated to the basic personality of the subjects, at least within the framwork of the experiment concerned. The relative conceptual isolation in which the new factor is usually presented has led to the accusation that in this kind of work the traditional cleavage between cognition and emotion is needlessly continued. Use of such expressions as "influence of needs or values upon perception" has given further nourishment to this interpretation. Murphy (1947) has characterized the point of view discussed by the phrase "needs keep ahead of percepts."

Examples of the second subvariety of the perception-dependent approach are given by a group of investigators who have come to conceive of personality as a whole after the pattern of what they have learned in studying perception proper. This role might well have fallen to the Gestalt psychologists had they been able to develop a sufficiently specified interest in problems of personality.[1] The challenge was, for some time, left in the hands of the characterologists. Among the perceptually loaded variables that have become prominent in this course of development is the one defined by the opposition of the *synthetic* and the *analytic* approach as adopted, among others, by Kretschmer and his school (notably in some later studies summarized in an as yet untranslated new chapter [13] on experimental type psychology in the 1936 and 1942 editions of his *Körperbau und Charakter)* and also represented by the *whole* versus *detail* emphasis in the evaluation of the Rorschach test (Rorschach, 1921); further pairs of opposites borrowed from the psychology of perception are *diffuse* versus *articulated* (Werner, 1940), *concrete* versus *abstract* (Goldstein and Scheerer, 1941), as well as such rather specific distinctions as *color dominance* versus *form dominance* (Kretschmer, Schroll, and others, and again Rorschach; see also the treatment in Thurstone's [1944] factorial study of perception).

A case by itself within this second group is E. R. Jaensch and his school (e.g., 1938). In his later years Jaensch has gone considerably beyond good evidence in postulating a "unity of style" within each individual so that a few simple perception tests would suffice for universal diagnosis. Although his tests are undoubtedly of greater potential relevance than most of the older psychophysical tests, none of them reaches the level of penetration of what has recently become known as projective techniques. Examples of the tests used by Jaensch are the adjustment of the individual to prismatic lenses which at first will make straight lines appear curved, the persistence of movement phenomena after viewing a rotating spiral, exaggerated reactions to binocular disparity, and other visual illusions, along with investigation of vivid "eidetic" images. Erratic responses are taken as a sign of general instability; there is a violent rejection of ambiguity in reactions of any form. The latter is taken as an expression of a pervasive "liberalism"

---

[1]Among the more recent expansions of the psychology of perception, the farthest advance into a special field of application under the Gestalt point of view has been made by the social psychology of Krech and Crutchfield (1948).

which Jaensch considers morbid in the perceptual as much as he does in the political sphere.

It is primarily the synesthetic or S-type that is said to display such liberalism. This is the type whose "spatial perceptions are unstable, loosened up, even dissolved. Normally the objects of the external world are given to the psychophysical organism of man in a univocally determined spatial order. To the points of the retina correspond firmly and univocally determined locations in visual space or, as this is usually expressed, the spatial values of the retina are fixed." (Note the gross incorrectness of this statement.) "This coordination between stimulus configuration and perceptual Gestalt is disrupted in the case of the S-type" (p. 37). Liberalism of every kind—and adaptability in general, which is being summarily depreciated—goes with a lack of strong ties, according to Jaensch: "The lytic S-type has no firm tie with reality. In fact he has no ties at all. He is the liberalist at large" (p. 44). "This social liberalism is paralleled by innumerable other forms of liberalism, all of them mentally rooted in the S-type: liberalism of knowledge, of perception, of art, etc."

In contrast, the firmness, consistency, and regularity of the desirable "integrated" or J-type is stressed over and over again. These characteristics, according to Jaensch, can be seen in the "elementary realm" of sensory phenomena as well as in the most complex cognitive and social attitudes. The J-type is said to accomplish his adaptation to the prismatic spectacles slowly and consistently, showing steady progress, whereas his undesirable counterpart, the S-type, is said to show in all the perceptual experiments irregularities, great latitude of reaction, instability, and jumpiness; his adaptation to the prismatic spectacles is said to proceed in a jerky fashion, with switching back and forth and a wide range of correction values.

Jaensch claims that the same tendencies exist in memory, imagery, and thinking. Thus, the free associations of the J-type are said to connect what belongs together, whereas those of the S-type connect what is separate, ignoring realistic relationships. The drawings of the J-type are said to be reality near, those of the S-type reality removed. In an experiment on the recall of pictures, the J-type is said to be more faithful and to like specific questions, whereas the S-type is said to recall a greater quantity and to give a report that is freer and of lesser fidelity—once more revealing, according to Jaensch, a morbid lack of ties to sensory reality. A rigid, rational superstructure and adherence to rational methods is said to be used by this type as a superficial safeguard against his instability on the more elementary biological levels.

The sampling technique and the statistical significance and validity of Jaensch's work are of the shoddiest kind and cannot stand up under scrutiny of even the mildest kind. As a mere theory, Jaensch's system is of interest to us for two reasons. First, his typology centers on concepts of ambiguity. Second, he postulates a connection between various areas of ambiguity in what he dogmatically considers the unitary "style" of liberalism, perceptual, cognitive, and social. As will be shown in this paper, all three of these liberalisms must be considered definite assets rather than liabilities, quite contrary to Jaensch's opinion. But he was probably right in seeing a connection between these apparently widely separated fields, although he himself has not gathered or intercorrelated material on all the aspects necessary to make such a statement, and although he has a most distorted valuation of the trait of liberalism. (For a criticism of the juxtaposition of machinelike precision and excessive subjectivity, see below.)

From Emotional Ambivalence to Cognitive Ambiguity; Personality Centering in the Present Approach

The approach used in the present paper differs from those outlined so far in that the problems to be discussed are originally developed and perfected in the clinical and social fields; they are reformulated and broadened here to absorb certain fitting elements of recent perceptual thought. It is this that we mean when we say that our approach is personality centered rather than perception centered.

The prime concern is to bring together a variety of aspects in order to study the generality or lack of generality of the personality patterns involved, that is, the readiness to spread from one area of manifestation to another. Can basic formal attitudes such as subjectivity, rigidity, fear of ambivalence and of ambiguity, etc., be taken as unified traits of the organism, or are we to find a more differential distribution, varying from one area to another?

A second advantage offered by the carrying of personality problems into perception is that tendencies which in the social and emotional fields are manifested in a vague fashion are rendered more clearly accessible to experimental verification.

It is hoped that by discussion of the same formal principles in all three, the motivational, social, and perceptual contexts, greater conceptual clarity can be achieved than through a discussion of any of those channels alone. Clarity will be added to the richness of motivational concepts by nailing them down on the more objective and precise perceptual level. As will be seen, differentiations lost or obscured in the globality of the motivational approach can be reestablished in this manner; on the other hand, problems in perception will gain in significance and fruitfulness if questions in personality and social psychology are allowed to help in the choice of problems. The gain is far from being restricted to the conceptual level. Important empirical relations are revealed along with clarification, throwing further light on the first-mentioned problem of the generality versus specificity of behavior as well as on problems concerning the interrelation of the levels of personality.

A third advantage is what may be called the reduction of social bias. By the shift of emphasis from the emotional to the perceptual area, certain preconceived notions which only too readily slip into the investigation of social and clinical issues can be greatly reduced and controversial issues delineated and at least indirectly decided on a more nearly neutral platform.

The last-named two advantages are, of course, contingent upon the first point in that any shifting of problems to other areas is valid only to the extent to which the mechanisms involved throughout these areas or levels tend to be similar within the same individuals. Only a beginning will be made in this paper toward answering this problem in an empirical manner. The major emphasis will lie on the following two points: (1) a development of the underlying reasoning from previous evidence based on the writer's own work as well as on sources from the literature; and (2) a showing of possible ways of attacking the problem experimentally. Experimental evidence as cited below, although scattered or preliminary and by no means conclusive thus far, partly points in the direction of the generality of the personality traits mentioned, partly is suggestive of compensatory relations which may make for the simultaneous presence of opposite tendencies.

The topic to serve as a medium through which this procedure

will be followed is given by what seems to this writer one of the basic variables in both the emotional and the cognitive orientation of a person toward life and what she has suggested be labeled "tolerance versus intolerance of ambiguity" (Frenkel-Brunswik, 1948a, 1948b, 1948c, 1948d).

The material evidence is based primarily on a project conducted at the Institute of Child Welfare of the University of California[2] and dealing with rigid adherence versus disinclination to ethnic prejudice in children, and the motivational and cognitive correlates of these social attitudes. This study has involved, to date, the construction of a series of scales for the direct and indirect measurement of prejudice and for the assessment of factors suspected to be related. Data have been collected from 1,500 public school children, 11 to 16 years old, in several samples. With 120 of these subjects, representing the extremes of prejudice and of freedom from prejudice, more intensive studies were conducted in terms of individual interviews and projective tests. Furthermore, the parents of the children interviewed were visited and likewise interviewed. Approximately 40 of the intensively studied children were further submitted to some of the experiments in perception proper and in memory, which are to be described below.[3] An advance report of some aspects of this project was given by the present writer not long ago (1948c, 1948d). Those of her collaborators who worked on the aspects discussed here will be mentioned in the proper context later in this paper.

The line of argument will now be outlined in somewhat greater detail. Starting from the observation that some of her subjects were able to tolerate emotional ambiguities better than others, the writer became involved in the question of whether this attitude of intolerance of more complex, conflicting, or otherwise open structures extends beyond the emotional and social areas to include perceptual and cognitive aspects proper.

The importance of individual differences in the insistence on unqualified assertions was first brought to the attention of the writer

[2]The writer is indebted to Dr. Harold E. Jones, the director of the Institute, for giving her the opportunity to carry out this project as well as for suggestions regarding its execution.

[3]While the project on social discrimination in children referred to here has some features in common with the project on adults (Adorno et al., 1950), it is distinguished from the latter by, among other things, the use of experiments and a greater emphasis on cognitive factors in general.

in a study on mechanisms of self-deception conducted at the University of Vienna before the war (1939). The greater the definiteness and lack of shading—that is, the greater the intolerance of ambiguity—in the self-description of favorable traits, the less were such assertions as a rule verified in the judgment of close acquaintances.

The background of the problem of ambiguity thus becomes related to the vast fund of knowledge supplied by psychoanalysis in connection with the development of the concept of "ambivalence," as defined by the coexistence, in the same individual, of love and hate cathexis toward the same object. The existence of ambivalence in a person and the further fact of this person's ability to face his or her ambivalences toward others must be considered an important personality variable. As in other areas of personality, psychoanalytic statements referring to content, such as attitude toward parents, repression of certain id tendencies, etc., are perhaps difficult of access to experimental verification. Here, however, we are dealing with experimentation concerning formal factors, such as intolerance of ambiguity, or rigidity, and the question of whether or not these attitudinal variables are restricted to the emotional area.

From here, a first step toward a more cognitively slanted reformulation is achieved by shifting to the problem of the recognition, by one and the same individual, of any actual coexistence of positive and negative features in the same object, e.g., in parents or other "in-groups." Ability to recognize such coexistences in all likelihood constitutes another important emotional-cognitive personality variable, which is not to be confused with emotional ambivalence in the original sense of the word. At the end of a scale defined by this ability stand those with a tendency to resort to black-and-white solutions, to arrive at premature closure as to valuative aspects, often at the neglect of reality, and to seek for unqualified and unambiguous over-all acceptance and rejection of other people. The maintenance of such solutions requires the shutting out of aspects of reality which represent a possible threat to these solutions. It is this problem of "reality adequacy" versus "reality inadequacy" which injects a distinctly cognitive element into the broader sphere of the problem of ambivalence.

Our material gives evidence of individual differences both in emotional ambivalence and in the readiness to face it, and in the more cognitive recognition of traits of conflicting values in others. Since the clinical aspects of the problems involved have been discussed in greater detail elsewhere (Frenkel-Brunswik, 1948a, 1948b, 1948c; Adorno et al., 1950), they will be presented here in a summary fashion only.

Some individuals are more apt to see positive as well as negative features in their parents and can accept feelings of love and hate toward the same persons without too much anxiety or conflict. Others seem compelled to dramatize their image of the parents in seeing them either as altogether good or as altogether bad. The following question suggests itself in this context: Is this second attitude an intolerance of an existing underlying ambivalence, or is it merely absence of ambivalence? Why do we doubt that a thoroughly positive description of the parents with denial of any negative features or discrepancies as given to us by some of the children is a true representation of the children's feelings? On what basis are we entitled to claim that the individual has repressed the negative side of an ambivalence out of some hypothetical intolerance of ambiguities and complexities?

We list here only a few of the facts which were used as the basis of such an inference. First, the description of the parents in the second type of case is often stereotyped and exaggerated, indicating a use of clichés rather than an expression of genuine feelings. The range of responses in such cases is rather narrow and without the variations commonly found in the description of real people. Only the more palpable, crude, and concrete aspects are mentioned. Thus we find a preponderance of references to physical and other external characteristics rather than mention of more essential and abstract aspects of the parents' personalities. Furthermore, a child relating only positive feelings while talking directly about his or her parents may at the same time reveal a negative attitude on manifestations which are more indirect. For instance, he may omit his parents from the list of people he wants to take to a desert island. Or, when describing parents in general rather than his own, e.g., in his responses to parental figures on the Thematic Apperception Test, he may stress the coercive and punitive aspects of parents. It is data of this and other kinds which induce us to state that the children concerned split the positive and negative

INTOLERANCE OF AMBIGUITY AS PERSONALITY VARIABLE 67

sides of their feelings and attitudes rather than become aware of their coexistence.

Both the exaggerated concreteness and the stereotypy of the descriptions can serve as diagnostic indices of dynamic states. The above considerations concerning the diagnosis of the "real" emotional state are a further demonstration of the greater conceptual power of the depth-psychological approach. The latter rests upon the inclusion of minimal cues as well as on material of an indirect type, such as projective techniques. For a more detailed discussion of the relationship of the underlying genotypic or conceptually more derived level to the manifest or phenotypic level of personality as relevant in this context, see Frenkel-Brunswik (this volume, Chapter 1; 1942).

Synopsis of a variety of data suggests that the attempt to master aggression toward parental figures who are experienced as too threatening and powerful is among the important determinants of the tendency rigidly to avoid ambiguity of any sort.[4] The requested submission and obedience to parental authority is only one of the many external, rigid, and superficial rules which such a child learns. Dominance-submission, cleanliness-dirtiness, badness-goodness, virtue-vice, masculinity-femininity are some of the other dichotomies customarily upheld in the homes of such children. The absoluteness of each of these differences is considered natural and eternal, excluding any possibility of individuals trespassing from the one side to the other. There is rigid adherence to these clearly delineated norms even if this implies restrictions and disadvantages for the own group. Thus, not only boys but also girls exhibiting the need for dichotomizing subscribe to restrictions for women rather than expose themselves to more flexible but at the same time more uncertain norms.

In line with this, in the type of home just referred to, discipline is experienced by the children significantly more often as threatening, traumatic, overwhelming, and unintelligible, as contrasted with an intelligent, non-ego-destructive type of discipline in the home with

---

[4]For a discussion of attitudes toward authority and the resulting patterns of life, see also Fromm (1941).

a more flexible atmosphere. Actually, in the home with a rigid[5] orientation the discipline is more often based upon the expectation of a quick learning of external, rigid, superficial rules beyond the comprehension of the child.[6] Family relationships are based on roles clearly defined in terms of dominance and submission. Some of the children live in a situation comparable to permanent physical danger which leaves no time for finer discriminations and for attempts to get a fuller understanding of the factors involved, but in which quick action leading to tangible and concrete results is the only appropriate behavior.[7] It is of course true that no child can fully master his environment. Global, diffuse, concrete, undifferentiated types of reaction have thus been described by Werner (1940) and others as characteristic of the child in general. It depends on the atmosphere of the home and the more specific expectations regarding the child's behavior, however, whether such reactions become fixated or whether progress toward higher developmental stages is encouraged. For the latter course a reduction of fear and a tolerance toward weakness in the child are necessary.

Further factors contributing to the rigidification of personality in children are the stress on stereotyped behavior, an expectancy of self-negating submission, and the inducement to repress nonacceptable tendencies. As a result we find a break and conflict between the different layers of personality which contrast sharply with the greater fluidity of transition and intercommunication between the different personality strata of the child in the permissive home. Repression and externalization of instinctual tendencies reduce their manageability and the possibility of their control by the individual, since it is now the external world to which the feared qualities of the unconscious are ascribed.

Data on the parents of the children in the rigid, intolerant group reveal that it is their feeling of social and economic marginality in relation to the group to which they aspire from which en-

[5] Few concepts in recent personality psychology have been used with such a variety of connotations as that of rigidity. Unless otherwise specified, in this paper the term "rigid" refers to the various kinds of intolerance of ambiguity discussed.

[6] Most recently, the relationship between frustration and rigidity was experimentally demonstrated by Christie (1949). In a task similar to that of Rokeach (1943) described below, subjects exposed to a frustrating situation given by an unsolvable reasoning problem persisted, more often than a nonfrustrated control group, in a set maladaptive to the task.

[7] For the relationship between frustration and rigidity, see especially Rosenzweig (1938).

sues the desperate clinging to external and rigid rules. These parents report significantly more often their own parents as foreign born, indicating perhaps that they still see themselves as entangled in the process of assimilation. They may well be furthering everything which they deem advantageous and repressing everything which they deem detrimental to this goal. Obviously, the less secure they are in their feeling of belonging the more they will insist on maintenance of the cultural norms in themselves and in their children. It is this rigid adherence to norms which furnishes the key to an understanding of all the various avoidances of ambiguities listed in this paper.

In order to reduce conflict and anxiety and to maintain stereotyped patterns, certain aspects of experience have to be kept out of awareness. Assumptions once made, no matter how faulty and out of keeping with reality because of a neglect of relevent aspects, are repeated over and over again and not corrected in the face of new evidence.

The spontaneous interview statements of children in the rigidly intolerant group show a tendency toward polarization similar to the one referred to above. Often this is done in moralistic terms, without any qualification or expression of conflicting feelings. The evidence from both direct and indirect material thus suggests that children who tend to make unambiguous statements, either of total acceptance or of total rejection, seem to be aware of only one of two aspects coexisting within their dynamic attitudinal make-up. A static superstructure appears to be superimposed upon a most conflict-ridden understructure, with resulting major discrepancies and stresses between the two levels. In this state of affairs the conflicting tendencies are isolated from each other and expressed only alternatively through different types of media, each of them representing a different layer of the total personality.

The fact that the tendency toward emotional dichotomizing in interpersonal relationships is related to dichotomizing in the social field is not a surprising one. In analyzing, say, the aspects contained in racial prejudice, one is first reminded of the more general dichotomy of in-group versus out-group in its more rigid form, which precludes the possibility of cross-passing. A further feature is that the criterion for the distinction is usually an external one, such as color or place in the social hierarchy. Moreover, the distinction tends to become a totalitarian one in that all of the "good" characteristics are ascribed to those of the in-group and all of the "bad" ones to the out-group. There is, finally, the introduction of a double standard of values as a further type of dichotomy. (For an analysis of the various dimensions of ethnocentrism, see Levinson [1949]; Adorno et al. [1950].)

In order to maintain the rigid and moralistically tainted distinctions just mentioned, one and the same trait—e.g., erudition or aggressive orientation toward success—is considered objectionable in the out-group yet definitely desirable in the in-group. There is little awareness of the ambivalent or ambiguous quality which these traits acquire by this double assessment. Both in-group and out-group are thus characterized by a gestalt which has great *Prägnanz* (is highly clear-cut), as was noted above for such concepts as that of masculinity and femininity. These gestalten are "closed" and cannot be modified by new experiences, which are immediately viewed from the standpoint of the old set and classified in the same way as the previous ones. Such tendencies as premature closure, jumping to generalizations on the basis of certain specific and external aspects, carrying over old sets, and the like, will become evident in the cognitive and perceptual reactions as they are evident in the emotional and social spheres. "Speed and strength of closure" turned out to be one of the major factors in Thurstone's (1944) analysis of perception. The question which is up for discussion in this paper is whether or not seeing gestalten which are too "good" in the sense of the principle of *Prägnanz* is an even more generalized type of reaction, although the seeing of relatively circumscribed and closed gestalten may be at the price of not being able to perceive the broader over-all connections.

One must add that a great variety of perceptual and cognitive processes may be considered as formal approaches to reality which may be very revealing of a person's style of life. The establishment of the relationship of these formal aspects to content is an important task of psychology. The question may be raised as to what are the consistencies and positive correlations, and what are the compensations in terms of behavior. It is such problems which led to the experiments discussed subsequently in this paper.

Concentrating on tolerance of ambiguity, the question takes the form as to whether those incapable of conflicting emotions—or of conflicting value judgments—are generally incapable of seeing things in two or more different ways. It is at this point that a well-worked-over area of psychological research is again being approached. This is the area covered by the concept of perceptual ambiguity *(Gestaltmehrdeutigkeit)* as originally defined by Benussi (1904) and as further developed in the well-known work of Rubin on figure-ground reversals and in the studies of the Gestalt psychologists proper (see Koffka, 1935). In its own right, this problem of cognitive ambiguity is of very broad scope. In its more recent ramifications it includes the problems posed by the fact that ambiguity of cognitive responses must be seen as a reflection of the uncertainties existing in the environment itself, thus opening up the field of "probability" as a new area of psychological research (see Egon Brunswik, 1943).

Academic research on ambiguity and on probability adjustment has discovered a number of important principles by which cognitive responses are linked to characteristics of stimulus configurations and stimulus combinations in the environment, such as to the relative size of the figure versus ground area, and the relative frequency of reward on the two sides of a rat maze, respectively. In turn, problems of personality patterns with respect to ambiguity such as those outlined in some of the preceding paragraphs were as a rule bypassed; in the typical case, individual differences in ambiguity reactions are rarely mentioned.

In the type of study with which the present paper concerns itself, this procedure is reversed. There is no more than a passing interest in the external conditions of ambiguity, basic in perception psychology. The entire development of the problem is under the aspect of personality. Issuing from this latter aspect, excursions are made into perception psychology, adapting some stock experiments or taking them as cues for new experiments but always subordinating them to patterns of personality differences as the basic problem, with an eye to developing them eventually as diagnostic tools or tests.

This personality-centered rather than perception-centered approach may be linked to certain further developments within psychoanalysis proper. An example of the occasional parallels between motivational and perceptual processes drawn in the psychoanalytic literature, which at the same time is related to our own problem, can be found in Fenichel's discussion of the compulsive character (1945). After an examination of the general dynamics of this syndrome Fenichel describes the need for being systematic and for clinging to definite systems as it occurs in the compulsive. This need, often manifested in the tendency to "type" and to classify in categories, is seen as protection against surprise and fear of drive impulses. Deviations from symmetry are not tolerated but are experienced as deviations from general norms, especially moral. Compare this depth-psychological explanation of the tendency toward symmetry with the one given by Gestalt psychology in terms of dynamic factors in the brain field and you have a further illustration of the difference between the personality-centered and the perception-centered approaches.

The clinically well-known mechanism of isolation found in the compulsive character can, according to Fenichel, lead to an inhibition of seeing gestalten and to a perception of a sum of elements instead. Related to this is said to be a preoccupation with small, insignificant detail, which is often found to be taken as a symbol for more important aspects of objects. In psychoanalysis, assumptions of this kind are not as a rule based upon actual experiments in perception or cognition. In some cases such experiments can easily be undertaken, however. In fact, the experiments referred to below bear decidedly upon the topics just described.

In order to investigate empirically how far basic personality trends found in the emotional and social sphere, such as ambivalence, are apt to spread beyond this area to include perceptual and cognitive aspects, it was decided to combine the personality studies of the children in our project on ethnic prejudice not only with an ascertainment of their social beliefs but also with an investigation of their perceptual reactions. To quote from the theoretical considerations in an advance report of 1945, the writer had been led "to expect prejudice to be associated with perceptual rigidity, inability to change set, and tendencies to primitive and rigid structuring of ambiguous perceptual fields. Well-tested experimental approaches are available for these variables. It only remains to use them in connection with susceptibility to prejudice"[8] (see also Frenkel-Brunswik, 1948c).

---

[8]The report from which this passage is quoted was written for the research department of the American Jewish Committee, which sponsored the first two years of the project on social discrimination in children mentioned above.

At first the problem was approached in a more summary fashion. Such traits as "intolerance of ambiguity," "distortion of reality," and "rigidity" were defined in a general manner, and each child was rated, without knowledge of his prejudice score, on the basis of a synopsis of the available clinical material. The same group which manifested extreme racial prejudice received on the average high ratings on these traits also.

Furthermore, children with a tendency to dichotomize in the social field on the basis of external characteristics—i.e., the ethnically prejudiced children—at the same time tend to subscribe to statements included in a personality inventory and expressly designed to reveal a dichotomizing attitude, a rejection of the different, or an avoidance of ambiguities in general. Examples of the statements used are:

People can be divided into two distinct classes: the weak and the strong.
Teachers should tell children what to do and not try to find out what the children want.
Only people who are like myself have a right to be happy.
Girls should learn only things that are useful around the house.
Refugees should be thrown out of this country so that their jobs can be given to veterans.
There is only one right way to do anything.

To this more general evidence of the relationship between emotional-social ambivalence and its repression on the one hand, and tolerance of cognitive ambiguity on the other, we now add a brief description of some relevant experiments, some of them still in a highly tentative state.

Differential Distortion of Reality in an Experiment on Memory

First a memory experiment will be discussed in which there is still some emotional and social involvement. Among other things, it will bring out closeness of opposites, a point which has been stressed above as an important characteristic of the personality-centered approach.

The task was the recall of a story. It was carried out in 1946 as a group experiment with 42 children in the sixth, seventh, and eighth grades to whom a number of tests developed in our above-mentioned project had been given. In this case, no selection of subjects was made in terms of their standing on the prejudice scale, so that the sample includes extremes as well as subjects of intermediate attitude.[9]

The "story"—actually a somewhat broadened milieu characterization—deals with the pupils of a school and their attitudes toward newcomers. In an introductory paragraph one short sentence each is devoted to examples of the boys in the school, labeling them by first names and giving one or two facts about each of them relating either to their individual habits or achievements—such as playing the violin or having been on a radio quiz—or to their fathers' occupation, economic status, religious affiliation, or ethnic and racial group membership. Of the 11 children thus introduced, one is a Negro and one is Jewish. The major part of the story starts out by listing three of the boys as newcomers to the school. It then proceeds to give short generalized sketches of the behavior of a number of the old-timers toward the newcomers in terms of aggressiveness versus protectiveness in the fighting that develops against the newcomers. The story ends with a description of the somewhat futile efforts of the newcomers to defend themselves. The entire material covers one and one-half double-spaced typewritten pages. With its many participants it is deliberately somewhat confusing. To render accuracy even more difficult, it was read to the children only once. After a short interval they were asked to reproduce it in writing.

In the context of the present paper we may conceive of the story as a piece of reality and ask ourselves what changes this reality undergoes in the memory of the children, especially in the direction of an elimination of ambiguities and other complexities.

As was to be expected, children scoring relatively high on prejudice mentioned the Negro boy significantly more often in an unfavorable context, with or without explicitly referring to his being a Negro, than did the less prejudiced. The negative characteristics

---

[9]The writer is indebted to Mr. Murray E. Jarvik and Mr. Donald T. Campbell for their participation in the construction of the experiment, and to Mr. Leonard Gordon for his assistance in evaluating the material.

ascribed to him were subjective elaborations on the part of the subjects concerned, since the story itself says no more about him than that his "father was a Negro and worked in a hotel."

The negativistic tendency in the distortion of story content on the part of the prejudiced children is not limited to the description of this particular boy with his minority status. The prejudiced children tend generally to recall a higher ratio of undesirable over desirable characteristics. This result is in line with the general overemphasis on negative, hostile, and catastrophic features found in the clinical data, the interviews, and the Thematic Apperception Test stories of the highly ethnocentric subjects.

It is further to be noted that in those scoring low on ethnic prejudice, the ratio of undesirable to desirable features recalled is closer to the ratio in the story itself. In short, low scorers stuck closer to the "truth," in this respect at least, than did high scorers. Over and beyond the hostility mentioned above, the distortions of the high scorers tend not only to be more frequent but also to be of a cruder nature. All this is revealed by the fact that 43% of the high-scoring children, as contrasted with only 8% of the low scorers, recalled exclusively that part of the story which deals with the fighting without mentioning any of the other themes (statistical significance is at the 1% level of confidence). It may be added that evidence from the interviews likewise points toward the relatively great attraction which fighting has for this group of children. In the recall of the prejudiced children the story gets generally more simplified and less diverse. Often a unified attitude of aggressiveness is assumed toward the newcomer, with the only theme, fighting, sharply focused on this group alone. It is in these extreme cases that the rooting of negativistic reality distortion in the tendency to avoid emotional ambivalence becomes most convincingly evident. The low-scoring children, on the other hand, tend to refer more often to the individual differences between the children, sometimes with an explicit emphasis on the content of the first paragraph of the story, which states that there are many kinds of children in this school.

The differential recall in the two groups of children is especially manifested in their answers to three more specific questions asked after they had written down their recall of the story as a whole. The last of these three questions called for a description of "the old-timer who stuck up for the newcomers." Of all those failing to answer one, but no more than one, of the three questions, the percentage of high scorers who omitted the last question was significantly higher than that of low scorers. On the other hand, a significantly higher percentage of low scorers omitted answering the second question, which asked for the description of "the stool pigeon," a boy with some undesirable characteristics.

Although the ratio of positive to negative characteristics mentioned by the low scorers is closer to the one in the story, their emphasis on positive and nurturant aspects sometimes leads them to omissions. Gross distortions of the kind often found in the prejudiced group are rare among them, however. The fact that low scorers on the whole approximate more correctly the actual configuration of stimuli will also be seen in the results of the perceptual experiments to be discussed below.

There are, further, still more general differences in the dealing with the story material which are of interest in this connection. The tendency to stray from the content of the story is in the high-scoring children combined with a tendency to remember faithfully certain single phrases and details. Some of the children in this group show predominance of either the first or the second type of reaction. As in the Thematic Apperception Test, some show a restricted approach concentrating on description of details of picture or story; others go off altogether, telling stories which have almost no relation to the material presented. Thus there is either a clinging to the presentation with little freedom and distance, i.e., a stimulus boundness in Goldstein's sense referred to above, or a neglect of the stimulus altogether in favor of purely subjective fantasies. It is in this manner that a rigid, cautious, segmentary approach goes with one that is disintegrated and chaotic, with sometimes one and the same child manifesting both patterns in alternation or in all kinds of bizarre combinations. As do negativism and distortion in general, both these patterns help avoidance of uncertainty, one of them by fixation to, the other by tearing loose from, the given realities.

Experiments on Perceptual Ambiguity

We now turn to a group of experiments in perception proper.

These are quite free from emotional and social content and are designed to help investigate whether or not such characteristics as intolerance of ambiguities are generalized. If such intolerance should turn out to be a formal characteristic of the organism independent of content, experiments on perceptual ambiguity could be used as diagnostic tools. We begin with preliminary experiments which showed a certain trend in the direction suggested in a relatively small number of subjects, although as a rule statistical significance was not scrutinized. This trend then was corroborated in further, somewhat modified experiments using more adequate numbers of subjects. In most cases the subjects were children in our project mentioned above who had scored extremely high or extremely low on ethnic prejudice. Unless otherwise specified, all the experiments discussed in this section were conducted between 1946 and 1948.

So long as experiments in perception dealt primarily with universal trends, the description of the sociological characteristics of the sample was comparatively irrelevant, or at least it seemed to be so. In entering the field of individual differences, however, the sociological attributes of the sample become decisive. Our own sample consisted mainly of a lower-middle-class group in an area restricted by covenant. In samples of this kind the rigid extreme is apt to be strongly preoccupied with the maintenance of his or her middle-class status and of the social distance from the ethnic minority groups and from the unskilled workers living near by. The experiments on ambiguity reported in this section were to a large extent conducted with such extreme individuals within our sample; because of their tenuous social position, greater over-all rigidity is found here than in samples belonging to other classes or exhibiting a higher educational level.

Against the general objection which may be raised to the effect that intolerance of ambiguity is nothing but lack of intelligence, the following may be said. First, the correlations between absence of ethnic prejudice on the one hand, and intelligence on the other, are generally low. Second, there is no reason why rigidity could not be considered a malfunctioning of intelligence, although it would seem to be a rather specific aspect of intelligence that may be involved.

In the first of the preliminary experiments a disk-shaped reversible figure-ground pattern was presented to 14 subjects. It was expected that prejudiced subjects would display a smaller number of spontaneous shifts, that reaction time in shifting would be longer, and that there would be a tendency to settle on one of the possible solutions. The answer to this may throw some light on the question whether subjects who exhibit rigidity in the emotional and social field are generally less likely to shift back and forth between alternative interpretations of an ambiguous perceptual configuration. The results of this experiment so far are not conclusive.

In another tentative experiment,[10] first the picture of a dog was shown, followed by a number of pictures representing transitional stages leading finally to the picture of a cat. At every stage the subjects were asked to identify the object on the given card. In spite of the fact that the cards were not very well drawn for the purpose, distinct trends became evident. The prejudiced group tended to hold on longer to the first object and to respond more slowly to the changing stimuli. There was greater reluctance to give up the original object about which one had felt relatively certain and a tendency not to see what did not harmonize with the first set, as well as a shying away from transitional solutions. Once this perseveration was broken, there seemed to be in this group either a spell of haphazard guessing or a blocking by the uncertainties inherent in the situation. It may well turn out upon further evidence that intolerance of perceptual ambiguity is related to a broader psychological disturbance of which prejudice—itself often a deviation from the prevalent code, especially in school—is but another manifestation.

Turning again to less specific situations, figural aftereffects of what is, or has temporarily become, the "familiar" seem to show

---

[10]The use of gradual transitions between objects of different kinds occurred to the writer in reading Goldstein's (1943, p. 309) description of certain schizophrenic patients who insisted on assigning "individual words" to each in a series of shades of green. Although the schizophrenics differ from the ethnically prejudiced in the degree of reality disturbance, the two seem to have in common a tendency to absolutize, or to absorb at one end of the scale, or to discard entirely differences which others will be able to integrate into a continuum of gradual steps. Relatively unstable stimuli representing intermediate stages between more clear-cut configurations have been common in experiments on the perception and memory distortion of form for some time. For suggestions regarding one of the experiments reported here the writer is indebted to Dr. Warner Brown.

Drawings representing transitions between objects more drastically different from one another than those mentioned above, such as a tree and a house, seem to be more suitable for our purpose.

INTOLERANCE OF AMBIGUITY AS PERSONALITY VARIABLE 79

generally a relatively strong resistance to change in this group. It is as if any stimulus—or what seems to be "the" stimulus in the person's interpretation—is playing the role of an authority to which the subject feels compelled to submit. Situations which seem to be lacking in firmness are apparently as strange, bewildering, and disturbing to the prejudiced as would be a leader lacking in absolute determination. With internal conflict being as disturbing as it is in this group, there apparently develops a tendency to deny external ambiguity as long as such denial can be maintained. Underlying anxiety issuing from confusion of one's social identity and from other conflicts is apparently so great that it hampers individuals in this group in facing even the purely cognitive types of ambiguity. The mechanism discussed is somewhat related to what Postman, Bruner, and McGinnies (1948) have called "perceptual defenses." A desperate effort is made to shut out uncertainties the prejudiced individual is unable to face, thus narrowing what Tolman (1948) has called the "cognitive map" to rigidly defined tracks. Persons with less severe underlying confusions, on the other hand, may be able to afford facing ambiguities openly, although this may mean an at least temporary facing of conflicts and anxieties as well. In this case the total pattern is that of a broader integration of reality without shutting off parts of it, and thus a more flexible adaptation to varying circumstances.

In a further experiment in which one after another in a progressive series of hues was to be named, the writer gained the tentative impression that prejudiced subjects again perseverate longer than the unprejudiced, in this case with a given color term, conceive of fewer and cruder steps along the scale, or tend toward one-dimensional rather than more complex systems of classification.

Another experiment, conducted recently along the general lines of the one with the cat-dog pictures just mentioned, is one by Norman Livson and Florine Berkowitz Livson. Numbers were used rather than objects, thus reducing the possibility of involvement with content. Two statistically significant differences were found (both at the 1% level of confidence) for a total of 42 of the children in our social discrimination project. One is the relatively slow recognition of numbers emerging from indistinctness, the other the relatively slow recognition of numbers changing from other numbers, by the ethnocentric group. Again, there was a prolonged clinging to the first impression, even though faulty, on the part of the prejudiced.

Rokeach (1943) investigated a problem of rigidity related to ambiguity. He used a Gestalt-psychological thinking problem involving the manipulation of three jars. A mental set was first established by presenting the subjects with a series of problems which could be solved only by a relatively long and complex method. The subjects were then presented with further problems which could be solved either by maintaining the original set or by using a more advantageous direct and simple method. A measure of rigidity was derived from the number of cases in which the established set was maintained and thus an inability demonstrated to restructure the field and to perceive the direct solution. The results presented by Rokeach indicate clearly that the children scoring extremely high on ethnic prejudice solve the new problems more rigidly than those extremely low on prejudice. Over and above the measure of rigidity, based on maladaptive perseveration, Rokeach utilized the amount of scratch paper used as an aid in solving the problems as a measure for concreteness of thinking. Those high on prejudice were found to use more scratch paper than those low on prejudice. A spatial problem also devised by Rokeach, calling for the finding of a shorter path on a map after a set for a longer route had been established, has further borne out the greater rigidity of the ethnically prejudiced.

The fact that the sample of children from our project on social discrimination who were used as subjects in the experiments of Rokeach had been studied with respect to a variety of personality characteristics made it possible to interrelate different measures of rigidity. Thus the rigidity scores derived from the simple arithmetic problems just referred to tend to correlate with over-all clinical ratings of children's rigidity based on their attitudes toward parents, sex roles, self, moral values, etc., as revealed in our clinical interviews. Similarly, significant correlations were found between rigidity scores gained by Rokeach and the total score on the personality inventory. This personality inventory had been designed to measure dichotomizing in emotional and social attitudes. It consists of a series of statements referring to attitudes toward authority, aggression, weakness, etc. A few statements from this inventory have been quoted above.

As mentioned earlier, intolerance of ambiguity must further be related to a reluctance to think in terms of probabilities and a preference to escape into whatever seems definite and therefore safe. Murray E. Jarvik adapted a technique developed by Egon Brunswik (1939b) in a probability discrimination experiment with rats in which food rewards were distributed with differing relative frequencies on the two sides of a simple T-maze. Jarvik presented a long series of pictures of white and Negro children to our ethnically prejudiced and unprejudiced children, asking them to state in each case whether they were dull- or bright-looking. After each response, the supposedly correct answer was given by the experimenter. For half of the children 75% of the whites and 25% of the Negroes were designated as "bright," and the rest as "dull," and vice versa for the other half of the children. A preliminary inspection of the data shows that the children extremely low on prejudice caught on to this probability learning situation more readily than those high on ethnocentrism; the latter tended to persist in their preconceptions, being less able to absorb the general trend of the information given.

Some of the traits mentioned in this section may be more fully ascertained by the use of such projective tests as the Rorschach, especially when the slant of interpretation given to these tests by Rapaport (Rapaport, Schafer, and Gill, 1946) is applied. Aside from a certain advantage of setting up specific experiments for specific variables, perceptual experiments of the kind described ordinarily offer a "reality" more clearly delineated, whereas projective techniques are purposely kept vague in a greater variety of directions. Since we were in the present context more interested in the handling and mastery of a well-circumscribed reality, and less in projections as such, the experiments listed have an edge over projective tests for our particular purpose.

Though the over-all trend of the data discussed in this section seems to indicate a certain generality, within the individuals concerned, of the approach to reality which we have subsumed under the term "intolerance of ambiguity," a much wider array of both techniques and population samples would be necessary to establish this generality with an adequate degree of definiteness. It must further be kept in mind that, as is pointed out elsewhere in this paper, compensation of rigidity by—often exaggerated—flexibility is probably as much present as is a positive correlation between different aspects of rigidity.

Detailed inspection of case studies which include both clinical data and data from experiments on such cognitive topics as perception, memory, and problem solving shows consistencies as well as apparent inconsistencies in this respect. For instance, there are perhaps some exceptional cases of children who score extremely high on the prejudice scale but manifest only an average amount of mental rigidity. The discussion of such inconsistencies would easily fill another paper. We shall give here only some indication of the complexity of the facts involved. In one of the inconsistent cases of the kind just described a boy's ethnic prejudice turned out to stem mainly from a marked physical marginality. His mother was loving and permissive, and her method of child training fitted better to the boy's relative mental flexibility than to his high prejudice. On the other hand, a girl who was most articulate in proclaiming a liberal ideology and who at the same time displayed more mental rigidity than is common in the unprejudiced turned out to be a member of a family which, though clinging in a dogmatic and militant way to a liberal ideology, did so with a great deal of inexorability and a lack of willingness to arbitrate with, or to accept, those who thought differently.

Rigidity, Discontinuity, and Chaos: The Closeness of Opposites

There is evidence, as pointed out above, for the fact that rigidity of attitudes constitutes a counterbalance to underlying conflicts often verging on chaos. Rigidity and chaos seem on theoretical as well as on empirical grounds more closely related than one might assume from a purely phenomenological viewpoint. Goldstein (1943) has pointed out the coexistence of rigid and disintegrated behavior in the same individual.

A combination of rigidity and chaos similar to that found in the cognitive and in the strictly emotional field is also present in the social field. In our own study the same children who adhere to the status quo and resist change tend to subscribe to statements which predict catastrophes, chaos, a total change in which everything is in flux. Examples of such statements are:

If everything would change, this world would be much better. Some day a flood or earthquake will destroy everybody in the whole world.

In fact, we find in the rigid children artificial isolation and separation of feelings and attitudes which belong together and at the same time fusion of attitudes which do not belong together. Apparently this is the way these children become restricted, in their awareness, to a small segment of their reactions to authorities, to the other sex, and to themselves. Many of the feelings which actually originate in their relationship with the parents are not seen in the original context but are displaced onto political leaders, minority groups, foreign countries, and so forth, leading to a personalization of the entire social outlook. There is on the surface a clinging to the ethnic, social, and sex identity. As may be seen especially from the indirect material, there is at the same time confusion about one's identity along all those lines. Underlying identification with, and envy of, the other sex as well as the out-group with its alleged pleasures and emotionality are clearly manifest.

It should be mentioned here that Werner (1946) conceived of "rigidity" as being caused by either too much isolation of the different subareas of the personality or by too much overlapping in the sense of a perseveration of certain elements throughout the entire mental life. The isolation and the keeping apart of sets as well as the tendency toward undue perseveration of the same set can serve the function of avoidance of complexities.

Another pair of attitudes closely connected with our topic is *concreteness* versus *abstractness*. It has been described in great detail by Goldstein and Scheerer (1941). The concrete attitude is one of being "bound to the immediate experience of the given thing or situation in its uniqueness." It can easily be seen how the escape into the concrete, the "boundness" to the specific stimulus, represents dealing with tangibles and certainties where everything opaque and complex can be avoided. We would like to add that too crude generalization and the inclination toward mechanical repetition of faulty hypotheses—an experiment on the latter has been referred to above—can serve the same function. Adequately flexible organization of the psychological field, as contrasted with orientation toward concrete detail with its close relation to disintegration and chaos, has likewise been discussed previously in this paper. Such pairs of cognitive opposites as concreteness versus abstractness, or the related one of objectivity versus subjectivity, must be reviewed in a somewhat new light to the effect that extreme objectivity and extreme subjectivity are concurrent rather than mutually exclusive attitudes.

The splitting off and exclusion from consciousness of unacceptable tendencies, such as aggression against authorities, fear, or weakness, may be considered as contributing to the general lack of insight, the rigidity of defense, and the narrowness of the ego characteristic of those intolerant of ambiguity. It must lead, furthermore, to all kinds of discontinuities as revealed especially in the attitude of the rigid person toward himself. We refer here to the occasional breaking through of an aggression, fear, or weakness of which there has been no awareness and which may have been attributed to someone else. Such a person attempts to keep these tendencies from interacting with other tendencies and with reality.

Another discontinuity concerns the subject's notion of development. The intolerant individual makes significantly fewer spontaneous comments on his own early childhood; upon inquiry a discontinuity between present and past self often becomes apparent. In the attitude toward one's sex role and parents, similar discontinuities have become evident. Verbalized love for the parents or an explicitly stated masculinity are contradicted by tendencies in opposite directions observed within the same material (see Adorno et al., 1950, Chapters 10 and 11).

It is apparently the great number of conflicts and confusions present in the prejudiced which leads to their resorting to black-and-white solutions. Too much existing emotional ambiguity and ambivalence are counteracted by denial and intolerance of cognitive ambiguity. It is as if everything would go to pieces if the existing discrepancies were faced. To avoid this catastrophe everything that might abet the uncertainty and opaqueness of life is desperately avoided by a selection of undisturbing, clear-cut, and therefore too general or else too concrete aspects of reality. Greater rigidity of defenses is necessary to ward off the danger of becoming completely overwhelmed by the repressed forces.

These considerations also show that intolerance of ambiguity is intrinsically equivalent to an oversimplified and thus reality-inadequate approach, characterized by the dominance of crude, relatively unessential aspects, and often combined with glaring omissions of fact. As long as we remain in the emotional and especially in the social field the evaluation of what is a reality-adequate or a reality-inadequate representation might be hard to judge. The fascist may accuse the liberal and the liberal the fascist of distorting reality. It seems very probable on the basis of our knowledge that our prejudiced subjects are mistaken about the existing relationships between ethnic group membership and certain personality traits. The least that can be said is that they exaggerate existing correlations and that they are frequently mistaken about the explanations of such correlations. On the other hand, a certain subtype of liberal tends to do the opposite, denying the existing relationships altogether, and with this implicitly the importance of the significance of social factors, such as membership in a minority group. All in all, we have the impression from our data that the liberals distort reality less. In order to demonstrate this, a shift to emotionally more neutral cognitive material had to be effected. The experiment on memory discussed above bears directly on this point, confirming our expectation.

The subtle but profound distortion of reality in the course of the elimination of ambiguities is precipitated by the fact that stereotyped categorizations can never do justice to all the aspects of reality. So long as our culture provides socially acceptable outlets for suppressed impulses, smooth functioning and fair adjustment can be achieved within the given framework. It must be kept in mind that the adjustment of this type of person depends on conditions which are comparatively narrowly circumscribed. Whenever differentiation and adaptability to change are required, this adjustment will run the risk of breaking down. Basically, therefore, avoidance of ambiguity and related mechanisms, directed as they are toward a simplified mastery of the environment, turn out to be maladaptive in the end.

The precise, machinelike, unswervingly unambiguous perceptual reaction glorified by Jaensch (1938; see also above) can thus be regarded as no more than a mixed blessing. In fact, many of the perceptual reactions of highest fidelity which seem so ideal to Jaensch must be considered as a rigid, if not pathological, stimulus boundness in the sense of Goldstein. Jaensch's favorite "integrated" type is in reality one who makes excessive use of the mechanism of isolation rather than one who sensibly interconnects different spheres of reality. It certainly is only a very superficial kind of integration a rigid person can achieve. On the other hand, proneness to interconnect the seemingly diverse by no means always constitutes an undue mixing up of issues; more often than not it will represent a creative establishment of essential relationships.

A case in point against Jaensch is the gross distortion of reality, such as overestimation of one's own strength and underestimation of that of the enemy as exemplified in Nazi ideology and behavior, with an utmost precision in work on technological detail. Fidelity in small matters often goes hand in hand with gross errors in the understanding of the most essential aspects of reality. Obviously, on the other hand, persons capable of creative efforts are bound to have small matters mechanized at the risk of being off the right track in a certain proportion of instances.

Much in the analysis of our material undertaken in the present paper may also be summarized in the statement that it is probably neither extreme stimulus boundness nor extreme subjectivity which is really helpful in understanding the world, but rather the classifying of concrete experiences under over-all guiding principles. There is ample evidence from various kinds of clinical material that the clinging to external stimuli is often a sign of anxiety, a "way out from the organism's unbearable conflict as a protection against the danger of severe catastrophe" (Goldstein, 1943). By contrast, the categorial or conceptual attitude is characterized by the ability or readiness to assume a mental set voluntarily, to shift voluntarily from one aspect of the situation to another, to keep in mind, simultaneously, various aspects, to grasp the essentials of a given whole, to break up a given whole into parts and to isolate them voluntarily, to abstract common properties, to plan ahead ideationally, to assume an attitude toward the "merely possible," to think or perform symbolically, and finally to detach our ego from the outer world.

To point out the fact that the extremely concrete, fixated orientation leads to disintegration of human behavior, Goldstein (1943) discusses the thinking of the schizophrenic and points out that this concreteness does not prevent the entering of subjective, changeable ideas and thoughts, but that this type of patient deals with ideas as if they were concrete things which belong to an object or situation. There is "an inability to maintain adequate boundaries," especially between the ego and the outer world.

Here we would like to stress, even more than Goldstein himself does, the paradoxical combinations which are found in the impared reaction of, say, the schizophrenic. The schizophrenic is not only very concrete but at the same time very general. That is, he transfers a specific property of a stimulus to many other stimuli. This tendency toward generalization may be connected with perseveration and may be due to the overlapping of different areas of personality. With Werner (1946) we may see in this overlapping, as well as in isolation, causes for rigidity. We thus might find rigid concreteness occurring together with rigid generalization; both have to be distinguished from an adequately abstract approach.

We may further point out in support of this that while Goldstein consistently stresses the concreteness of the schizophrenic, Kretschmer (1942) thinks of the schizoid primarily as given to abstraction, while it is its opposite, the cycloid (related to the manic-depressive), who is seen to be more concretely oriented. The greater ability for abstraction on the part of the schizoid type is, among other things, said to be manifested in his ability to concentrate more fully on certain characteristics of the stimulus to the neglect of all others. If the task is to reproduce colors he will succeed in doing so, whereas the cycloid will tend to recall letters along with colors. The schizoids are declared to be superior in sorting and parceling out, whereas the cycloids tend toward global and total impressions, concentrating on concrete objects as a whole. The free associations of schizoids to a given word are more logical in the formal sense, whereas those of the cycloids are more affective, more direct, and more fluent. In all, the thinking of the cycloid is seen to be less precise and logical than the thinking of the schizoid; the cycloid is said to show more realism, more love of detail, less differentiation between relevant and irrelevant features.

Whereas in the present study the main emphasis was on environmental factors, Kretschmer stresses constitution as a determinant of differences in cognitive and emotional behavior. Our evidence regarding environmental factors must not be allowed to detract from the possibility of constitutional differences in rigidity and frustration tolerance, although they may well turn out to be of a different kind from those emphasized by Kretschmer.

It is interesting to observe that Kretschmer seems to interconnect ability to abstract with autism. As he points out, the schizoid ignores in his abstractions what seems not to fit. Although Goldstein is far from being blind to this fact, he still stresses more the connection between concreteness and autism—rather than that between abstraction and autism—and seems to think that they tend to occur together in the same individual. Evidence presented in this paper suggests that extreme concreteness and extreme generalization may well go hand in hand and are both relatively primitive forms of reaction.[11]

Realization of the possibility that apparent opposites such as extreme abstractness and extreme concreteness, or extreme subjectivity and extreme objectivity, may be psychologically closer together and more apt to combine with each other in the same subject than any of them would with an intermediate position along the same scale may be traced back to psychoanalysis. To be sure, in psychoanalysis this pattern is discovered primarily in the field of emotion, through the phenomenon of ambivalence. Conscious love of extreme and exaggerated intensity is viewed with the same suspicion by the psychoanalyst as are extreme feelings of hate.

One of the characteristics of the perception-centered outlook of most personality psychologies based upon cognititve categories is that they tend to ignore this fact and to stick to the more obvious policy of naïve dichotomizing in which opposite extremes are conceived of as true polarities.

It is only where work has been centered on the study of normal and abnormal personality organization that the closeness of opposites and the juxtaposition of the intermediate as against either or both of the extremes begins to make itself felt along with that between one extreme as against the other. Personality-centered research would, at least to the present writer, seem to be bound to give great prominence to the idea of the closeness of opposite extremes. Results of research designed with an eye on genuine prob-

---

[11]For animals the relationship between organically induced mental deficiency on the one hand, and a decrease in the variability of behavior which is one of the most outstanding characteristics of the concrete attitude on the other, has been described by Krechevsky (1937).

lems of personality dynamics will of necessity force upon the investigator the recognition of this basic relationship. Thus in studying mechanisms of self-deception the writer (Frenkel-Brunswik, 1939) found that exaggerated verbal emphasis on certain ideals of conduct and related extremes of protestation and of other linguistic expression were indicative of shortcomings rather than of strength with respect to the traits in question in the subjects concerned. In a quite different context (Frenkel-Brunswik, 1942) it was shown that the need for aggression may either be openly expressed—one extreme—or else lead to general tenseness with a minimum amount of overt aggressiveness—the opposite extreme—within a system of "alternative manifestations." If exaggerated aggressiveness is openly manifested, this in its turn often correlates with indications of a need of an opposite kind, for instance, the need for dependency.

An interesting parallel to the phenomenon of grossly alternative behavioral manifestations just referred to has been described for the physiological domain of the bodily expression of emotions by Jones (1935).

It must be emphasized here that expression of genotypically identical needs or drives through alternative manifestations which are phenotypically far apart from, or even opposite to, each other by no means detracts from the possibility of the generality of a certain basic personality feature. Thus rigidity in one respect may go with flexibility in another; yet they both may actually be part of a dynamically coherent personality make-up. In fact, it may even be impossible—in an almost logical sense of the term—to remain extremely rigid, or objective, or concrete, without at the same time making up for it by extreme flexibility, subjectivity, or abstractness in some other respect compensatory to the first. The problem of whether individuals differ primarily with respect to over-all rigidity or with respect to the differential distribution of rigidity within the various aspects of personality thus appears in a new light and acquires even greater urgency.

Uniformity of style of a person in the sense just described would then be defined in terms of such formal characteristics as, say, being extreme or given to exaggeration in any direction within any or all dimensions of conduct. Such concepts as ambivalence or fear of ambiguity, being at least in part descriptive of certain aspects of the closeness of extremes, are thus automatically included with these formal characteristics. On the basis of the earlier study of self-deception mentioned above (Frenkel-Brunswik, 1939) as well as of the evidence on the ethnically prejudiced referred to throughout this paper, one may indeed be led to believe that the formal elements of personality style are not subject to censorship—in the psychoanalytic sense of the term—in the same manner as is the more concrete content of wishes and instinctual tendencies. Since it is only the content which is directly threatening, the form in which it is set may not seem in need of being censored. If this holds true, formal style elements, such as exaggeration, easy generalization (as contrasted with salient specificity), intolerance of ambiguity, and the like, would be of greater penetrating power within the personality, more nearly alike on the surface and at greater depth, and thus of greater generality and greater diagnostic validity than such content elements as, say, sex, aggression, the Oedipus complex, and the like.

Conclusion

In this paper an attempt was made to discuss denial of emotional ambivalence and intolerance of cognitive ambiguity as but different aspects of what may be a fairly coherent characteristic. An underlying emotional conflict between glorification and hostility in the attitude toward parents, sex, and one's own social identity, previously demonstrated in children inclined toward rigid social dichotomizing as revealed by ethnic prejudice, is taken as the impetus for experiments in memory, perception, and related topics, devised to test tolerance of ambiguity on an emotionally more neutral ground. There is some indication of a prevalence of premature reduction of ambiguous cognitive patterns to certainty in the prejudiced subjects, as revealed by a clinging to the familiar, or by a superimposition of one or many distorting clichés upon stimuli which are not manageable in a more simple and stereotyped fashion. There is some indication that in the case of distinct intolerance of emotional ambivalence one can as a rule locate at least some aspects of intolerance of cognitive ambiguity, although these may often be more apparent on a level higher than that of perception proper.

More detailed study of single cases, however, reveals that social and cognitive intolerance are far from being inseparable even in the extreme groups. Furthermore, it seems likely that in specific contexts flexibility in one perhaps essential respect may have to be compensated for by rigidity in other perhaps relatively unessential respects. On the other hand, the clinging to the familiar and precise detail can go hand in hand with the ignoring of most of the remaining aspects of the stimulus configuration, resulting in an altogether haphazard type of approach to reality. (The over-all equivocal relationship between emotional and cognitive factors and abilities has been discussed by the present writer elsewhere [this volume, Chapter 1].)

Emotional ambivalence, and related reciprocities of the kind just referred to, help to imbue personality-centered study of cognition as exemplified in this paper with the realization of such important dynamic principles as the closeness of opposites. Thus lack of distance and too much distance from culture, parents, and other stimulus configurations seem to be more closely related to each other than is either of these two extremes to what we may term a "medium distance" from these situational elements.

From these complexities and compensations let us turn once more to positive correlation. In general, severe repression of certain tendencies such as aggression toward authority, fear, weakness, or elements of the opposite sex in oneself, finds its parallel in an externalized image of these tendencies as projected onto others and in a narrowness and rigidity of consciousness. There is more than an empirical affinity between the strength of hostility, of power orientation, of externalization, and of rigid stereotyping on the one hand, and the intolerance of ambiguity on the other; there is a similar affinity between the orientation toward love and the acceptance of drive impulses on the one hand, and a general flexibility on the other. The struggle between these two orientations is basic to our civilization; its individual members display these two patterns in varying proportions and changing configurations.

3

PERSONALITY THEORY AND PERCEPTION

The present symposium is one among an increasing number of manifestations of the convergence of personality and perception research. But instead of taking this new trend for granted, we may inquire how these two lines of research, until recently widely separated, could have come together. We may ask which developments within the field of personality on the one hand, and within the field of perception on the other, make such a rapprochement possible, a rapprochement which is significant for psychology as a whole. Instead of making perception the starting point, as has been the case in the symposium as a whole, I shall reverse the order and take the development of and changes within personality theory as the point of departure for discussion. I shall then attempt to indicate how this development has served as a basis for bridging over into the field of perception. Some attention to problems of motivation, ego structure, and reality adaptation, as well as to problems of social influences upon personality, will have to precede all this, since they define the elements upon which any personality theory must draw. Previously in this symposium (especially in Blake, Ramsey, and Moran, 1951; Bruner, 1951; Cameron, 1951) these elements have been traced throughout their interweavings with perception. The general plan of procedure here will be to discuss them first in relation to the clinical level and then to apply them to the empirical findings on the interrelationship of personality with perception and cognition.

The lumping together of perception with other, more general

First published in *Perception: An Approach to Personality*, ed. R. R. Blake and G. V. Ramsey. New York: Ronald Press, 1951, pp. 356-419.

modes of cognition requires a word of justification. The argument in favor of sharper differentiation stresses that in perception one is confronted with external stimuli actually present, whereas cognition deals with inferences from such data. Granted that there is a continuum, with relatively clear-cut perception on the one end and relatively pure theoretical constructs on the other, we must not overlook the fact that there is some element of inference in every perception, and that conceptual constructs always relate to perceptual data (see Hilgard, 1951; Dennis, 1951).

The absence of a fundamental difference between the more direct and the more indirect modes of cognition must especially be stressed in the personality-centered type of research in thing perception, which by its very definition deals with individual differences as elicited by vague or ambiguous rather than clear-cut stimulus configurations. Even more this is the case for self-perception and the perception of others—*Fremdwahrnehmung* in the sense of Scheler (1923)—both topics of focal interest and widely discussed in the present symposium. Although there can be no doubt that the self or the social partner constitutes an actually present perceptual stimulus, there can likewise be no doubt that there is a substantial contribution on the part of inferential, more broadly cognitive factors, along with the obvious emotional factors, to perceptual responses as global, as vacillating, as vague, and at the same time as vital as is self-perception and the perception of others.

FROM SURFACE TO DEPTH[1]

GENERAL CONSIDERATIONS

Interest in the dynamics of human behavior in its full complexity appeared on the scene of psychology rather suddenly, and chiefly under the influence of psychiatry and psychoanalysis. The suddenness was a result of the fact that those interested in personality as a unit did not choose to wait until academic psychology, using experimental and laboratory techniques, arrived step by step at the same goal by studying the relatively simple units customarily involved in this latter approach. Unhampered by the difficulty of objectifying the tangled relationship between overt behavior and the patterns of

[1] Many of the issues in the present and in the next section have been documented in greater detail in two previous publications (Frenkel-Brunswik, this volume, Chapter 1; 1942).

underlying dynamics, the new and vital trend in the study of personality proceeded to an understanding of what has long been considered basic and important about human beings by physicians, philosophers, artists, and poets.

More concretely, this trend consisted in a turning away from the more segmentary approach of, let us say, the earlier form of behaviorism with its emphasis on overt responses to immediate stimuli. Mainly under the influence of psychoanalysis, a bold attempt was made in the direction of interpretation in terms of underlying dynamics, overt reactions being relegated to the role of mere steppingstones for inference. There is no doubt that this branch of psychology, in avoiding the errors of an overcautious and stimulus-bound approach, has often fallen into another error, that of overinterpretation and of drawing far-reaching conclusions on the basis of insufficient material evidence. At present a steadily improving balance between these two extremes is being attained.

Before entering into a discussion of the present status of personality research and theory, however, the writer would like to underscore once more the powerful impetus which the psychology of personality has received from psychoanalysis. The shift of emphasis from the level of external, overt manifestation to the level of motivational dynamics, stemming from psychoanalysis, has opened the way to highly fruitful explanations and predictions and thus is chiefly responsible for the establishment, within psychology, of a scientific discipline which really deals with personality. Data which looked from a phenotypic point of view like a mass of unrelated and even contradictory expressions became ordered, meaningful, and unified when the motivational approach was introduced. By conceiving of seemingly diverse behavioral reactions as alternative manifestations of one and the same dynamic force, many an apparent inconsistency was successfully resolved. By this method central motivations can be established and consistent themes in a person's life uncovered.

It was psychoanalysis which first made us question the validity of the literal meaning or face value of a manifestation per se. In this manner we have come to acknowledge that exaggerated friendliness may hide destructive tendencies, that heterosexual promiscuity may be a defense against homosexual desires, or that apparent indifference may conceal a strong interest. An intense striving may thus find expression in no more than subtle and inconspicuous manifestations. On the other hand, the most conspicuous behavioral features may in certain instances have little dynamic significance or lasting effect. Dynamic concepts, as Lewin (1926) points out, "circumscribe a whole range of possibilities of manifestations."

Quite aside from the question of the material correctness or incorrectness of any specific extrapolations into central dynamics as made by psychoanalysis, one must recognize that it has succeeded in conceptually integrating in a general manner an apparently chaotic variety of behavioral reactions relevant to life. These novel groupings of symbols or mechanisms of substitution are sufficiently known so that we need not go into the far-reaching implications of the theory of the instincts and their modification by early interpersonal relationships. In the present symposium, much of the content of psychoanalysis relevant in this context has been discussed by Bronfenbrenner (1951). The layer of the instincts is here made accessible by analyzing materials relatively removed from the rational sectors of the personality, among them free associations, the content of dreams, and transference and symbolism in general. In all this, the interest in the adult was centered on diagnosing the persistence of infantile or archaic tendencies.

Since about 1930, the picture of psychoanalytic endeavors has somewhat departed from this original type of emphasis. Before discussing these changes, we must first come back to the importance of motivation for the psychology of personality. The influence of needs, of irrational tendencies and motives, upon perception has been stressed all through this symposium, most explicitly by Miller (1951) and Bruner (1951). In view of such agreement, it seems justified to take some time for a more detailed discussion of human motives and the methods of their ascertainment.

Our knowledge of motivation is established by means of a complex process of inference and interpretation, utilizing the most minute cues as well as gross features of behavior. Instead of grouping phenomena together on the basis of their overt similarities, we have learned from psychoanalysis to group them on the basis of genetic or symbolic similarities. Delving into depth in this manner has brought us awareness of rules and laws quite different from those found on the surface. To quote from Anna Freud

(1936, p. 7): "In the id the so-called 'primary process' prevails; there is no synthesis of ideas, affects are liable to displacement, opposites are not mutually exclusive and may even coincide and condensation occurs as a matter of course."

POLARITIES IN PSYCHOANALYSIS

Similarly, in discussing the vicissitudes of instincts, Sigmund Freud (1915a) deals with such crucial mechanisms as the reversal of an instinct into its opposite. He speaks of such changes as the replacement of a passive aim (for instance, to be looked at) by an active aim (to look at), or the reversal of a content as found in the change of love into hate.

In general, Freud believes that our mental life is governed by three polarities, namely, subject-object, pleasure-pain, activity-passivity, in each of which one opposite pole may be replaced by the other.

We as psychologists may add that the closeness of opposites found by observing the vicissitudes of the instincts actually turns out to be a general personality characteristic. Let us take from one of our studies the example of a delinquent boy, Jeff, whose overdaring, aggressive masculinity is interpreted as a counteractive façade for his basically insecure and passive attitude. The assumption of his underlying passivity may help us to understand a larger sector of his behavior. Thus, we will not be surprised to find in his Thematic Apperception Test stories gratuitous endings in which the hero is apt to get things without much effort on his part, as well as a generally passive attitude toward his environment, perhaps especially toward other men. We may find feminine identification and interest in getting food or in being fed. As long as we assume only the existence of aggressiveness, we may understand only the criminal acts of Jeff. However, if we add the hypothesis of underlying passivity, the content of other less conspicuous but not less crucial aspects of his behavior, as well as the content of his fantasy, free associations, etc., become intelligible to us.

We might also bring to bear a specific example in the opposite direction, Merle, whose exaggerated friendliness may serve, or may even be the direct result of, strong destructive tendencies. Quite often in life real motivations cannot be shown openly. The distinction between manifest personality and inferred motivational personality seems to be especially important in our culture. In the two examples given, cultural pressures are at work in opposite directions. Merle, in reality a boy identified with middle-class values, was found to have developed defense mechanisms against his hostility. Jeff, a lower-class delinquent boy, was found to have tried exhibiting the tough and rugged façade he believes his environment expects of him. We have endeavored to indicate in both cases how a variety of behavioral features must be taken as circumstantial evidence in sizing up the subject.

AN ANALYSIS OF ALTERNATIVE BEHAVIORAL MANIFESTATIONS OF MOTIVATION

In trying to nail down the differences between the depth-oriented and the more conventional psychological approaches, one must point to the fact that psychoanalysis and psychiatry usually fall short of making fully explicit the relationship between the inferences involved and the observational data. For concrete illustration, I shall refer here briefly to a monograph which I published some years ago (Frenkel-Brunswik, 1942) as a part of the University of California Adolescent Growth Study (for a general description of the entire study see Jones [1939, 1943]). This monograph had the double aim of showing the predictive value of motivational hypotheses and of demonstrating the relationship of motivation to behavioral data.

The California Adolescent Study collected over a number of years such data as physiological measurements, achievement-test scores, ratings by adult raters of the subjects' behavior in social situations, the subjects' self-reports, and projective material. Correlations between the observed behavior of the children on the one hand, and their self-reports and fantasy material on the other, were found to be on the whole rather low; this is not surprising if one considers that these two sets of data reflect different aspects of personality.

The writer's assumption was that if we introduced motivational ratings, they might be found to account for apparently diverse manifestations, and that an important lead for uncovering relationships might lie in comparatively few but fundamental characteristics of the subjects, as might be brought out in such ratings. The judges, who had known the children over a period of eight years, were asked to forget about the manifest behavior of the children and to group them according to assumed motivation rather than according to similarities of displayed techniques. The aim was to obtain intuitive, interpretive ratings based on wide knowledge of the children's behavior. Explicitly excluded from inspection, however, were indirect performances, such as self-reports and projective materials, in order to maintain the independent status of these for purposes of comparison. There were only nine motivational categories, most of them selected from Murray's list of needs. Since Murray's list covers different levels of personality, we selected from this list mainly drives we considered the most basic, such as "aggression," "abasement," and "succorance."

The results of our analyses show that this perception in depth is probably not inferior to surface perception so far as interrater agreement is concerned; this bears out the impression that in day-to-day living we tend to perceive not only the social techniques of those with whom we come in contact but their basic motivations and purposes as well. What is more, our results supported the original assumption that the drive ratings are of considerable advantage in organizing the previously collected data on overt behavior observed in social situations. As will be shown later, they also help to predict and explain the perception of self, of others, and of the thing-world.

It seemed from the outset that different classes of behavioral expressions not related to one another were often related to the same drive, apparently as "alternate manifestations" of that drive. A statistical analysis of our material, based on a total of 95 subjects, in terms of multiple correlation corroborated the hunch that two phenotypically unrelated, or even diverse, types of manifestations can be related to one and the same set of dynamic factors. To give an example: Overt behavioral ratings on "exuberance" and "irritability" were found to intercorrelate negatively with one another and thus to be relatively incompatible; however, both these behavioral traits showed some positive correlation with the ratings on the drive for aggression. The multiple correlation between aggression and the two diverse behavior features was found to be relatively high, thus establishing the principle of alternative manifestations of a drive. For our boy subjects, the quantitative results are shown in the following schema of alternative manifestations. The gain of the multiple over the two basic, zero-order correlations, checked in all such cases by means of the Wherry shrinkage formula, was found to be statistically significant.

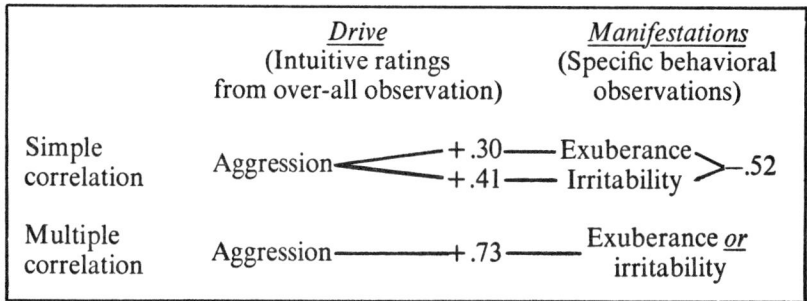

Figure 1. Alternative Manifestations of the Same Drive

Less drastically, the following patterns point in the same direction. For boys, the intercorrelations of "energy output," "social participation," and "leadership" on the one hand, with "irritability" on the other, are −.27, −.30, and −.38 respectively. The corresponding correlations of these items with ratings on the drive for aggression range from .32 to .46. Multiple correlations, however, are between .66 and .75. Leadership is here the more direct expression of the drive for aggression, whereas tenseness and anxiety are manifestations of aggression of lesser phenotypic similarity to the underlying motive.

In short, adolescents whose ratings on the aggressive-drive cluster are high are likely to be either maladjusted, tense, and anxious, or else successful in their overt social activity, say, as leaders; or they may even display both manifestations.

Since in the examples mentioned thus far the relationships described involve negative intercorrelation of the two (or more) overt manifestations with one another, the simultaneous presence of both manifestations will be somewhat less likely than if the intercorrelations were zero or positive. Such patterns thus tend, to a certain extent, toward an exclusive "either-or" rather than toward what may be called an "and-or" type of alternative manifestation.

An example of the latter type is the following: in the girls of our group the behavioral traits of "altruism" and "insecurity" were found to be uncorrelated. Ratings on the drive for abasement, however, were found to correlate about .53 with both of them. The joint multiple correlation with ratings on abasement is .75. Girls tending toward abasement thus seem to have the choice between sublimating their abasement in altruism and being insecure, but there also is a good chance that they will be both altruistic and insecure.

Analogously, but in the opposite direction, certain manifest features, especially those concerned with adjustment, seem to originate in a variety of underlying motivational conditions. For example, for the general behavioral trait "insecurity" (the opposite of "security feelings"), combinations of ratings on the need for abasement, succorance, absence of need for achievement, and presence of the need for escape in girls and for aggression in boys, yield third-order multiple coefficients of .78 for girls and .83 for boys. In girls none of the basic coefficients surpasses .53, and in boys none of them surpasses .62.

Drive ratings furthermore show good relationships to independent data such as self-reports and projective material, indicating that these ratings can contribute to predicting the behavior of the subjects in situations which do not enter as a basis for the drive inferences. Self-perceptions and self-reports do not mirror behavior directly, to be sure; but they are interlaced with some of the underlying drives and thus indirectly bear on behavior related to these drives. For example, the low correlations between maladjustment in actual behavior and in the self-reports can be accounted for by the fact that only where maladjustment stems from, or is coupled with, a strong drive for abasement will it be frankly admitted in the self-reports. There were linear correlations of about .5 between ratings on the need for abasement and self-reported maladjustment; whereas actual maladjustment as rated by clinicians tended to show curvilinear relationships to self-reported maladjustment, with both the best- and the least-adjusted children perceiving themselves as optimally adjusted.

Our analysis further revealed positive correlations between our motivational ratings and ratings on the same drives based on projective material. In contrast to this, Sanford et al. (1943) found no relation between ratings of what they termed "manifest needs" and need ratings based on Thematic Apperception Test stories. In our opinion this is due to the fact that anything manifest represents only the unrepressed, and thus often less dynamic, aspect of the motivational tendencies. Resorting to the concept of manifest drives actually implies a return to a straight behaviorism and its endless lists of "habits" which are of little use for purposes of parsimonious reduction.

To avoid these pitfalls, we have gone so far as to advocate reserving the concept of motivation, or of underlying "drives," for the realm of inferential constructs which go beyond, or "behind," the gross features of behavior (Frenkel-Brunswik, this volume, Chapter 1; 1942). It is only such qualities which would seem to deserve the designation of "depth." Among the drives in our list all show alternative manifestations in the sense described above with the exception of the need for "achievement." Although ratings on the drive for achievement probably reflect a basic personality orientation toward certain long-term effects—as may also be indicated by the existing correlations with other rated drives as well as with behavioral features—a striving for achievement may by its greater closeness to the ego with its reality orientation lend itself less to indirect, phenotypically heterogeneous manifestations than, say, a striving for aggression, dependence, or escape.

Our results have lent support to the assumption that the concept of underlying motives supplies us with an instrument which, due to its particular level of abstraction, or depth, is helpful in uncovering relationships and consistencies in the field of personality, provided that the relation between inferred drives and behavior has been analyzed and the meanings of the former have been specified operationally. While the issue of underlying dynamics was first clearly raised by psychoanalysis, it is in the tradition of academic psychology that the necessity to relate the dynamic concepts to behavioral data is being stressed. But it is this same tradition which is apt to overemphasize the importance of behavior as such.

Referring once more to our example of the boy who was rated high on underlying need for aggression and low on overt aggressive behavior, we must stress that both types of data are relevant; he certainly would be another kind of boy if his drive for aggression were coupled with overt aggressiveness, but he would even more certainly be another kind of boy if his surface friendliness were due to a genuine lack of aggressive drive. To cite another example: sadism and masochism may be closely related, but the effects may be as far apart as the impacts of a mass murderer and a saint upon society.

In the manner described, the problems of overt behavior which make up the core of traditional psychology, such as social adjustment, or perceptual and cognitive mastery of reality, must all be brought within the scope of personality research and personality theory. Here psychology will meet with a trend which has developed within psychoanalysis proper, namely, the partial turning away from depth toward an ego psychology.

From Depth Back to the Surface

SHIFTS TOWARD THE EGO AND THE MASTERY OF REALITY IN PSYCHOANALYSIS AND PERSONALITY THEORY

The exclusive interest in the central region of the personality as displayed by psychoanalysis in its beginnings proved to be too narrow to catch all the essentials of personality. As long as psychoanalysis concentrated its efforts upon the id, that is, the unorganized, primitive, pleasure-seeking system of instinctual drives, the resulting reduction left too little space for further differentiation in social terms. There was relatively little interest in the question of what a person had made out of his complex, that is, whether a drive pattern had, in spite of conflict, been successfully worked out to socially approved achievement, as in art, or whether it had led to a highly unsuccessful adjustment. Yet, as we indicated in the previous section, it is of far-reaching importance to have learned that in both cases similar drive patterns could have been at work and that underlying central forces might have differed from each other only in shades.

On the other hand, restriction of interest to the id actually means a depreciation of the functions directed toward the mastery of reality—the ego—to the role of mere diagnostic data. It also means that the environment as a stimulus enters the scope of investigation mainly insofar as it permits a repetition of childhood reactions to father, mother, and other persons in the past social environment of the child.

As we have said above, psychoanalysis has been undergoing a change in this respect, thus rendering irrelevant many of the older objections. Anna Freud (1936) herself seems to consider the early stages of psychoanalysis as limited to the central, but she emphasizes at the same time the shift toward the ego, which is defined in psychoanalysis as the agent governing the relationship of the individual to actual reality and responsible for the obtained results:

> There have been periods in the development of psycho-analytical science when the theoretical study of the individual ego was distinctly unpopular. Somehow or other, many analysts had conceived the idea that, in analysis, the value of the scientific and therapeutic work done was in direct proportion to the depth of the psychic strata upon which attention was focussed. Whenever interest was transferred from the deeper to the more superficial psychic strata—whenever, that is to say, research was deflected from the id to the ego—it was felt that here was a beginning of apostasy from psycho-analysis as a whole. The view held was that the term *psycho-analysis* should be reserved for the new discoveries relating to the unconscious psychic life, i.e. the study of repressed instinctual impulses, affects and phantasies. With problems such as that of the adjustment of children or adults to the outside world, with concepts of value such as those of health and disease, virtue or vice, psycho-analysis was not properly concerned. It should confine its investigations exclusively to infantile phantasies carried on into adult life, imaginary gratifications and the punishments apprehended in retribution for these. . . .
>
> When the writings of Freud, beginning with *Group Psychology and the Analysis of the Ego* and *Beyond the Pleasure Principle,* took a fresh direction, the odium of analytical unorthodoxy no longer attached to the study of the ego and interest was definitely focussed on the ego-institutions. Since then the term 'depth-psychology' certainly does not cover the whole field of psycho-analytical research [pp. 3-4].

Other contributors to this symposium, especially Bronfenbrenner (1951), have pointed out that this shift toward the ego in psychoanalysis brings us closer to cognition and perception. As Sigmund Freud (1923) wrote:

> It is easy to see that the ego is that part of the id which has been modified by the direct influence of the external world, acting through the perception-consciousness. In a sense it is an extension of the surface differentiation. . . . Moreover, the ego has the

task of bringing the influence of the external world to bear upon the id and its tendencies and endeavors to substitute the reality principle for the pleasure principle which reigns supreme in the id. In the ego, perception plays the part which in the id devolves upon instinct. The ego represents what we call reason and sanity in contrast to the id, which contains the passions.

Freud is explicit in his judgment that the function of the ego is not to be limited to external perception but includes internal perception as well. Though in his view the concept of the ego is not identical with that of perception—parts of the ego are considered to be unconscious—perception certainly is one of its main functions. (Parenthetically one may add that the animistic language of the psychoanalysts can easily be translated into a more objective and operational language.)

Parallel to the increased interest in the ego, attention in therapy is no longer being focused exclusively on transference effects of early infantile contents but is directed more and more frequently to resistance stemming from the ego; censorship operating in dreams is considered as crucial a material as their latent content, and modes of defense are as much studied as the impulses against which they are erected.

The function of the ego is seen mainly as the achieving of a compromise between the instincts on the one hand, and reality and ethical and moral demands on the other, as well as in the accomplishing of a synthesis of the three institutions of id, ego, and superego. Thus Anna Freud (1936) stated: "No longer do we see an undistorted id-impulse but an id-impulse modified by some defensive measure on the part of the ego" (p. 8); and "Were it not for the intervention of the ego or of those external forces which the ego represents, every instinct would know only one fate—that of gratification" (p. 47).

Impulses are exposed to rejection and criticisms and are modified under the pressure of the reality principle, which is considered by Sigmund Freud (1911) a basic "principle of mental functioning." The neurotic is described as "turning away from reality," as "being alienated from actuality," and as being unable to dethrone the pleasure principle in preference to a safeguarding of reality.

Since, with the study of the ego and the defense mechanisms, psychoanalysis moves into the field of psychology, we may turn briefly to these defense mechanisms, especially since much of the experimental work to be reported in the second part of this chapter builds upon our knowledge of defense mechanisms. Anna Freud mentions 10 defense mechanisms: regression, repression, reaction formation, isolation, undoing, projection, introjection, turning against the self, and reversal; the tenth mechanism, pertaining to the study of the normal, is sublimation. The first nine defenses are considered as pathogenic and as closely related to the formation of neuroses and psychoses. However, all of them are found, at least to some degree, in the development of the normal personality.[2]

In this chapter we are interested in the defense mechanisms mainly from the cognitive angle. Denial of painful sensations and facts represents the grossest falsification of reality and is thus found more often in young children. We find, however, milder degrees of denial in adults, where a truth can be known without its full implications being apparent or where "screen memories" may substitute for original memories. All manner of compromises between one's memory and the tendency toward denial can be observed and have in part been studied experimentally.

It is internal dangers rather than external ones that are the prime source of the mechanism of projection, through which the unpleasurable is seen as outside instead of inside. Paranoid patients produce the crudest projective misinterpretation of reality. To a certain degree, however, this mechanism is called upon to explain misunderstanding of actual reality in the direction of unconscious needs.

Repression consists in an unconscious forgetting or in the failure to become aware of internal impulses or of events connected with the impulses considered to be objectionable. The sex instinct seems to lend itself mainly to repression, whereas aggressive impulses elicit other types of defense mechanisms. The mechanism of repression is most clearly exhibited in hysteria.

What has been said so far can provide a basis for extensive personality-centered research in cognition and perception both in normals and in the pathological. Thus we would expect more omissions of reality on the part of the hysteric and more commissions of distortion on the part of the paranoid patient. More pre-

---

[2]The summary of defense mechanisms given here and in the following discussion is based on S. Freud (1915a, 1915b), A. Freud (1936), and Fenichel (1945).

cisely, we may find distortion of reality in the paranoid combined with faithful stimulus boundness, the latter constituting an attempt toward the restitution of a reality experienced as slipping.

Still different results would have to be expected in the case of the compulsive and obsessive patient, where we would be likely to find a series of actions one of which would be a direct reversal of the other—undoing—with frequent repetitions to make sure that the original impulse is undone and with continuing doubts that this has really been achieved. In the mechanism of isolation prevalent in the compulsive, parts are recognized as such, but they are kept apart by interjecting spatial or temporal intervals or by using other techniques, such as, for instance, the isolation of an idea from its emotional context. The so-called detached, logical thinker may often be warding off anxieties by isolation and may thus miss many important relationships and restrict his creativity. From an examination of the general dynamics of the compulsive syndrome, Fenichel proceeds to a description of the need for being systematic and for clinging to definite systems as it occurs in the compulsive character structure. This need, often manifested in the tendency to "type" and to classify in categories, is seen as protection against surprise and fear of drive impulses. Deviations from symmetry are not tolerated; they are experienced as deviations from general norms, especially moral ones.

Perhaps we should emphasize at once that we are far from considering different forms of perception and cognition merely as a result of different ways of warding off instinctual anxiety. We shall expand on this later. Here we are more concerned with stressing the provocative angles under which the cognitive approach has been put by psychoanalysis.

We may now conclude our discussion of the mechanisms of defense by pointing to reaction formation; this mechanism involves a definite change of personality away from the feared impulse. Cleanliness, when developed in this manner, will be exaggerated, but there will be a persistent occasional breaking through of dirtiness. The same holds true for kindliness, which often represents a true reaction formation against hatred. The origin of these types of defensive attitudes is indicated by the rigidity which they assume and by the occasional breaking through of the original impulse. These original tendencies may be seen with exceptional clarity in the case of the disintegration of a reaction formation.

In spite of the fact that various psychoanalysts have attempted more or less explicitly to describe the clinical data which are the basis for inferences about defense mechanisms, much remains to be done in this direction. In any event, defense mechanisms seem to be among the functions which are relatively accessible to direct observation. It is as yet open to question, however, which types or aspects of defense mechanisms should be studied in the laboratory and which should be handed over to other, more clinically oriented psychological techniques or should be left to be checked in the therapeutic procedure only. We shall have more to say about this after the discussion of some experimental material.

The increasing concentration on the ego and the defense mechanisms renders partially invalid the objection, often leveled against psychoanalysis, to the effect that reduction to instincts was carried too far and that what all people have in common was stressed too much, while important differences were neglected. So long as psychoanalysis concentrated on instincts, there undoubtedly was some validity to the objection made by Allport (1937) that in psychoanalysis "needs are disembodied and depersonalized to a greater degree than is justified in elements that are to serve as the radicals of personality." But we find psychoanalysis now increasingly concerned with needs as modified by the defense mechanisms. This is a step which introduces a great deal more in the way of differentiation and which connects human behavior not only to its internal sources but also to external realities. The defense mechanisms may be recruited to explain at least partially such differences as the one between a masochist who remains a sexual pervert and a well-disciplined monk, to use an example of Allport's. With the increasing study of the defense mechanisms we thus find in psychoanalysis an increasing emphasis on the study of character formation.

The definition of anxiety may serve as a good example of the change of framework in psychoanalysis. Anxiety was first seen mainly as the result of dammed-up sexual instincts. Later, however, anxiety—at least in its lesser degrees—was seen also, among other things, as a signal for the use of protective measures, as an anticipation of the future. In other words, it has come to be considered as an indicator of an increased alertness of the ego toward reality.

All this, however, meets only partially the above-mentioned objections against psychoanalysis. It may still be argued that, by and large, psychoanalysis has considered defense mechanisms and character structure mainly under the defensive aspect and relatively little under the aspect of positive adaptation. This is admitted by one of the most orthodox psychoanalysts, Fenichel (1945, p. 52). Freud (1925) also was aware of this fact, and this was the reason why he did not regard psychoanalysis as a closed system. Rather, he conceived of psychoanalysis as needing other types of psychology to complement it:

> By itself this science is seldom able to deal with a problem completely, but it seems destined to give valuable contributory help in a large number of regions of knowledge. The sphere of application of psycho-analysis extends as far as that of psychology, to which it forms a complement of the greatest moment.

The approach merely hinted at by Freud was taken up by his students. Hartmann (1939) goes far beyond the view of the ego as a mere defense against instinct. Taking intellectualization as an example, he stresses that a phenomenon of this kind cannot be completely defined by considering it only as a defense; it is also characterized by properties and laws which result from the primary orientation of the intellect toward mastery of the external world. Even in cases in which the process of intellectualization was first developed as a defense, it can become independent of the source and serve a different, exclusively constructive function. The same holds even more for perception, of course.

In general, memory, learning, and other mental capacities are no longer seen as developments in the conflict between the ego and the instincts or in the conflict with love objects; rather, they are seen primarily as adjustive mechanisms. Allport originally thought of his principle of functional autonomy as at variance with psychoanalytic theory; but now we find him in agreement with a student so faithful to Freud as Hartmann.

Hartmann and some of the other psychoanalysts are in a sense discovering many of the phenomena which for a long time have been the exclusive concern of psychology and the social sciences. We should welcome this state of affairs; we should even be grateful that psychoanalysis for a long time ignored these aspects of human behavior which are so obvious to the psychologist. It was this oversight which made it possible for psychoanalysis to concentrate upon a formerly neglected aspect of human behavior and to introduce a novel, crucial, and, in the true sense, dynamic aspect into the study of human nature.

Changes similar to those within the psychoanalytic movement can be observed within the fields of personality theory and research. At first, the principal methods in this field were the so-called projective techniques, mainly the Rorschach and Thematic Apperception tests. They were designed to reach the deeper layers of the personality by making reality vague and unclear, thus providing an opportunity for the projection of the "private world," to use a term suggested by L. K. Frank (1939). Thus, these deep and subjective tendencies replaced the reactions of the subject to the standard objective world as the focus of attention. Now a shift is taking place—as this symposium bears witness—with the personologists increasingly interested in perception and cognition. They thus return to the fold of general psychology only to find that, in the meantime, general psychology itself has faced in the new direction of an interest in personality.

CHANGES IN THE SOCIAL SCIENCES AND IN SOCIAL PSYCHOLOGY

Before discussing this matter further, we must follow another trend of personality theory which, similarly to the interest in cognitive processes, leads away from the preoccupation with the deep, the private, and the subjective. We refer to the problems of social adjustment and the whole realm of topics included under the label of "personality and culture."

First, we must stress the positive contributions which psychoanalysis has made to these topics, at the same time trying not to lose sight of the limitations of these contributions. Let us emphasize that it was Freud and psychoanalysis which first pointed out the intimate interaction of biological and social factors in the individual. Thus, such processes as sucking, bowel movement, and masturbation, considered as purely biological phenomena before the advent of psychoanalysis, have been woven by the latter into the fabric of social interaction. Sucking is considered not only as a means for getting food but also as a means of experiencing and expressing affection and aggression, and the process of bowel movement is seen as being utilized by the child in his struggle with the parents and with authority in general. Dreams, which were considered as private and meaningless before Freud, are now used as a basis for a reconstruction of the most decisive and subtle aspects of interpersonal relationships. These aspects also permeate perception, as will be remembered from the discussion of the defense mechanisms.

While psychoanalysis stresses in the development of the individual his contact, or rather his clash, with society, it does not as a whole concern itself with the characteristics of society as such nor with social institutions so far as they appear as independent of the single individual. Here again psychoanalysis attacks only the most intimate aspect of the problem, namely, how social influences—mainly represented by parental figures—disturb and modify the deepest layers of our biological and instinctual lives. Social influences are seen as a series of traumata which bring to a halt and discontinue instinctual expansion. The concept of sublimation is adduced to explain how the energies of the ungratified instincts are transferred to socially constructive goals. This concept, however, remains relatively sterile and vague in the writings and teachings of psychoanalysis. We hear very little about the satisfactions which may be derived from successfully adopted social roles and identities.

In the meeting of psychoanalysis and anthropology we are able again to discern the change from depth to surface which we have sketched for the meeting of psychoanalysis and psychology. Róheim, one of the first psychoanalytically oriented anthropologists, sees most cultural phenomena as deriving from early traumata in infancy (1943). The handling of the child's needs and the approach to child rearing in general are definitely not seen by Róheim as part of the broader social structure. On the contrary, the social structure is seen as the result of the ways a few individuals handled their own and their children's instinctual problems, ways which they transmitted to the other members of the tribe. The specific traumata inherent in the different methods of upbringing and enforced renunciations are said to form the basis for customs and religions. Again, this point of view, though one-sided and incomplete, has enriched anthropology and the social sciences in a decisive way. It points the way to increased emphasis on child development in different cultures, toward searching for unified themes in the private modes of experience as well as in religion and ideology. It leads to the inclusion of such materials as dreams, free associations, and projective materials in general in the study of personality and culture. This approach, in combination with the original emphasis of the social sciences on historic tradition, on the ways of subsistence, on the organization of society, has led to a more fruitful understanding of the individual in his society.

Further examples of this type of synthesis are the works of Fromm (1941), Kardiner (1939), Kluckhohn (1949), Erikson (1945), Mead (1949), and Linton (1945).

One of the special fields of the social sciences which is increasingly influenced by psychoanalysis to the benefit of both is social psychology. Changes are along lines similar to those in the social sciences in general. An increasing number of social scientists have moved away from the exclusive use of public-opinion polls and are concerned with relating social attitudes to personality as well as to sociological factors. The work of Stagner (1936), of Hartley (1946), of Allport (1935), and our California studies on ethnic prejudice (Adorno et al., 1950; Frenkel-Brunswik, 1948c) may be cited as examples. The latter combine methods and outlook of social psychology with those of clinical psychology.

For example, in the California studies we were primarily interested in a certain subject's social attitudes, say, his attitude toward Roosevelt, and not only as a basis for understanding his attitude toward, say, his own father. But we probably would never have been able to understand the range and subtlety of the subject's attitude toward Roosevelt had we not been guided by the findings on his attitude toward his father. Social attitudes and social techniques are at least as real as the underlying motivation, but often we need to speculate on the latter to understand the former.

CHANGES IN THE PSYCHOLOGY OF PERCEPTION

Not only the social sciences but also general psychology, as we have mentioned above, changed under the impact of psychoanalysis and the science of personality. General psychology, especially represented by the fields of learning, perception, and other aspects of cognition, seemed at first untouched by so-called dynamic psychology. More recently, however, these fields have been invaded. We find Murphy (1947), Murray (1933), Sanford (1937), Bruner,

Postman, and others (Bruner and Goodman, 1947; Postman, Bruner, and McGinnies, 1948), and Sherif (1936) among the pioneers who have looked at perception mainly from the angle of needs. Murphy designates the fact that cognitive processes move in the direction of needs as "autism" and stresses that "all cognitive processes are apparently continually shaped in greater or lesser degree by the pressure of wants" (1947, p. 365). "There is no standard objective world except through our slow yielding to a rather painful compromise process." Fear, hunger, need for conformity, and values have been explored as determining perception.

Again we find here, on a smaller scale and in a more rapid succession, steps of development parallel to those described previously for psychoanalysis and for personality research. The reality which the cognitive processes are supposed to transmit to us has in the past been interpreted by general psychologists as something reflected in perception in an absolute and universal manner. An important system of the psychology of perception which deals exclusively with the veridical functions of the cognitive processes is that of Egon Brunswik (1934). This system represents a crucial progress over the classical psychophysical approach insofar as it is oriented toward the perceptual conquest of the world of physical and social objects, whereas psychophysics is arrested in mediation and stimulus boundness without reaching the functionally important part of the stimulus world. More specifically, it is the orientation toward "thing constancy" which reintroduces the "distal" reality lost in the traditional psychophysical approach. Another example of a functional approach to perception is represented by Hilgard (1951) in his contribution to the present symposium.

The next step, the discovery of autism, shows us how subjective and shifting this conquest of reality is when exposed to changing systems of needs, with their power to select or distort many aspects of perceptual reality.

Summarizing, we may say that "reality," first lost in psychophysics, was reinstated in the work on the constancy problem, but became again lost in a one-sided emphasis on motives as determinants of perception. The last step seems paradoxical in view of the fact that psychoanalysis, which had been an influence in this emphasis away from reality, itself stressed the reality orientation of perception as soon as it had come around to deal with the matter.

Still more recent workers in the field of personality and perception have managed to balance their interest in the mastery of reality, in the perceiver's different ways of handling it effectively, with an interest in subjective distortions. As may be seen from this symposium and the Symposium on Personality and Perception in the *Journal of Personality* (September and December, 1949), we are now about to reach a fruitful compromise by combining the study of the veridical and the subjective functions of the cognitive processes.

Another line of thought which converges into the synthesis of personality and perception research is that of such German typologists as Kretschmer (1942), Jaensch (1938), Goldstein (1936), and Werner (1940). Relatively little interested as they are in both the influence of needs on perception and in the veridical functions of perception, they have stressed over-all styles of personality as expressed in behavioral patterns as well as in the cognitive approach to the environment. Among the perceptually loaded variables that have become prominent in this course of development is the one defined by the opposition of the "synthetic" and the "analytic" approach as adopted, among others, by Kretschmer and his school and also represented by the "whole" versus "detail" emphasis in the evaluation of the Rorschach test; further pairs of opposites borrowed from the psychology of perception are "diffuse" versus "articulated" (Werner), "concrete" versus "abstract" (Goldstein), as well as such rather specific distinctions as color dominance versus form dominance (Kretschmer, Schroll, and others, and again Rorschach; see also the treatment in Thurstone's factorial study of perception [1944]).

Not only are most of the major theories in German academic psychology rooted in perception (see the Gestalt psychologists, and the constancy approach of Egon Brunswik and of others), but the same holds for the German psychology of individual differences, as exemplified by the typologists just mentioned as well as by William Stern (1935).

The work of Rorschach, the Swiss psychiatrist (1921), represents a merging of psychoanalysis and the work of the German typologists. Unlike the materials used by the German typologists, Rorschach used his vague inkblots in order to get as much projection as possible and proceeded to an interpretation at least in part along the lines of his psychoanalytic orientation.

In the workshop of the clinical psychologist we find all these trends combined. Case histories are collected and combined with the results of a battery of tests, which include projective materials as well as intelligence and concept-formation tests.

We have seen that with the greater emphasis on perception and cognition, as well as on social factors, personality theory is reintroducing the manifest personality or phenotype. Perceptual and cognitive performances as well as social attitudes are being carefully and systematically observed and are used not merely for extrapolations into the deeper layers. On the contrary, speculations about the deeper layers are considered as detours necessary for the prediction of what is in the end our greatest interest, namely, the so-called surface behavior, whether this consists in a political attitude or in the solution of a cognitive task. Expanded understanding of human behavior in the sense just indicated will contribute to a dynamic ego psychology considerably beyond the contribution of psychoanalysis in this field. Precisely at which points and to what extent the dynamic ego psychology, which seems now to emerge as the major interest of psychologists, is based on the dynamic ego psychology developed by psychoanalysis and precisely how much change the topic has undergone under the impact of psychology proper can better be discussed after the presentation of some experimental and empirical material, to which we now proceed.

Perception of Self and of Others

We now enter into the discussion of the empirical material by way of problems in the perception of the self and of others, using some of our California studies as examples. In the framework of this symposium the problem of the perception of the self and of others has already been introduced by Carl Rogers (1951) with an emphasis mainly on the changes that occur in the course of a successful therapy. Our emphasis, however, will be on a comparison of self-perception with actual behavior as observed by others. We will ask ourselves what factors of adjustment and motivation determine the accuracy or distortion of our self-image, and what are the cues by which we can tell whether or not self-descriptions and descriptions of others are representative of actual reality. We hope to answer some of the questions posed in this symposium by Bruner as to the conditions under which certain aspects of the self become more salient in our perception than others. In the final sections we will deal with the reality adequacy of thing percepts and concepts in their relation to personality factors.

A STUDY OF MECHANISMS OF SELF-DECEPTION

Our first example is a study conducted by the present writer some years ago at the Psychological Institute of the University of Vienna (Frenkel-Brunswik, 1939). Its aim was to compare the actual conduct of a group of students, as observed by four independent judges, with the students' own statements about their conduct. Besides asking the students to describe their own behavior, we also inquired about the "guiding principles" of their conduct in general and their "demands upon the environment," that is, the way they perceived their immediate working environment and what changes they would like to make in it. These three types of query represented three different degrees of directness in approaching the personalities of the students concerned.

The results, based on about 40 subjects, showed that the functional realities of one's own behavior are distorted when they enter consciousness and are verbally reported. This holds true, above all, so far as shortcomings of the subjects are concerned, but it is also true for positively valued traits.

The most striking mechanism found here was "distortion into the opposite." For example, one of the students was characterized by all the judges as lacking in sincerity. The student himself declared he was "sincere under all conditions."

There are marked statistical correlations between the tendency to perceive oneself in an extremely favorable light on a certain personality characteristic, such as popularity or sincerity, and an opposite, unfavorable rating on the same characteristic by the judges. In general, it is social maladjustment as rated by the judges which correlates with the presence of this mechanism of self-deception. Intellectual ability as rated by the judges is relatively unrelated to the tendency of "distortion into the opposite." This may be regarded as supporting the assumption of the relative independence of intelligence and emotional adjustment. Moreover, there was no evidence of such a mechanism of distortion into the opposite in regard to the trait of scientific ability.

A second mechanism of self-deception as found in our material is that of "exaggeration." In the case of the subject quoted above who delcared himself to be "sincere under all conditions," one is reminded of Shakespeare's warning that "the lady doth protest too much." Indeed, exaggerated formulations—as here the denial of guilt—were found to be statistically symptomatic of the absence rather than the presence of the asserted trait.

A third, more subtle mechanism found was that of "omission." In this case the subject did not mention a positive or negative characteristic of his which the judges had especially noted as displayed by him.

There was, fourth, a kind of apologetic camouflage constituting an attempt at justification of a defect. For instance, one of the subjects, characterized by the judges as extremely aggressive, stated about herself, "I do not let myself be intimidated."

"Minimizing" is still another, fifth, mechanism. Here a trait is seen by the subject in an unconcealed way but is minimized by his regarding it as not very strong or by his shifting the emphasis away from it by mentioning it relatively late in his self-characterization. Thus, in the case of one student all the judges had noted first of all in their list of traits that he was extremely social-minded, altruistic, and self-sacrificing. The subject himself said, "I try to help others if I can," but he put down this statement only after he had listed nine other traits in the description of himself.

On the whole, we have found more self-deceptions, in the sense defined here, in the area of more generalized behavioral dispositions than in that of the more palpable particulars of conduct. Thus there is relatively little illusion about one's own behavior in concrete situations, such as the bringing back of books to the library on time. Reality testing is easier and more obvious in such situations than it is in the case of the more generalized traits. Only in pathological cases do we find false self-perceptions concerning relatively unambiguously defined, concrete behavior. Thus, one student, diagnosed as an incipient schizophrenic, explained his lack of contact with other students by his being so seldom at the Institute, while the observers agreed that he was regularly present, although without actual participation.

By comparing the language of the self-perceptions with that of the perception and description of others, we find that, in the case of our Viennese students, self-reports were more concerned with (often spurious) motivational aspects of behavior, while the reports of the judges were focused more upon the overt social effects. Though the two sets of descriptions may thus deal with somewhat different topics, we may still speak of self-deceptions, since our subjects were explicitly asked to talk about their overt behavior. It would seem to be very difficult for one to see his own behavior without introducing immediately the aspect of motivation with its implicit element of justification. We function as judges of the behavior of others, but rather as doctors or mothers when we are viewing the behavior of ourselves.

What has been said for the perception of one's own behavior holds even more true in the case of the guiding principles of conduct listed by our subjects. Declaration of such principles often turned out to represent a compensation for behavioral shortcomings rather than a reflection of strength. As in the case of the behavioral traits, we can make a list of the guiding principles in the order of their probability of being actualized in real behavior. Thus, we find that "sincerity" listed by a subject as a guiding principle is negatively related to real sincerity, and "to be helpful" is not at all related to being helpful in reality.

On the other hand, what may be called the principles of achievement were found to be lived up to in almost every instance in which they had been mentioned by the subjects. Achievement, like intelligence, thus seems to be more interlocked with conscious design or purpose than is emotional or social conduct.

Shortcomings in social and personal attitudes are often not directly represented by conscious guiding principles but are rather expressed or signalized there in a diametrically opposite way. The ultimate aim of this inverse signalizing is probably a modification of behavior. A compensatory function of the guiding principles is also indicated by the fact that overemphasis, e.g., use of superlatives and repetition, was found to stand more often for a shortcoming than for a strength in the area concerned. The production of a great number of explicitly formulated guiding principles for one's behavior likewise often was found to go with its opposite, that is, with lack of fortitude of character.

In the perception of the environment and the demands for

changes in it as expressed in the protocols of our subjects we find different types of statements. One group may be called "matter-of-fact," indicating, say, the demand for more books in the library, a demand which, according to the judges, was undoubtedly justified.

Another group of statements demands that the environment meet the subject's own personal shortcomings without his seeming to realize his own defects. For example, a subject considered as very aggressive by the judges demanded that others should be more friendly. His wishes for reform seemed to be directed exclusively toward the environment, so that he might live in it with as little friction as possible.

Finally, a third type of statement asks help of the environment in overcoming the subject's own shortcomings, which are here less repressed than in the case mentioned previously. For instance, one of the subjects, rated as lacking in self-discipline, demanded a much stricter organization of the Psychological Institute.

In the manner described, the demands which are made upon the social environment, and the general way this environment is perceived, seem to give a better picture, in an indirect, projective way, of the real dynamic forces within the person than is contained in his own self-reports. These demands indicate a comfortable way in which these shortcomings, which as such remain unperceived, could be remedied. It would appear that we do not always see ourselves as we are but instead perceive the environment in terms of our own needs. Self-perception and perception of the environment actually merge in the service of these needs. Thus, the perceptual distortions of ourselves and the environment fulfill an important function in our psychological household.

CASE STUDIES OF SELF-DECEPTION IN ADOLESCENTS

Our seond example of mechanisms of perception is based on an analysis of material on three girls which I carried out as a part of the University of California Adolescent Growth Study referred to in the first section of this paper. This analysis—not hitherto published—shows in somewhat greater detail some of the mechanisms in the perception of the self and of others just described and relates them to the general dynamics of the personality. As mentioned above, a schematic description and evaluation of the adolescents' overt behavior as well as of their underlying motives had been made by adult observers and by their classmates. This had been done over a period of eight years. Detailed material about the self-evaluation of these children, concerned with the way they saw themselves and described their way of behaving, their feelings, and their status, was also available. In the focus of our attention for the present purposes will be the devices which are used on the different levels of personality to secure mental balance by settling at least temporarily on a certain self-image as well as on a certain image of one's environment.

On the behavioral observation ratings done by the staff of the Adolescent Study one of our three girls, Nell, was usually rated high on "talkativeness" and "display." Nell was thus seen as a girl who was rather uninhibited in vying for the attention of others. That no doubts entered her mind concerning the appropriateness of her behavior is indicated by her marked degree of "poise," as noted by the adult observers. However, she was one sigma below average in "relaxation," and there were signs of "anxiety" which might indicate underlying insecurity, although Nell was considered to be, on the surface at least, a carefree and cheerful girl.

The observers further rated Nell as having an "unpleasing expression," as being "unattractive," and as "unpopular" except for a period in the eighth grade when she achieved some degree of popularity. Though she never really achieved popularity, she was rated consistently high on "social interest" and on "initiative." Her ratings on "good-naturedness" were usually below average, giving further evidence of her egocentricity. She received especially low ratings, almost two sigmas below average, on "calmness," "cooperativeness," and "contentedness." Also below average were her ratings on "tolerance," "earnestness," "responsibility," "constancy of mood," and "social insight." She was more than one sigma above average in "exploitiveness." All this points to the picture of a restless, impulsive, tense girl who was highly inconsiderate of others and, in general, lacking in responsibility. This impression is further confirmed by Nell's being above average on all the items expressing overactivity, social striving, and aggressiveness, that is, on "self-confidence," "bold behavior," and "self-assertion." She was also above average on "busyness," "initiative," "activity," and "quick comeback," as well as on "drive for social contact" and "attention-gettingness."

There were no striking developmental changes in Nell's behavior pattern during the years of the study. The only consistent trend was one of slight improvement during the end of her school career. It was in the eleventh grade that Nell was for the first and only time rated as above average in "relaxation" and "good-naturedness." Her rating on "awareness of the audience" rose at this time from one sigma below average to one above average, indicating an increasing sensitivity and concern about the impression she made. After developing this awareness, a slight improvement with respect to her adjustment could be found.

We next turn to the data indicating the way Nell was seen by her classmates. The Reputation Test (sometimes called the "Guess Who")[3] provides a means of determining the reputation a certain child has with his fellow students on a series of personality attributes.

Nell was rated by her classmates as very low on grown-up behavior and high on being restless, attention-getting, and talkative. Again, Nell's reputation improved in the ninth and tenth grades, when she was considered as happy, enthusiastic, and as having a good sense of humor.

So far we have discussed how Nell has been rated by others, both adults and classmates. Now we turn to Nell in her function as a judge of herself and of others. The Reputation Test is also a test of self-evaluation, since every child is asked to consider himself for inclusion in his list of names for each trait, in addition to being judged by his classmates.

Though Nell was not rated by the others as popular, she herself considered that she was popular. It is important to note in this context that in her judging of others Nell used a concept of popularity which deviated from that of the group. Her unusual method of judging the popularity of others reveals, even more than do her illusory direct judgments of her own popularity, her personal liability in this area. Her way of judging becomes clear from the following facts. Although Nell agreed with the group in rating the girls whom she considered popular also as happy, enthusiastic, friendly, and daring, she differed from the group in linking popularity with talkativeness, with being assured with adults, and with

---

[3]Extensive use is made here of the "clusters" of traits which Tryon (1939a) developed on the basis of the Reputation Test.

attention-gettingness. Recalling her own high standing on the last three items, we find in her association of these traits with popularity, when she was judging others, an indirect revelation of—and at the same time a defense against—these weaknesses existing in herself. Furthermore, unlike most of the girls, Nell associated tidiness and good looks with lack of popularity; she herself was rated low on tidiness and good looks, and it is obviously for this reason that she did not consider these traits as necessary for popularity. She saw the unpopular girl as tidy, not talkative, not attention-getting, and shy about making friends. Only in the last of these items did her conception coincide with that of the group. Here she could afford to have an undistorted judgment because she herself was not shy. On the whole Nell showed a marked inclination to judge her classmates unfavorably.

We have seen how Nell, in her judgments of others, revealed herself indirectly by projecting her own weaknesses onto them. In her direct statements about herself all defenses were activated. She put herself down as being a popular, good-looking girl who was a leader, active in games, friendly, talkative—we remember that she evaluated talkativeness as being an attribute of popular girls—and happy, as well as assured in class and with adults. Her classmates agreed with her about herself on talkativeness, happiness, and enthusiasm, especially in the last years in school. But she was not considered as popular, nor as good-looking (average or below), nor a leader. She also considered herself as daring at a time when she got a marked rating for being afraid. She mentioned herself as being assured in class, though she usually received either no mention or a negative score on this trait from others. The one year in which she received a positive score on being assured in class she did not mention herself on that item, whereas when she was rated negatively she paradoxically put herself on the positive side. In the seventh grade, when her reputation for being attention-getting was at its height, she claimed she was not attention-getting; but in the eleventh grade, when for the first time none of her classmates mentioned her as attention-getting, she, for the first time, admitted that she liked to be the center of attention.

Nell's realization of her weaknesses when she was in the eleventh grade is especially enlightening in view of the fact that it was in this period that her external behavior showed the first signs of increasing insight and contemplation.

With the exception of such isolated instances of partial insight as the one just discussed, however, Nell may be said, on the basis of the material presented here, to reveal a number of mechanisms of self-deception. First, she displayed the crudest of the mechanisms of distortion into the opposite. In Nell's case the distortion went in the direction of ego inflation and maximation, implying a complete denial of an unfavorable reality.

Second, there is evidence of the mechanism of projection. She described her classmates in an unfavorable light, thus indirectly blaming the others for whatever difficulties might arise. Furthermore, by degrading the others she apparently hoped to lift herself up.

A third mechanism detected in Nell is distortion and omission in judging others. As described above, her conception of a popular girl was found to differ from that of the group in a way which made more possible her inclusion in this classification. As far as omission is concerned, Nell, in spite of rating herself as popular, did not make much use of this category in judging others. In spite of her overt denial, she apparently felt some uneasiness on this issue and thus preferred to bypass it.

From the point of view of developmental stages, we find that in Nell both the mechanisms of self-deception and the aggression against others seemed most marked at the ages of 13 and 14. In those years she considered herself as good-looking, having older friends, being tidy, friendly, happy, enthusiastic, and social. To others, especially to boys and to her friends, she attributed negative characteristics. But this was the year in which no one selected her as a friend. At the age of 16, on the other hand, her mechanisms of self-deception and projection appear to have been toned down, while at the same time her behavior improved. Of the total of 72 mentions of herself, which Nell made over a period of eight years on the Reputation Test, all but 11 were positive. Those 11 negative judgments were made during the last two years, when in fact she was about to be accepted by the group.

Another of the instruments used in the California Adolescent Study, the Adjustment Inventory,[4] was intended as a broad and

---

[4]The Inventory (Tryon, 1939b) consisted of several series of items, including a number of sections from tests reported by Rogers (1931) and by Symonds and Jackson (1930). Examples are the checking of three wishes or aspirations, or of any number of fears, out of prepared lists; the naming of three persons to share one's life on a desert island; there also was a check list of self-evaluations and corresponding wishes concerning one's personality and social relations. The categorization of the material was in the hands of Tryon (1939a).

systematic approach to self-evaluation. The children were asked to rate themselves on approximately 600 specific items at yearly intervals over a period of seven years beginning with the fifth grade. While the Inventory has since proved of somewhat limited value when responses are taken at face value, it gains new significance when interpreted as material on self-perception and as indirect evidence on motivation

In line with results on the Reputation Test, Nell's score on "social adjustment" as based on self-evaluation was usually somewhat above average (about one sigma), the major exception being in the eleventh grade, when it was below average. As noted above, this was the year in which Nell's behavior actually improved. The rest of the time she grossly overestimated herself, especially her acceptance by others. As before, however, Nell's answers to the more indirect questions reveal her ardent but partially frustrated social ambition and her doubts that everything was well in her relationships with others. She thought that the other boys and girls were often mean, snobbish, and "stuck-up."

Nell's score on "personal inferiority" was likewise most of the time well above average, demonstrating once more that Nell evaluated her personal attributes positively. There was a marked tendency toward ego inflation, as reflected, for example, in her aspirations. Every year but one, Nell wished to be a movie star, a choice which was made by only a small proportion of the children. This choice is especially conspicuous in view of the fact that Nell was consistently rated as below average in good looks. Only rarely did Nell mention vocational aspirations that were more realistic, and when she did so her aspirations became very modest. Again, however, in the last year in school Nell seemed less self-satisfied.

Her "school adjustment" as seen by herself stayed, with the exception of the fifth grade, well above average. She herself, however, complained almost every year about being told that she was "too noisy and talks too much" and about "not having a chance to recite in class." Instead of facing her restlessness and her drive to exhibit herself, she felt herself unjustifiably restrained by her teachers. It was only in these indirect complaints that Nell indicated difficulties in her relation to the teacher. Five out of the seven times she filled out the Adjustment Inventory, she considered herself as "a girl who is very much liked by the teachers," and only twice did she consider herself as completely rejected, adding that she did not wish to be liked by them. Here is one instance in which an extreme affirmation of an alleged asset alternates with an extreme denial, showing the closeness of the two extremes to one another and indicating an insecurity in this respect. (For a general discussion of closeness of opposites, see this volume, Chapter 2.) Nell's insecurity was justified, since we know from other sources that she was not very highly regarded by the teachers.

Nell's responses in regard to the items which deal with the attitude toward family show marked ambivalence. She expressed a great deal of attachment to her family in the direct questions, e.g., in her preference to go home after school, a preference which she shared with only 10% of the girls; but she usually omitted her family when asked about the three persons she would take to a desert island, while most of the girls did choose some family members.

In a study of Nell's case, based on home interviews, Mary C. Jones describes the eager social ambition of Nell's parents, especially of her mother, and the pressure put upon Nell to fulfill this ambition. On the basis of the behavioral data, we have seen that Nell identified with the attitude of her mother and displaying the same social ambition. However, in her reactions to the indirect questions concerning her attitude toward her family, such as the one about companions on a desert island mentioned above, Nell revealed her wish to escape from this pressure and her resentment about not getting enough love and affection. As will be seen later, the type of ambivalence toward parents which is not utterly conscious and accepted very often goes with an inclination toward black-white solutions and an avoidance of emotional and cognitive ambiguities in general.

We have said before that exaggeration is one of the most important signs of compensatory as contrasted with representative statements. The number of exaggerated responses in the Adjustment Inventory is measured by the category "overstatement." Nell is found to do a great deal of overstating. Her overstatements usually expressed an extreme satisfaction with herself. As mentioned above, she judged herself as very well liked, as very bright, very well dressed, having very much fun, and the like. On the few occasions when Nell thought she was lacking in a positively valued characteristic, she overdramatized this lack and denied emphatically the wish to be different.

Nell yielded extreme responses not only in judging herself but also on the corresponding questions indicating her wishes and ideals. When both self-description and aspirations are extreme, there is very little room for discrepancy between the two. The average child shows more discrepancy, yet neither his self-description nor his aspirations customarily go to such extremes as those reached by Nell. We recall here Rogers's (1951) statement stressing the diminishing discrepancy between ideal self and real self after successful therapy; we should like to add that the absence of such a discrepancy is probably not always a sign of adjustment. It is certainly not such a sign in Nell's case.

Along the same line are some of the findings in our studies on ethnic prejudice (Frenkel-Brunswik, 1948c; Adorno et al., 1950). Prejudiced persons, who as a group are less well adjusted than the unprejudiced, reveal less awareness of discrepancy between real and ideal self than do the latter. Here is a minor point of difference between Rogers's and our findings on self-perception. Otherwise our results are remarkably similar and mutually confirmatory.

Aside from overstatement, there is still another category in which Nell, in spite of her displayed self-satisfaction, revealed an underlying anxiety. At the time she reached the climax of her apparent satisfaction with herself, she also rose above the average on the category "fears." More specifically, her fears reflected the notion of a threatening, aggressive environment. In the eleventh grade, which will be remembered as a period of increased insight, more correct self-perception, and more effective mastery of difficulties for Nell, her "fears" decreased to one sigma below average.

A second case we should discuss briefly is that of Joyce, a girl who, in contrast to Nell, was highly successful though somewhat egocentric and lacking in basic adjustment. Her success started about the sixth or seventh grade when she got the highest ratings on popularity, poise, and social prestige and low ratings on the tendency toward display. Later there are indications that, behind Joyce's smooth social façade (she was two sigmas above average on this trait), there were some preoccupations which interfered with her ability for good object relations. At the age of 16, Joyce was rated one sigma below average on "cooperativeness" and one sigma above average on "exploitiveness." These ratings indicate that, in spite of her remarkable success, her social adjustment was on a superficial level. But at first no one besides herself seemed to know much about her inner difficulties. One of her more palpable reactions was that her judgments of herself on the Reputation Test were rather distorted. In contrast to Nell, Joyce showed a total of only 41 judgments about herself, and 24 of these were negative. In spite of the fact that she received the highest possible score on "tidiness" and "good-lookingness," she gave herself a negative score on these items.

Not only did Joyce point in her judgments to liabilities where she actually possessed assets, but she realistically faced her true weaknesses. In the sixth and seventh grades she had credited herself with a sense of humor, but from the ninth grade on she indicated that she had no appreciation of jokes and no sense of humor. It was precisely at that time that her reputation for "having humor" dropped rather drastically. Since she frequently ascribed to girls she considered popular certain characteristics which she thought she lacked, such as being active in games, assured in class, happy, good-looking, and having an appreciation for jokes, we can assume that she really thought she was not liked. Her way of perceiving others may be used as an indirect check on her self-judgment to the effect that she was unpopular.

We find Joyce's self-judgments shot through with understatement and self-minimization when we compare them with judgments made about her by others. We have every reason to believe that this tendency on her part was due not to a mere display of modesty but to real insecurity. The means of defense here was not verbal ego maximation as in Nell, but a strong striving toward all kinds of actual success. This striving was successful but, at the same time, insatiable and therefore never really satisfied. Because of her actual success Joyce could afford to admit to herself her underlying weaknesses.

It might be interesting to speculate further about the source of Joyce's tendency to understate her assets and to dramatize her shortcomings. One source might be the lack of actual personal equipment, not so much as compared with reality, but as compared with her aspirations. These, we find, were most unrealistic. On the Adjustment Inventory she expressed, in the course of the years, the wish to be a princess, an aviator, a movie actress, a singer, and the like. In her self-perception she obviously compared herself with the aspired-to self more than with the real self. From this predicament she apparently attempted to escape into a "make-believe world"; in fact, in her self-reports during the first three years, she admitted this. Her wish, in the eighth grade, "not to grow up" points in the same direction.

In the sense that she understood her real shortcomings earlier than her classmates did, Joyce's unfavorable judgment of herself in certain respects was an anticipation of her reputation with others in later years. In the end she did lose status with the group to a certain extent, although she continued to be rated more favorably by others than by herself. According to an analysis of Joyce's case by a clinician, there seems to be more agreement between her picture of herself and the diagnostic picture presented of her than between either of these pictures and her social façade as reflected in her reputation. As seems to be quite often the case, Joyce perceived herself more with the eyes of a clinician than with the eyes of a surface-behaviorist. The latter point of view, reflected in the ratings of manifest behavior discussed earlier in this chapter, brings to the fore the "persona," that is, the social role the individual has grown into, rather than the core of personality.

Although Joyce's inner difficulties did not lead to depressions, they did find expression in "fears." It is especially interesting that the number of Joyce's fears increased sharply in the course of her last three years in school. At this time an increase in the expression of her basic difficulties was to be expected. It occurred. Perhaps the fact that she was, at least in some respects, very successful, enabled her, in contrast to Nell, to face some of her inner maladjustments. Whereas Nell's lack of awareness functioned as a defense to reduce tensions that would arise from an objectively very difficult situation, Joyce's conscious perception seems to have had an opposite function. Her acute awareness of shortcomings and her generally negative attitude toward herself seem to have acted as a warning rather than as a defense mechanism. She actually needed these warnings because external assets, such as her good looks and general attractiveness, made her life appear smoother—at least for a while—than it actually was.

To repeat: Both Nell's and Joyce's perceptions of their own behavior and of their acceptance by the group were at variance with the actual facts as stated by close acquaintances, both adult observers and classmates. Nell's exaggeratedly inflated picturing of herself—as revealed by overstatement, contradictions between answers to direct and indirect questions, and a distorted perception of others—was clearly of a defensive and compensatory character. While Joyce's distortions went in the opposite direction, that of gross understatement, the unusual number of negative statements in her self-evaluation should serve to caution us regarding the actual and direct validity of her self-perception. As was the case with some of our Viennese subjects, her statements signalize possible dangers and pitfalls which in fact toward the end of her school years started to disrupt even the external social adjustment which she at first so grossly underrated.

To conclude this section, we may highlight a few points from the material on a third case, Ann, who differed from the first two girls in being unusually free of self-deceptions. From the beginning Ann was rated, by both adults and classmates, as cooperative, good-natured, unexploitive, responsible, and even-tempered. These judgments weve coupled with extremely low ratings on the tendency toward display. Here is a perfect picture of personal and emotional adjustment. Ann's social adjustment, specified under the headings of sociability, expressiveness, and effect on the group, started at about average but rose consistently as she grew up.

During the seven years of observation Ann made only 27 mentions of herself on the Reputation Test in contrast to Nell's 72 and Joyce's 41. Of these 27 judgments, 19 were positive and 8 were negative. This seems an unretouched, balanced proportion. As for the few discrepancies between self-mentions and mentions by classmates, we find Ann for the most part on the modest side.

There is only a single area in which Ann seemed to be subject to self-deception, and that is sex adjustment. At the same time, this was an area of comparative maladjustment for Ann. As noted by the adult observers, her interest in the opposite sex was below average; in a girl this is often linked with masculine identification. Support for this assumption as applied to Ann is that she showed an unusual tendency to attribute masculinity to girls whom she considered popular. Furthermore, until her last year at school Ann consistently gave the boys more favorable ratings than the girls and at the same time tended to attribute to boys rather than to other girls the same characteristics she attributed to herself.

DRIVES AS DETERMINERS OF THE PERCEPTION OF SELF AND OF OTHERS

Turning back to our initial topic, the importance of motivational considerations for the understanding of personality in general and of perception in particular, we will conclude our discussion of the three cases by referring to the ratings these children received on underlying motives as introduced in the study of alternative manifestations of drives presented above. This will throw light on the causes of the differences among them with respect to self-perception.

Although Nell's own evaluation of her behavior and status was found to be at odds with the evaluation of her specific overt behavior by other observers, such a discrepancy ceases to exist when we compare her self-perception with her drive pattern as rated intuitively by trained adult observers on the basis of prolonged close acquaintanceship. (As has been mentioned above, the self-reports were not included as a basis of these ratings.) It is especially her need for an inflated ego image that becomes evident in these overall ratings. Nell was rated high on the drives for aggression, for recognition, for dependence, and for escape, whereas she was rated low on the drives for autonomy, for achievement, and for abasement. Unrelentingly driven toward success without the ability really to work for it, and without benefit of the dampening influence of abasement, she escaped into a shortcut and into deceiving herself about what she had actually reached among all the things she desired. Her high degree of aggression had become evident primarily through her way of judging her environment.

Joyce, on the other hand, received only an average rating in aggression. We remember that, in accordance with this, she did not put projective blame on the environment fov her own weaknesses. Her excessive self-blame can be understood best in terms of the relatively high rating she received on the need for abasement. This latter rating may seem to be in contradiction to her external success; but we must recall that she did not enjoy her success and that she seemed headed for some sort of dramatic upheaval in her personal life. (This actually came to pass later on, after she had left school.) Joyce also received the highest possible rating on the drive for escape. Accordingly, we found her escaping from real obligations through all kinds of means such as external success or the exaggerated and unrealistic level of aspiration. This high level of aspiration was one of the few characteristics she shared with Nell. More basically, it was the drive for escape which she shared with Nell and which in both must be held responsible for the lack of real adjustment. Unlike Nell, Joyce was not rated high on the drive for dependence, and this may account for her relative indifference toward her social success.

Our third case, Ann, received the lowest possible rating on the drives for aggression and for escape, and next to the lowest on the drive for recognition. She was markedly above average on the drive for achievement. This drive was sharply differentiated in our study from the drive for recognition and was meant to refer to the desire to do a good job rather than to receive approval. Ann was also rated above average in her drive toward affiliation with others. It was perhaps precisely the relatively weak strivings for aggression, escape, and abasement which accounted fov Ann's comparatively undistorted perception of herself and of others.

Again, intuitively rated drives seem better able to explain self-reports than does the observed manifest behavior. However, all these types of material are needed fully to explain self-perception. Only by considering Nell's low social standing in class and her poor social techniques, together with her strong drives for escape, recognition, and aggression, and her low ratings on the dvive for abasement, can her particular pattern of mechanisms of self-deception be understood. The same holds in reverse for Joyce. Obviously, it is the combination of social and behavioral with motivational realities which determines the perception of the self and of others.

The data just reported support the general assumption that the perception of the self—or more specifically, the perception of the self as related to actual behavior—is a crucial index of personality adjustment. We also found that in cases where self-perception was distorted there was a tendency to project the unaccepted tendencies onto other persons. It is evident that the problem is of special importance for the therapist, the clinician, or any other person involved in making judgments of others.

THE CLINICIAN'S BIAS IN PERCEIVING THE SUBJECT

Still another aspect of the analysis carried out by the present writer at the California Adolescent Growth Study was aimed at analyzing the personal equation which enters into the judgment of the clinician (Frenkel-Brunswik, 1942, Chapter 4). Such influences would be expected especially in interpretive judgments, of which the ratings of motivational tendencies discussed in the first section of this paper constitute an important special case.

The question is how the personality of the rater as well as his theoretical background is apt to influence his percepts of the children. More specifically, there are three separate problems here that demand discussion. Drive ratings may be influenced differentially by (1) the way in which the drive is conceived by the judge; (2) the degree to which the child is liked or disliked by the judge; and (3) the intensity of the drive in question in the personality of the rater. In the study under attention there were three independent women judges, the "rating personalities" of whom could in this manner be compared with one another.

In order to investigate the implicit definitions of any of the drives rated in terms of other drives, intercorrelations of the ratings of the children on each of the drives were computed for each judge separately. As an illustration, let us consider, for each of the three judges separately, the interrelationships of the ratings she made on the drive for autonomy with those she made on other drives. In the case of one judge there was a sizable negative correlation of "autonomy" with "social ties" and also with "succorance"; that is, in the opinion of this judge, these drives are to a certain degree mutually exclusive. In the case of the second judge neither of these two correlations, nor any of the others for that matter, was significantly negative. The ratings of the third judge showed positive correlations of "autonomy" with "aggression," a pair which in the ratings of the other two judges exhibited no relationship. In other words, there was no uniform conception of the drive for autonomy; the discrepancies apparently arose from the fact that the various judges differed in their opinions about whether this drive constituted a reaction formation or not. On the matter of the interdependency of the remaining drives under consideration, the judges differed somewhat less than on the drive for autonomy. On the whole, the varying conceptions of a given drive did not seriously interfere with interrater agreement, which for the most part turned out to be satisfactory.

A similar examination of the explicit emotional attitudes of the raters toward the subjects seemed to indicate that these attitudes had even less effect upon interrater agreement than the varying conceptions of drives. After completing the ratings on drives, the judges were asked to indicate on a five-point scale their liking of or dislike for each of the children involved. Correlations of these preference ratings with the drive ratings given by the judges to the children were computed for the individual judges. Many of the coefficients were close to zero, indicating that in the case of several of the drives the ratings were not tied up with verbalized emotional preferences. Exceptions occurred in connection with the drives for aggression, for escape, and for succorance; here negative correlations were found, indicating that dislike went with high ratings on these drives.

It is interesting to note that the judge who showed in her ratings of the children the highest correlation between ratings of dislike and ratings of aggression and succorance did not show any poorer judgment about the drive for aggression when agreement with the other judges is taken as a measure of accuracy. Thus, on the basis of a comparison of her ratings with those of the rater least prejudiced against the drives in question, we can say that at least in this instance an extreme aversion toward a certain drive did not go with an unusual bias of judgment. It is reassuring to find that a judge's freely admitted liking or disliking of a subject did not necessarily distort her perception. There are slight variations among the judges with respect to this matter, however.

This leads us to our third problem, that posed by the question of how far the presence or absence of a drive in a judge himself influences perception of the same motivational tendency in others. Murray (1938) found a slight tendency toward rating by contrast, that is, a rating of people as if they were different from oneself. Sears (1936) found that persons who have insight into a trait in themselves rate by contrast and those who repress the awareness of a trait in themselves rate by projection.

In order to obtain further evidence on this matter, each of the three judges was rated by the other two on the same list of drives on which they had rated the children. They also rated themselves on the same list. Bearing out the findings of Sears, the rater who showed the best insight, as indicated by the least amount of discrepancy between her self-ratings and the ratings given to her by the others, showed a slight tendency to rate the children by contrast. Also consistent with Sears's results are the findings in the case of another of the judges who had somewhat less insight than the remaining two and who tended to rate the children by projection. The third judge, however, presented a picture differing from that to be expected according to Sears, as she combined good insight with some tendency toward projection. In agreement with the results of the Vienna study on self-deception previously reported in this paper (Frenkel-Brunswik, 1939), there was a tendency on the part of the judges to give extreme ratings to the children on those drive variables on which they disagreed most with the other raters regarding their own status.

On the whole it seems that, within the limits of the Adolescent Study material, the tendency toward rating by projection was stronger than the one toward rating by contrast, that the raters showed a stronger tendency to project when rating children of their own sex than when rating children of the opposite sex, and that the tendency to project their personality as seen by themselves was stronger than the tendency to project their personality as seen by others. This last result, however, may hold true to a greater extent for raters with self-insight than for those without.

Similarities between judges were computed, and it was ascertained that two of the judges tended to give subjects more similar ratings on those variables in which they themselves were more similar. This trend seemed by no means consistent for the remaining two possible combinations among the judges, however.

In brief, we must acknowledge that there are various subjective factors that seem to influence the perception of others even in clinically trained observers. These factors could be averaged out by using large and representative samples of judges. An encouraging feature is the fact that the three raters showed satisfactory interrater agreement in making highly interpretive judgments about the children, even though a personal equation had entered into these judgments.

In the theoretical parts of this paper the question was posed whether or not defense mechanisms of the type described in this section are the same as those described in psychoanalysis. It is our opinion that at least in part we are dealing with the same mechanisms. To be sure, psychoanalysis is chiefly concerned with defenses established in early childhood against instinctual dangers. In our case the defenses are mainly against loss of self-esteem. In a formal sense, however, the two types of mechanisms are very similar. Projection, for example, is in both cases defined as the ascribing to the environment of what is internal and at the same time unpleasant. This similarity holds especially for the mechanisms discussed in the present section, which involve a mobilization of defenses against such vital issues as lack of popularity and the like. The similarity holds to a lesser degree fov laboratory experiments, where success or failure is usually of little relevance.

INTOLERANCE OF AMBIGUITY AND DISTORTION OF REALITY IN PERSONALITY-CENTERED STUDIES OF PERCEPTION

RIGIDITY AND THE PROBLEM OF UNITY OF STYLE

The importance of individual differences in the tendency toward unqualified assertions was brought out in the discussion of mechanisms of self-deception. As a rule, however, the greater the definiteness, exaggeration, and lack of shading in the description of favorable traits in oneself the less often were such assertions verified in the judgments of close acquaintances. Let us now turn to cognition and object perception proper, as studied in a project on social discrimination in children (Frenkel-Brunswik, 1948c; this volume, Chapter 2).

A certain inability, in the perceptual and cognitive approach of an individual, to tolerate more complex, conflicting, or open structures might, is seemed, also occur to a certain extent in the emotional and social areas. Proceeding from the observation that some persons can tolerate the coexistence of love and hate less than others can and that these persons seem to tend toward perceiving people generally in terms of positive or negative halos and dichotomies rather than allowing for independent and continuous variability of traits, we attempted to ascertain just how pervasive this disposition might be by undertaking a number of experiments on memory, concept formation, and perception proper.

Results so far collected support the conjecture that, by and large, such tendencies as the quest for unqualified certainty, the rigid adherence[5] to anything given—be this an authority or a stimulus—the inadequacy of reaction in terms of reality, and the like, operate in more than one area of personality. It can be demonstrated, further, that such specific forms of reaction as orientation toward concrete detail (stimulus boundness) tend to occur again and again within a person in contexts seemingly far removed from each other. Inclination toward mechanical repetition of faulty hypotheses, inaccessibility to new experience, satisfaction with subjective and at the same time unimaginative, overconcrete, or overgeneralized solutions, all appear to be specific manifestations of a general disposition which holds sway among certain groups of persons, such as the ethnically prejudiced, in their approach to emotional and social as well as more purely cognitive problems.

Before going into the discussion of individual cases which show different degrees and patterns of acceptance of ambiguity, let us summarize a few more general findings. We found evidence, in certain groups of our subjects, of intolerance of ambiguity in the perceptual as well as in the emotional and social areas. In these persons there is, on the surface, a rigid, unambiguous adherence to cultural and conventional values, but this is combined with an underlying destructiveness directed toward these same values; this combination of opposites is in contrast to the establishment of a healthy "medium distance" to the culture.

In a similar manner, an underlying ambivalence toward the parents is split into a positive and a negative side and expressed through alternative media, e.g., stereotyped and exaggerated admiration in response to direct questions, combined with the conception of punitiveness and harshness in parents revealed in the indirect material. Medium distance is again lacking, and feelings are expressed in terms of the ends of a continuum rather than of a continuum proper.

Furthermore, perceptual stimuli not too familiar and lacking in firmness and definiteness seem to be more disturbing to the rigid,

---

[5]Recently Cattell and Tiner (1949) have pointed at some of the confusions in the use of the term "rigidity." In the present chapter the term is used in two definitely interrelated meanings. One is the traditional usage, referring to perseveration and resistance to change (see also Rokeach, 1943). The second usage is as an abbreviation for "intolerance of ambiguity" as discussed in this chapter.

prejudiced group. In experimental situations involving a change of stimuli, this disturbance is expressed either in a persistent use of the name of the object originally shown or in a bout of random guessing. In either case there seems to be an effort to replace the vague by known and structured objects.

In brief, the group of which we speak here shows emotionally dramatized responses to middle-class values, parents, outgroups, and people in general as well as to perceptual and cognitive material, especially if it is vague or otherwise threatening. The choice is between total acceptance and total rejection; if the two coexist, they do so in different layers of the personality.

Rather than a conscious coexistence of acceptance and rejection, leading to qualified feelings and statements, however, we find avoidance of complexities on the surface, with chaos lurking behind and breaking through the rigidly maintained façade. With internal conflict being as disturbing as it is in the rigid group, there apparently develops a tendency toward denying external ambiguity as long as such denial can be maintained. Underlying anxiety issuing from the confusion of one's social identity and from other conflicts is apparently so great that it hampers persons in this group in facing even the purely cognitive types of ambiguity. The mechanism discussed is somewhat related to what Postman, Bruner, and McGinnies (1948) have called "perceptual defenses." A desperate effort is made to shut out uncertainties the prejudiced person is unable to face, thus narrowing what Tolman (1948) has called the "cognitive map" to rigidly defined tracks.

Persons with less severe underlying confusions, on the other hand, may be able to afford to face ambiguities openly, although this may mean at least a temporary facing of conflicts and anxieties as well. In this case the total pattern is that of a broader integration of reality, in which no parts are left out, and thus a more flexible adaptation to varying circumstances.

The lack of integration and the resultant break between the conscious and unconscious layers in the rigid person, as compared with the greater fluidity of transition and of intercommunication between the different personality strata in more flexible persons, appear to have the greatest implications for the respective personality patterns. The shutting out of certain aspects of feelings and of inner reality in general must be seen as the root of the distorted perceptions and judgments of outer reality shown by the rigid group.

In spite of the rather consistent recurrence of elements of rigidity in various areas, there is thus no all-pervasive unity of style in this pattern of personality. In listing the attitudes which go together in the same persons, we are in the end faced with the coexistence of rigid perseverative behavior and a haphazard, disintegrated, random approach. Another related phenomenon seemingly at odds with the principle of personal unity concerns the discrepancies from one level of personality to another. Further to elaborate a point discussed above, we may say that, in our prejudiced subjects, the negative side of the feelings toward parents is repressed without losing its dynamic force, only to be transferred at least in part to other objects, such as minority groups. The clinging to definite dichotomies and demarcation lines apparently reduces the conflict on the conscious level but at the same time increases the underlying confusion. The conception of a unity of style within the personality can be restored by defining styles in a more complex manner, say, by the inclusion of opposites within the same pattern.

Paradoxically, the prejudiced person, who, by virtue of the mechanism of isolation, displays less integration of the different aspects of personality, at the same time often shows more consistency of reaction; the subjective factors eventually invade and disrupt even those forms of reaction which in the unprejudiced have largely managed from the start to remain determined by objective reality. Of course, one may interject that reality adequacy is the consistent response of the mature person. This is, however, a kind of consistency which at the same time is inconsistent insofar as it varies to a higher degree with changing stimuli. Along the same line we may observe that normal subjects, in performing simple perceptual tasks, show but small individual differences, whereas a psychotic person may behave in a very atypical manner yet remain true to a form of his own, whether this be extreme deviation from the stimuli or a compensatory, in essence equally "unrealistic," slavish clinging to its irrelevant details.

CASE STUDIES IN PERSONALITY AND PERCEPTION

Over and beyond these general considerations which must warn us against a superficial implementation of the unity-of-style principle, consistencies as well as inconsistencies of a more specific kind can be found in individual cases. We have selected from the above-mentioned project on social discrimination in children a few specific cases and will now examine their social, emotional, and cognitive reactions.

We turn first to the case of Bob, a 13-year-old boy high on ethnic prejudice whose outstanding characteristic is his desire to conform. His entire outlook is one of intolerance of ambiguity. His statements in response to questions covering a variety of topics reveal his rigid adherence to conventional values and his great anxiety about making the grade. His conceptions about people show that he draws clear lines of demarcation between the "right" and the "wrong" people. He has a tendency to resort to black-white solutions, achieve premature closure on a restricted basis with respect to evaluative aspects, and to arrive at unqualified over-all acceptance or rejection of other persons. Thus, he thinks that Americans are only "those born here" and he considers it would be best "if all the different races all went back to their own states."

In general, Bob's approach, in discussing social and political problems as well as values in general, consists of what we may call "poor hypotheses"; he reveals a relative lack of information and a highly stereotypical kind of thinking, and he repeats himself a great deal. Asked what a perfect boy is, he answers, "He's clean. Well, he has clean clothes, and he combs his hair, and he keeps his ears clean." Asked what the worst job would be for a man, he answers, "I wouldn't like to dig ditches. Well, it doesn't give you a very good standing." It should be added that the more rigid children tend to answer this question by referring to a fixed social hierarchy, whereas the other children think of jobs in terms of whether one likes them or not.

Bob dichotomizes sharply between weakness and strength, between the feminine and the masculine, and so forth. His preoccupation with physical strength is further revealed in the interview as well as in the Thematic Apperception Test. This preoccupation appears in a general way, as well as more specifically in admiration for his father, whom he considers strong, and in his contempt for his mother, whom he considers weak. Bob's reactions in the perceptual and cognitive tasks are consistent, to a large extent, with the over-all clinical picture. Though there is a great deal of conformity and compliance in Bob, we also find tendencies toward explosive aggression, which are expressed in fits of rage.

The first experiment to be discussed here in relation to the case of Bob is one undertaken by Norman Livson and Florine Berkowitz Livson in connection with our study on social discrimination in children. The experiment was somewhat similar to one by the present writer that had involved transitions from the picture of one familiar object—a cat—to that of another—a dog—(see this volume, Chapter 2, p. 78) and bore out its tentative results. The Livsons presented the subjects with a series of cards showing numbers slowly emerging from indistinctness; then certain numbers presented would, on successive cards, change into other numbers.

It was found that the unprejudiced group recognized the changes significantly earlier than the prejudiced. Bob's response in this experiment was very cautious, as evidenced by the fact that he did not present any perceptual hypotheses before the fourth card, or relatively late as compared to the group as a whole. Once he had ventured a guess, however, he clung to it even if objective support was not forthcoming. He did not correctly recognize changing numbers before the twelfth card, whereas correct response on the ninth card was the average.

In another experiment, undertaken by the same investigators, blank spaces had to be filled in with words previously memorized. Bob was on the whole careful. His one error was that of filling in a wrong word which was implicitly suggested by the experimenter. Submission to the experimenter thus proved even stronger than faithful adherence to the stimulus.

Though Bob manifested a rather consistently careful, restricted, and conservative attitude toward the stimulus in the experiments just discussed, his behavior was different in an investigation of concept formation conducted with the children of our study by Marvin Hyman. It involved an adaptation of the well-known Vigotsky Test in which blocks are to be ordered according to certain abstract principles. Bob made an unusual number of mistakes. He began with a good hypothesis, but when he could not work it out fully his behavior disintegrated in the direction of concreteness, repetitiveness, and randomness. Examples are the fitting together of only two blocks at a time, without orientation toward an over-all principle. Bob produced seven such random arrangements. He did not respond to the attempts at correction made by the experimenter, since he seemed unable to grasp the principle involved and continued to repeat his trials based on bad guesses. The number of corrections he made is third highest in the total group. He was found never to repeat one of his rare good hypotheses, but he did so frequently with poor hypotheses. Though prejudiced children generally tend to take a longer time to make a correction than the unprejudiced, Bob made his corrections in a relatively speedy way. This was due, however, to a relatively large number of undirected trials and errors. As is the case with most children in the prejudiced group, the quality of his hypotheses was not high. It took Bob almost 40 minutes to arrive at the right solutions, which is unusually long for his age.[6]

Bob generally tended to turn from a careful and restricted approach to a haphazard one when the situation became too difficult to master. We have noted above, on the basis of his clinical data, that his otherwise docile and obedient pattern was occasionally disrupted by breakthroughs of explosive aggression; the same docile and restricted approach found to be dominant in his perceptual reactions is thus analogously disrupted by disintegrated behavior when the strain of coping with the task becomes too great.

In his responses to the Thematic Apperception Test, Bob showed the same cautious, unimaginative, and careful approach that he displayed in the interviews and on the other cognitive tests. He tended to be preoccupied with the details of the pictures rather than being ready to let go and tell a story. We find references to "nice, clean boys," and to "smart men who can get through life pretty easy." He says in response to a picture which shows white and Negro children playing together, "If I saw all the others playing with a nice Negro boy, I guess I would too." This quotation shows that the basis of Bob's prejudice is mainly conformity. From his other responses to the test, as well as from the interview, it seemed to be evident that a further contributing factor is his desire to overcome his weakness.

In the light of our assumption, developed elsewhere (see this

---

[6]The ages of the children given in this paper are those at the time of the clinical explorations. The experimental data referred to here were gathered more than one year later.

volume, Chapter 2), to the effect that there is a correspondence between such social factors as the type of discipline used at home and the way children approach perceptual stimuli, it may be of interest to refer to a few points from the interview with Bob's mother. As far as Bob's upbringing is concerned, his mother seems to be defensive: "He rather had to be forced to do things— to eat and go to bed and go to sleep. He isn't so willing to cooperate." All kinds of measures were used to make him cooperative. "When he doesn't come home in time—if he is more than 15 minutes late, he can't go next time with that boy when he wants to. . . . I am forever after him. Personal appearance, too. I think we do nag him for that."

Asked about her own upbringing, the mother says: "I wouldn't disobey, oh boy! I feel that way right now [about parents]. I can't get my children to obey like that." She describes her own mother as follows: "She was a good little German woman, busy having children. . . . She was very strict, I should say." Her father is described as follows: "He was German, too. All my grandparents were born in Germany. He was the strict one. A hard-working man, had definite ideas and you couldn't change him. They were good, honest people." (Father too severe?) "Yes, I really felt so. I guess he really couldn't help it, though. Gosh! We couldn't do anything, we didn't have any privileges. . . . All our folks were for morality, didn't drink or go to nightclubs and things. My husband's parents were strict with him. He was kept in the yard until he was twelve years old."

Bob's mother verifies our description of his aggressive behavior: "He really gets mad, wild. He just stamps off, is mean, hateful in his talking, but it doesn't last long. He's just like his father that way." She further substantiates our assumption about his dependency: "I notice him. He follows the boys he is with whether they are good or bad. It's a problem of choosing friends, I think."

All this indicates that Bob may have been under great pressure during his childhood. His mother's insistence on quick obedience and his ensuing fear of punishment may well have led him to handle situations in an abbreviated and stereotyped manner. This is, as mentioned above, a frequent contributing factor in the patterns found among our rigid, prejudiced group to which Bob belonged.

It is of interest to note that Bob also shared with others of our rigid children some constitutional weakness. This may be another factor contributing to their rigidity. Bob's mother told us that he was "premature one month, so he wasn't strong and had a slow start." Greenacre (1941) has emphasized the fact that premature children lack the necessary equipment to cope to a satisfactory degree with the requirements of the initial stage of their lives. She assumes that this, along with unfavorable factors in the social environment, occasions increased tensions and inadequate mastery of life. In a similar vein, our interviewer remarked that Bob always appeared to be tired and undernourished and that a physical checkup uncovered a state of serious anemia. His mother told us, further, that he was always a "crybaby" and that he had pneumonia when he was two years old. Physiological insufficiency together with harsh discipline at home may go a long way in explaining the oversimplified, rigid, and often panicky form of reaction found in Bob.

Now we turn to the case of Joan, a 12-year-old child with an extremely low questionnaire score on ethnic prejudice. Her more informal remarks about social issues revealed great flexibility, open-mindedness, tolerance, permissiveness, and the attempt to weigh all aspects of the matters presented. Even her remarks about Hitler were more restrained, qualified, and less aggressive than those of most of the other children: "Well, he wasn't exactly the kind of man you would want to rule your country. I guess he wasn't the right kind of man to rule any country." Her open-mindedness and inclusiveness were expressed in her suggested remedy for conflicts between different countries: "Oh, we would visit one another's countries and study more about them." She was inclined to say positive things about everybody and everything. Asked about Negroes, she referred to a ". . . lady who has become very famous, she taught school . . . and she brought a lot of education to this country." She thought one ". . . might study them and give them a chance to prove that they are equal by giving them better schools and better places to live." She was against segregation of whites and Negroes. "I don't think it's quite right, because they are human and like us except for their color."

The pupils Joan liked were "ones that seem to get along with everyone, good in their school work." The absence of any fixed set was especially apparent in her answer to the question, "What would be the best job for a man?" She replied: "Well, that just depends on what he is fit for. The job he can do best probably." To the question, "What would be the worst job for a man?" she replied, "Well, a person that probably couldn't do a job and happened to be put in the wrong place and if it was serious it might take other people's lives." She did not mention a specific job as good or bad but gave a broader definition which provided latitude for a number of variables which had to be considered. To the question, "What do you want to be when you grow up?" she answered: "I don't know exactly now. But I think it's going to have to do with animals." Again, there is no need to give too definite an answer.

Joan had difficulty in expressing aggression against anybody except herself. To the question, "How would you change yourself if you could?" she answered with a longer list of desired traits than most of the children: "Oh, try to behave better, try to get along better with my friends, be able to play better in sports, oh, be able to get better grades; just be able to get along." In the light of available objective evidence, this self-perception was faulty only in that it minimized Joan's real assets.

In the experiment with the slowly emerging numbers she made the right guesses relatively early, close to the average of the unprejudiced and generally flexible group. She was somewhat cautious in making these early guesses, however. This caution is rather characteristic of unprejudiced children, who in general seem better able to accept ambiguity instead of having immediately to transform it into something definite, as do many of the prejudiced. (The total number of hypotheses given in response to ambiguous stimuli tends to be larger for the prejudiced than for the unprejudiced.)

In spite of her caution in the face of ambiguous figures, Joan responded very easily to changes in the stimulus configuration. This distinguished her from Bob, who lacked her flexibility and, though cautious most of the time, on occasion became extremely incautious.

Joan showed considerable aptitude in remembering a list of words without making errors. In spite of the unusual precision of her whole performance, she saw no necessity for sticking to the original order of words in her recall, however. During the entire series of experiments she was rather critical of her own performance.

In the Luchins type of experiment involving water-container problems (1942) which Rokeach (1943) adapted for these children, Joan very quickly found the set necessary for solving the original tasks; what is more, she was also quick in solving further tasks in this context by switching to the shortcut which becomes possible at this later stage rather than clinging rigidly to the method established at the beginning.

On the concept-formation test mentioned before, Joan's performance was very different from Bob's. She started with a good but not fully adequate hypothesis. When corrected once by the experimenter, she stopped altogether for 10 minutes. This was most unusual for the group as a whole. On the basis of observations in a variety of situations, we found that such pausing and thinking was more likely to occur in unprejudiced than in prejudiced children, however. When unprejudiced children were blocked, they waited and reconsidered the problem, whereas the prejudiced rushed into random activities or gave up the problem altogether. Joan had the independence to remain in the suspense of thinking in spite of some pressure on the part of the experimenter toward action. After pausing for 10 minutes, she found the right solution without any further trial and error. Whereas Bob made 15 rather random corrections, apparentl? without any overall hypothesis, Joan made only three corrections in all. Whereas Bob did not repeat his original good hypothesis but repeated a poor hypothesis four times, Joan repeated a good hypothesis only twice and never made a poor one. In all, she thus received a much higher ranking on the quality of her performance than did Bob.

Joan had in common with Bob a certain cautiousness and lack of readiness for adventure in her approach to problem solving. This was further manifested in her relatively descriptive approach on the Thematic Apperception Test. Here a comparative lack of initiative was again common to both. However, Joan's performance was much the superior of the two and showed much higher flexibility.

These similarities and partial differences recur in a somewhat analogous manner in the patterns of aggression exhibited by Joan and Bob. Their similarity lies in the fact that both Bob and Joan repressed aggression. The difference lies in the strength of aggression, which was much greater in Bob, as manifested in his fits of rage and in an extreme rejection of people. More rigid defenses were necessary to keep this aggression down. Joan's aggression was of a mellower quality, as witnessed by a genuine love for her parents and the acceptance of other people in general. Whatever aggression might have been present in Joan, she was unable to verbalize it save against herself. Had her aggression been given freer expression, she might well have been more imaginative.

That Joan's aggression was in reality mild rather than merely repressed was revealed in her deep acceptance of parents and people, a fact supported by all the indirect and direct material, including the interview with the parents. There was, in fact, a very permissive and affectionate atmosphere in her family. Bob repeated his submission to, and rebellion against, stern parental authorities in his approach to perceptual stimuli, whereas Joan had a flexible relation to both parental and stimulus authorities.

Bob was on the whole an example of a more cautious and conservative type of prejudiced boy whose approach to social and personal issues had been mainly governed by conformity. Another 12-year-old boy, Jerry, represented the near-psychopathic type of prejudiced boy whose outstanding characteristics are recklessness and aggressiveness, with conformity taking a second place. His performance on the perceptual and cognitive experiments thus showed more consistently an adventurous and uncautious approach than that of Bob. In response to the ambiguous stimuli he immediately made a large number of guesses, many of them altogether on the wrong track, but he got the right solution earlier than Bob. In his approach to the concept-formation task he made approximately as many random arrangements and corrections as Bob, with an even larger total number of hypotheses. Four of these hypotheses were good and six were bad, but he repeated both types frequently. Unlike Bob, he did not get any final solution. (Only nine children of the total group of 44 who were given the test did not reach the right solution.) The over-all rating of the quality of his guessing was, however, not any better than Bob's.

Clinically, Jerry exhibited a pattern closer to the fascistic or prefascistic type than did Bob. About his choice of a profession he said, "I like adventure. I intend to be a policeman when I grow up, on the homicide squad. That has been my ambition for a long time." In discussing his friends in the neighborhood, he manifested marked contempt for those he considered weak: "There is one around the corner that's a softy. There is another boy twelve years old. He's a softy too. Anybody can take him." The only time

Jerry exhibited any affect during the interview was when he talked about the necessity of wearing glasses, expressing his concern that this might interfere with his being taken into the police force. He showed open rejection of people, including his parents. He rejected his parents mainly because they were old. (His parents were actually much older than the parents of his classmates.) He showed contempt for his father because "he has to take pills all the time. He could only eat milk; he has a milk stomach. . . . I take after my dad in temper. He has a vile temper." About girls Jerry said, "They are gold-diggers," and a perfect friend was "somebody that doesn't tell things behind your back." At the same time this boy was much concerned with conventional values. For instance, he felt very defensive about his family's not having a car and said quite formally, "Circumstances forced us to sell our car." In discussing his wish to be a policeman, he stated, "People look up to you and it gives you a good feeling."

The mixture of recklessness and aggressiveness on the one hand, and fear and anxiety on the other, further became apparent in Jerry's Thematic Apperception Test stories. We found a number of aggressive themes. However, Jerry alternated between rushing into these themes, telling them with a high degree of confidence, and the excessive use of such words as "probably," "well," "maybe," coupled with a tendency to modify and change his plots and a readiness to take back what he had said.

A GENERAL RIGIDITY SCALE AND ITS RELATIONSHIP TO PATTERNS OF PERCEPTUAL OUTLOOK

In connection with the discussion of their approach to perceptual and cognitive tasks, it may be of interest to consider briefly the standing of Bob, Joan, and Jerry on a scale designed to measure general personality rigidity.[7]

We find both Bob and Jerry agreeing with a number of items representing a rigid, white-black approach to life. Whereas Joan disagreed, both of the boys agreed with the statement: "There are just two kinds of boys, the regular guys and the no-goods." (Of the

---

[7]This scale was developed in 1945 and 1946 as part of our project on Social Discrimination in Children. The writer is indebted to Murray E. Jarvik and Milton Rokeach for their assistance.

PERSONALITY THEORY AND PERCEPTION 147

whole group of 300, 70% of the prejudiced and 45% of the unprejudiced children agreed with this statement.)

Bob's perseveration and rigidity were revealed in his agreement with the following statements: (1) "A person should always stick to a decision he makes." (Of the prejudiced children 50% and of the unprejudiced children 45% agreed with this statement.) (2) "Order and cleanliness are just about the most important things in life." (About half of all the children agreed.) (3) "There is only one right way to do anything." (Of the prejudiced children 73% and of the unprejudiced children 56% agreed.) (4) "Take care of the pennies and the dollars will take care of themselves." (About 60% of all the children agreed.)

In the same vein, Bob disagreed with this statement: "It does a kid good to be lazy once in a while." (Only about 30% of the children disagreed with this statement.)

Bob's hierarchical conception of human relations is expressed in his agreement with the following statements: (1) "Parents should always tell the children what they should do." (Of the prejudiced children 36% and of the unprejudiced children 24% agreed.) (2) "The world would be perfect if we could put on a desert island all the weak, crooked, and feeble-minded people." (Of the prejudiced children 45% and of the unprejudiced children 22% agreed.) (3) "Appearance usually tells us what a person is really like." (Of the prejudiced children 66% and of the unprejudiced children 58% agreed.)

Bob's underlying aggression is revealed in his agreement with such items as: (1) "Criminals should be more severely punished." (About half of the children agreed.) (2) "Brothers and sisters are more trouble than fun." (Of the prejudiced children 35% and of the unprejudiced children 26% agreed.)

Jerry checked many of the above items representing conventional values which Bob checked, and in addition he subscribed to a number of items expressing a less conventional and more fescistic ideology with which Bob disagreed. Examples of such items are: "People who are leaders are usually born to be leaders and the others are born to do what the leaders say." "It would be better if the teachers would be more strict." "A good leader should be strict with the people under him in order to gain their respect." (One third to one half of the children subscribed to these items.)

With only a small minority of the children, Jerry subscribed to items which express superstition, such as: "The position of the stars at the time of your birth tells your character and personality." (Only 12% of the prejudiced and 8% of the unprejudiced subscribed to this statement.)

Jerry also subscribed to statements which express a self-defensive attitude and pride: "An insult to a person's honor should always be punished," and "It is best never to admit defeat." (Of the prejudiced children 42% and of the unprejudiced children 31% agreed with the latter statement.)

Jerry's antifeminine attitude led him to subscribe to items like the following: "Girls play up to teachers and that is why they get better grades," and "Boys should play only with boys; only a boy can understand a boy." (Only 27% of the prejudiced and 18% of the unprejudiced children agreed with the latter statement.)

In many ways Jerry was even more rigid than Bob. He agreed that: "It is best to have regular hours for everything," and "It is best to do some things at the same time and in the same way each day." (Approximately half of the children agreed with these two statements.)

Jerry's readiness for adventure and quick judgment were expressed in his agreement with such items as: "It is best for a person to make up his mind quickly," and "It is usually pretty easy to judge other people." (Approximately one third of the children agreed with the first item, and predominantly the prejudiced children agreed with the second.)

With a minority of the children, Jerry further subscribed to the item: "If everything should change, things would be much better." (Only 33% of the prejudiced and 23% of the unprejudiced agreed.)

The last three items indicate an affinity with haphazard action and chaos, often found, as in Jerry, in combination with extreme rigidity. This combination is revealed not only in Jerry's pattern of response to the rigidity scale but also in his perceptual and cognitive problem-solvmng approach.

Joan's emotional and cognitive flexibility, which has been revealed in the clinical data as well as in her problem-solving approach, was also expressed in her disagreement with most of the items indicating rigidity and in her agreement with such items as:

"It is interesting to be friends with someone who thinks or feels differently from the way you do," or "It feels good to stand up against a group and defend someone who has been picked on."

It is noteworthy that the frequency of agreement with the items which are designed to measure rigidity, egocentrism, externalization, and the tendency to dichotomize decreases significantly with age. The developmental argument can be called upon here to point toward the emotional and intellectual immaturity of the prejudiced child. The items which correlate with prejudice are the same as those to which the younger children subscribe more often than do the older ones. Some of the trends which are connected with ethnocentrism are thus natural stages of development which have to be overcome if maturity is to be reached. There is a surprising similarity between the tendencies found in our prejudiced children and those described by Piaget (1926, 1932) as the chronologically earlier stages of moral and intellectual outlook.

In going back to our main line of argument, we may repeat briefly that Bob's and Jerry's rigidity in approaching perceptual and cognitive tasks was found to correspond with a high standing on a scale measuring rigidity in different spheres of life. The reverse holds for Joan.

Though Bob and Joan and Jerry showed some consistent differences in their social, emotional, and cognitive outlook, such clearcut separation does not hold to the same degree in all cases. Another boy, Dick, who was also high on prejudice but who differed somewhat in his personality make-up from Bob and Jerry in the direction of being more manipulative and exploitive rather than conformist and aggressive, showed at the same time less rigidity in his perceptual reactions. The protocol of his responses to the emerging numbers was barren, but he recognized the final numbers not later than average. On the concept-formation task he also performed quite well, and he showed only a mild degree of rigidity on the water-container experiment. Thus, in Dick the in-group versus out-group dichotomy does not go with an unusual degree of rigidity in the total personality make-up and in the cognitive approach.

On the other hand, we also find unprejudiced children who show relative rigidity in their perceptual approach. This may be due either to an atypical general rigidity of personality or to an increased anxiety and a blocking on the tasks concerned, these tasks being often less congenial to unprejudiced children than they are to the prejudiced.

In this group we found an unprejudiced girl, Pat, whose poor performance was probably mainly due to a lack of interest in this aspect of reality, since her orientation was mainly toward people. Personality consistency in Pat's case was clearly disrupted; the general quality of her performance in social and human tasks did not agree with her low performance level on simple cognitive tasks. In most cases of this kind, however, a more detailed phenomenological analysis of the cognitive approach, especially in tasks of higher sophistication, revealed features which go quite well with the over-all clinical picture. For examples of apparent or real disruption of personal consistency on a much broader scale, it may suffice to point to well-known examples of creative men in whom intellectual or artistic achievement has served as a compensation for a barren and restricted life lacking in emotional maturity.

Form and Content

The traditional concepts of "form" and "content" are notoriously relative and of a shifting meaning. Yet they will prove very useful in rounding out our discussion. Without ettempting to make a sharp distinction between them, we will include under "content" such issues as attitude toward parents or authority in general, generalized motivational tendencies like aggression or dependence, such instinctual realities as heterosexual or homosexual development, and social adjustment. By "form," on the other hand, we shall understand the different ways in which such motivational categories are handled. Here we are thinking mainly of the defense mechanisms which determine the differential destiny of sex and aggression. Related to the defense mechanisms and also subsumed under formal categories are the general perceptual and cognitive modes or styles in the approach to the social and object world, as discussed in this chapter, and finally the linguistic or related semantic properties of statements.

Form Less Subject to Censorship than Content

It is the writer's opinion that relationships can be ascertained between the contentual and formal aspects of behavior in spite of the complexities involved. These relationships are especially important in personality studies in well-developed cultures, where it is usual for many motivational tendencies to be modified and distorted under the impact of external and internal censorship. It will be maintained here that the formal elements of personality style, since they are not as directly threatening as its content, are not subject to censorship in the same manner as is content and that they, therefore, can be used as powerful tools in diagnostic procedures. The above-mentioned study on mechanisms of self-deception, as well as some of the later evidence cited, seems to suggest that such formal style elements as exaggeration, easy generalization (as contrasted with salient specificity), intolerance of ambiguity, and the like may be of greater penetrating power within the personality, more nearly alike on the surface and at greater depth, and thus of greater generality and greater diagnostic validity than such content elements as, say, sex, aggression, the Oedipus complex, and the like.

Whereas in our discussion the relations between form and content concerned have so far remained more or less implicit, we will now conclude with an attempt to make some of these relations explicit, thereby summarizing our findings and adding some new material. Not only has the perception of each individual a formal side all its own which is a reflection of his total personality, but by virtue of the possibility that peculiarities of perceptual style may be less subject to repression they may furnish substantial cues for the intuitive perception as well as the more explicitly cognitive diagnosis of these total personalities by others.

The theoretical introduction to this paper was concerned in a general way with the problem of how certain motivational tendencies may be camouflaged from perception by others by a façade of phenotypically opposite character. Next we discussed a number of concrete examples of formal characteristics which help us to discern whether a certain social façade or verbal statement is representative of, or else compensatory to, the social realities and the dynamics of motivation. Among the major formal cues used in the interpretation of such phenomena were, more specifically, the following: exaggeration; absoluteness of emphasis; intolerance of ambiguity; the predominant use of the extreme values of what actually are continua; such inconsistencies as are found in the comparisons of general with specific features of behavior or of verbal statement, or in the comparison of responses to direct questions with those to indirect questions; the occasional breaking through of a pattern of denial; deviations from the perceptions, from the concepts, and from other answers which constitute the norm for the group as a whole; stereotypy; concreteness; small range of variability in response; repetition; and all manner of rigidity. Allport (1942, p. 132), in discussing the work on self-deception described above, states that, if it is extended, "it may not be too much to hope that psychologists will one day produce a 'Guide to Rationalizations and Projections' to assist users of personal documents in discovering those passages in which the narrator is, in the narrow and specific sense of the term, deceiving himself."

CLOSENESS OF OPPOSITES

We found, in the work referred to, that in self-description a statement is often indicative of its opposite. Closeness of opposites emerged, on the basis of several of our studies, as one of the general formal principles in personality organization. One may trace back to psychoanalysis the original realization of the possibility that apparent opposites may be psychologically closer together and more apt to combine with each other in the same subject than any of them would with an intermediate position along the same scale. To be sure, in psychoanalysis this pattern is discovered primarily in the field of the instincts and the emotions, and mainly through the phenomenon of ambivalence. Conscious love of extreme and exaggerated intensity is viewed by the psychoanalyst with the same suspicion as are extreme feelings of hate. On the basis of more strictly psychological evidence, we must now proceed from the emotional to the perceptual-cognitive sphere and include with the dynamically interchangeable opposite extremes such pairs of formal classifications as extreme rigidity and extreme fluidity, extreme abstractness and extreme concreteness, extreme subjectivity and extreme objectivity, and so forth.

FORM AND CONTENT IN AN EXPERIMENT ON MEMORY

The existing relationships between more specific motivational contents and their formal accompaniments may be illustrated by the following example. In an experiment on memory distortion (this volume, Chapter 2), it was found that the children who recalled mainly the aggressive aspects of a story that had been told to them also tended to show a series of formal features, especially a tendency to alternate between rigid stimulus boundness (for example, literal repetition of certain phrases) and a complete neglect of the stimulus in favor of purely subjective fantasies. A selective memory for aggressive content was here combined with poor form; the latter consisted either in an overcautious, segmentary, and rigid approach, or else a disintegrated and chaotic one; sometimes one and the same child manifested both patterns in alternation or in a variety of bizarre combinations.

More research will be necessary before we are able to tell what kind and degree of aggression are apt to sharpen our cognitive tools and what kind is likely to diminish or destroy our ability for cognitive mastery. On the basis of data from different contexts, the present writer is inclined to think that it is the destructive, not ego-integrated, contents and forms of aggression which go with poor cognitive mastery; true to the principle of the closeness of opposites, extreme degrees of repression of aggressive tendencies may not be much better; it will probably be the milder and ego-integrated varieties of aggression that will be found to be most closely connected with increased cognitive capacity.

FORM AND CONTENT IN PROJECTIVE TESTS: CASE MATERIAL AND STATISTICAL RESULTS

In proceeding to an analysis of the interrelationships between motivational content and cognitive form found in projective material, we may begin by adding a further example on the topic of aggressive preoccupation just discussed. The Thematic Apperception Test stories of an extremely prejudiced preadolescent boy, Karl, who was one of the subjects of the Adolescent Growth Study, were concerned with murder and gore to a much greater extent than is usual in stories of children of his age. More specifically, the implicit recurrent theme in his stories seemed to be that neither the role of the aggressive man nor that of the passive one is workable. The man who is passive and in possession of some fortune is usually attacked in some surprising way—from behind or while asleep—and is destroyed. The aggressive man, on the other hand, is regularly caught by the police and sentenced to life imprisonment at least, though more often he is executed in the electric chair. In one of these stories the "crooked place was turned into a big Safeway store," a clear revelation of Karl's deep-seated longing that all the dangerous men should be removed and that he should be allowed to be passive and surrounded by food, without fear of aggression and the ensuing necessity for being aggressive himself. This was also the way he imagined girls to live. Though the girls in the stories were in a more enviable position, even they were not always safe. In almost every one of his stories Karl mentioned food and money.

Of the two types of men, the passive and the aggressive, Karl really felt closer to the former. In one story he described in detail how a passive boy was always being hit by a tough boy who "had taken exercises from a guy that helps you make muscles." We thus have evidence of insecurity about masculinity and of feminine identification; the latter is also manifested in the occurrence of many phallic symbols and castration threats and in Karl's apparent embarrassment about his body build and genital organs. In a story in which he described a swimming scene, he was careful to point out that the boys had swimming suits under their clothes and thus did not have to strip naked. Karl's stories were not only exaggerated versions of the stories common among the prejudiced boys in general but were also similar in some ways to the stories of overt homosexuals.

The formal correlate to this pattern of content in Karl's stories was as follows. His narration was long and flowing, an uninhibited and uncontrolled stream of free association. We note here a kind of fluidity which goes with a low form level. The stories were neither coherent nor structured, and what seemed like imagination was really a kind of ruminative repetition of the same scenes over and over again. The repetitiveness extended even to such details as numbers. The stories were, furthermore, utterly unrealistic as far as general probability was concerned; they were full of bizarre elements and strayed away to a marked degree from the subject matter of the picture which, after the first few sentences, was frequently lost from sight entirely.

Karl's perceptual outlook was thus upon a world which, on the one hand, was full of aggressive men and other dangers, although it offered, on the other, an abundance of food and other infantile gratifications; quite fittingly this content went with a lack of grasp of reality and of logical consistency so far as the formal level was concerned. The connecting link was a general immaturity which extended to content and form.

A not fully published statistical analysis of projective material on extremely prejudiced and extremely unprejudiced adult women done in collaboration with Reichard (1947; Frenkel-Brunswik, 1948a) yielded findings of a similar kind. In the Thematic Apperception Test stories there were significantly more acts of destructive aggression, such as killings, rape, etc., in the stories of the prejudiced group as contrasted with milder forms of aggression, such as quarreling, in the stories of the unprejudiced group. Prejudiced women, significantly more often than unprejudiced women, perceived parental figures as unloving and punitive rather than as benevolent, and they made significantly more frequent reference to supernatural forces. On the formal side it may be said that the prejudiced women made much greater use of moralistic terms, such as "bad," "good," "criminal," and the like, than did the unprejudiced. The former tended to view people from an evaluative, distal point of view rather than from a motivational, central one.

On the Rorschach test the same prejudiced group showed some tendency toward poorer form level and more rigidity than the unprejudiced. The results have further indicated that "prejudiced subjects tend to be less productive mentally, less responsive emotionally, and less original than unprejudiced subjects. They tend to be more inhibited and more compulsively overmeticulous" (Frenkel-Brunswik, 1948a).

The problem of the affinity of certain content and form elements in the Thematic Apperception Test stories first became fully clear to the writer some time ago in the context of a number of longitudinal case analyses undertaken at the Institute of Child Welfare of the University of California (Frenkel-Brunswik, this volume, Chapter 1; 1948a, 1948b). The approach has not at present reached the quantitative stage of evaluation. Thus, the following listing of patterns is based on an inspection of case material rather than on statistically conclusive findings.

The content of the Thematic Apperception Test stories of a 12-year-old boy, Tom, revealed an ambivalent preoccupation with the problem of male authorities. In many of his stories total submission, to the point of self-destruction, was advocated; it was not the authorities but rather the victim of coercion and deprivation who was considered the culprit. In a few stories there was an indication that achievement—for instance, becoming a famous surgeon—would be the solution of the authority problem. We find, furthermore, on the content side a frequent mention of money and possessions.

As to form, Tom's stories were of good quality, realistic, and of high logical consistency. There was good intellectual penetration of the problems involved without, however, much sign of imagination or familiarity with the world of fantasy. Further characteristics of his stories were frequent expression of doubts and suggestions of alternative stories.

The very few stories in which Tom expressed aggression against male authorities were made unreal by an introductory remark that what was to follow dealt with a picture rather than with reality; these stories were somewhat more incoherent, less logical, and less realistic than those in which no aggression of this kind occurred. They did not, however, tend to become particularly improbable; they were, rather, real life put into the garb of fiction.

Tom not only repressed his hostility against his father but also his strong love for his mother. In a story about a mother and her baby, the baby came too close to the railing of a balcony, fell off, and was "crippled for life. . . . Something happened to its leg." Here is still another type of formal element than those discussed so far; it may be called the mechanism of "symbolic translation." From the total context of Tom's stories the assumption may be ventured that the balcony stands for the mother, and coming too close to the mother implies the danger of being crippled. The ensuing ambivalence, especially toward the father figure, seems to be connected with alternative formulations and ramifications. Thus, in one of the stories which started with the statement, "This is the picture of a woman," we were told that the husband had been shot. Quite in contradiction to this version—and contradictions were very rare in this boy's stories—we heard two sentences later that "The husband wasn't killed—just wounded—and unconscious." Tom apparently did not dare to kill the husband of the woman. On the other hand, the hostilities were there. And he corrected himself again by saying, "He was wounded very badly, however." Considering both content and form, a highly developed compulsive syndrome, quite unusual for this age, must be assumed in Tom.

One of Tom's classmates also showed a great deal of hostility toward his father, although on a more immature level. In one of his stories he described in the following circumstantial—not to say high-flown—style the death of a husband: "Something dear to her left her in a very drastic way."

In a third boy in the same group the love for the mother was more uninhibited; it was expressed directly as well as indirectly, orally as well as genitally, with the husband left out completely most of the time. At the same time the rich, undisciplined, yet highly original fantasy indicated the prevalence of the dream world. Though the stories were unrealistic, they suggested the potentiality of great creativity. Whether these creative fantasies and unconscious resources will be channeled into real achievement and a better grip on reality or whether they will disrupt the integration of this boy's personality will depend on forces favorable or unfavorable to the development of his ego strength.

The stories of still another boy in this study, the last to be mentioned here, showed a passive sensuousness combined with a great deal of expansion on concrete and palpable impressions such as the enjoyment of a landscape, of the act of smoking, of resting, and of related physical sensations. His stories neither posed nor solved big or dramatic problems nor did they show a flight into imagination. On the content side we find this boy passively, and seemingly without conflict, oriented toward men. It was the men in his stories who gave affection and who took care of children. One father took care of 30 children. On the basis of all his stories, the assumption that this boy may become an overt homosexual does not seem far-fetched. Though Thematic Apperception Test stories of overt homosexuals seem to show an orientation toward sensation, they are by no means always as well organized and lacking in bizarre elements as are the stories of this boy.

We may conclude the discussion of form and content in the Thematic Apperception Test stories with a reference to two contrasting girls. In one case there was an uncontrolled, undisciplined, unimaginative flow of free associations combined with an infantile preoccupation with the mother, especially with feeding and being fed. The stories of the other girl showed a creative, subtle, and differentiated view of human relations combined with a genuine interest in love and heterosexuality, in spite of overtones of an undue attachment to the father.

FORM AND CONTENT IN INTERVIEWS OF ETHNOCENTRIC SUBJECTS

Relationships between form and content similar to those just discussed were also found on the basis of interviews (Adorno et al., 1950; Frenkel-Brunswik, 1948c). On the content side, in ethnically prejudiced adults and children certain attitudes such as overt acceptance were found coupled with underlying aggression toward parents, authority, and society in general, fear of weakness, passivity, and sex impulses. Rigid forms of defenses have to be erected against many of these tendencies; one of these is the mechanism of projection, by which much that cannot be accepted as a part of one's own ego is externalized. As discussed in the previous section, a pervasive rigidity and intolerance of ambiguity, as well as a distortion of reality, are among the further formal characteristics related to the contents just mentioned.

Whether such tendencies as aggression or homosexuality are accepted or not determines the forms of their expression. Aggression which is accepted will be relatively mild, tending toward regular release and toward verbal expression, and it will be directed toward the objects which were the original targets of the aggression. Unaccepted aggressive tendencies, on the other hand, will assume a destructive and explosive character and will tend toward all-or-nothing expressions.

The inability to accept one's self will in due course interfere with an adequate perception of one's self and of others. Instead of viewing himself as a unit in continuous development, the prejudiced subject tends to offer apologetic "explanations" in terms of unscrutinized accidental, hereditary, or physical factors. The inability to accept one's self finally altogether prevents a social-psychological outlook and leads to an unscientific or pseudoscientific outlook on man and society. Furthermore, when one's fears and wishes are not integrated and not modified by reality, in the way indicated in the first part of this chapter, autistic thinking in goal behavior and an unrealistic view of means-end relationships results.

On the preceding pages an effort was made to provide material and discussion by which the relationship between such contents as aggression or the attitude toward authority on the one hand, and the formal elements of the perceptual and cognitive approach on the other, would be approached in some detail. It may be emphasized, again on the basis of case studies rather than of conclusive quantitative evidence, that most of those among the prejudiced subjects who performed well on some of the relatively simple perceptual and cognitive tasks discussed in this chapter nonetheless revealed signs of rigidity in their performance. Here we are reminded of the frequently noted technological abilities of the German Nazis. Those in this group who performed poorly were often found to slide into overfluidity and disintegration. The unprejudiced subjects, on the other hand, tended more toward creative flexibility, although they sometimes displayed utter blocking in the solving of the tasks concerned.

Many other findings and topics could, and perhaps should, be discussed under the heading "form and content." The writer is thinking primarily of such findings in clinical psychology as those by Rapaport (Rapaport, Schafer, and Gill, 1946), Schafer (1948), and others concerning the relationships between Rorschach and intelligence test results on the one hand, and life histories and patterns of emotional and cognitive disturbances on the other; also of some of the developmental problems discussed by Werner (1940), Piaget (1926, 1932), Charlotte Bühler (1935), and others involving the establishment of developmental stages from the point of view of both content and form. Unfortunately, a comprehensive discussion of all this cannot be attempted in the present framework.

This chapter may conclude with a few remarks on possible trends in future research. The study of personality in its relation to perception must certainly be considered a going concern. We shall probably have a period in which every imaginable perceptual experiment will be related to every imaginable personality variable. Often these two types of variables will not be clearly differentiated from each other, either theoretically or experimentally; the fact that sometimes the same term is used for both will give the a priori illusion that real relationships are involved.

In spite of such pitfalls—pitfalls which endanger undertakings in every field of research which becomes fashionable—we can look forward with confidence to important discoveries along these lines. Probably they will come especially from those who attempt to formulate and clarify their problems thoroughly before rushing into the computing of correlations. All this will necessitate the increasing use of identical sets of subjects for a variety of assessments, as was first attempted at the Harvard Clinic (Murray et al., 1938) and the OSS Assessment Center during the war (OSS Assessment Staff, 1948). The choice of the subjects will have to be carefully determined both from the sociological and the psychological point of view, since now we are less concerned with normative and more concerned with differential problems.

A great need, and one which the writer hopes will be filled in the future, is that of research on children. On the motivational side, the original drives are most openly accessible and least modified by cultural pressures on the child. Considering that children present such excellent opportunities for direct verification of the basic assumptions of psychoanalysis, it is surprising that so few of the psychoanalytically oriented psychologists have worked with them. Furthermore, an analysis of the more complex perceptual and cognitive approaches to reality can be achieved with the least interference in children. The ready accessibility of different developmental stages leads most naturally to an analysis of the forms of cognition; this has been attempted with particular penetration by Werner (1940) and Piaget (1926).

Thus it would seem that the most promising avenue of approach should be the one which combines emphasis on general personality variables, both motivational and cognitive, with an emphasis on developmental aspects. In any event, there can be little doubt that this is a most challenging period in psychology.

4

PSYCHOANALYSIS AND THE UNITY OF SCIENCE

The Broadening of Operationism

Freud's first formulations of his ideas in the sphere of personality aroused a clamor of protest which has never entirely subsided. More recently, however, we can observe a shift in the type of criticism leveled against psychoanalysis. Once the initial shock ensuing from Freud's discoveries had been overcome, scientists were in a better position to look at the structure of the theory of personality proposed by psychoanalysis, and the more recent scrutinies of the system appear to be concerned to a greater extent with its formal or methodological characteristics than with its content. Thus we hear that the method employed by psychoanalysis is a subjective rather than an objective one; that hypotheses and facts are often confused; that the psychoanalytic propositions do not lend themselves to scientific verification; that concepts like super-

---

Some of the contentions of this paper were first presented at the Symposium on the Experimental Approach to Psychoanalytic Theory held at the Meeting of the American Psychological Association in 1950, and also at seminar meetings in the Universities of California, Chicago, and Michigan in 1951 and 1952. Some of the theoretical parts of the paper in its present version were read at the Berkeley Conference for the Unity of Science, July, 1953, and at the San Francisco Psychoanalytic Society. First published in *Proceedings of the American Academy of Arts and Sciences,* 80: 273-347, 1954. ©1954, American Academy of Arts and Sciences.

The philosophical arguments brought forth in this paper derive from some of the teachings of logical positivism. The writer is indebted primarily to her teacher in the philosophy of science, Moritz Schlick, in whose seminars and discussion groups she participated during and after her studies at the University of Vienna. In effect, this paper constitutes a return to an assignment, suggested to the writer some 20 years ago by the late Otto Neurath, to clarify the standing of psychoanalysis in the framework of the Unity of Science movement inaugurated by him at that time.

ego, ego, and id are foisted on us as entities in a manner characteristic of the prescientific stages of inquiry and formulation; that many of the attempts to verify psychoanalytic assumptions have actually failed.

The common theme of these charges seems to be a dissatisfaction concerning the relationship between concept and fact, or between theory and observation, in psychoanalytic theory. We are not suggesting that all of these strictures are unjustified. Before examining concept formation as it occurs in psychoanalysis and existing attempts at confirmation of psychoanalytic hypotheses, we should, however, first like to recall, in a more general way, some of the more recent teachings concerning the relation between theory and observation. We should like to show that some—though by no means all—of the criticisms raised against psychoanalysis are based on misconceptions about this relationship. Many of the objections against psychoanalysis have their origin in an overnarrow interpretation of the version of scientific empiricism commonly known as operationism with its stress on the rooting of all concepts in concrete manipulations and observations (Bridgman [1928]; for a summary of psychological applications see Stevens [1939]), and generally in a vaguely antitheoretical attitude, rather than in a legitimate criticism of psychoanalytic theory. This holds especially for the criticism originating in psychology proper.

As operationism is an offshoot of some considerations in physics, many critics of psychoanalysis explicitly point to the physical sciences as providing an ideal model for the formulation of theory, psychoanalytic or otherwise. However, this is in most cases done without full realization of the extent of certain changes in the conception of theoretical structure which have taken place in the field of physics itself. These developments in physics made it necessary to modify the requirements stated in the older forms of empiricism and positivism. Thus Einstein (1944) does not demand that all abstract terms of science should be interpreted in terms of sense observation, and he designates as "structural" those elements of a theory which deal only with the relationship between the symbols.

> In order that thinking might not degenerate into metaphysics or into empty talk, it is only necessary that enough propositions

of the conceptual system be firmly enough connected with sensory experiences.

It was Schlick who as early as 1920 stressed the departure from the phenomenally given as one of the foremost accomplishments of Einstein's theory. Schlick emphasized the importance of both "observational" and "auxiliary" concepts such as electric forces. Since the latter are also measurable, he was at that time even inclined to consider them to be as "real" as colors and tones. He changed his position later, however. At the present time we witness a return to Schlick's critical realism (1918) within the movement of logical positivism, notably by Feigl (1950). Instead of the phenotypic approach we now acknowledge what Philipp Frank (1941) has labeled the nonpictorial type of theorizing. The inability of our imagination to follow the notions of a four-dimensional space is only one of the most trivial examples of this. Frank points out that the earlier ultrapositivistic requirement, according to which all principles of physics should be formulated by using only observable quantities, has been replaced by a weaker requirement: now it is merely postulated that from these principles mathematical conclusions could be drawn that would be connected by semantic rules with statements about observable facts. Einstein speaks of "the ever-widening logical gap between basic concepts and laws, on the one hand, and the consequences to be correlated with our experiences, on the other."

Along similar lines move Hempel's (1952) formulations concerning the necessary revisions of operationism and empiricism:

> But it is precisely those fictitious concepts rather than those fully definable by observables which enable science to interpret and organize the data of direct observation by means of a coherent system which permits explanation and prediction.

There is increasing realization of the fact that scientific theories are the product of our imagination even though the system must have a rooting in observable fact and experience remains the ultimate and sole criterion of its adequacy. Different levels of description and theory can be defined by the closeness of the concept to, or remoteness from, observable facts. Hempel gives a vivid description of the relationship between a scientific theory and the observational data.

> The whole system floats, as it were, above the plane of observation and is anchored to it by rules of interpretation. These might be viewed as strings which are not part of the network but link certain points of the latter with specific places in the plane of observation. By virtue of those interpretive connections, the network can function as a scientific theory: from certain observational data, we may ascend, via an interpretive string, to some point in the theoretical network, thence proceed, via definitions and hypotheses, to other points from which another interpretive string permits a descent to the plane of observation.

A comparison between the developments in physics and the situation in psychoanalysis is certainly not in all respects justified. While we must grant to the psychoanalytic system many more elements of a truly scientific theory than most philosophers of science realize, it still remains true that psychoanalysis contains many metaphors, analogies, and confusions between constructs and facts of which it can and must in the end be rid.

However, some parallels between recent developments in physics and psychoanalysis can be pointed out, and these have implications for the problem of what are the requirements for a confirmation of psychoanalytic propositions. Modern physics and psychoanalysis have in common a turning away from the "natural" to a "fictitious" language. And the common result of this policy is that a wider and simpler network of interrelationships within observable data is ultimately being achieved. Freud introduced a number of fictitious constructs, such as unconsciousness, id, superego, repression, death instinct, and so forth. Although we may grant that psychoanalysis, in trying to avoid the error of an overdescriptive, segmentary, and specific approach, has sometimes fallen into the error of overinterpretation and of drawing far-reaching conclusions from fragmentary evidence, we still contend that at one point the jump into theory which Hempel advocates must be made. The fact that theoretical constructs of the kind mentioned above refer only indirectly, and not completely at that, to observable data must therefore not be made the basis of an objection against psychoanalysis as such. It would constitute a serious misunderstanding of scientific theory construction were we to go along with the all too frequent type of criticism of fictitious constructs recently exemplified by Ellis (1950) who, in referring to such concepts as id and superego, writes as follows: "Many professional workers will immediately object that while they have frequently come across sex-desires, guilt-feelings and conflicts in their patients, they have never had the pleasure of greeting an ego or superego."

At the same time we must stress that the links to the observational data must be specified. Freud started with rather specific observations concerning hysteria and repression of the sexual content in hysteria. While at the beginning of his psychoanalytic explorations Freud kept close to the data and introduced constructs which he needed more directly for description and explanation of his data, he later became more speculative. From these speculations he derived a number of theorems which he then tested in his clinical observations. Then he became speculative once more to an extent which may be considered controversial, as we shall see in our discussion of the death instinct.

The Concept of the Unconscious

There are two aspects of psychoanalytic theory which must be held apart. The first is given by its formal aspects, that is, the way the constructs are defined and the relationship between the various concepts. The second consists in the problems of verification or confirmation of psychoanalytic statements. We will begin with a discussion of the way Freud himself introduced some of his crucial concepts and will concentrate on two of the most basic and at the same time most controversial, that of the unconscious and that of instinct. Later we will turn to an analysis of these concepts from the point of view of recent notions about scientific concept formation.

As far as the definition of basic concepts is concerned, many critics of psychoanalysis have objected to an alleged lack of sophistication in Freud concerning the philosophy of science, and to his tendency to "reify" his concepts. The quotations from Freud that follow are brought forth as evidence to the contrary. They are to demonstrate how keenly aware Freud was of logical and epistemological problems, a fact often forgotten under the impact of the carelessness with which some of his followers use his terms.

About the function and nature of definitions in science, Freud has the following to say:

> The view is often defended that sciences should be built up on clear and sharply defined basal concepts. In actual fact no science, not even the most exact, begins with such definitions. The true beginning of scientific activity consists rather in describing phenomena and then in proceeding to group, classify and correlate them. Even at the stage of description it is not possible to avoid applying certain abstract ideas to the material in hand, ideas derived from various sources and certainly not the fruit of the new experience only. Still more indispensable are such ideas—which will later become the basal concepts of the science—as the material is further elaborated. They must at first necessarily possess some measure of uncertainty; there can be no question of any clear delimitation of their content. So long as they remain in this condition, we come to an understanding about their meaning by repeated references to the material of observation. . . . Strictly speaking, they are in the nature of conventions; although everything depends on their being chosen in no arbitrary manner, but determined by the important relations they have to the empirical material—relations that we seem to divine before we can clearly recognize and demonstrate them. It is only after more searching investigation of the field in question that we are able to formulate with increased clarity the scientific concepts underlying it, and progressively so to modify these concepts that they become widely applicable and at the same time consistent logically. Then, indeed, it may be time to immure them in definitions. The progress of science, however, demands a certain elasticity even in these definitions. The science of physics furnishes an excellent illustration of the way in which even those "basal concepts" that are firmly established in the form of definitions are constantly being altered in their content [1915a, pp. 60-61].

Freud further stresses the fact that we also make use of certain "complicated postulates" to guide us in dealing with psychological phenomena. Freud is aware of the fact that our observations are guided by explicit or implicit theoretical assumptions. Thus most clinical descriptions found in Freud employ the inferential construct of the unconscious. Freud proceeds from the common observation that an idea which is now present in consciousness may become absent in the next moment, and may become present again, after an interval, unchanged and from memory rather than as a result of a fresh sensory perception. It is this fact which leads Freud to the "supposition" that during the interval the conception has been present, although in a "latent" stage. In this he follows such famous precedent as that of Plato or Herbart. Freud argues that an unconscious conception is one of which we are not aware, but "the existence of which we are nevertheless ready to admit on account of other proofs or signs" (1912, p. 22).

Among other things it is posthypnotic suggestion which is brought forth as evidence for the importance of the distinction between conscious and unconscious. According to Freud no account of the posthypnotic execution of an order, received during hypnosis and of which there is no recollection, can be given unless we assume a condition of latency, or of unconscious presence, of the command. Freud further points out that not all the idea reemerges into consciousness, but only the conception of the act to be executed.

From the standpoint of modern logic of science, there is nothing objectionable about the notion of latent or unconscious tendencies, at least not so long as we do not insist on assigning them to "the mind" in a metaphysical sense. A comparable situation obtains in physics when we observe that a physical object at one time exhibits magnetism—that is, when a piece of iron is present in its vicinity—and that it does not do so when this condition is not fulfilled. Magnetism thus is what Carnap (1936, 1937) has called a "dispositional concept." The precise logical nature of concepts of this kind in relation to psychoanalysis will be taken up later. Suffice it to say here that such composite terms as unconscious hostility or dependency describe a disposition to display aggression or dependence under specified conditions, for example in therapy. We may remember in this context the definition of behavior given by Carnap at another occasion (1938) which includes the just-mentioned processes with which psychoanalysis deals:

> It must be made clear that the term behavior has a greater extension here than it tended to have with the early behaviorists. Here it is intended to designate not only overt behavior which can be observed externally but also internal behavior, that is, processes within the organism; in addition, it includes

dispositions to behavior which may not be manifest in a given special case; and finally it includes certain effects of overt behavior upon the environment.

In addition to the posthypnotic execution of hypnotic suggestions as a means of confirming unconscious factors as determinants of behavior, the transition of latent processes into manifest behavior may also be observed more directly in the psychoanalytic procedure. Freud considers the assumption of unconsciousness as necessary because the data of consciousness are "exceedingly defective." Conscious acts alone do not enable us to account for the parapraxes and dreams of healthy persons and of the mental symptoms or obsessions in the sick. Our most intimate daily experience introduces us "to sudden ideas of the source of which we are ignorant, and to results of mentation arrived at we know not how" (1915c, p. 99). All these conscious acts are said to remain disconnected and unintelligible if we are determined to hold fast to the claim that every single mental act performed within us must be consciously experienced. On the other hand, it is pointed out, they fall into a demonstrable connection if we interpolate the unconscious acts that we infer. The gain in meaning and connection is considered by Freud a perfectly justifiable motive, one which may well "carry us beyond the limitations of direct experience."

In Freud's opinion it is the very assumption of unconscious processes which enables psychoanalysis to take its place as "a natural science like any other." He goes on to explain that these processes are "in themselves just as unknowable as those dealt with by other sciences such as physics and chemistry" (1940). And Freud remains in the spirit of the natural sciences when he states that "it is possible to establish the laws which those processes obey and to follow over long and unbroken stretches their mutual relation and interdependences" (p. 36).

The introduction of the term "unconsciousness" thus is done in the service of good scientific procedure and with explicit reference to its rules. The relationships between consciousness, preconsciousness, and unconsciousness are described in detail by Freud, and he designates this field as the topographical aspect of psychoanalysis. Latent ideas which are capable of entering consciousness without any special resistance are called preconscious, while the term unconscious is reserved for ideas "with a certain dynamic character" which are kept "apart from consciousness in spite of their intensity and activity."

The concepts of conscious and unconscious thus emerge as signification of "particular systems and possessed of certain characteristics." Freud was keenly aware of the fact that he was building a formal model containing the different systems with a specification of the relationships between them. The following quotation shows how far he was from a reification of his concepts:

> We might still attempt to avoid confusion by employing for the recognized mental systems certain arbitrarily chosen names which have no reference to consciousness. Only we should first have to justify the principles on which we distinguish the systems and we should not be able to ignore the question of consciousness, seeing that it forms the point of departure for all our investigations. Perhaps we may look for some assistance from the proposal to employ, at any rate in writing, the abbreviation Cs for consciousness and the Ucs for the unconscious when we are using the two words in the systematic sense [1915c, p. 105].

From then on Freud consistently used these symbols, as if to underscore the fact that they refer to mere abstractions. Freud further points to the fact that by the introduction of the different mental systems he has departed from the descriptive academic psychology and that the consideration of "mental topography," which means the indication "in respect of any given mental operation within what system or between what systems it runs its course," has won psychoanalysis the name of depth psychology.

Freud thus introduced the concept of the unconscious as an abstract, hypothetical construct (see the discussion later) which is specified by its relationship to other concepts, such as consciousness and preconsciousness, and to which a partial empirical interpretation is given by reference to free associations, dreams, and occurrences during therapy. In order to establish the relationships to observational data, many subsidiary hypotheses such as those concerning the nature of the therapeutic process and of dreams are necessary. In his later writings (notably 1933, 1940) Freud prefers to use the term "unconscious" as denoting mental qualities rather than systems, at the same time replacing it by the more obviously dispositional term "id" for the major purposes of the theory. "We will no longer use the word unconscious in the sense of a system and to what we have hitherto called by that name we will give a better one which will not give rise to misunderstanding. We will call it henceforth the Id" (1940, p. 33).

These and related formulations of Freud are in our opinion less lucid than the ones discussed before. The reason for Freud's proposal to shift from the interpretation of the unconscious as a "system" to that as a "mental" quality lies in his later discovery that not only the "id" but also part of the "superego" and "ego" are often unconscious. In our opinion this discovery does not necessarily interfere with an interpretation of the unconscious as a system with specific dispositional characteristics. Incidentally, it may be helpful in the early stages of discovery to designate certain patterns of behavior in terms of special and relatively fixed classifications such as id, ego, and superego. Today many of the earlier statements of psychoanalysis may be reformulated in terms of behavioral patterns in such a manner that the facets of behavior connected with the biological processes are differentiated from those which are the result of cultural taboos.

There is no reason to assume that Freud's writings necessarily improved as time progressed. It is interesting to speculate whether Freud first felt the need of thinking of the unconscious as an abstract system, and then his increasing familiarity with the manifestations which were to be explained by the term once chosen made him view these attributes as mental qualities. In his paper on "existential hypotheses," Feigl (1950) has pointed out that at the beginning of a science it is often difficult to judge which concepts represent mere conventions and which refer to specific entities. Although Freud never explicitly designated the concept of unconscious as a mere convention, in his above-quoted interpretation of the unconscious as a system to be designated merely by letters or letter combinations it seems to entail more conventionalist connotations than in his later writings. In view of Freud's original intent in introducing the concept of the unconscious, such criticism as the following by Ellis (1950) seems unjustified:

It is now (thanks to Freud) a well established clinical fact that human beings have thoughts and feelings of which they are unaware or unconscious. But to collect the processes under the term unconscious, used as noun and implying a specific entity in itself, is more confusing than revealing.

In discussing the localization of mental processes, Freud points out that the objection may be raised that these latent recollections can no longer be described as mental processes but that they correspond to residues of somatic processes. Against this he holds that the conventional identification of the mental with the conscious is thoroughly impractical since it forces us "prematurely to retire from the territory of psychological research without being able to offer us any compensation elsewhere." He concludes that we shall therefore be better advised to give prominence to "what we know with certainty of the nature of these debatable states" (1915c, pp. 99ff.).

Freud goes on to acknowledge that a "rough correlation of . . . the mental apparatus to anatomy . . . exists." But in his opinion every attempt to deduce from these facts a localization of mental processes has completely miscarried. He points to the "hiatus which at present cannot be filled, nor is it one of the tasks of psychology to fill it." Our mental topography, he concludes, has for the present nothing to do with anatomy; it is concerned not with anatomical locations, but with "regions in the mental apparatus" irrespective of their possible situation in the body. The fact that, at least for the time being, a physiological interpretation of his concepts has not become possible is stressed by Freud again and again. While at the beginning Freud was intensely dominated by neurophysiological thinking, the decisive progress in psychoanalysis occurred not until after he freed himself from the search for such analogies and turned to more openly psychological models. However, Freud always considered this step as temporary and as necessitated by the present imperfect state of the biological sciences.

We cannot do more than give a few examples of the many-sidedness of Freud's models. Thus Freud goes into great detail in discussing the fate of ideas and affects in terms of a "given volume of excitation," developing the point of view which he has called "economic." In an earlier paper Freud characterizes this energy as "something having all the attributes of a quantity although we possess no means of measuring it." He adopts Helmholtz's principle of conservation of energy. Siegfried Bernfeld (1944) has amply pointed out Helmholtz's influence on Freud. The energy withdrawn from a conscious idea when it is repressed is used for an anticathexis of the same idea, which makes for keeping the idea out of consciousness. Freud uses the various formal relations between the different systems to give an explanation for the subvarieties of repression occurring in hysteria, phobia, and other forms of neurosis. In the discussion of an animal phobia which constitutes a substitute for the hate of the father, Freud (1915c) compares the real fear of an animal with the neurotic one. The latter is "fed . . . from the springs of unconscious instinct" and is "obdurate and extravagant in the face of all influences brought to bear from the system Cs, . . . thereby betraying its origin in the system Ucs."

There are said to be several differentiating characteristics between the *Ucs.* system and *Cs.* system. The conscious ideas comprise the "concrete idea" plus the "verbal idea" corresponding to it. By linking the two, a higher form of organization can be achieved. The processes of the *Ucs.*, on the other hand, are little related to reality. They are subject to the pleasure principle, and the external reality is substituted by an internal reality. There is exemption from mutual contradiction and the outcome depends mainly upon the degree of strength of these processes and upon the "degree of their regulation by pleasure and pain." Or, as Freud says later, we deal here with mobile and unbound energies. The processes of this system are "not ordered temporally," are not altered by the passage of time. All these characteristics are grouped together under the heading of "primary processes." These are genetically succeeded by the "secondary processes" which occur within the *Cs.* system. This latter system binds the primitive energies through reality control.

The derivatives of the *Ucs.* act especially through dreams and free association as intermediaries between the two systems. Closer study of the derivatives of the *Ucs.* will altogether disappoint our expectations of a schematically clear division of the one mental system from the other. A good illustration of inferences from the "manifest" to the "latent" content is given by the following quotation on dream interpretations:

The dreamer's associations bring to light intermediate links which we can then insert in the gap between the two and with the help of which we can recover the latent material of the dream and "interpret" it. It is not to be wondered at that this work of interpretation (acting in a direction opposite to that of the dream-work) fails occasionally to find a completely certain conclusion [1940, p. 54].

In defending all these complexities Freud stresses the aim of merely translating into theory the results of observation. He points out that there is no obligation to achieve at our very first attempt a theory that "commends itself by its simplicity, in which all is plain sailing." Freud argues that we must defend complexities of the theory so long as we find that they fit in with the results of observation; and we must not abandon our expectation of being guided in the end by those very complexities to recognition of "a state of affairs that is at once simple in itself and at the same time answers to all the complications of reality" (1915c, p. 122f.). There is an obvious similarity between these and many of Freud's earlier-quoted programmatic utterances, and those of logical empiricists; this adherence extends here to the postulate of simplicity and becomes even more pointed by the relegation of simple structure to a distant ideal state of affairs.

The Concept of Instinct

Next to the concept of the unconscious it is that of instinct which has been objected to most vigorously in the face of claims of psychoanalysis for consideration as a science. According to Freud, the concept of instinct is a "conventional but still rather obscure" one. Considering mental life from a biological point of view, an instinct appears to Freud as both the "mental representative" of the stimuli emanating from within the organism and as a "measure of the demand made upon the energy of the latter in consequence of its connection with the body" (1915a, pp. 61, 64). Statements concerning animal drives like hunger or sex would not seem to require any special justification so long as they remain mere descriptive summaries of factual behavior. However, the further elaboration of the concept of instinct as representing a special kind of energy and a constancy principle for this energy, as well as the more specifically psychoanalytic doctrine of the far-reaching transformations and disguises, particularly of the sex instinct, renders the concept of instinct a much more involved one, leading Freud to the following simile: "The theory of the instincts is, as it were, our mythology. The instincts are mythical beings, superb in their indefiniteness. In our work we cannot for a moment overlook them, and yet we are never certain that we are seeing them clearly" (1933, p. 131).

There are several ways in which this statement may be interpreted. Freud may have had in mind that the concept of instinct is hypothetical in spite of the fact that we are aware of some of the instinctual impulses. In this case the term "mythology" may be misleading. What Freud probably had in mind over and beyond the interpretation just given is the lack of knowledge about the basic biological processes which underlie the instincts, and consequently a certain lack of clarity in his own instinct theory. Although we must grant that this is true, we must add that the sections dealing with infantile sexuality and with the description of the psychosexual stages of development belong to the most lucid and most powerfully executed parts of Freud's system.

After differentiating and defining the "impetus," "object," "source," and "aim" of instincts, Freud undertakes to classify the instincts, pointing out that there is "obviously a great opportunity here for arbitrary choice." In this enterprise we should not neglect to ask whether instinctual motives do not admit of further analysis in respect to their sources, so that only those primal instincts "which are not to be resolved further" could really lay claim to the name (1915a, p. 67).

Pursuing the psychological description, Freud summarizes the distinctive characteristics of instincts by pointing out that instincts have in a high degree the capacity to "act vicariously for one another" and that they can readily change their objects. Thus they are capable of activities widely removed from their original modes of attaining their aims, such as in "sublimation" (p. 69).

The very fact that the concept of instinct covers a wide variety of behavior and permits of many manifestations accounts for its explanatory value. Only if Freud had ascribed to every variety of manifest behavior a corresponding instinct would he have rendered this concept superfluous and circular. Freud nonetheless expresses some doubt whether the psychological approach alone will afford any decisive indication for the distinction and classification of instincts. He himself wavered in his classification of instincts. At first he differentiated the sex instincts from the ego instincts (self-preservation). The ego instincts include further all the countersexual forces such as guilt feelings, ethical ideals, etc. However, later, Freud viewed "egoism" or "narcissism" as of the same libidinal character as sex. He therefore gave up his original classification of instincts, and later he distinguished Eros and Death, in which process aggression acquired a primary status not further deducible.

The "death instinct" is Freud's perhaps most controversial speculation. It assumes that there is a basic tendency in living organisms as well as in inorganic systems toward self-destruction, reduction of tension, and Nirvana; in contrast to this, Eros represents initiative and hunger for stimulation. Even such an ardent follower of Freud as Fenichel (1945) tends to the belief that the death instinct is a superfluous and far-fetched concept even in the explanation of such facts as depression, masochism, and guilt feelings. According to Fenichel, "external factors that disturbed the principles innate to the organism" could be adduced instead of a separate "genuine self-destructive instinct." However, definite judgment on this matter should be postponed. Freud himself stressed that much will depend on results of future biological research. Freud's own tentativeness concerning these assumptions is strikingly expressed in the following passage, showing, at the same time, once more Freud's astuteness in matters of the philosophy of science:

> One may surely give oneself up to a line of thought, and following it up as far as it leads, simply out of scientific curiosity, or—if you prefer—as *advocatus diaboli*, without, however, making a pact with the devil about it. . . . At all events, there is no way of working out this idea except by combining facts with pure imagination many times in succession and thereby departing far from observation. We know that the final result becomes the more untrustworthy the oftener one does this in the course of building up a theory, but the precise degree of uncertainty is not ascertainable. One may have gone ignominiously astray [1920, p. 190f.].

A large part of psychoanalytic theory deals with the vicissitudes of the instincts and their transformations, such as reversal into the opposite, repression, and sublimation. These concepts do not pose the same logical questions as, for instance, the concept of the unconscious; they refer to interrelationships among facts and successions of patterns, all of which are more or less directly observable. But since these transformations include a very long span of time and permit of alternative manifestations, we soon get involved in problems of the methods of verification and confirmation; these we shall take up in later sections. Here we should like to give just an example of how Freud arrives at the assumption that such traits as exceptional orderliness, cleanliness, parsimony, and obstinacy, in adults, are related to anality and the process of bowel movement in early childhood, thus constituting aspects of the instinctual pattern of anal eroticism. Freud first observed the repeated coexistence of the traits mentioned and then turned to the history of the persons who exhibited them. These were found to have been in the habit of refusing to empty the bowel, deriving an incidental pleasure from the act of defecation. Since these peculiarities tend to disappear once childhood has passed, the anal zone seems to have lost its erotogenic significance; but the constant appearance of the traits listed may, according to Freud, be brought into relation with the disappearance of the anal erotism of the persons concerned. Freud proceeds to show the theoretical relation between the trait syndrome and activities related to the anal zone. The triad of cleanliness, orderliness, and reliability is said to give exactly the impression of a reaction formation against an interest in things that are unclean and intrusive and ought not to be on the body. Freud refers to the saying, "Dirt is matter in the wrong place." He admits that to bring obstinacy into relation with interest in defecation seems no easy task, but points to the fact that infants can very early behave with great self-will about parting with their stools (1908, p. 45). Freud introduces materials from ancient civilizations, myths, fairy tales, dreams, and superstitions as a further means of verification of the anal theory by demonstrating that in these archaic modes of thought money comes into a close relationship with excrement.

The correlation between the three traits of cleanliness, orderliness, and obstinacy has been statistically confirmed by Sears

(1936). In the psychoanalytic system these empirical relations are not disconnected from such theoretical considerations as those on infantile sexuality and repression. Freud's scientific procedure can be illustrated once more by his theoretical deduction of the observation that one may expect but little of the "anal character" in adults who have not repressed the erotogenic quality of the anal zone, as for example certain homosexuals.

In addition to the evidence from genetic sequences and from symbolic materials like dreams and myths, Freud attempts to support the transformation of the original interest in excrement and dirt into a later interest in cleanliness and orderliness by referring to the occasional breaking through of the older attitude in spite of the fact that a reaction formation took place, and to the exaggeration of the new attitude which from the point of view of "economy" seems to indicate a struggle against a force in the opposite direction. An independent empirical study which has led me to a systematic inventory of criteria of this kind will be discussed below.

While Freud gave prominence to such physical activities as oral and anal ones and considered them as prototypes and models for other types of activities, the neo-Freudians consider these bodily activities as but one manifestation of broader social events. Only a large and at present unavailable body of data could help us to choose between these alternative hypotheses. On the basis of the evidence accumulated thus far it would seem that although bodily events have a distinction of their own, they still are capable of being, and actually are, modified by the larger cultural contexts in which they obviously are embedded.

The material discussed in this and the preceding section seems to warrant the conclusion that Freud was aware of the principal problems of theory construction and of the philosophy of science. On the whole he introduces his concepts very carefully, distinguishing what we now call the postulatory from the operational elements of the theory and allowing their interplay as he moves along. However, some more formal attempts in the direction of an axiomatization of the psychoanalytic system would be quite useful. We are not speaking here of a logical or quantitative formalization in the strict sense but merely of the more systematic differentiation between basic assumptions and their derivations. For example, a combination of the assumptions of infantile sexuality and of repression may be able to cover many of the more specific theorems in psychoanalysis. As we have seen, Freud himself has derived the concept of unconsciousness from his observations about repression. Such an attempt at a systematization of psychoanalysis would be helpful in uncovering the logical contradictions, empirical gaps, insufficient evidences, and related flaws inherent in the system. In spite of its suggestive character and in the main logically appropriate approach, in many aspects psychoanalysis still remains programmatic, as Freud himself has so often emphasized.

It must furthermore not be forgotten that Freud often talks in an abbreviated manner, for example when he speaks about the "existence of the unconscious" or when he uses such expressions as "the superego, or the ego" being such and such, or doing this and that. However, this manner of speech does not, as a rule, lead to serious consequences. Freud always continued to work on the improvement of his concepts and their relations to each other, and to check them against observational data. The two procedures are often combined in his writings, but mostly it is not difficult to discern which definitions are "syntactical" and which "semantical."

In spite of Freud's caution and his fine sense for scientific procedure, psychoanalytic theory remains vague in many places. Freud is aware of this fact; in one place he speaks of the "superb indefiniteness" of the term "instinct." But he tries to defend concepts of this kind when he says:

> We can claim for them the same value as approximations as belongs to the corresponding intellectual scaffolding found in other natural sciences and we look forward to their being modified, corrected and more precisely determined as more experience is accumulated and sifted. So too it will be entirely in accordance with our expectations if the basic concepts and principles of the new science (instinct, nervous energy, etc.) remain for a considerable time no less indeterminate than those of the older sciences (force, mass, attraction, etc.) [1940, p. 36].

In this context we may recall a statement made by Otto Neurath to the effect that "new ideas of scientific importance start mostly with vague and sometimes queer explanations," and we should heed his advice that "one can love exactness and nevertheless consciously tolerate a certain amount of vagueness" (1938, p. 21), advice which he apparently considers necessary to give to an empiricist.

Pointing to the frequent use of analogies, many critics of Freud feel, and not entirely without justification, that Freud at times exceeded the legitimate degree of vagueness. Freud himself thinks that some of the difficulties in his speculations concerning the life and death instincts come from our being obliged to operate with "metaphorical expressions peculiar to psychology (or more correctly psychology of the deeper layers)."

Freud assumes that some of the shortcomings would disappear if for the psychological terms we could substitute "physiological or chemical" ones. Freud explicitly states that until then we have to deal with analogies, and that analogies "prove nothing." Their function is to make one "feel more at home" (1933, p. 103).

We come here to perhaps the most serious objection that can be raised against the psychoanalytic system. This is given by Freud's occasional use of analogies which seem to go distinctly beyond the heuristic stage. In discussing the unconscious, Freud himself raises the question whether or not he is merely dealing with animistic analogies. He points out that the psychoanalytic assumption of unconscious mental activity may be nothing but a further development of that primitive animism which caused our own consciousness to be reflected in all around us (1915c, p. 104). After some further deliberation, however, Freud rejects his own objection, and we must agree with him as far as the particular case in question is concerned.

There also are many mechanistic analogies in Freud, although these are mostly used for the explicit purpose of stating mere formal similarities. One becomes impressed by the carefulness with which Freud avoids an oversimplified and uncritical dualistic psychophysical parallelism. He speaks of the "insoluble difficulties" of psychophysical parallelism, or of interactionism for that matter, and often prefers to talk about the psychological versus the physiological "language," or about physiology as slated some day to supersede psychology, rather than about causal relationships between two metaphysically distinct systems.

While the analogical procedure is not suited for purposes of ultimately proving a scientific hypothesis, it must be stressed that the function of analogy is more important in psychology than it is in physics. In physics pictorial types of relationships are available as an important heuristic guide prior to the establishment of abstractly and objectively defined terms used in theory construction. In the early stages of scientific theory construction, such as we are witnessing in psychoanalysis, in which the abstract terms are not yet fully defined, the analogy plays an important role in the discovery and communication of relationships. Their use by Freud turned out to be extremely fruitful, perhaps because it was coupled with a sense of responsibility for scientific procedure which led to his being aware most of the time of the stage of scientific inquiry and testing in which he happened to be involved.

Remoteness from the Phenotype

Freud's turning away from the directly observable, obvious, face-value picture of personality and from its common-sense interpretation, which is illustrated in his use of the concepts of unconscious and of instinct, is one of the most impressive and at the same time one of the most bewildering aspects of psychoanalytic theory. This departure from the obvious, directly observed phenomenon which we shall now study in its relational aspects has taken two different forms. First, there is an attention to certain relationships which had remained largely unexplored before the advent of psychoanalysis. Observations of pathological states prompted Freud to explore infantile sexuality, dreams, the psychopathology of everyday life, the seemingly irrational types of symptoms, both normal and neurotic, and eventually fairy tales, myths, and works of art. All these unusual types of data were exposed by him to scientific inquiry. The second surprise element in Freud's approach lies in the unusual and unfamiliar interpretations which were given to familiar data of overt behavior. In either case certain forms of behavior were examined in a wider genetic and dynamic context and inferences drawn which went beyond—and often were in seeming contradiction to—the obvious gross characteristics of behavior. Sometimes these gross characteristics are called "phenotypical" in psychology, in a modified usage of the familiar biological term. The inferences concerned are in line with the departure from the immediate pictorial appearance in modern physics to which we have referred in the introductory section.

To many critics it has seemed disturbing that in certain psychoanalytic contexts extreme friendliness is interpreted as a sign of hostility, extreme tidiness as a sign of preoccupation with dirt, or extreme boredom as a sign of intense interest. However, this seeming discrepancy with observation does not mean that there is no set of specified conditions and rules which determine when friendliness is to be interpreted as friendliness and when as aggression. We will discuss those specifications in a moment. But we must anticipate there that it often turns out that if we draw our inferences from a greater variety of manifestations, using maximal as well as minimal cues, instead of taking verbalized statements or social techniques as directly valid, we arrive at a more fruitful and unified interpretation of personality which furnishes an improved basis for long-range predictions. We may go so far as to say that it is the very shift from the level of external, overt manifestation to the level of motivational dynamics which opens the way to a science of personality. This shift is altogether the merit of psychoanalysis.

In some previous discussion of psychoanalysis the present writer (this volume, Chapter 1) has suggested that it is primarily the interpretive extrapolation into a hypothetical central region that justifies the use of the label, "depth psychology," as contrasted with the more conventional surface psychology which concentrates upon the directly accessible gross features of behavior or of experienced phenomena at their face value.

Scientific inference concerning central processes, that is, the assumption of internal states on the basis of external evidence, cannot be defended unless it is based on a wide variety of circumstantial evidence. In this sense central inference had never been truly attempted before psychoanalysis. Correspondingly psychoanalysis, especially in its beginnings, comparatively neglected not only the surface observations in their specific identity but also the so-called distal achievements—that is, end results—of behavior (see Chapter 1). As was pointed out by Egon Brunswik (1952), the major objective criteria for units of action in psychology, such as those suggested by Albert P. Weiss, Hunter, Tolman, and Hull, are explicitly and implicitly based on a recognition of "vicarious functioning" of behavioral means relative to the same distal goal.

The approach of psychoanalysis shows important differences from this approach to behavior, both falling short of it and going beyond it. The regrouping of manifest observable facts was at least in the beginnings of psychoanalysis undertaken exclusively in terms of "cause" or "need" rather than in terms of "effect" (as would be the case in Tolman's [1932] purposive behaviorism). Not only are there alternative manifestations to the same need in psychoanalysis, there are even alternative goals to the same need. The chief differentiating characteristic of psychoanalysis is to have pointed out sameness of cause rather than sameness of end. Thus the conscious or unconscious aspects of our reactions are not in the same way alternative as, for instance, running or swimming toward the same goal, to cite one of Tolman's experimental examples. One may argue that if somebody gives up the goal of, say, playing with dirt, for, say, painting, still the same goal is perceived. Against this objection it could be pointed out that such sublimated activities as painting represent a scattering to essentially shifted forms of adjustment and behavioral effects in spite of their asserted relatedness, in a genetic manner, to the same primitive instinctual tendencies.

In the discussion of Freudian theory, the influence of Darwin is usually stressed. Freud himself made some remarks to this effect in his autobiography (1925). This influence is certainly discernible as far as his theory of evolution is concerned. However, unlike that of Darwin, Freud's view and classification of behavior phenomena is not based on criteria of "adjustment."

In discussing Darwin's influence on Freud, Bergmann (1943) stresses as a positive feature the naturalistic approach and as negative what he calls the teleological aspects of the Freudian doctrine, that is, explanations from the point of view of a goal, such as survival. It will be remembered that we have taken the opposite stand, that is, that psychoanalytic explanations are oriented primarily toward causes rather than toward ends.

The relative absence of distal result reference, that is, of emphasis on fixed goals and environmental effects in Freud's theory, which the present writer has pointed out from the standpoint of academic psychology (Chapter 1), has also been noted by some of Freud's most devoted intimates. Using somewhat different means of conceptualization, Anna Freud (1936) has pointed out that at least in the more orthodox forms of psychoanalytic theory and diagnosis all efforts concentrate backward into "depth," that is, toward the common "historical" origin of the various manifestations. More recently, Suzanne Bernfeld (1951) has related this predilection of Freud for "digging" into the past of the individual to his fondness for archaeology, which she has shown to have been his only major hobby.

In defense of the depth-psychological type of approach it must be emphasized that the temporary abandonment of concern with the reaching of goals has turned out to be an eye-opener for all the vastly different manifestations which may be linked functionally to an assumed common drive. One of the most fruitful consequences of this seems to me to be that it now becomes possible to link the motivational patterns thus uncovered not only to gross features of behavior but also to minimal cues. It is crucial that neither the gross nor the subtle features are taken "at face value" in this process. One of the main advantages to be gained from the concept of drives would be lost if we failed to transcend the straight description or direct categorization of behavior. Quite aside from the validity of the psychoanalytic inferences, one is forced to recognize that they have shown a great resolving power in bringing together conceptually the most diverse varieties of apparently unrelated behavioral features.

The exclusive emphasis on manifest behavior and its further effects proved to be sterile both in the study of personality and in the earlier, static classificatory systems in psychiatry. It is to a large extent the fact that in our culture basic impulses must be disguised or transformed to pass individual and social censorship which makes it necessary to unearth the hidden themes of motivation. Academic psychology dealt chiefly with types of behavior in which there is more continuity all through the course of life, and was less concerned with the kind of behavior which gets drastically deflected and changes the basic form of manifestation as development proceeds.

In the majority of cases it is verbal behavior such as dreams, free associations, and the like, rather than overt motor behavior which psychoanalysis takes as the basis for drive interpretations. This does not mean that psychoanalysis is "introspectionistic," however. As everyone knows, it is precisely through psychoanalysis that we have learned to doubt the face value of introspection. In behaviorism we often find the tacit assumption that motor behavior is superior to verbal behavior as a validating criterion of constructs. This predilection for overt behavior as the final measure of validity is not justified. We can "lie" with gestures as well as we can with words, either deliberately or as a matter of unrecognized practice. If we observe the motor behavior of two people in their interaction we may be more misled about their basic attitudes toward each other than if we study the verbal statements they make about each other.

However, the shift of emphasis from overt behavior to underlying dynamics was too radical in psychoanalysis. Even though it remains true that the variety of isolated behavioral manifestations is too diverse for scientific penetration, integration in terms of unorganized, instinctual dynamics alone is too universal an integration. While academic psychology and sociology tended to abstract only the gross features of behavior whenever they tried to cope with the unmanageable variety of behavioral manifestations, psychoanalysis did not altogether avoid the pitfall of motivational relativism and a genetic dissolution of overt adjustmental values. Most of Freud's thoughts are concerned with the innate instinctual development, while the discussion of the modification of the instincts under the restrictions and disapproval of the environment takes a secondary place. Such widely different patterns of social adjustment as that of, say, a criminal and a lawyer, a "saint" and a sexual masochist, are not adequately differentiated from one another in terms of the psychoanalytic theory of instinct taken in and by itself. Although it is of utmost importance to become cognizant of what these socially so diametrically opposite patterns may have in common, the differences existing between them must also be accounted for in any full-fledged and behaviorally oriented theory of personality. The concept of "sublimation," adduced in psychoanalysis to explain the transformation of certain instinctual energies into socially accepted channels and goals, remains vague and the conditions of this mechanism appear not to be fully specified in psychoanalytic theory. This shortcoming has been noted by some orthodox psychoanalytic theorists also.

In fairness to Freud it must be stressed that he made a definite effort to move from his predominant orientation toward the unconscious, irrational, and "archaic" to a consideration of so-called reality factors in his psychology of the ego and of the defense mechanisms. Some of the differentiations just mentioned are introduced there. However, Freud subordinated the development of the ego with its reality-oriented behavior under the supremacy of the id factors, that is, under the internal, biologically determined instinctual inpulses: "It is easy to see that the ego is that part of the id which has been modified by the direct influence of the external world through the perception-consciousness" (1923).

Freud tends to view character structure from a defensive point of view, and social influences as a series of traumata which bring to a halt or discontinue instinctual gratification and expression. While providing an understanding of an important aspect of the individual's attitude toward society, this view does not do justice to all the satisfactions gained from moving along constructive social avenues.

Within psychoanalysis, it was Heinz Hartmann (1939) who first stressed explicitly the partial independence of such outwardly adjustive processes as perception, learning, and thinking from the instinctual processes. In general, psychoanalysis has undergone, during the last few decades, some modification in the direction of including just those problems which it previously neglected. However, psychoanalytic expansion in this direction has been more programmatic than real, and there are a number of problems which can be solved only by an explicit integration of psychoanalysis with psychology and with sociology. The conceptual tools of psychoanalysis just are not sufficient fully to explain rational and social behavior (see this volume, Chapter 1). If we were to deny this we would obscure the essential theoretical contribution of Freud. Some of the resistances against admitting psychoanalysis to the circle of respectable sciences may well be based on an unrecognized transfer from the realization of the failure of psychoanalysis to deal adequately with reasoning behavior.

While the neglect of certain environmental factors in Freud's theory can hardly be questioned, there are, at the other extreme, such overt behavioral psychologists as Skinner (1953), who tend to look askance at the assumption of special internal dynamisms and attempt to offer an explanation of the facts observed by Freud in terms of direct relationships between resultant behavior and the stimulus environment. However, a translation of the psychoanalytic concepts into the terminology of such a stimulus-response approach, useful as it may be in certain contexts, has its difficulties and limitations. The specific contribution psychoanalysis may be able to make to stimulus-response psychology by stressing the function of internal agencies is best illustrated by means of the superego concept. Although the superego designates that aspect of our behavior dispositions which is most markedly determined by the transmission—via stimulus-response learning—of cultural norms and ethical standards, psychoanalytic theory at the same time stresses the irrational distortions which the external authorities undergo in the process of their absorption into the superego. Thus arises the seemingly paradoxical picture of a superego which originates outside—being an introjection of parental authorities and of the norms they represent—and which then becomes endowed with all kinds of unsocialized subjective tendencies (such as aggression) so that the end effect is frequently an irrational and unconscious distortion of the very values it is supposed to represent. Thus our moral feelings can probably not be fully explained by external cultural factors; they must be seen as reinforced by the internal, hostile feelings with which, in our childhood, we projectively imbued parental figures.

The very fact that moral behavior and especially moral feelings cannot be derived exclusively from the cultural institutions as learned by the example of adults makes it understandable that patterns of behavior acquired in childhood are often intensified in old age by means of some processes of internalization, in spite of the fact that they are not reinforced in later life and should therefore, according to the accepted principles of learning theory, slowly succumb to extinction. In 1942 the late Professor Hull, the foremost formalizer of classical learning theory, expressed to me his puzzlement about these facts and the difficulty he had in explaining the superego by his learning theory. Recent learning theories have paid some attention to these problems without, however, giving a fully satisfactory resolution (see Shoben, 1948). Skinner's above-mentioned reservations against psychoanalysis, on the other hand, seem to stem not so much from an involvement with classical learning theory as from a more general antitheoretical position which is directed against both psychoanalysis and learning theory.

It is interesting to note that quite generally Freud's major contribution to the understanding of social phenomena does not lie in the writings in which he deals directly with sociological phenomena. Here as elsewhere it is his personality theory which, in spite of its limitations, seems to emerge as the most powerful influence in the end. Thus, while such sociologists as Durkheim (1894) stress conformity to the social institution as something unequivocally positive, psychoanalysis helps us to distinguish the genuine from the compensatory conformity. At the behavioral level, the compensatory type of conformity is characterized by a compulsive, all-or-none character. It is excessive because it compensates for feelings of uncertainty and the attendant fear of becoming an outcast, and because it often serves the function of covering up the underlying resentment toward the social system as a whole, unconscious as this resentment may be. The compulsive conformist tends to adhere to the letter rather than the spirit of the social institutions. This tendency issues from a distortion and simplification of the system of norms and commands in the direction of what one may call unidimensional interpretation. Rules are adopted or enforced which are largely nonfunctional caricatures of our social institutions, based as they are on a misunderstanding of the ultimate intent of these institutions. The absence of a genuine incorporation of the values of society accounts for the rigidity of the conformity; at the same time it accounts for a certain unreliability, a readiness to shift allegiances suddenly and completely to other, sometimes diametrically opposite authorities or standards. In this and in most other ways the compensatory conformist defeats the very purposes which are inherent in any genuine adherence to a principle. The potential of psychoanalysis eventually to become involved in the systematic treatment of behavioral results after all, is shown to best advantage in the uncovering of fake mechanisms such as that just discussed.

As we have seen, the major emphasis of psychoanalysis is on internal causes; these include, in the language of psychoanalysis, "subjective fantasies" and generally the differential meanings external events acquire for the individual. Freud began to make progress in his understanding of hysteria only after he had given up the idea of a simple environmental causation of the disease by the traumata to which the patients themselves referred. Freud points out that only after the factor of the hysterical fantasies had been introduced did the structure of the neurosis and its relation to the patient "become conspicuous." Since the relationship of these fantasies to external factors is most complex and ambiguous, it seems in the long run far more parsimonious to assume the internal mechanisms postulated by psychoanalysis and to try to specify them operationally as fully as it is possible at a later time. Contrary to Skinner, we believe that such assumptions do not carry us outside of the "bounds of natural science." On the other hand, we do agree with Skinner on the point that the "looking inside the organism for an explanation of behavior" can easily lead to a neglect of environmental factors, and we readily acknowledge that it has done so in the case of psychoanalysis.

The Explanatory Value of Psychoanalysis: Motivation and Behavior

In spite of the one-sidedness of the depth-psychological approach, the unique contribution of psychoanalysis lies in the unified explanation of personality. Diverse classes of behavioral manifestations are subsumed under more general principles. Behavior is no longer defined in terms of its symptomatic characteristics but is viewed from a causal-genetic point of view.

The tangled relationships between overt behavior and the patterns of underlying "dynamics" have posed numerous methodological difficulties to objectification. There have been two major types of inadequacy in approaching these difficulties. First, some investigators worked on the basis of a tacit assumption of a perfect one-to-one correspondence between motivation and action. The concept of motivation thus is rendered a merely descriptive one; in fact, it becomes nothing but an unnecessary duplication of behavior rather than a truly explanatory, inferential construct imbued with some degree of independence. The scientist or diagnostician must avoid such direct projection of behavioral trends back into the subject without due consideration of the ambiguities inherent in the relationships between drives and behavior. To indulge in such projection in an almost postulatory fashion as is sometimes practiced would expose us to the accusation of circularity. A second and somewhat obsolete type of spurious attempt at explanation is given by the introduction of dynamic concepts which are so remote from behavior that they cannot be confirmed either directly or indirectly.

To help resolve the methodological problem involved in the definition and measurement of motivation separately from, and in a certain sense independently of, isolated bits of specific behavior, and at the same time to illustrate the way in which motivational tendencies can be operationally based on certain intercombinations of observed behaviors, the present writer (1942) has undertaken a statistical demonstration of the explanatory and predictive character of psychoanalytic concepts based on the systematic study of a large number of adolescents extending over a period of several years. For a limited set of problems, this was to be an empirical verification of psychoanalysis and was to take the place of the case-centered and thus necessarily somewhat fragmentary and often casual inferences of motivation customary in psychoanalysis. A direct intuitive assessment of underlying motivation was made, and these drive ratings were compared with the specific and directly observable behavioral techniques used by the subjects. Considering the fact that verbalized self-reports and short-sample behavioral techniques often reveal the phenotypic façade of a person rather than the genuinely dynamic tendencies of his behavior, several clinicians, closely familiar with the group of adolescents in question over a number of years, were asked to rate them with respect to the strength of their basic motivation as abstracted from a synopsis of a wide variety of long-range behavior contacts. By introducing motivational ratings we hoped to be able to account for apparently diverse manifestations, and hoped that, just as in psychoanalytic theory, an important lead for uncovering relationships might lie in comparatively few but fundamental characteristics of the subjects brought out in motivational ratings. Different classes of behavioral expressions seemingly not related to one another were found to be related to the same intuitively inferred drive, apparently as alternate manifestations of that drive. To give an example: overt behavioral ratings on "exuberance" and "irritability" were found to intercorrelate negatively with one another ($r = -.52$) and thus to be relatively incompatible; however, both these behavioral traits showed some positive correlation ($+.30$ and $+.42$) with the ratings on the drive for aggression. The so-called multiple correlation between rated aggression and the two diverse behavior features was found to be relatively high (+.73), thus establishing the principle of "alternative manifestations" of a drive. Our results can be more generally stated by saying that a knowledge of the type of drive variables stressed in psychoanalysis seems to hold good promise for behavior prediction of the "either-or" type just described statistically, which is in essence the either-criminal-or-lawyer type of prediction of which we have spoken in our above example from the discussion of psychoanalysis.

The results also indicate that we could not arrive at the underlying motivational variables by such conventionally used statistical means as factor analysis, at least not in its various forms customary to date. These and related techniques provide us with clusters of behavioral manifestations which intercorrelate highly with each other. The fact that certain manifestations may fully substitute for others renders the relationship in psychoanalysis that we are looking for much too complex to be handled in this simple manner. The type of evaluation of underlying motivations considered here allows for alternative manifestations of the same motivation or instinct which are negatively correlated or which may even be mutually exclusive even though probably genetically related.

The linking of the motivational ratings to behavioral manifestations constitutes at the same time a "rational reconstruction" of the so-called "intuitive" inferences made by the clinicians. This is done by the statistical establishment of the cues which they as a group used for their ratings. The relatively satisfactory interrater agreements which were obtained for the motivational ratings are a further indication of the fact that we are capable of perceiving not only the surface manifestations in their own right, but also the underlying personality structure. We "see" not only whether or not a person shows a friendly front but also whether his friendliness is genuine or "phony."

In the present context we are primarily interested in establishing those aspects of behavior that can be predicted on the basis of motivation ratings or a psychoanalytic appraisal of the underlying instinctual structure and those that cannot be predicted on such a basis. Since results suggest that the same underlying motivation may lead to a wide range of behavior, the further specification must hinge on other than "dynamic" factors. Among these further factors determining whether, say, underlying aggression is worked out in a socially constructive form or in neurotic symptoms, such extraneous factors as social and economic or occupational conditions will probably play a major role.

In summary, the study of motivation and behavior just reported constitutes an attempt to move from the level of the description of overt behavior and expressional techniques to the level of inferential hypotheses along basically psychoanalytic lines by discounting incidental effects of transient situations and by regrouping the forms of behavior in terms of common dynamics. In this manner we do arrive at comparatively few underlying tendencies which account for a wide array of behavioral manifestations seemingly unconnected with each other. It may be added that further evidence shows that we also arrive at predictions about fantasies of our subjects which are markedly superior to predictions based on the direct use of overt behavior. In our empirical work our assumption of the increased economy and greater explanatory value of constructs relating to underlying dynamics has been justified by means of a multiple-correlational analysis.

The one major way in which academic psychology has attempted explanations of behavior is by means of physiological models. So far not too many predictions from such models have been deduced, however; and those that have been refer to rather simple types of behavior, e.g., the laws of so-called gestalt perception or some of the basic mechanisms of learning. It is hardly an exaggeration to say that we may disregard these types of explanation as far as the field of personality is concerned. The nonphysiologically oriented learning theories have introduced, in somewhat piecemeal fashion, a number of constructs originally restricted to relatively simple types of behavior. There have been many attempts to expand learning theory to the area of problems covered by psychoanalysis. As we have exemplified above by means of the example of the progressive nonreinforced internalization of the superego, it seems doubtful that the commonly employed principles of learning are capable of explaining all of the major discoveries of psychoanalysis, the efforts of Gustav Bergmann (1943), of Dollard and Miller (1950), and of others notwithstanding. I shall come back to this point later.

The view that psychoanalysis is explanatory in contrast to most of academic psychology, which moves at the level of description, may be supported by reference to Feigl's theoretical discussion of levels of explanation. Feigl (1949) distinguishes four levels of scientific discourse. The first is the level of description, dealing with specific statements, logically in singular form, by means of which is stated what is directly observed. The second level is that of empirical laws, that is, of generalized functional relationships between relatively directly observable magnitudes. The third level, called first-order theories, involves a set of assumptions from which empirical laws can be derived. It is only by means of theory that a unification and an understanding of the functional relationships between facts as expressed in empirical laws can be achieved. While in first-order theory the constructs used are homogeneous with the operationally defined concepts used in the empirical laws, the constructs of the theories of the second order—the fourth level in Feigl's hierarchy—are heterogeneous to the empirical regularities which the theory purports to explain; an example is the physiological explanation of regularities of overt behavior. Feigl places psychoanalysis at the third level in this scheme, that is, at the level of first-order theories, together with the theories of Tolman and Hull. Although we follow Feigl to this point, the question remains whether or not a certain group of psychoanalytic concepts such as that of the unconscious should be considered to be as heterogeneous to behavior as are physiological constructs or explanations. It should be noted in this context that Feigl's somewhat restrained preference for physiological explanations of behavior is evident in all his writings. It is the assumption of the unconscious which establishes the major difference between psychoanalytic theory construction, on the one hand, and Tolman and Hull, on the other.

Before continuing the discussion of the properties of psychoanalytic concepts we should like to deal briefly with some more vaguely philosophical arguments which question the explanatory value of psychoanalysis. Toulmin (1948) argues that the psychoanalytic explanations constitute an account of "motives rather than of causes," since they provide the patient with plausible reasons for his neurosis and do not necessarily relate to objective facts. Expanding this argument, Flew (1949) states that Freud as a working psychoanalyst makes patients realize what their unconscious motives, purposes, and intentions are, and then proceeds as a theoretician to assume that the inferred unconscious processes are capable of producing real symptoms, while only "real" physiological and neurological processes could do such a thing and mere inferred unconscious processes have nothing to do with causes. Arguments of this kind stem from confusions about the nature of concepts; here we may follow Dingle (1949), who in his answer to Toulmin and Flew takes the point that the concept of the unconscious is in no way different from that of the atom or of light.

Far from identifying the reported motive and the objective explanation of behavior, the major merit of psychoanalysis is to have differentiated the two and to have unmasked and "discredited" as to their explanatory value the subjective experiences of motivation. The "manifest" phenotypic characteristics are now taken to provide only the indirect cues for inferences concerning the "latent" genotypic (conditional-genetic) forces of motivation.

In all the efforts to distinguish manifest behavior and latent motivation, surface and depth, our path is full of obstacles, some of which go beyond the merely methodological ones encountered in the procedures of scientific verification. One of these additional difficulties is a semantic one. The vocabulary of everyday language does not furnish us consistently with two separate sets of terms, one for overt behavior and the other for underlying motivation. Unless we are ready drastically to depart from familiar usage of terms, we must use "friendliness" for both the basically friendly outlook on life and for the techniques of friendliness—genuine or fake—by which this basic outlook may be implemented or pretended. The same holds for such terms as "aggression," "submissiveness," etc. Qualifying adjectives are needed to specify the meaning of the word "friendly" or "aggressive" in each case it is used. In the first place, such double usages make for unmanageable clumsiness; second, and more important, is the fact that they present a challenge to our claim that the splitting up of the vocabulary is really necessary.

This dilemma is in a formal sense similar to the one presented by the dual meaning of our common perceptual terms, which was pointed out by Egon Brunswik (1934). These terms too tend to have double reference, one to the personal and somewhat variable perceptual response, and the other to the interpersonal measured physical stimulus that underlies the so-called corresponding response with some, but by no means perfect, regularity. Examples are phenomenal versus measured size, shape, color, pitch, and so forth. Phenomenal size or shape can be experimentally shown to depend in a multiple fashion on a variety of measured sizes or shapes in our surroundings or at the retina. The same holds for color, and subjective pitch has since the time of Helmholtz been known to depend on both the frequency and the intensity of sound, so that "pitch" is no longer admissible as a synonym or translation for "frequency." If in view of these tangled relationships the conceptual separation of perceptual stimulus and response can be said no longer to constitute a case of entities superfluously multiplied, neither can, we may add, the separation of behavior and motivation with their similarly tangled relationships. Each time separations of this kind had to be substituted for previous identifications in the history of science, there was irrational, emotional resistance against the recognition of the equivocations or ambiguities involved. These resistances remind the present writer of the syndrome of "intolerance of ambiguity" she has found to be a major characteristic of the authoritarian personality (see this volume, Chapter 2).

Certainly, both our "motivations" and "behaviors" are constituted from overt behavior, as both stimuli and perceptual responses constitute different types of observational experiences. But motivations are arrived at through a synopsis of the constant elements in many bits of behavior, while the latter are momentary manifestations. The important point is that the two sets are to some extent operationally independent, and that they turn out to be actually independent to a surprising degree by the frequency of alternative manifestations of identical motivations, and vice versa. An independent nomenclature for the levels will in the end have to be established. This would remove much of the temptation to fall back into an oversimplified single-level treatment of the motivational aspects of behavior as is still present in such recently suggested concepts as that of "manifest need." For example, it can be shown (this volume, Chapter 1) that Murray's frequently quoted list of "needs" (1938) is by no means free of duplications of overt behavior patterns, his own warnings to the contrary notwithstanding.

In the process of the conceptual differentiation between motivation and behavior a further semantic aspect will have to play an integral part. We mean the use of minimal cues such as those to be described later in this paper as an indication of the frankness or "genuineness" of behavioral expressions.

The problem of genuineness of behavior which has proved so crucial for the considerations in this section is comparable to that of strict "correspondence" versus "noncorrespondence" between a certain stimulus variable and a certain response variable in perception to which we have referred above, and thus to the problem of the accuracy or correctness of perceptual performance.

ARE PSYCHOANALYTIC CONCEPTS HYPOTHETICAL CONSTRUCTS OR INTERVENING VARIABLES?

In a paper which has attracted much attention in the literature on psychological theory, MacCorquodale and Meehl (1948) proposed to distinguish between "intervening variables" as quantities obtained by specified manipulations of the values of empirically observed variables, and "hypothetical constructs" which involve assumptions about an additional entity, process, or event not directly observed. Statements dealing with intervening variables contain no terms which are not definable either directly or by reduction sentences in terms of empirical variables. According to MacCorquodale and Meehl, they represent nothing more than shorthand summaries about observables and contain no inferences about the occurrence of unobserved events. Carnap's dispositional concepts are given as an illustration of intervening variables, while "electron" is given as an example of a hypothetical construct. While it is admitted that the statements about electrons also are supported by observations, these are said not to exhaust the entire meaning of the sentences about electrons.

In the field of psychology, hypothetical constructs are illustrated by MacCorquodale and Meehl by physioneurological models of behavior. A parallel is drawn between intervening variables and "abstracta" in the sense of Reichenbach (1938), and hypothetical constructs as corresponding to Reichenbach's "illata." To the latter inferred entities belong such constructs as other persons' "minds." These are inferred on the basis of our sensory impressions, but statements involving them are not reducible to sentences about impressions; they have what Reichenbach calls a "surplus meaning." MacCorquodale and Meehl assume surplus meaning only in case an effort at explanation from another domain is made. Thus physiological explanations of behavior are assumed to have surplus meaning in the behavioral frame of reference only, not in the framework of physiology proper.

In the rather sketchy application of their distinction to psychoanalysis, MacCorquodale and Meehl point out that psychoanalysts originally introduced such terms as libido, censorship, and superego as intervening variables, claiming them to be conventionalized designations of observable properties; but they add that in the course of further discussion there usually is an unnoticed shift in the direction of using them as hypothetical constructs. The authors point to certain elaborations of the concept of libido which Freud first introduced as an abbreviation for a set of sexual needs but then proceeded to describe as "flowing," as being "dammed up," as "tending to regress to early channels," as "being converted" into anxiety, and as "making its energy available" to the ego. The authors do not object to the concept of libido on the grounds that it refers to unobservables, but merely because the postulates concerning existential properties are not explicitly announced. A further argument which MacCorquodale and Meehl raise against the "hydraulic" analogy of the libido as used by Freud is that analogies of this kind would have to consider the knowledge now available in physiology. They continue to argue that no known properties of nervous tissues could correspond to these hydraulic properties and that the nervous system does not contain tubes and pipes.

Although we find the distinction between intervening variables and hypothetical constructs useful because of its emphasis on differences in the degree of indirectness of evidence, we at the same time consider it in many ways misleading. First, the authors seem to conceive of hypothetical constructs mainly as assumptions about physiological processes. They do not discuss what seems another frequent type of hypothetical construct, that is, one in which the actual properties are neither at present determined nor expected to be determined in the foreseeable future.

Second, by reiterating that intervening variables are definable in terms of observables, the authors fail to stress that statements containing intervening variables can, at least in principle, no more be exhausted by statements about observables than can those about hypothetical constructs. We recall here the changes in the views on verification which occurred within the school of logical positivism. To quote Carnap (1936, 1937):

> If by verification is meant a definite and final establishment of truth, then no synthetical sentence is ever verifiable. We can only confirm a sentence more and more. Therefore we shall speak of the problem of confirmation rather than of verification.

According to Carnap, even such simple sentences as "There is a piece of white paper on the table" need an infinite number of operations and statements to be verified. Empirical laws are not verifiable since they refer to an infinite number of instances while all observation is finite.

According to this view, the difference between universal and particular statements must be minimized. It also follows that the interpretations of the testability criterion in terms of complete verifiability or of complete falsifiability are inadequate and too restrictive. This holds especially for the physical disposition terms referred to above, such as "magnetic" or "electrically charged"; these are introduced by means of so-called reduction sentences which, in spite of their function as operational links, have the character of partial or conditional definitions. They are not definitions in the strict sense of the word, however; they are fragmentary specifications of meaning. Following Carnap, Hempel (1952) states explicitly that sentences containing disposition terms cannot be fully translated into statements about observables; they involve "open" terms and require an indefinite series of conditions to be tested.

It seems to follow from these considerations that intervening variables in the sense of MacCorquodale and Meehl, referring as they do to a generalized variety of conditions, are likewise elements of "explanation" even though they are of a less tentative and less "theoretical" variety than hypothetical constructs. Since the examples given by the authors for hypothetical constructs are almost exclusively concerned with physiological explanations of behavior, it is not quite clear whether or not their distinction coincides with Hempel's between theoretical constructs introduced by postulates, on the one hand, and concepts introduced by definitions or reduction chains based on observation, on the other. In practically all of the concrete instances of theory construction in science it is not an easy task to decide whether a given concept has been arrived at primarily on the basis of theoretical considerations or primarily by observation. This holds especially for such a relatively immature theory as psychoanalysis. We would venture to guess that Freud, guided by some relatively fragmentary initial impressions, arrived at many of his constructs in a process of building a theoretical structure, with empirical interpretation lagging somewhat behind. A careful reading of Freud makes it quite clear that more space is devoted to the definition of theoretical constructs, such as superego, ego, and id, in terms of their structural relations to each other than by reference to the relations of these various constructs to observation.

The distinction between intervening variables and hypothetical constructs may to a certain extent be preserved in the face of the above arguments by differentiating between two kinds of surplus meaning. The first kind could briefly be labeled "observational surplus"; it is given by the inexhaustibility of possible tests to be applied in the confirmation of an empirical statement and therefore is present in all intervening variables. The second we will call "existential surplus"; by this we mean primarily the hypothetical transcendence beyond the existential frame of reference in question, such as when a microstructure is adduced in the explanation of macrobehavior.

The involved character of the above considerations makes it difficult to decide whether in psychoanalytic theory we deal mainly with hypothetical constructs or with intervening variables. For example, the concept of unconsciousness may be classified as a hypothetical construct if it is meant to refer to a theoretical system, not yet determined in physiological terms but with the claim that one day it will be determined. In this case it involves the assumption of an entity which goes beyond the behavioral framework per se and from which many particular occurrences are being derived. On the other hand, if we conceive of the unconscious wish to kill one's father, or the unconscious wish for failure, then we have before us what may be considered intervening variables, since reduction to the if-then type of statement seems possible for all cases involving the use of these terms. Many of the psychoanalytic terms are disposition terms; they refer to latent qualities which become manifest only under specified conditions. As disposition terms they are intervening variables in the sense of MacCorquodale and Meehl. As we have seen, however, their definition remains incomplete and open since we cannot specify all conditions and manners in which latent tendencies become manifest. For this reason it may be preferable not to consider a disposition predicate as defined by the total number of reduction sentences formulated at any given stage of a science. The actually stated conditions of testing constitute as a rule but a limited selection at which we may have arrived by an informal process of ingenuity, leaving the possibility open for the discovery of new conditions to be added to or substituted for the old ones.

Since intervening variables share with hypothetical constructs the fact that excess value is being added to the observed phenomena, their distinction should be viewed as one of degree rather than of principle. However, while Bergmann, in a recent survey of theoretical psychology (1953) which appeared after the relevant parts of the present paper had been written, goes so far as to obliterate the distinction altogether, the present writer would favor retaining it as a gradual one. Hypothetical constructs are higher-order concepts from which intervening variables can be derived. In Feigl's scheme of explanations, mentioned above, the disposition terms have to do with empirical regularities, while hypothetical constructs may furnish the constructions by which the disposition terms are unified. But again we must stress that disposition terms as such already contain unifying principles, although there remains a difference in the degree of accessibility to confirmation which may be ascribed to the heterogeneity of the hypothetical constructs relative to the observations to which they are adduced.

The fact that intervening variables are not fully defined and fully interpreted in terms of observation raises the question whether inferential concepts should be employed at all. Against such a restriction we hold that overly specific or narrow concepts are usually not very helpful. Psychoanalytic theory is far from succumbing to this danger. It abounds in both intervening variables and hypothetical constructs, the specification of which often falls short of even the more liberal requirements adopted in this paper.

However, Freud's use of a mentalistic and phenomenalistic language creates the erroneous impression that he stayed closer to the verbal behavior of his patients than he actually did. These and other phenomena and symptoms were used by him as a basis for the construction of genuinely inferential concepts, although the connecting links between the two levels were not always made explicit. The indicated narrowing of the gap between intervening variables and hypothetical constructs may support our tendency to reduce the stringency of the requirements for the establishment of hypothetical constructs.

Here we must add a few critical remarks concerning MacCorquodale and Meehl's requirement that hypothetical concepts which refer to physiological entities must correspond to our present-day knowledge in physiology. The progress of empirical science would be unduly hampered if all our explanatory terms had to be specified fully in terms of the discipline from which they are taken. Progress in physics has been greatly furthered by the use of often wild-sounding assumptions or models. We have seen that Freud was fully aware of the fact that in view of the state of the biological sciences he could not utilize knowledge from physiology and anatomy; yet he did not hesitate to improve his own models, and was amply rewarded. His hydraulic model, mentioned above, led to a fruitful conception of psychological relationships, and such visualizations as that of the dammed-up libido having to use devious channels when blocked led to a deeper penetration of the relationships involved and to improved predictions. Similarly, to think of repression in terms of "keeping something down" so that stronger forces are necessary to counteract the repressed force, often leading to an intensification of the counteractive forces, seems to be a more productive way of thinking about the processes involved than would be a purely descriptive statement about a sequence of certain events. As far as the possibility of an eventual reduction of these analogies to physiological observation is concerned, Freud was, as we have seen, most helpful. The question of the reduction of psychoanalysis to physiology is, however, an empirical and not a logical one.

In the literature there seem to be differences of opinion about whether science tends to proceed from hypothetical constructs to intervening variables or in the opposite direction. The question is raised as to which of the two represents the more mature stage of scientific development. It seems that scientists, especially those with great ingenuity, have frequently proceeded from observations directly to hypothetical constructs and have derived the intervening variables later, although sometimes the procedure was reversed. The most fruitful policy seems to be that of an alternation between the cultivation of the images and constructs with all their richness of meaning and a concerted effort toward a more precise observational specification of the terms involved. There can be no doubt that the ultimate function of science is the achievement of these greater specifications and clarifications. For the sake of the continued creativity of the scientific process, however, it is important to keep in mind that the specifications do not always reflect the full content of the original meaning. Thus Freud at first made relatively specific observations about repression of sex instincts; these observations stimulated him to introduce the concept of the unconscious; only after that did he proceed to specify a number of other mechanisms which account for the transformation of unconscious material and which constitute the heart of the Freudian theory. The oscillation between hypothetical constructs and intervening variables seems to afford a protection against both a too-narrow operationalism and the dangers of meaningless generalization.

Attempts at Confirmation of Psychoanalytic Hypotheses

As we have seen, the elements of overt behavior and of inferred motivation vary to a certain degree independently. But since the underlying motivation is often unconscious and cannot, therefore, be verbalized by the subject, and since it also is disguised by the behavioral techniques used by the subject, there are difficulties inherent in the observation and measurement of the underlying motives. By referring to concepts more removed from the immediate data, psychoanalysis has lengthened the chains of intellectual and experimental work which connect the principles with the protocols or observation. We may recall the statement of Philipp Frank (1941) that in modern physics greater ingenuity is needed to find ways of verifying the theories in question, and that this fact is a result of the greater abstractness of concepts. He has pointed out how easily the statements of traditional Newtonian physics could be verified by observation since they were a direct formulation of our everyday experience, obvious and plausible to common sense. He goes on to explain that "in Einstein's general theory of relativity, however, the description of the operations by which the quantities involved could be measured becomes a serious and complex task. It becomes an essential part of the theory" (pp. 19-20).

Psychoanalysis thus shares with physics in the fact that their statements do not lend themselves to direct and obvious confirmation. In either case, the highly interpretive statements involved do not carry the rules of their confirmation as obviously with themselves as do descriptive statements. The situation in psychoanalysis was further complicated by a certain tendency—leading obviously into a blind alley—to attempt an isolation of some of its statements which could only be understood in the context of other statements, and by some futile attempts to find an *experimentum crucis*. But there is also increasing realization of the fact that more stress should be placed on the verification of predictions than of the theories themselves.

Several possible ways to circumvent the methodological difficulties involved in the approach to the latent level will now be discussed briefly.

Let us begin with attempts at verification based on the therapeutic process. The ego defenses which are at work to prevent the patient from consciously facing many of his basic tendencies or conflicts are being gradually removed in this process, so that a more correct picture of the underlying dynamic realities emerges. Many promising attempts are being made to render the therapeutic diagnosis and procedure accessible to intersubjective scrutiny. Recording of the procedure allows submission of the material to more than one observer, a checking of predictions, and a comparison of interpretations and evaluations, the latter being stressed especially by Kubie (1952).

One of the most important aspects in the objectification of psychoanalytic knowledge in general will be the making explicit of the cues which the therapist uses in his interpretations. At the same time this will help to reduce the subjectivity of the individual interpretive process. Freud's benign yet sophisticated outlook on the dangers of interpretation may be illustrated by the following quotation:

Our justification for making such inferences and interpolations and the degree of certainty attaching to them of course remain open to criticism in each individual instance; and it is not to be denied that it is often exceedingly difficult to arrive at a decision—a fact which finds expression in the lack of agreement among analysts. . . . For in psychology, unlike physics, we are not always concerned with things which can only arouse a cold scientific interest. Thus we shall not be so very greatly surprised if a woman analyst who has not been sufficiently convinced of the intensity of her own desire for a penis also fails to assign an adequate importance to that factor in her patients. But such sources of error, arising from the personal equation, have, when all is said and done, no great significance. If one looks through old textbooks upon the use of the microscope, one is astonished to find the extraordinary demands which were placed upon the personality of those who made observations with that instrument while its technique was young, and of which there is no question today [1940].

Next is the experimental approach to underlying motives. This approach has thus far been satisfactory only in certain specific directions. Since the ego defenses are nearer to the surface, they have proved particularly attractive for experimental investigation. Thus we find a number of experiments aimed at verifying psychoanalytic statements on fixation, regression, repression, and projection. Sears (1936) and more recently Hilgard (1952) have summarized and discussed many of these experiments. It is interesting to note that Sears comes to the conclusion, and we follow him here, that hypotheses on fixation and regression have been better confirmed experimentally than those on repression and projection—and, we would add, better than those on reaction formation. This agrees well with one of our contentions made above. Fixation is indeed a descriptive concept referring either to persistent attachment to a certain love object or arrest on a certain developmental level. We may refer here to an experiment with newborn rats (Wolf, 1943). For a period of a few weeks some were blindfolded and the others had their ears stopped. When, after full growth was attained, the rats were put under stress, the first group developed functional seeing difficulties, and the second group functional hearing difficulties. In this experiment it was possible to isolate early trauma and to show the ensuing fixation and regression. Blindfolding and ear-stopping at a later date did not lead to the same consequences, which is in line with psychoanalytic emphasis on the earliest phases of infancy. The effect of certain infantile frustrations was demonstrated by Hunt (1941). Rats starved in early infancy were found to eat and to hoard more food in later life than those who had been fed satisfactorily while young. By producing different types of conflict in animals, Masserman (1943) studied some aspects of the origin of neurosis in animals, and even the effects of what amounted to various types of therapy. Only a relatively small segment of psychoanalytic theory can be effectively tested with animals, however.

The relation of frustration to regression has also been demonstrated in children. Barker, Dembo, and Lewin (1941) first induced a group of children to play with parts of toys, the gaps to be filled out in imagination. Then the children were shown a fuller and more attractive set of toys through a glass window. Their approach to the available toys as well as their general behavior deteriorated markedly after this frustration.

The relative difficulty of studying experimentally such further mechanisms as repression or reaction formation has above been ascribed to the fact that the concepts involved derive from the more inferential and abstract parts of psychoanalytic theory. Repression was originally described by Freud in connection with the handling of threatening id impulses, primarily those of sex and aggression. Complex conditions, such as those involved in the analysis of transference, are required before what was repressed can become conscious. Most of the frequently adduced experiments dealing with such facts as memory for overtly pleasant or unpleasant words cannot be brought to bear on psychoanalytic assumptions of this kind, for these are concerned with quite a different matter. Since repression proper extends to the ideational content originally connected with the forbidden instinct, the selection of words which are consciously pleasant or unpleasant for the average person may have very little dynamic relevance for a particular subject. Furthermore, contrary to widespread belief, Freud did not assume that only the pleasant is remembered. In *Beyond the Pleasure Principle* (1920) he discussed the tendency of children to reproduce anxiety-inducing experiences in play as well as in dreams in order to achieve mastery of the traumatic situation.

Misunderstandings of psychoanalytic theory have arisen when in the manner described statements concerning repression, which originally were intended to refer to unconscious—that is, inferred rather than overt—processes, are erroneously taken as purely descriptive statements of conscious contents. As in physics, a simple identification of statements containing disposition terms with statements about manifest events is not permissible.

Some of the leading learning theorists, such as Dollard and Miller (1950) and Mowrer (1950), have contributed challenging and life-near experiments conceived in the genuine spirit of psychoanalysis. Certain mechanisms, such as regression, fixation, and displacement, were effectively demonstrated by these experiments. Sharing a "historical" outlook with psychoanalysis, the learning approach has highlighted microscopically such mechanisms as reinforcement or generalization which are also implicit in psychoanalysis. However, learning theory cannot completely explain why in certain contexts we learn as little as we do, as psychoanalysis has impressively demonstrated. Maier's (1949) assumption of two different mechanisms of behavior, the motivation and the frustration behavior, constitutes a recognition of the same kind of fact; in Maier's system only motivation behavior is the learning type of behavior, frustration-instigated behavior is not.

The general reason why the typical psychological laboratory experiment is not well suited to the purpose of verifying or disproving psychoanalytic hypotheses is its preoccupation with the isolation of relatively irrelevant variables and with psychological tasks which have little to do with the vital processes psychoanalysis is concerned with and in which even success or failure is usually of little relevance. Much of this preoccupation is avoided in the so-called projective techniques with all their subvarieties in which the meaning or story "theme" imputed by the subject to ambiguous pictures is made the basis of interpretation, as well as in certain of the more complex memory experiments and in some further related types of procedure. All these techniques give access to dynamically relevant material and the transformation it undergoes when it passes into consciousness chiefly because they do not insist on the unattainable requirement that the subject drop his defenses to help our effort to study his unconscious. The defenses, as well as the tendencies against which these defenses are erected, are revealed in a more indirect manner. Along the same lines, Kubie (1952) has advocated the study of materials brought forth in free association, in hypnosis, and under the effect of certain drugs.

Still other experimental studies have verified such seemingly far-fetched psychoanalytic assumptions as symbolism. We are thinking here primarily of experiments by Schrötter (1912) and by Betlheim and Hartmann (1924) at the Vienna Psychiatric Clinic in which stories with crude sexual content were told to uneducated hypnotized subjects and to Korsakoff patients. These stories were dreamt about or reproduced in memory with the spontaneous use of symbols for sexual content in conformance with standard psychoanalytic assumptions. A similar study was conducted by Brenman (1942), who asked her subjects to recall fairy tales they had heard during childhood. The reproductions showed omissions and distortions in the direction of the emotional needs of the subjects as ascertained by the Thematic Apperception Test and by hypnosis.

Turning now to the genetic approach, the study of psychosexual development in its various stages assumed by psychoanalysis (oral, anal, phallic, etc.) has been attempted by Blum (1949) with the use of 12 cartoons depicting a dog, named "Blacky," as engaging alone or with his parents or siblings in all the activities assumed to be relevant for the various libidinal stages. The interpretation of the cartoons has been found to correlate with the psychodynamic pattern of the subject. Again, the subject is less on guard and less apt to protect himself, describing as he does the activities of a dog rather than those of a human. Still, the interpretation of the Blacky Test remains much more uncertain than the author assumes.

It has been pointed out by many observers that although psychoanalysis is mainly genetically oriented and explains much of adult behavior in terms of early childhood experiences, most of this knowledge is based on a reconstruction from the therapy of adults rather than on direct observation of the child. Such a classic psychoanalytic summary of the development of mental and instinctual processes as Fenichel's uses almost exclusively examples from neurotics and psychotics to discuss what happens in childhood. Observation of children would seem the more fruitful, as the instinctual processes have not yet undergone the transformations which are supposed to occur under the pressure of family and social institutions. The ultimate requirement for a dynamic child psychology remains the ascertainment of the interrelationships of early childhood events to later personality structure, and only a so-called longitudinal study planned under the auspices of genuinely psychoanalytic modes of thought and extending over several decades could give an adequate answer. How to get hold of all the events which acquire meaning for the growing child and how to interpret these events, especially in the preverbal stage, still offer staggering methodological difficulties.

FORMAL CRITERIA IN A STUDY OF SELF-DECEPTION

In an experimental study of mechanisms of self-deception this writer (1939) attempted to make the ego defenses themselves the focus of exploration. Self-descriptions—as well as asserted "guiding principles" for conduct—were compared with descriptions of the subjects' actual behavior by detached observers well acquainted with them. The distortions in a person's self-appraisal were found to be greatest in the areas of actual behavioral shortcomings. The defense mechanisms of the type described in this study can be shown to be in a formal sense very similar to those described in psychoanalysis, although the emphasis is mainly on the defenses against loss of self-esteem rather than on defenses established in early childhood against instinctual dangers. Projection, for example, is in both cases defined as ascribing to the environment what is internal and at the same time rejected. In the area of overlap with psychoanalysis lie especially our self-deception mechanisms of distortion into the opposite, minimization, rationalization, and projection. These mechanisms make it possible for the person to see himself, say, as highly sincere even though he is judged by others to be highly insincere.

The findings of this study help to throw light on the problem of the function of consciousness in behavior. The inverse signalizing given by the mechanism of distortion into the opposite is frequently also expressed in the so-called guiding principles of conduct, for a report of which we also asked. The ultimate function of this inverse signalizing in consciousness, especially in its latter form, is probably the modification of behavior. We find, furthermore, projective types of distortion, exemplified by a subject judged to be very aggressive who at the same time demanded that others be more friendly. One of the subjects rated as lacking in self-discipline demanded a much stricter organization of the institute to which he belonged. Thus sometimes the function of consciousness seems to be of a defensive and compensatory character, protecting the person from a painful truth which he has been unable to face. This is in harmony with the general view psychoanalysis takes of consciousness. In other cases we found a conscious realization of shortcomings in oneself which were not perceived by others until later because they were hidden behind a well-functioning façade.

Our next step was to establish criteria by which we could ascertain whether in a given case the underlying motivational and behavioral realities were distorted or faithfully mirrored in consciousness. This brings us to certain semantic aspects of our results and their diagnostic implications. For example, we found that self-descriptions which do not correspond to the social realities are formulated in an exaggerated way. This exaggeration was found to be symptomatic of the absence rather than the presence of the asserted desirable trait. The use of such linguistic devices as superlatives, generalizations, and repetitions was found to be statistically concomitant with a shortcoming rather than a strength in the area concerned. The greater the definiteness and lack of shading and the greater the intolerance of ambiguity in the self-description of favorable traits, the less often as a rule were the traits concerned found to be present according to the judgment of close acquaintances. A list of "formal" cues of this kind, derived from our material (including some later studies) and useful in the interpretation of the truthfulness or sincerity of behavior or of self-reports, include the following: exaggeration; absoluteness of emphasis; intolerance of ambiguity; predominant reference to the extreme values of what actually is a continuum; inconsistency of general with specific features in behavior or in verbal description, or of responses to direct as compared with indirect questions; the occasional breaking through of a pattern of denial; deviations from the perceptions, concepts, and other answers which constitute the norm for the group as a whole; stereotypy; overconcreteness; small range of variability in response; repetition; and all manner of rigidity.

It may be assumed that these formal characteristics are less subjected to censorship than is the type of instinctual content studied in psychoanalysis proper. They may, therefore, in certain contexts be of greater diagnostic value than are symbols and other direct disguises for content elements.

In the approach just described we have taken a path around the person's self-perceptions and around the disguises his basic tendencies undergo in his own awareness or overt behavior by having other observers evaluate the dynamic realities of the subject on the basis of his overt behavior. Another method relies entirely upon the statements a subject gives about himself, but involves such a broad matrix of his statements that we are enabled to discern, with the help of the formal semantic criteria derived from the previous type of approach, whether or not the behavioral realities are consciously or unconsciously distorted. An example of this procedure is the interpretive evaluation of interview material. Thus the authoritarian child tends to begin with assurances of great admiration and love for the parents in reply to rather general questions but proceeds to reporting episodes of victimization and injustice in answer to more specific questions (see this volume, Chapter 2). A somewhat similar inconsistency is seen in an ethnically prejudiced child who, though relating only positive feelings while talking directly about his parents, omits his parents from the list of persons he would take with him to a desert island.

In comparing the interview with the projective techniques concerning their power of penetration to the dispositional layer, we find that while in some persons, especially in those in whom underlying tendencies are near the surface yet not quite conscious, the projective material seems to highlight certain dynamic tendencies in a particularly direct and dramatic fashion, other persons appear definitely less differentiated on projective tests than they do in their reactions to direct interviews.

Psychodynamics and Cognition

One of the areas best suited for the testing of some of the psychoanalytic hypotheses as well as for the expansion of our knowledge of dynamic ego psychology is that of perception and of cognition in general.

In academic psychology, perception and cognition were first approached under the aspect of the universal laws of general psychology including psychophysics, and with an emphasis on a cognitive "task" and the subject's way of solving it. In the foreground of attention stood the adaptation to reality. Individual differences were at first neglected, and their tracing back to the varying histories and motivations of individuals has hardly come into its own even today. For a long time the dominant tradition was that of association psychology with its conception of the human mind as a *tabula rasa*. Gestalt psychology was the first to introduce an organismic factor of cognitive organization, but this in turn was derived from the assumed general structure of the physiological apparatus rather than from more specific genetic sources, be they intellectual or emotional. Thus the cognitive processes continued to appear mainly as transmitters of characteristics of the physical stimulus, and all distortions appeared as reflections of certain characteristics of the cognitive system itself.

Beginning the 1920s there appeared on the German psychological scene typologists such as Kretschmer (see 1942) and Jaensch (1938) who claimed the existence of over-all styles of personality which would be manifested in a variety of cognitive patterns. Investigators in this group likewise tended to pass by motivational factors. Related to this typological approach is the approach via the pathology of thinking as represented by Bleuler (1911), Kurt Goldstein (Goldstein and Scheerer, 1941), and Cameron (1947). Under these auspices pathological, especially schizophrenic, thought patterns are described primarily in their illogical properties or as lacking the appropriate abstractness. It is pointed out how symbols are treated as realities, and how thought processes show instability of organization "with a relative inability to exclude contradictory, competing, or irrelevant reactions (overinclusion)" (Cameron). In still another related approach the emphasis is on developmental aspects of cognition. Stages of thought patterns are differentiated mainly from the standpoint of coherence of organization or adequacy to reality, and seen as determined by maturation. Piaget (1926), Werner (1940), and others stress the egocentric, syncretic, diffuse, physiognomic, rigid, and at the same time labile character of the thought processes in the child or the immature person. These latter descriptions begin to resemble the notions concerning primary processes as entertained in psychoanalysis.

Still further, and more distinctly under the influence of psychoanalysis, are the studies dealing with the influence of motivation on perception, often summarized under the label of autism. Yet it must be remembered that within academic psychology autism in motivation and cognition is on the whole not conceived as the result of early psychosexual experiences and dynamic mechanisms; the emphasis is mostly on temporary or otherwise personality-alien factors defining a single motivational force in relative isolation. Such forms of motivation as want, fear, experimentally induced reward or punishment, and other social values are superimposed upon a problem rooted in the tradition of the general psychology of cognition. In all the approaches listed so far in this section we find what may be called a "cognition-centered" orientation, that is, a basic dependence on the outlook, problems, and techniques developed in general psychology or descriptive psychiatry.

In the context of psychodynamics proper, on the other hand, we must think of a quite opposite type of approach, one in which problems are primarily organized about our notions of the motivational core of the person and are only secondarily extended to the field of cognition. This kind of approach we may call "personality centered." Such an orientation lays stress on the irrational, unconscious, and archaic layer of the personality, the discovery of which constitutes the major contribution of psychoanalysis in its basic function as depth psychology.

As mentioned above, Freud was well aware of the vicissitudes of the id under the influence of reality. Still, he viewed the functioning of the ego and character structure under the aspect of defensiveness more than under that of adaptiveness. Although it is assumed that in the course of development an objective, reality-adequate approach supersedes the primal undifferentiated, wish- and fear-ridden outlook, the primary process is not assumed to lose its dynamic significance; according to Freud (1927) the voice of the intellect remains low even though it is also seen as persistent. Taking off from Freud, several psychoanalysts have formulated challenging hypotheses concerning the relationship between thought patterns and underlying dynamics, however. These have far-reaching implications for the timely problem of the psychodynamics of acceptance or rejection of scientific theories.

We may illustrate this by means of Reik's (1951) cogent analysis of ecclesiastical dogma. According to him, the dogma of the trinity is a compromise formation which achieves the unification and reconciliation of what appears to be a logical contradiction. This dogma makes it possible to award Christ, the son, a position beside or really above God, the father, and at the same time to preserve the unique position of God as the father. Reik believes that in every dogma there is an attempt to unify opposing impulses; in the historical development of dogma there is an alternation between the prominence of the repressing agencies and the return of the repressed ideas. The emphasis placed on the certainty of the dogma originates in the defensive battle against doubt and heresy. As in the obsessional idea, the mechanisms of dogma are those of generalization, displacement, isolation; the transfer of doubt to insignificant detail serves to prevent the latent meaning of the obsessional idea or of the actual dogmatic statement from becoming conscious. Contradictions in both dogma and obsessional thinking can be explained by the oscillation between two opposing poles or by ambivalence, which, as Freud has pointed out, plays so large a part in obsessional neuroses. There is a stress on the differences resulting from the privacy of the obsessional ideas, which are usually kept hidden or unconscious, and the proclamation of religious doctrines, which endeavor to become official and public.

In his detailed phenomenological account of the thought patterns and total approach to life of the masochistic personality, including the cultural aspects of masochism, Reik (1941) stresses the significance of fantasy—the suspense factor and the demonstrative and provocative features of this syndrome. In consequence of his lively imagination the masochist is prone to anticipate punishment and the anxiety connected with it and thus tends to prolong the suspense. Masochism is seen as induced by social forces and by their intimidation of the ego in fantasy. The masochist seems to acknowledge the demands of reality but at the same time he defies them by an exaggerated obedience which turns the meaning of the demand into its opposite.

Fenichel's (1945) hypotheses concerning certain patterns of perception in compulsives (some of which were empirically verified by Rosenberg [1953]) have considerable bearing upon the present discussion. Over and above such relatively well-known features as magic thinking, the mechanism of isolation, displacement onto small detail, and the compulsion to doubt, Fenichel considers the "inhibition in the experiences of gestalten" an important characteristic of compulsion neurotics. He points out in detail how isolation separates constituents of a whole and prevents the compulsive person from awareness of the whole, and how the thinking in compulsive categories represents a caricature of logical thinking since isolation does not serve the purpose of objectivity but rather that of defense. In order to exclude the possibility of surprise, compulsion neurotics have a tendency "to make false generalizations, to classify hastily all ideas into certain mutually exclusive categories, and then to get into a state of doubt concerning the nature and evaluation of the categories." In emphasizing the predilection of compulsives for symmetry, Fenichel draws on the work of Ferenczi and Schilder. All these characteristics of perceptual and of thought processes are seen in the context of such instinctual orientations as ambivalence toward authority and the wish to keep a balance between the id and the superego.

In any application of the multilayer approach to thinking we are bound to go beyond the face value of the phenomena and to be sensitized to such formal principles as that of the closeness of opposites, hinted at earlier in this paper. This closeness is the direct result of the modification of the original aim by defense mechanisms. Freud himself (1915a) has dealt with the reversal of instincts into their opposite. He speaks of such changes as the replacement of a passive aim—for example, to be looked at—by an active aim—that is, to look at. The reversal of a content, as found in the change of love into hate, constitutes a similar pattern. Our mental life is seen as governed by three polarities, subject-object, pleasure-pain, activity-passivity, in each of which one pole may be replaced by its opposite.

In my own work on cognition, closeness of opposites could repeatedly be observed. A certain inability to tolerate complex, conflicting, or open structures was observed in the perceptual and cognitive approach of ethnocentric and authoritarian persons (see this volume, Chapter 2). This "intolerance of ambiguity" might, it seemed, be repeated in the more purely emotional sphere in the same manner as it is found in the social area. Ranking our subjects according to their intolerance of emotional ambivalence and their tendency toward perceiving others in terms of positive or negative halos and dichotomies rather than allowing for independent and continuous variability of traits, we attempted to ascertain just how pervasive this intolerance might be. This was done in a number of experiments on memory, concept formation, and perception proper.

Results so far collected support the conjecture that such tendencies as the quest for unqualified certainty, the rigid adherence to the given, the inadequacy of reactions in terms of reality, and so forth, to a certain extent tend to spread between the various areas of personality. It can be demonstrated, further, that such specific forms of reaction as "stimulus boundness," that is, the pedantic orientation toward concrete detail, tend to recur within a person in contexts seemingly far removed from each other. Inclination toward mechanical repetition of faulty hypotheses, inaccessibility to new experience, satisfaction with subjective and at the same time unimaginative, overconcrete, or overgeneralized solutions, all appear to be specific manifestations of a general disposition. It seems to matter little whether the authority to which there is submission is that of a person or that of a physical stimulus. In each case the choice seems to be between total acceptance and total rejection; if the two overlap, they do so in different layers of the personality. Avoidance of conscious coexistence of acceptance and rejection which could lead to qualified feelings and statements, and of other complexities, is confined to the surface level, however, with chaos lurking behind and breaking through the rigidly maintained façade. With internal conflict being as disturbing as it is in the rigid person, there apparently develops a tendency toward denying external ambiguity as long as such denial can be maintained. The clinging to definite dichotomies and demarcation lines apparently reduces the conflict at the conscious level but at the same time increases the underlying confusion. In the nonauthoritarian type of intellect, on the other hand, the total pattern is that of a broader integration of reality; no parts are left out, and thus a more flexible adaptation to varying circumstances is achieved.

It is the lack of integration and the resultant break between the conscious and unconscious layers in the rigid, authoritarian person, as compared with the greater fluidity of transition and of intercommunication between the different personality strata in the more flexible person, which appear to have the most far-reaching implications for the respective personality patterns. The shutting out of certain aspects of feelings, and of the inner strata in general, must be seen as the source of the distortion of the external perceptions and judgments. In spite of the recurrence of common elements in various areas, there is no obvious or simple "unity of style" in this type of personality, at least not so long as we take this term in the sense in which it is used by such typologists as Jaensch (1938). At least in part this is the result of the many repressions and of the break between the conscious and unconscious levels discovered and explored by depth psychology (Freud, 1915c). Thus there is a coexistence of such seemingly incompatible opposites as rigid perseverative behavior with an overfluid, haphazard, disintegrated, random approach, of compulsive overcaution with the tendency toward impulsive shortcuts to action, of chaos and confusion with orderly oversimplification in terms of black-white solutions and stereotypy, of isolation with fusion, of lack of differentiation with the mixing of elements which do not belong together, of extreme concreteness with extreme generality, of cynicism with gullibility, of overrealism with irrationality, of self-glorification with self-contempt, of submission to powerful authorities with resentment against them, and of stress on masculinity with a tendency toward feminine passivity. But it must be remembered that, say, stimulus boundness, that is, a pedantic orientation toward concrete detail, does as little justice to the problems and principles inherent in any cognitive task as does its opposite, overgeneralization. An abstract attitude stressing over-all principles is better suited for the penetration of the structure of the concrete and particular data than is exclusive attention to these data in their concreteness. A concentration on the literal meaning of a stimulus datum often entails a distortion of its essential contextual characteristics. The same situation obtains in science where the imaginative, subjective, or intuitive elements with which facts are viewed are of crucial importance for their intellectual mastery.

Styles of thought both in philosophical and scientific thinking must be assumed to be determined by both psychological and social factors. For instance, in psychology an altogether different type of person is usually attracted to the psychoanalytic system from those who show signs of wishing to escape into the palpable, concrete, and obvious forms of thinking. Besides the emotional resistance to psychoanalysis, the entire problem of the remoteness from data must be considered here. While some scientists feel safest when they are very close to the data, other feel safest when there is no reference at all to factual data; still others can tolerate the medium levels of abstraction. Prejudgments of an emotional and cognitive nature enter the picture. The problem of social factors is especially acute now, when we are witnessing a new upsurge of the search for absolutes in the wake of the anxieties and tensions inherent in our time. There can be little doubt that the choice between such philosophical positions as idealism, rationalism, and empiricism is likewise dependent on underlying personality factors. The same may be said for such ethical positions as absolutism, relativism, pessimism, optimism, and so forth.

A further approach to the depth-surface relations which this writer has followed up in some detail is the evaluation of the stories given in response to Murray's Thematic Apperception Test referred to above (1938) in the direction of relating the dynamic conflicts to formal characteristics of imagination and thinking. There is evidence that good intellectual organization of the stories often goes with a medium degree of aggression. Underdeveloped aggression tends to impair intellectual penetration and overdeveloped aggression tends to lead to disorganization. The evidence so far collected seems further to suggest that advanced psychosexual development in preadolescence, e.g., the prominence of the Oedipal conflict, tends to go with realism and originality, and that the coloring of the personality structure in terms of orality or anality is a further determinant of the formal quality of the production. Thus one of the adolescents under study who had progressed as far as the Oedipal stage but not beyond it, and who at the same time still manifested some of the genetically earlier oral traits, displayed marked imagination and creativity in the sense of a true grasp of reality, whereas the more purely infantile orality in another boy was accompanied by a sterile type of rumination about the topic of food. Preadolescents who are relatively mature in their psychosexual development tend to produce either imaginative fairy-talelike stories which show creative understanding of real relationships at a symbolic level or very realistic stories which reveal differentiated cognition. Children who display intolerance of ambiguity and are fixated at earlier stages of development tend to display either impoverishment of thought processes or unrealistic stories full of rambling repetition which do not add up to any organized sequence of events. All this is not to say that certain abilities may not develop to a certain degree independently of instinctual and emotional conflicts. It is not only the drive which must be assumed to determine the fate of ability, but also the ability which must be assumed to determine the fate of drive (see this volume, Chapter 1).

In conclusion, the vastness of the area of cognition and of imagination in which the contribution of instinctual vicissitudes and of internal mechanisms in general is crucial must not be underestimated, however. The internal dynamisms which psychoanalysis has described, mainly in the domain of sex and aggression, must be assumed to reach into all fields of psychology, including the seemingly remote one of scientific cognition. Over and above the external observations and the given abilities to organize and to create, our thinking is undoubtedly strongly determined by such defense mechanisms as isolation, repression, displacement, rationalization, and so forth. From our own work we reported interrelations between an ego-alien and not accepted ambivalence toward parental figures on the one hand, and an intolerance of cognitive ambiguity coupled with rigidity on the other. Psychosexual development in general seems to be an important determinant of content and quality of imagination. A complete picture of personality must refer both to the pattern of basic motivations and to the manner of manifestation of the motivational tendencies. For prediction we need both depth and surface. While psychoanalysis has been asking, "Which drive?," and general psychology has been asking, "Which effect?," a unified psychology must ask, "Which effect out of which drive?" To a certain extent Allport's (1937) principle of "functional autonomy" may hold; that is, there may be partial independence of cognition and social adjustment from genetic and instinctual factors. Emphasis must at the same time be laid upon the interrelationships between the two areas, however, and upon a multilayer approach to all psychological phenomena. The psychologist may be able to contribute to our insights into these depth-surface relationships considerably beyond what psychoanalysis has developed so far. With an added knowledge of underlying dynamics we will be the better equipped to identify and to integrate over-all organizing principles of overt adjustment. Thus the phenotype is reintroduced without losing sight of dynamic aspects. We must take the detour over the genotype to understand the phenotype. Freud (1925) was clearly aware of this fact, and that was the reason why he did not regard psychoanalysis as a closed system. Rather, he conceived of psychoanalysis as needing other types of psychology to complement it:

> By itself this science is seldom able to deal with a problem completely, but it seems destined to give valuable contributory help in a large number of regions of knowledge. The sphere of application of psychoanalysis extends as far as that of psychology, to which it forms a complement of the greatest moment.

Psychoanalysis, Ethics, and Rationality

Since the true or alleged ethical implications of a scientific theory tend to determine its acceptance and further destiny, any discussion of the scientific involvements of psychoanalysis must remain incomplete without a consideration of its ethical relevance. It has frequently been objected against psychoanalysis—although perhaps more often in the past than in the present—that its orientation is fundamentally unethical and that it aims at the dissolution of morals. Arguments of this kind were raised not only by philosophers in search for a system of absolute, transcendental values but also by empirically oriented social scientists and psychologists of major stature, for example Max Weber (1904-1905). According to his wife and biographer, Marianne Weber (1950), Weber saw in psychoanalysis an expression of a tendency to loosen up our basic ethical principles. She gives a vivid picture of how they both were impressed by the necessity of the acceptance of ethical norms, laws, and obligations, and how disturbed they were by any movement that seemed to challenge this necessity. In this context we find a number of references to Freud. In a long letter written in 1907 Weber tried to justify his negative attitude toward an article by one of Freud's followers in which reference is made to Freud's system as a psychiatric or "nerves" ethics characterized by the prevalence of the hygienic point of view (1950, p. 417). It is essentially the claim, made by some of the followers of Freud, that psychoanalysis represents a new kind of ethics which Weber found objectionable.

Weber also criticized the application of psychoanalysis to religion (Freud's major works on this topic had not yet appeared at that time). Indeed, Freud's predilection for genetic and biological explanations of social and cultural phenomena including ethics can best be illustrated by his conception of religion. The reader will remember our reference, in the preceding section, to Reik's views on religion, which in essence are similar to those of Freud. Freud points out that the search for consolation in the face of threatening feelings of inadequacy and helplessness to which religion provides the answer is nothing new in the life of the person, since everyone had found himself in a similar situation of helplessness as a child vis-à-vis the parents. The longing for a strong father is seen as closely related to the longing for God. The wisdom and goodness which are attributed to the deity reduce anxiety concerning the dangers of life, and moral order and justice are secured in fantasy even though they may rarely be fulfilled within existing human cultures.

According to Freud, the substitution of the scientific spirit for the earlier religious beliefs is a rather complex and long-drawn-out process. Freud favors a purely rational justification of cultural commands as a social necessity. In anticipating objections to this view Freud points to the apparent contradiction between his assumption of the domination of the person by instincts and passions, on the one hand, and his substitution of reason for emotion as a basis of obedience to culture, on the other. He tries to dispel these anticipated objections by explaining that the intellect is our only means of mastering our instincts, and that in turn mere threats and anxiety are rather ineffectual in the strengthening of intellectual functions. Again we are reminded that the voice of the intellect, though low, does not cease until it is heard.

While Freud tends to explain such social phenomena as religion primarily by reference to dynamics within the individual, most anthropologists and sociologists, notably Durkheim (1894) and Weber (1904-1905), prefer explanations in terms of processes conceived as involving society as a whole. In Durkheim's writings there is an emphasis on respect toward religion as an essential concomitant of respect toward normative rules, customs, and basic values. Religious rituals are seen as an expression of common values and of the moral unity of a society. We may refer to G.E.C. Catlin's remark (in his Introduction to the English translation of Durkheim, 1950) that "unlike Freud he [Durkheim] does not make this God a projection of the individual consciousness or nature."

A similar contrast exists between Freud's view that the moral level of a group can be preserved only when the group keeps the characteristics of the individual, and that of Durkheim, who assumes that there is nothing moral in the individual as such; it is society in its own right which is possessed of superior moral authority.

To both Durkheim and Weber, religion, far from being seen as an illusion or epiphenomenon, appears as a formative factor in social organization. Weber's (1904-1905) analysis of the relationships between capitalism and Protestant ethics is but one of the several examples he offered to illustrate the power of religious ideas. Weber assumes that religious feelings, interests, and experiences are worked out differently in different societies; and he is mainly interested in the rational consequences of these religious ideas for social and economic action. Although he gave much attention to an analysis of the rational aspects of organizations like bureaucracy, ultimately this rationality is traced to religious ideas outside of reason.

Both Durkheim and Weber have repeatedly been accused of rationalism, albeit both see the foundations of society in fundamentally nonrational moral qualities. Freud, on the other hand, has been criticized for having given too much prominence to the irrational, while in fact his one hope is the overcoming of the irrational in a society built on reason. Here is an illuminating reversal in the role played by reason when we proceed from the direct verbal formulations made by the authors mentioned to an analysis of the actual function of reason in their theoretical edifices. Freud neglected to explore reason directly and challenged the potency of reason in guiding human conduct. But in his evaluations of the goals of human development he had an exalted esteem for reason, and his understanding of the vicissitudes of unreason sharpened his grasp of the fundamental nature of reason; in this more crucial respect he was a believer in reason in the best sense of the word. Weber and Durkheim, on the other hand, appear primarily—although by no means exclusively—oriented toward the rational aspects of social conduct. However, one cannot but feel that their grasp of the power potential of reason in human affairs is blunted by an overrarefied idealization of the interplay of rational forces. There is a resulting uneasiness about reason, perhaps not atypical of the twilight of the enlightenment philosophy and of the Victorian age; in the end we find group cohesion and morality seen as hinging upon emotive patterns.

The ultimate recognition of reason by Freud notwithstanding, the original concentration of psychoanalysis on the discovery of the dynamic importance of the primitive, unorganized system of instinctual drives and of their derivatives has led—as was mentioned above—to a far-reaching neglect of consideration for social and interpersonal phenomena. It is largely this diversion of attention from the functions of reason in psychoanalysis which has given the semblance of ethical relativism. Actually, as we have seen, psychoanalysis was so overwhelmed by its epoch-making discovery of the role of irrational forces that the explicit exploration of reasoning processes appeared as the lesser challenge by comparison, even though it was reason and not the irrational that held the top spot so far as the evaluative attitude of psychoanalysis is concerned.

Even within all the reservations that psychoanalysis has voiced against an overly naïve rational interpretation of ethics, it merely turns against the assumed major executive principle of the traditional forms of ethics rather than against the basic constructive content of ethics. This particular executive principle is the mechanism of repression. Most prepsychoanalytic ethical systems assume that socialized behavior is largely dependent upon such inhibitory devices as the looking away from evil, or its denial, or the mastery of its most blatant overt manifestations through strength of will. From psychoanalysis we have learned about the inefficiency and the dangers of these various forms of repression;

and we have also understood why emphasis on sainthood and the techniques of the inquisition so often go hand in hand.

As far as both the goals and the effective means of execution of ethics are concerned, psychoanalysis lays stress on the importance of consciousness, integration, and maturity. If we recall for a moment all that is considered an essential ingredient of maturity in psychoanalysis, such as rationality, the overcoming of aggression, the development of cooperativeness, the ability to love and to work, and the courage openly to face inside and outside threats which oppose these characteristics, we readily see that we are confronted with standards which are certainly not lower than those expounded in the traditional systems of ethics. In psychoanalysis, every neurosis is *ipso facto* considered as failure at satisfactory moral control. The traditional systems of ethics attempted to strengthen consciousness and conscience against the invasion of instincts, and that remains their important historical contribution; however, through psychoanalysis we have become aware of the fact that such strengthening can be achieved only by facing and by working through, rather than by merely condemning, the forces which threaten our conscious personal and social values. From this latter viewpoint, the mortal sin is self-deception, and lack of insight in general, rather than a lack of repression.

It is one of the greatest and least appreciated contributions of psychoanalysis to have seen not only that for genuinely ethical behavior the antisocial instincts must be made conscious and integrated into a more encompassing system, but also that the major controlling instance of the primordial id impulses and thus the alleged major guardian of morals, the superego, may be a source of unconscious sadistic and primitive tendencies. Thus not only the id but also the superego must in the end be subordinated to the more reasonable prescriptions of the ego.

The noxious aspects of the superego derive from the internalized and archaically interpreted or distorted cultural taboos. To use an expression of Fenichel's (1945), in the superego the ego is confronted with an often "irrational representative of reality." Thus, if the neurotic person keeps punishing himself for sins he has never actually committed, for, say, mere feelings of aggression, a total relativism concerning real social action may easily develop. Unconscious moral tendencies stemming from rigid repressions generally turn out to be unrealistic, unadaptable, infantile, and out of touch with social realities. They represent a mere caricature of moral standards which may become destructive of the individual and of his society. These destructive effects of repression may occur in several different ways, frequently combined with each other. The desired yet unaccepted instinctual impulses may remain split up and unmodified, pushing to return and to break through the brittle defenses. Or an irrational superego may remain ego alien and nonintegrated with the conscious personality, thus perpetuating a pattern of conflict and tensions which may easily undermine the person's conscious and social intentions as well as his self-esteem. There may, finally, be a tendency to project the guilt stemming from a severe superego onto others; this may lead to the establishment and the persecution of scapegoats in social behavior, or to inequities in the objective appraisal of novel types of approach or theory in scientific behavior.

It hardly needs to be made explicit that rationality cannot be construed to imply amorality and freedom from obligation. On the contrary, genuine ethical behavior involves a comprehension of the issues involved, a facing of all uncertainties and conflicts and of one's own guilt, and a readiness to accept the anguish involved in such an open confrontation. Irrationality and the tendency toward destruction of one's self and of others, on the other hand, are often combined with a short-range overrealism and an orientation toward immediate material benefits. Similarly, steering clear of a compulsive quest for certainty in science does not imply cynicism and morbid doubt. On the contrary, obsession with certainty is a characteristic of irrational problem solutions, and the need for absolutes turns out to be combined with basic disbelief and general distrust.

Some recent writers seem resigned to the fact that only what is irrational, absolute, and dogmatic is capable of inciting enthusiasm and of motivating to action, whereas the rational, many-sided approach is seen as inherently inhibitory and as leading to a barren and sterile conception of life or of science. Against this we must hold that persons who are more open to reason and to facts are in general at the same time those who have a more differentiated internal life and deeper and more reliable—though often relatively calm—emotions. They are at the same time those who, even though less fanatic and less compulsive, show more consistency, conviction, and dedication in their principles and ideals. In application to scientific discourse we may stress that extreme or highly obvious positions lend themselves more readily to compact verbal formulation and thus give the false impression of eliminating the perplexities of an unresolved problem situation. Such definite and unqualified statements are especially suited to being put into the service of either very concrete or else excessively general assertions. In the task of the positive formulation of a theory, on the other hand, we must face the difficulties intrinsic in the complexities, ambiguities, flexibilities, and less fetching logicalities of the structures at hand, in a manner well exemplified by the stark yet subtle, daring yet not wayward, policies of psychoanalytic theory construction.

As far as conduct proper is concerned, the distinction between the manifest and the latent, which is one of the most basic achievements of psychoanalysis, provides us with the tools for a differentiation between genuine and spurious ethical behavior, even though the latter may be hidden behind a moralistic façade. But psychoanalysis does much more than that; it also provides us with an understanding of the sources of these forms of behavior, by pointing to their roots in relatively early phases of childhood, notably in the degree and type of identification with the parents and in the conscious or unconscious, hostile or loving, character of the relationship established with them. When Freud says that "what began in relation to the father ends in relation to the community," he may have put his finger on one of the most crucial determinants of our social and moral attitudes. The contribution psychoanalysis has made to a deepened understanding of the ethical behavior of individuals can be expanded into important insights into the historical development of the great systems of ethics. The need for a metaphysical system of absolute values, the insistence on the freedom of will, as well as unbridled relativism and cynicism, are set in their proper context within a system of personal need dynamics under psychoanalytic scrutiny.

Summary

An appraisal of the scientific legitimacy and operational status of psychoanalytic concepts must first consider certain fundamental changes in the views concerning theoretical structure which have taken place within physics itself as the model discipline for the unity of science and for operationism. Both Philipp Frank and Einstein have pointed to the ever-widening gap between observation and theory; there is increasing realization of the fact that the basic concepts and principles of science must be formulated in an abstract, "nonpictorial" language which seems to belie its origin in the world of direct perceptual experience. Much of the seeming absurdity of psychoanalytic assumptions is resolved by setting them side by side with established physical constructs which in many cases are as much in opposition to the perceptually given as are those of psychoanalysis to the data of manifest, "phenotypic" introspection.

An attempt is made to demonstrate that such basic psychoanalytic concepts as that of the unconscious or of the instinct are either theoretical constructs introduced by postulates, or are concepts defined by reduction chains. According to Carnap, the latter designate "dispositional predicates." Originally the concepts of the conscious and unconscious signify particular systems possessed of certain dynamic characteristics, calling for a specification of their relationships within the over-all formal model. Dreams or subsequent free associations are used for the establishment of intermediate links which can be inserted in the gap between the two systems and with the help of which we can recover the latent material in a process of interpretation.

Freud can be shown to have been familiar with the basic outlook of the philosophy of science. This is evident in his acknowledgment of the fact that the major function of his constructs is the filling out and the integration, in the manner just indicated, of the "exceedingly defective" data of consciousness, as well as in the judiciousness of his use of partially defined or temporarily unspecified hypothetical model systems. In doing so, Freud stresses that only by means of the assumption of the unconscious can the laws of the conscious processes be established, and that it is this very assumption which enables psychoanalysis to take its place as a natural science. His creative scientific daring is maintained in the face of, and in essential keeping with, the basic requirements of scientific empiricism rather than, as some of his critics would have it, in ignorance of these requirements or in wanton arbitrariness. The far-reaching influence of Helmholtz's physicalism and of the physiology of the late nineteenth century upon Freud has been demonstrated by recent students of the history of psychoanalysis.

While the psychoanalytic system comes closer to a truly scientific theory than most observers realize, psychoanalysis still contains many metaphors, analogies, and confusions between construct and fact which must in the end be eliminated.

The psychoanalytic concept of instinct is complicated by the assumption of far-reaching transformations and disguises, particularly of the sex instinct. But again Freud pursues an essentially operational course when he points to the capacity of the instincts to "act vicariously for one another" and readily to change their objects. It can be argued that the explanatory value of the instincts lies in this emphasis on the variability of their activity, of which the mechanisms of repression, reversal into the opposite, and sublimation are some of the more striking examples. Only in the case of an assumed strict correspondence between instinct and manifest behavior would the concept of instinct become circular or superfluous as an unnecessary duplication of behavior.

When Freud ascribes some of the difficulties in his speculations concerning the instincts to our being obliged to operate with "metaphorical expressions peculiar to psychology," we must add in his behalf that for the type of problems with which psychoanalysis deals the mentalistic (introspectionistic or animistic) vocabulary constitutes the precise counterpart of the pictorial vocabulary which has been stressed as a legitimate or at least tolerable ingredient of the earlier stages of physical science.

One of the most bewildering aspects of psychoanalytic theory is the turning away from the obvious face-value picture of personality as it derives from introspection or from the direct, "phenotypic" observation of external behavior segments. An example is the reinterpretation of overt friendliness as a sign of underlying hostility, or of extreme tidiness as a sign of preoccupation with dirt. The discrepancy disappears with the specification of a set of fixed or variable conditions which determine when overt behavior is to be interpreted as genuine and when as manifesting some heterogeneous latent factor.

Since scientific inference concerning central processes—that is, the assumption of internal states on the basis of external evidence—cannot be defended unless it is based on a wide variety of circumstantial evidence, central inference can be said never to have been legitimately attempted before psychoanalysis. It can be shown that on the negative side of the ledger psychoanalysis, especially in its beginnings, has comparatively de-emphasized both the surface manifestations in their specific identity and, what is more, the so-called distal achievements of behavior. These latter "results" of behavior in turn play the dominant role in such neobehaviorist systems as that of Tolman. The regrouping of manifest observable facts as undertaken by Freud centers on sameness of "need," that is, sameness of assumed internal cause, while in the case of Tolman it centers on sameness of effect and in the case of Egon Brunswik's theory of perception it centers on sameness of external object. By virtue of this incompleteness psychoanalysis did not altogether manage to avoid the pitfalls of motivational relativism and of a genetic dissolution of overt adjustmental values. But it must also be stressed that in psychoanalysis we find a legitimate reconstruction of objective causes and not only a pseudo explanation in terms of subjectively experienced motives, as some critics have tried to argue.

It must further be pointed out that the assumption of the dynamisms of the "inner man" to which such behaviorist critics of psychoanalysis as Skinner have objected can be shown to increase the parsimony of the scientific description of behavior patterns. Even more crucial is the fact that these extrapolations from overt behavior help to select the most relevant though often less conspicuous aspects of behavior which would otherwise be lost in the infinite range of possible observation. The relatively great explanatory and predictive value of hypotheses dealing with underlying motivation, which can be demonstrated statistically by means of multiple correlations, may be based on the fact that the selectivity just referred to enters crucially into the formation of these hypotheses. It may be added that from the standpoint of logical analysis there is no alternative but to be behavioristic in any psychological endeavor; neither the so-called subjective fantasies in which psychoanalysis is interested nor any other "introspective" events in others can be constituted except by reference to the manifest physical observation of organisms.

While Feigl places psychoanalysis at the third of the four levels of explanation he distinguishes, thus grouping it together with the relatively descriptive behavior theories of Tolman and Hull, it seems that at least a certain group of psychoanalytic concepts including that of the unconscious goes beyond this level by involving what Reichenbach calls surplus meaning. Using a distinction recently injected into psychological theory by MacCorquodale and Meehl, this group of concepts would seem to be "hypothetical constructs," in contradistinction to the "intervening variables" which are thought of as resting exclusively on the values of a specified set of empirically observed data. In their own rather sketchy analysis the authors point out that such terms as libido, censorship, and superego were in psychoanalysis originally introduced as intervening variables, that is, as conventionalized designations of observable properties, but that there was frequently an unnoticed shift toward hypothetical constructs. In their arguments the authors tend to overlook the fact that statements containing intervening variables are by no means exhaustible by statements concerning their observational basis. Both Carnap and Hempel have made it explicit that sentences containing disposition terms cannot be fully translated into sentences about observables. Since we cannot specify all conditions and manners in which latent tendencies become manifest, dispositional statements involve "open" terms and require an infinite series of conditions in order to be tested. The distinction between intervening variables and hypothetical constructs may, in our opinion, nonetheless be retained in a modified form as a gradual one involving different degrees of indirectness of evidence, or different kinds of surplus meaning. Possible relationships to the distinction made by Carnap and Hempel between postulatory theoretical constructs and concepts more directly reducible to observation are pointed out. Guided by some relatively fragmentary initial impressions, Freud seems to have proceeded rather directly to the building of a theoretical structure, with empirical interpretation lagging somewhat behind; in the definition of such theoretical constructs as superego, ego, and id, the major emphasis is on their structural relations to each other rather than on their relations to observation.

In turning to the problems of the objective verification of specific psychoanalytic hypotheses by means of experiments carried out in the formal tradition of psychology proper, two types of approach may be distinguished. One, and the more customary of the two, takes its start from the particular hypothetical mechanisms for which psychoanalysis has coined its most salient key terms. In analogy with an observation made by Frank for the field of physics, the more inferential and abstract parts of psychoanalytic theory, such as the hypotheses concerning repression, projection, and reaction formation, turn out to be less readily accessible to experimental confirmation than the more descriptive ones, such as those concerning fixation and regression. Some of the experimental studies have verified even such seemingly far-fetched psychoanalytic assumptions as symbolism.

A second type of approach, one which the present writer has tried to develop for a number of years, concentrates on the principle of alternative manifestations of motivational tendencies. This principle describes the basic pattern of interrelationships between the two strata involved in all psychoanalytic theory, the manifest and the latent, and can be shown to underlie most if not all of the specific mechanisms just mentioned. The possibility of analyzing statistically the tangled relationships between the two strata after imbuing them with some degree of operational independence is illustrated by studies dealing with motivation in its relation to overt behavior segments and with certain mechanisms of self-deception. In the former study a comparison of over-all motivational ratings with specific behavioral manifestations is used for a "rational reconstruction" of the cues underlying the so-called intuitive inferences made by the clinicians; the same general procedure would apply in the case of the more explicit and more scrutinizing inferences concerning motivational dynamics made by the psychologist as a scientist rather than as a synoptic rater. In the study of self-deception certain formal criteria of distortion, which may take their place alongside the more content-oriented type of diagnostic criteria favored in psychoanalysis proper, were established by means of a semantic analysis of the subjects' responses.

The verification of psychoanalytic hypotheses rests only in small part on the systematic evidence furnished by academic psychology. Psychoanalysis itself has provided confirmatory empirical data of overwhelming scope, ranging from the wealth of evidence given by individual patients to a synopsis of dream mechanisms, of lapses of tongue and of memory, of pathological symptoms, and of certain relevant features of folklore, myth, and other cultural phenomena.

Regardless of how imperfect psychoanalytic theory may be in its formal structure, it has no rival among psychological theories as far as the range of both its evidence and its explanatory power is concerned. Learning theory, which is the only other serious contender in such a contest, is equally ambitious in its claim to universality and at the same time more formalized than is psychoanalytic theory. It shares with psychoanalysis the "historical" outlook as well as some basic explanatory principles. But it falls short in accounting for such crucial facts as neurotic inaccessibility to "reinforced" experience which psychoanalysis has so impressively demonstrated and explained, or for the progressive strengthening of the superego in spite of the absence of appropriate reinforcement.

An effort is further made to relate the motivational aspects dealt with in psychoanalysis to certain cognitive problems. Acceptance of the ambiguous relationship between motivation and manifestation which is the chief discovery of psychoanalysis requires cognitive "tolerance of ambiguity" on the part of the scientist. Relations to the principle of the closeness of opposites, and to the analysis of concretistic, compulsive, and dogmatic patterns of perception and thought by such orthodox psychoanalysts as Fenichel and Reik, are pointed out. The necessary complementarity of the study of motivation and of cognition within a full-fledged system of psychology is elaborated on in its relationship to the complementarity of the depth and the surface approach within the psychology of motivation itself. A more formal aspect of the interrelatedness of the psychology of motivation and of cognition is given by the semantic difficulties arising from the employment of a partly identical nomenclature for the latent and manifest strata in commonsense language; as pointed out earlier in the paper, these difficulties are analogous to those arising in the psychology of perception in consequence of the confusion of stimulus and response terminologies as inherited from traditional philosophy.

A concluding section deals with the ethically constructive aspects of psychoanalysis. Psychoanalysis combines the genetic reduction of infantile conscience to irrational patterns with a stress on personal maturity and rationality as the adult ethical ideal. Some applications to the problem of the acceptance of scientific theories are made.

5

INTERACTION OF PSYCHOLOGICAL AND SOCIOLOGICAL FACTORS IN POLITICAL BEHAVIOR

The theoretical models developed to deal with the interaction of sociological and psychological factors in the formation of political behavior indicate a wide divergence of opinion. At one extreme are a group of scientists, mainly psychiatrists and anthropologists, who see most social phenomena as deriving from the subjective experiences of the individual. The specific traumata inherent in different methods of upbringing and in the resulting renunciations imposed upon the child are regarded by them as the formative basis for customs, religions, social attitudes, and so forth. Some specific examples of their point of view may be found in attempts to explain war as an expression of the destructive instincts, or capitalism as a manifestation of the anal syndrome. But at the other extreme are proponents of the view that the social structure is independent of the single individual and that individual behavior can be explained and predicted in terms of membership in classes and groups as they have developed historically, mainly on the basis of mode of subsistence.

Failing to agree with either of these extreme points of view, one may argue that any speculation about the causal interrelation of sociological and psychological factors in the group and in the individual must recognize the fact that these factors have been artificially isolated and abstracted and that no exclusive factual

---

This paper is a somewhat expanded version of one presented as part of the Symposium on Sociological and Psychological Problems Involved in the Study of Social Stratification and Politics, at the 47th annual meeting of the American Political Science Association in San Francisco in August, 1951. First published in *American Political Science Review*, 46:44-65, 1952.

primacy can be given to any of the aspects in a pattern so closely interwoven. An inquiry into the totality of the social process must consequently consider the structure of the social institutions as well as the different ways in which the economic and social organization is experienced by, and incorporated within, the individual.

A more fruitful question than that of factual primacy of factors is the one which inquires to what degree the conceptual tools of psychology and of sociology are equipped to describe the various phenomena in question. Accepting Parsons's assertion that social institutions and the standardized behavior derived from these institutions comprise the major content of sociology (1948), we shall deal in this paper with the origin and change of institutional patterns with very little, if any, reference to psychological concepts. On the other hand, when we turn our attention to the functioning of the institutions and their influence on man and his social behavior, psychology will be predominant.

Lasswell's *Psychopathology and Politics* (1930) was a pioneer study which tried to integrate psychological and political concepts, and Fromm's *Escape from Freedom* (1941) was another outstanding attempt at such a synthesis. (The influence of Fromm's work on the recent group study of *The Authoritarian Personality* [Adorno et al., 1950] can be seen very clearly.) Other valuable attempts to synthesize psychological and sociological aspects have been made by Kardiner (1939), Linton (1945), Kluckhohn (1949), and Mead (1942). In the present writer's previous studies (Frenkel-Brunswik, this volume, Chapter 1; 1942), she has stressed the importance of differentiating the motivational aspect of social behavior from its effects and adaptive value; and we shall take up this distinction, with its implications for political behavior, in the next section. Here we need only emphasize that both social behavior and personality structure are important links in the network of societal interaction, with sociology and psychology representing different levels of organization and of abstraction. As we proceed further, we shall encounter the necessity of differentiating sublevels within psychology as well as within sociology. In making, as we can and must, the distinction between the concepts of psychology and those of sociology, it is necessary to keep in mind that the study of individuals in their personality structures is but one of the many methods by which the social structure can be revealed. However, a deep and penetrating study of individuals may often tell us more about the themes of a contemporary society than will a surface description of the existing institutions.

It is intriguing to follow the reverberations of social patterns within the most intimate realms of individual life. We know a little, but not enough, of how social and technological changes play upon neurotic symptoms and how they find their way into the most bizarre delusions of psychotics whose very disturbance is their obvious remoteness from the social realities. And the findings of research on the "authoritarian personality" [1]—a pattern most relevant to the contemporary social scene—have revealed, among otler things, such trends as self-alienation, mechanization, standardization and stereotypy, piecemeal functioning, intolerance of ambiguity, lack of individuation and spontaneity, and a combination of irrationality with manipulative opportunism. These features, discerned in the psychological study of individuals, are closely akin to some of the features inherent in the process of industrial mass production and the machinery by which it operates; the functioning of social institutions seems clearly to be illuminated by studying how they are realized within the individual.

However, we cannot continue to develop concepts of mental health and integration without reference to the economic and social realities. This means that, in addition to the assessment of the rational and manifest purposes of social institutions, we must assess their irrationalities, inconsistencies, and latent meanings in order to know what kind of behavior we may expect from individuals. The complete appraisal of an individual, the evaluation of his adjustment, his sanity or insanity, implies a knowledge of the social realities, whether these are rational or irrational. All therapeutic techniques and therapeutic goals must be in accord with these realities.

Thus we come to ask what kind and degree of integration of the internal "personality agencies" we can expect from individuals who live in a period of increasing division of labor and of part-functioning in the manufacturing process, from individuals increasingly controlled by outside forces which must remain opaque and unin-

---

[1] This and many subsequent references are to the material about and treatment of this concept in *The Authoritarian Personality* (Adorno et al., 1950).

telligible to them, with the value of the family challenged and many other traditional values in decay, with social changes too rapid to be genuinely assimilated, and with an emphasis on success and competition which compels the individual to a degree of externalization that is only too likely to interfere with internal integration. To make this picture even more complex, the rewards of competition and initiative are increasingly diminished as participation in, and belonging to, big organizations become more important.

On the other side of this picture are forces which to a certain degree counteract the threatened disintegration. The same individual who has to meet the challenges just listed is exposed to a great variety of strivings and attempts, the goal of which is penetration to the fundamentals behind the confusing and shifting surface, and which promise new kinds of stabilities and salvations. Furthermore, the rising number of choices offered the individual in the course of the progress of industrial society may compensate for the restrictions stemming from the same process.

While social institutions in this manner undoubtedly influence the reactions and orientations of individuals, political institutions, such as that of democracy, conversely must be formulated with reference to psychological realities. How should democratic values be made vital to men of various socioeconomic and national backgrounds? What degree of rationality, of tolerance of the complexities and conflicts inherent in the democratic process, can be expected of them? How much need for absolutism and dogmatism do we find in the various countries? How can democratic values be stated so that misinterpretation both in the direction of totalitarian absolutism and in the direction of a too far-reaching relativism will be avoided? Some of these questions can be answered by considering the type of personality for whom totalitarian forms of government have special appeal. The political attitudes of this personality group can also serve as paradigms to illustrate the interaction of psychological and sociological variables. But first we must turn briefly to the psychological tools, conceptual and methodological, which are at our disposal in describing man in his society.

I. GENERAL CONSIDERATIONS IN A SCIENCE OF PERSONALITY

Interest in the dynamics of human behavior in its full complexity appeared on the scene of psychology rather suddenly, and chiefly through the influence of psychiatry and psychoanalysis. The suddenness was a result of the fact that those interested in personality as a unit became weary of waiting until academic psychology, using experimental and laboratory techniques, could proceed beyond the study of the relatively simple sensory or motor units with which it customarily dealt. Behaviorism in its earlier forms was not really open to questions of motivation, since it emphasized directly observable ("manifest" or "overt") responses to immediate stimuli, rather than the internal dynamics of personality or the broader context and background of behavior with its consequences that point beyond the momentary situation. In fact, however, the distinction between the manifest and the inferred motivational personality is of the utmost importance in studying our culture. In any advanced culture a person's real motivations quite often have to be disguised or transformed in order to pass individual and social censorship. Nevertheless, as common observation itself bears witness, as a rule they do not cease to exist and to exert influence. (For example, it is well known that exaggerated friendliness may serve, or even be the direct result of, strong hostile tendencies.) For this reason, the shift of emphasis from the level of external, overt manifestation to the level of motivational dynamics, stemming from psychoanalysis, has opened the way to highly fruitful explanations and predictions, and ultimately to the establishment of a stratified psychology of personality as an exact science.

The concept of underlying motivation supplies us with an instrument which, because of its particular level of abstraction or depth, is helpful in uncovering hitherto unrecognized relationships and consistencies in the field of personality—under the provision, of course, that the relations between inferred drive and overt behavior have been analyzed and the meanings of the former specified in objective, "operational" terms. This type of analysis has been extended from the customary casuistic to the more useful statistical stage in a study on the interrelationships between motivation and behavior (Frenkel-Frunswik, 1942). A group of adolescents, known to a group of observers over a period of many years, was rated by the latter on the basis of underlying motivation rather than on the usual one of displayed social techniques. The results supported the original assumption that such "intuitive" drive ratings are of considerable advantage in organizing a great body of data consisting of descriptions of behavior, of so-called projective materials (such as perceptual responses to inkblots or stories told upon the showing of a picture), of self-reports, and of other surface material. In fact, by conceiving of seemingly diverse behavioral reactions as alternative manifestations of one and the same dynamic force, we are able to resolve successfully many apparent inconsistencies. Central motivations can be established and consistent themes in a person's life can be uncovered. It often turns out, if we draw our inferences in this way from a great variety of manifestations (using gross as well as minimal cues) instead of taking verbalized statements or social techniques as directly valid, that we arrive at a more fruitful and unified interpretation of personality, and that such interpretations provide an improved basis for long-range predictions of the socially relevant aspects of behavior.

Having stressed the importance of the motivational approach, we must point out that this emphasis should not lead us to ignore the clear effects which behavior has upon society (see Chapter 1). In a complete description of personality, both aspects, the manifest and the motivational, must necessarily be included. Psychoanalysis and psychiatry cannot be entirely acquitted of the charge of having gone to the extreme of a one-sided emphasis on motivation. In the past, especially, it has very often appeared that a diagnosis of, say, underlying aggression was all that mattered, and the question of whether the underlying hostility led in a compensatory fashion to great achievement or to criminality seemed to be of little importance. In our discussion of political behavior we shall see the necessity of viewing behavior both from the motivational angle and from the angle of manifest appearance and observable results. This is a step which makes possible a great deal of differentiation because it connects human behavior not only to its internal sources but also to external realities. We shall see that, in order to understand fully the reactions of individuals to social issues, we must keep these differentiations in mind and must use this multilayer approach.

In our opinion, Freud's signal contributions to sociology and political science are his interpretation of human behavior from the angle of its latent, unconscious, irrational, and archaic aspect, and his emphasis on the formative influence of early childhood, dreams, and fantasies. It was also Freud who first pointed out the intimate interaction of biological and social facts in the individual, although he has sometimes been accused of a too far-reaching biological orientation. Such processes as sucking, bowel movement, and masturbation, considered as purely biological phenomena before the advent of the dynamic approach to personality, have been woven by psychoanalysis into the fabric of social interaction. From the newer viewpoint, sucking appears not only as a means of getting food but also as a means of experiencing and expressing affection and aggression, and the process of bowel movement is seen as one which is utilized by the child in his struggle with his parents and with authority in general. We now realize that cultures in general, and individual parents and children in particular, use these biological processes as a medium to induce or to express such social attitudes as submission or stubbornness, generosity or retention, and so forth. Similarly, dreams, which were considered as private and meaningless before Freud, are now being used as a basis for a reconstruction of the most decisive and subtle aspects of interpersonal relationships.

The ways in which Freud dealt with social problems, however, are undoubtedly insufficient. His direct writings on the origin and structure of society (1913, 1939) have been justly criticized for their speculative and ahistorical nature. Indeed Freud, who introduced the historical aspect into the consideration of the individual, did not himself make use of this aspect in describing primitive societies, while, in addition, the close analogy which he drew between the maturational stages of the individual and the maturational stages of societies appears to a large extent unwarranted by fact. Social influences are seen as a series of traumata which bring to a halt and discontinue gratification and expression of instinctual strivings. Though this image of civilization as a pattern of forces chronically interfering with the individual and leaving him mutilated is not altogether without point, it certainly is too narrow. The concept of sublimation, adduced to explain how the energies of the ungratified instincts are transferred to socially constructive goals, remains relatively sterile and vague in the writings of psychoanalysis, and very little has been said about the satisfactions which may be derived from successfully adopted social roles and identities. This omission indicates that the environment enters the scope of traditional psychoanalytic investigation mainly insofar as it permits a repetition of childhood reactions to father, mother, and other persons in the child's past social environment. Yet social attitudes and social techniques are at least as real as underlying motivation and early childhood, even though we may need to speculate on the latter in order to understand the former. For example, in our own studies, which were focused primarily on the subject's social attitudes (Adorno et al., 1950), our inquiry into his attitude toward, say, Roosevelt, was not undertaken in order to increase our understanding of his attitude toward his own father. But it is true that we probably would never have been able to understand the range and subtlety of our subject's attitudes toward Roosevelt had we not been guided by the accumulated and integrated findings of psychoanalysis on attitudes toward fathers, father substitutes, and father figures.

II. THE AUTHORITARIAN PERSONALITY: A DESCRIPTION ON FOUR LEVELS

The distinct personality pattern which emerged from two Berkeley studies[2] and which we have chosen to call "the authoritarian personality" will serve as a concrete example to illuminate in a more specific way the interaction of psychological and social factors. In our present description of this personality pattern, we shall first use the resources and language of clinical psychology. This approach alone will cover two levels, that of overt social behavior and that of underlying motivation; the discrepancy between the two has been shown to be one of the major characteristics of the authoritarian character. Our subsequent discussion, in this context, of the authoritarian's ways of perceiving and thinking will not introduce a really new level of description, since these matters may be classified with overt behavior as the directly observable reactions of the individual. A third level may be designated as social-psychological, since we shall deal here with attitudes toward social institutions and social roles. Finally, a

[2]Adult subjects were used for the project which resulted in *The Authoritarian Personality*. Children are the subjects of a second project, carried out at the Institute of Child Welfare of the University of California by the present writer with several collaborators. For preliminary reports of the latter, see Frenkel-Brunswik (1948c; this volume, Chapter 2).

fourth level of description will be from the sociological point of view, examining the authoritarian personality within the various social and occupational groups. Here some reference will be made to the political and social organization as historical background of the phenomena studied.

Totalitarianism as a politcal attitude held by Americans lends itself especially well to these four levels of description. Since the prevalent political organization in America is not a totalitarian one, such an attitude must be explained psychologically as well as sociologically. In countries where totalitarianism is a pervasive form of enforced organization, the importance of psychological factors involved in the choice of ideology is greatly reduced, for only when the existing institution leaves room for genuine preference do psychological and sociological factors become important (see Frenkel-Brunswik, 1948a, 1948b).

It is easy to anticipate that it will be impossible to give a pure psychological or a pure sociological description. We attempt here such an artificial isolation in order to demonstrate the relative contribution of the two types of conceptual organization. Naturally, the relatively lopsided descriptions which we have thus chosen to give will yield incomplete pictures. Only when taken together will they constitute an approximately comprehensive determination.

The material evidence of the two Berkeley projects mentioned above takes its start from questionnaire scales designed to elicit responses to a variety of slogans or statements involving social and political attitudes, with special emphasis on "ethnocentrism"— commonly known as racial or national prejudice—including attitudes toward parents, authority, conventional values, criminality, superstition, fellow men, fate, etc. Individuals found to be either extremely high or extremely low on ethnic prejudice were subjected to further study by intensive interviews and by the so-called projective techniques, such as the Thematic Apperception Test. The interviews delved, among other matters, into the subjects' images of various social "outgroups," their spontaneous ideas and conceptions of major political and social events, of religion, of parents and childhood, of friends and of people in general, and of their experiences with, and expectations of, the other sex.

Intercombination and synopsis of results from the various methods employed show that intolerance toward one minority group correlates with intolerance toward other minority groups. This rejection of everything that is "different" goes hand in hand with an undue glorification of one's own group; it is for this reason that the term "ethnocentrism" was introduced. This attitude in turn is related to a broader sociopolitical outlook which can be described as a kind of pseudo conservatism, since it combines rigid adherence to the status quo with readiness to use force for the restoration of what is extolled as, say, "the true American way of life." Because these various attitudes are closely interrelated, such terms as "authoritarianism," "ethnocentrism," "prejudice," and "antidemocratic" attitude will be used interchangeably throughout this presentation. It should perhaps be noted that the studies, well under way before the end of the last war, concentrated mainly on the fascistic form of totalitarianism, then in the foreground of interest.

CLINICAL DESCRIPTION

The distinct personality syndromes of the two extreme groups, those "high" and those "low" on ethnocentrism, evolve in the main from the analysis of the interviews for which the present writer was mainly responsible. The method of evaluation represents a compromise between individual case studies and quantification (see Frenkel-Brunswik, 1948a, 1948b). As much as possible of the richness and intricacy of the material was encompassed by a number of specially instructed raters. A number of broadly conceived categories, such as submission to family and degree of aggression and repression, were set up on the basis of a preliminary survey of the interviews. Each subject was then rated on these categories by clinically trained persons who did not know whether the person in question had an authoritarian-ethnocentric or a democratic orientation; the diagnosis of attitudes toward family, sex, etc., thus was always a "blind" one.

The description which follows is a statistically substantiated composite picture; few, if any, persons exhibit at the same time and to a marked degree all of the traits listed under either of the two syndromes. From a psychological point of view, an over-all summary of the authoritarian personality must first stress the great number of discrepancies and discontinuities—seldom conscious, to be sure—which can be found in this type of person. The ethnocentric person is less likely than the ethnically unprejudiced to face within himself such emotional tendencies as ambivalence, passivity, fear, aggressive feelings against parents and authorities, and instinctual impulses which are considered "bad" or immoral. Because he usually fails to integrate these tendencies with the conscious image he has of himself, he rather tends to ascribe them to the outside world and to fight them there. Closely related to this tendency is his moralistic condemnation of other people. For him the world itself comes to appear as a dangerous and hostile place, to be viewed with distrust, suspicion, and cynicism. An undercurrent of panic is evident in his fear that food and other supplies may run short and that he may be left helpless in the face of danger, which he is all too ready to anticipate. Asked to retell a story in which aggressive as well as friendly characters were described, the prejudiced children as a group recalled a greater number of aggressive characters, whereas the unprejudiced children recalled a greater number of friendly characters, than had been mentioned in the story originally read to them. Moreover, the total distortion of reality—here the original story—was greater among the ethnocentric children (this volume, Chapter 2, pp. 73-76).

It is easy to understand that persons so fear-ridden will tend to be unusually manipulative and exploitive in their relations with others. Fellow men become, to borrow a term from Fenichel (1945), mainly "deliverers of goods." Thus, along with the self-centered overpersonalization of the social scene, human relationships become depersonalized. The kind of material-magic dependency just described extends not only to people and authority but also to inanimate forces; ethnocentric subjects subscribe more often to superstitious beliefs. It seems to be important for them to use devices by which they can get evil and dangerous forces to join them on their side. Such support should be considered a substitute for an underdeveloped self-reliance; and it is apparently this same feeling of helplessness, together with underlying destructive impulses, which leads the ethnocentric subject to agree more often than others with questionnaire statements which describe or predict doom and catastrophe, the spread of contagious diseases, and so forth.

The prejudiced person's attitude toward work shows an externalization similar to that just noted in his attitude toward people and animistic forces. He is indifferent toward the content of work and lays emphasis upon work mainly as a means to success and power.

Prejudiced persons also tend to create and adopt extreme and mutually exclusive pairs of values such as dominance-submission, cleanliness-dirtiness, badness-goodness, virtue-vice, masculinity-femininity, and so forth. They consider the absoluteness of such dichotomies to be natural and eternal and so exclude the possibility of any intermediate or overlapping position. Their adherence to these delineated norms is likely to be rigid, even though it may imply restriction and disadvantages for their own group. Thus it is that not only the prejudiced men but also the prejudiced women favor restricting women to narrowly defined fields of activity which are considered to be "feminine."

In an attempt to understand these rigidities and dependencies, we may turn to the childhood situation of our authoritarian-minded subjects. Here we find a tendency toward rigid discipline on the part of the parents. They demand that their children learn quickly the external, rigid, and superficial values which they themselves have adopted but which are beyond the comprehension of children. This insistence may be explained by the fact that faithful execution of prescribed roles and the exchange of duties and obligations is, in the families of the prejudiced, often given preference over the exchange of free-flowing affection. In telling of their parents, ethnocentric children tend to think in the category of strictness and harshness, whereas the unprejudiced tend to think primarily in terms of companionship. We are led to assume that an authoritarian home regime, which induces a relative lack of mutuality in the area of emotion and shifts emphasis onto the exchange of "goods" and of material benefits without adequate development of underlying self-reliance, forms the basis for the opportunistic type of dependence of children on their parents which is described here, and that the inherent general stereotypy is an outcome of this orientation.

However, it is of great importance that, although he tends to submit to the authority of his parents on the surface level, the authoritarian child harbors an underlying resentment against them. Along with conventional, stereotypic idealization of the parents, we find indications that the child feels, without being fully aware of it, that he has been victimized by them. Frequently ethnocentric children tend to begin, when speaking of their parents, somewhat vaguely and on a note of general admiration; but the praise is likely to be followed by descriptions of specific episodes of neglect, unjust discipline, and the like. Fear and dependency seem not only to discourage the child from conscious criticism of his parents but further to lead to an acceptance of punishment and to an identification with the punishing authority.

It is especially the male authoritarian who seems intimidated by a threatening father figure; and we may note here that our material shows the family of the ethnocentric person to be more often father-dominated, whereas that of the unprejudiced is more frequently mother-centered. However, since in the prejudiced home the closeness of the parent-child relationship is based more on fear than on love, and since the punishments and rewards meted out must seem inconsistent to the child, no genuine identification with parents or real internalization of values can be achieved.

The ambivalent submission to the parent of the same sex, especially that of the son to the father, and the ensuing latent homosexuality are often counteracted by a rigid display of the accepted characteristics of one's own sex and by repression in oneself of tendencies of the opposite sex. The prejudiced man tends to think of himself as active, determined, energetic, independent, tough, and successful in the competitive struggle. We may find here parallels to the well-known Nazi emphasis on virility. Of course, there is no room in this ego ideal for passivity and softness, and strong defenses are accordingly erected against these attitudes in general, with the result that only their opposites are established in consciousness. Nonetheless, inclinations toward dependency and a far-reaching passivity—although they remain unaccepted and ego alien—are evident. There is reason to speak of a sexual marginality of the ethnocentric man and to recall also the sexual deviations observed in the Nazi "elite."

In addition to the dichotomizing of sex roles per se by the prejudiced, we also find among them dichotomous sex attitudes in a broader sense of the term, such as the sharp opposition of "sex" versus "marriage," of "pure" versus "low" women, and so forth. This explains why the prejudiced woman clings to a self-image of "femininity" defined by subservience to, and adulation of, men at the same time that she shows evidence of an exploitive and hostile attitude toward men.

To summarize our description thus far, in our extremely ethnocentric subjects, both adults and children, we find surface conformity lacking integration and expressing itself in a stereotyped approach devoid of genuine affect in most areas of life. This tendency toward a conventional, externalized, shallow type of social relation has a generally pervasive character in the authoritarian personality. Even in the purely cognitive domain, as we shall see, ready-made clichés tend to take the place of spontaneous reactions.

PERCEPTION AND THINKING

In the foregoing we have seen that the authoritarian personality tends to resort to black-white judgments and to unqualified and unambiguous over-all acceptance or rejection of other people. In his descriptions, whether of ingroup or outgroup, of parents, or of a political leader, this person displays both stereotypy and lack of differentiation—in short, an all-or-nothing approach. His opinions are "closed" and cannot be modified; new experiences are immediately viewed from the standpoint of the old set and are classified in the same way as the earlier ones.

The rigidity of the ethnocentric person which is implied in this presentation seems to a certain extent to be a generalized personality trait. Experiments on perception and thinking carried out with the children in our study show that stimuli which are unfamiliar, ambiguous, or subject to change are experienced by the prejudiced as strange, bewildering, and disturbing, much as they would be to a leader lacking in absolute determination (see this volume, Chapter 2, pp. 76-82). Children in this group tend either to jump to premature conclusions or to hold on rigidly to a familiar stimulus and to ignore the changes that may prevail. In the retelling of the story mentioned above, the ethnocentric children reproduce literally some of the phrases but misrepresent the essence of the story more often than do the unprejudiced children. Clinging to a concrete, isolated detail of reality and overgeneralizing are two alternative ways of avoiding complexity and of making things definite at the expense of the existing facts. Indeed, with the ethnocentric child, the intolerance of ambiguity seems to pervade the solving of problems ranging from those of parent-child relationship and sex roles to simple perceptual and intellectual tasks. In the course of these attempted solutions a subtle but profound distortion of reality must necessarily take place, since stereotypic categorizations can never do justice to all of the aspects of reality.

The implication of this intolerance of ambiguity and of complexity for political behavior cannot be stressed too much. It is obvious that difficulties will be encountered in explaining democratic values to persons who have the need for a definitely structured social outlook and for organization in simple and clear-cut hierarchical, rather than equalitarian, terms which exclude the possibility of free and dynamic exchange of influences.

In this connection a German psychologist, Jaensch (1938), perhaps the foremost exponent of Nazi ideology in psychology, praises precise, firm, regular reactions which are unambiguously tied to external stimulus configurations. He refers to the physics of Einstein as a type of science "without consideration of reality" and with a tendency to "dissolve all reality into theory" and contrasts this type of approach with the more desirable "concretely oriented German physics." Jaensch misses the point that more abstract attitudes, oriented toward over-all principles, often are better able to penetrate to reality than is an exclusive attention to facts in their concreteness. In our experiments with authoritarian-minded children, we were able to demonstrate that an overrespect for the concrete did not do justice to the problems and principles inherent in the conceptual tasks with which our subjects had been confronted. As was pointed out above, an overconcrete attitude often turns into overgeneralization; and both are seen to be inferior approaches compared with the method of abstract thinking.

Our observations have led us to believe that the adjustment of the authoritarian person is confined to narrowly circumscribed conditions. It is precisely his extreme conformity, rigidity, and need to ascribe all his own weaknesses and shortcomings to a scapegoat which account for the restricted conditions of his functioning. In fact, Jaensch has considered adaptability and tolerance of tentativeness to be signs of degeneration:

> In case of racial mixture, nature has to leave everything uncertain and in suspense; the individual at birth may be endowed with nothing fixed and certain but only with the uncertainty, indeter-

minability, and changeability which would enable him to adjust to each of the various conditions of life. The opposite is true if an individual possesses only ancestors who from time immemorial have lived in the North German space and within its population. From the biological point of view, it is not only extremely probable but certain that such an individual will live under the same environmental conditions as his ancestors. The characteristics necessary for this, therefore, may be safely placed in his cradle as innate, fixed, and univocally determined features [pp. 230ff.].

Like many of Jaensch's contentions, this one is far from being empirically verified. Though it is sometimes true that the ethnically marginal person is more adaptable, this position often leads to greater rigidity. But we shall have more to say about this point in the following sections.

Concerning the democratic-minded person, it may suffice here to emphasize that he is generally better able to face uncertainties and conflicts, as indeed he must in order to master the physical and social realities. Readiness to recognize, to accept, and to master diversities, conflicts, and differences in oneself and in others, as contrasted with the need to set off clear demarcation lines, was found to be one of the most basic distinguishing criteria of the two opposite patterns in our studies.

SOCIAL-PSYCHOLOGICAL DESCRIPTION

We may now turn back and interpret much of what we have said about the authoritarian personality pattern in the light of a further fact, that is, his rigid conformity to cultural clichés. It must be stressed that this conformity does not consist in a genuine identification with traditional values. Our evidence points to the fact that the authoritarian person has frequently lost his roots in tradition and has made an attempt to compensate for this loss by a rather nonfunctional, forced, and rigid conformity. This surface conformity to externalized values can be observed in a variety of spheres of life. One of the earliest expressions is to be found in his attitude toward parents. His conception of sex roles[3] is likewise highly conventionalized, with emphasis on activity, determination, toughness, and success in the masculine ideal, and on passiv-

---

[3] For detailed exposition of the concept of "role," see Linton (1945) and Parsons (1948).

ity and subservience in the feminine ideal; and in all personal relationships preference is given to restricted roles rather than to vaguely defined ones. Thinking in hierarchical terms—such as dominance versus submission, orientation toward power and success, dichotomizing of sex roles, and the like—would have to be considered part of this conformity. In fact, most of the dichotomies which imply valuation, such as good and evil, strength and weakness, dirtiness and cleanliness, masculinity and femininity, can be seen as mirroring a conventional inventory of social clichés. The ethnocentric group, which desperately wants to "belong" and to be successful, acts as custodian of these distinctions, keeping them always in mind as the approved vehicles by which its most obsessively cherished goals may be reached.

The moralistic conventionalism of the authoritarian personality characterizes not only the more conservative type within this group but also the lunatic fringe and the psychopathic variety. A set of interviews with the highly ethnocentric among prison inmates has shown that on certain levels this group ardently identifies itself with the prevalent conventional values and condemns ethnic outgroups on the basis of their deviations from these values.[4] These interviews show widespread preoccupation with external social goals, a preoccupation constantly directed toward the narrow and steep ascent to a higher social status. Since the persons so absorbed tend to identify themselves with a group which is socially and economically superior to their own, it follows that their sense of belonging to the privileged groups is extremely tenuous. Their level of aspiration is often quite fantastic; in certain cases the intellectual and artistic aspirations have even less basis in reality than had those of some of the Nazi leaders. It is the discrepancy between the status aspired to and that achieved which leads to the feeling of social and economic marginality.

Because of their real or imagined marginality, some persons feel persistently threatened with being degraded in one way or another. It is in defense against the possibility of being grouped with the underdog that identification with the privileged groups is so insistently asserted. Apparently the great number of conflicts and

---

[4]The interviews, conducted by W. R. Morrow, are described in *The Authoritarian Personality* (Adorno et al., 1950).

confusions concerning personal, sexual, and social roles are responsible for determined efforts to eliminate uncertainties in all contexts of life; yet our interview material furnishes ample evidence that chaos and violent destructiveness lurk behind the rigid surface, posing dangers to the very society to which there seems to be conformity.

The concept of social marginality includes both sociological and psychological aspects. Authoritarianism correlates less well with actual socioeconomic status (as will be shown later) than with subjective dissatisfaction with one's status; and therefore, on the basis of our material, we must expand the concept of marginality to cover sexual and physical marginality as well. In passing, we may refer to the case of a boy in our study who, though from a liberal home, reveals attitudes of extreme ethnocentrism. The interview material points to a history of illness and ensuing feelings of physical inadequacy as probable reasons for his need to assert his superiority by designating the outgroups as inferior.

As mentioned above, external criteria, especially social status, are the yardsticks by which the ethnocentric person tends to appraise people in general; these criteria furnish the grounds on which he either admires and accepts or rejects his fellow men. The ethnocentric person tends to take cognizance primarily of whether people's behavior is appropriate to alleged social roles, and tends to ignore the intrinsic values of the people themselves. He takes social institutions so literally that his personal orientation and behavior reflect in many ways the basic structure of certain gross features of our civilization. The relative uniformity in the personality structure of persons in the ethnocentric group is derived from this adoption of status and role values. However, this does not mean that the behavior and feelings of these persons represent our social institutions in *all* of their essential aspects. We have evidence that, in their reactions to perception, thinking, and memory tasks, ethnocentric persons show great fidelity with respect to concrete details but tend to miss the over-all problem (see this volume, Chapter 2, pp. 73ff.). A similar quality can be discerned in their interpretations of social institutions. Among other distortions, they tend to simplify the meaning of these institutions and interpret the predominant values too homogeneously and too absolutely in the direction of status values, ignoring other trends in the civilization. In the final analysis, rigid adherence to conventional values turns out to be no more than a superstructure beneath which operate many tendencies which are self-destructive of the society to which superficial conformity has been achieved.

It was, to repeat, psychoanalysis which introduced the differentiation between manifest and latent content, a distinction which is seen to be especially important for an understanding of the authoritarian personality. In the tradition of a pre-Freudian social psychology, we would have to take exaggerated conformity at its face value and would thus overlook the fact that it stems from feelings of social insecurity and resentment and that it can switch dramatically into its opposite. Both conformity and its reverse, chaotic upheaval, are considered by the authoritarian person to be useful means for gaining power, and he will give preference to whichever appears more likely to succeed.

SOCIOLOGICAL CONSIDERATIONS

In the preceding few pages we have begun to discuss some psychological findings in more nearly sociological language. It is now appropriate to inquire whether or not the feeling of social marginality, which is so characteristic of the ethnocentric person, is related to distinct socioeconomic factors. In an attempt to determine the sociological factors in the background of the authoritarian personality, we used a variety of approaches.[5] A questionnaire was used to ascertain the political preferences, group memberships, and incomes of our subjects. An analysis of the responses to questions on political party preference indicates that no relationship exists between ethnocentrism and preference for either the Democratic or Republican Party as such, but that New Deal Democrats and Willkie Republicans obtain significantly lower scores on ethnocentrism than do members of the traditional wings of the Democratic and Republican Parties. The correlation of .5, obtained with the groupings just described, shows, however, that there is considerable individual variability. Further analysis reveals that in the middle-class groups the rela-

---

[5] The material of this and the following two paragraphs is based on Ch. 5, prepared and written by Levinson, of *The Authoritarian Personality*. The remainder of the present section is based on material from the project on Social Discrimination in Children referred to above.

tion between ethnocentrism and political preference is much closer than in working-class groups. Different people seem to support a given political group for different reasons, and inquiry into the basis of selection is as important as establishing group membership. There is, furthermore, a significant difference in degree of ethnocentrism between those who agree with the politics of their parents and those who disagree. As we might expect from the psychological data, the subjects who disagree with their parents on politics are significantly lower on ethnocentrism than those who agree.

Economic and social stratification may to a certain degree determine party preference, but they seem to have little to do with such social and political attitudes as ethnic prejudice. We find that members of a CIO union had a slightly higher mean score on ethnocentrism than a Parent-Teacher Association group composed largely of middle-class members of a relatively high educational level. Members of a women's club were substantially higher on ethnocentrism than were a group of members of the League of Women Voters. In the latter instance, neither actual class nor educational level differentiated the two groups; but such factors as upward economic mobility, pseudoconservative values, and the like, did.

There is a slight tendency for the lowest and highest income groups to score higher than the middle-income group on ethnocentrism, while within the latter ethnocentrism seems to decrease as income increases. These relationships, however, are so tenuous as to support the hypothesis that economic factors as such are not closely related to ethnocentrism so far as individuals are concerned. These findings are in line with those of other observers (e.g., Bendix, 1951) to the effect that economic factors alone are insufficient to account for the occurrence of fascist movements. We must view the economic and sociological factors in the light of their meaning to the individual and to society as a whole if we are to increase their predictive value.

Over a period of time the present writer was able to collect extended data on the socioeconomic history of the families of extremely ethnocentric and of nonethnocentric children. One of the chief purposes of obtaining this material was to see whether or not the feeling of marginality which is so important to ethnocentrism is determined by sudden changes in the socioeconomic status of the families. The assumption in collecting such data was that loss of status might undermine a person's social security and that gain in status might lead to all kinds of attempts to maintain the gain. This hypothesis has been only partially confirmed in the sense that families with a long history of privileged socioeconomic status seem to be on the whole less ethnocentric than families with unstable histories; but instability of status, per se, goes almost as often with tolerance as it does with ethnocentrism.

For the most part the families studied had been recruited from lower-middle-class and middle-class sectors of the population. As a group, the ethnocentric families do not differ to any marked degree from the more democratic-minded families in purely economic terms, i.e., difference in income, housing conditions, number of cars, radios, etc. However, within the group studied, the few persons whose living conditions fell decidedly below middle-class standards were mostly ethnocentric and those whose conditions were definitely above them were mostly liberal. Since the neighborhood of the schools from which our subjects were drawn would indicate middle-class identification on the part of all of the families studied, the differences in ethnocentrism which we observed may thus hinge upon the relation of level of status aspiration to actual status rather than upon status per se.

Ethnocentrism also seems more closely related to the occupational affiliation of families than to purely economic factors. The parents and grandparents of unprejudiced children are significantly more often from professional fields, such as medicine, law, teaching, the ministry, etc., than are those of ethnocentric children. We may refer here to Daniel Lerner's (1951) finding that a certain proportion of the Nazi elite, especially the propagandists, were intellectuals, or, as he put it, more precisely "alienated intellectuals." This is not as contradictory to our findings as it may seem at first glance. Some of our authoritarian subjects display intellectual, or rather pseudointellectual, and artistic ambitions which—according to their own report—they were unable to realize because they were cheated of their opportunities. However, whereas in Germany this type of pseudo intellectual possesses a certain accepted occupational status of his own, in America he is likely to turn to some kind of substitute occupation, such as working in a garage or being a waiter, and he is therefore often listed under occupational groups other than artistic or intellectual ones. In the relatively rare cases where the father or grandfather of our ethnocentric subjects comes from one of the professions, it is likely to be the engineering profession.

These results point to a certain relationship between education and freedom from prejudice. Information, and especially information along the lines of social science, is by no means directly related to economic factors, however. The crucial factor seems to be a certain psychological receptiveness accompanied by accessibility to facts. This is why experiments have shown that extensive information about minority groups does not markedly alter the beliefs of ethnocentric persons.

We find, furthermore, a higher percentage of nonethnocentric families among the small merchants in our sample and a higher percentage of ethnocentric families among the workers. This circumstance may be an indication that the small merchant in America, in spite of the big monopolies, does not yet feel basically threatened. (In Germany, as we know, the small independent lower-middle-class groups contributed the greatest number of Nazi followers.) Among employees as a whole, we find an even distribution of ethnocentric and unprejudiced families. In particular, however, the salesmen, policemen, firemen, etc., are more frequently among the prejudiced, while bus drivers, accountants, and goverment workers are more frequently among the unprejudiced. Some of these relationships can perhaps be explained psychologically. Thus, choosing the occupation of salesman may indicate self-promoting tendencies and choosing that of policeman may reveal identification with authority and aggression, whereas choosing to be a bus driver may be related to enjoyment of this kind of activity as an end in itself.

In general, the ethnocentric person tends toward a more unstable history of work than the nonethnocentric. He seems to be less rooted in his daily task, and there is a greater discrepancy between aspiration level and performance. Another possible source of excessive status concern may be seen in the fact that the parents of our ethnocentric children report significantly more often than the others that their own parents were foreign born (especially Italian and German), indicating perhaps that they still see themselves as enmeshed in the process of assimilation.

While these socioeconomic considerations throw some light on our problem, the fact remains that certain families or individuals accept their objective social marginality cheerfully while others develop rigid defenses against it; the latter apparently have to reject the "outgroups" in order to demonstrate that they themselves are not weak or different. Economic deprivation may be one differential factor, but undoubtedly there are others. Thus we found in our study that certain families are preoccupied with the maintenance of their middle-class status and of the social distance from ethnic minority groups who may live nearby, while other families of similar socioeconomic level show no similar tendencies. At the same time the political attitudes of the two groups—similar in socioeconomic history as they often are—range from extreme ethnocentrism to a stable liberalism. Perhaps the foregoing paragraphs can be illustrated by the following concrete examples, which describe the backgrounds of one of our most prejudiced and of one of our most unprejudiced children:

> The socioeconomic histories of the two families show great similarity. The father of the unprejudiced child, whom we shall call "Joan," had at the time of our interview just sold a small restaurant which he had come to consider a bad investment. His professional history includes managing a store, selling insurance, and working in a restaurant as waiter and cook. He is a college graduate as is his wife, a trained musician who is now a schoolteacher. Joan's maternal grandfather, according to his daughter, was first "a small town doctor where he was a dictator and patriarch to the population. He entered the army as a medical officer and liked the opportunity which it gave him for expressing authority." Joan's mother apparently received a great deal of warmth from her own mother, but she rebelled against her father. Joan's father was born in Yugoslavia, the son of a leader in a liberal party who was a pharmacist by profession and whose function in the community was similar to that of a doctor. Though the father's occupational history, especially as compared with that of his parents and that of the parents of his wife, could have led to a feeling of social marginality, this family actually does not seem to be dissatisfied with its present

status; much of the time of its members is devoted to such pursuits as supporting the liberal causes of the community, participating in discussion groups, and so forth.

Very different are the psychological characteristics and social beliefs of another family with a similar socioeconomic history. The father of "Karl," one of the most ethnocentric boys in our study, is a mechanic. Karl's mother was born in this country, and so was her father, while her mother was born in England. Karl's maternal grandfather was a doctor, as was the case with the unprejudiced Joan's maternal grandfather. But while the marriages of Joan's grandparents were stable on both sides, Karl's maternal grandmother had divorced her husband shortly after Karl's mother was born. In fact, Karl's mother had a succession of stepfathers of whom one, who was a combination of actor and coal miner, played the most important role for her. Karl's father and his own father were born in this country, whereas the child's paternal grandmother came from Germany. The paternal grandparents died when Karl's father was four years old, and his father was reared by grandparents "who were rich but not generous with their money." (They owned a large farm and a wholesale liquor store.) Both of Karl's parents had been exposed to strict discipline. Though Karl's father is a mechanic, he asserts that his occupation is only temporary since he is likely soon to make a big mechanical invention. This aspiration remains on a fantasy level since there is little evidence of any concrete work toward the goal. Similarly, Karl's mother, who works as a waitress, thinks that some day she will compose music or write a novel. She finished the eighth grade, whereas the father's education stopped even before he had reached this level. It would lead too far here to go into the details of the political beliefs of Karl and of his family; suffice it to say that they were definitely on the fascistic side.

Future publications will include further cases in which socioeconomic background fails to account for political and ethnic attitudes, along with others which can readily be understood in such terms.

III. CONCLUSION

By way of summary, it has appeared inadvisable to attempt any far-reaching compartmentalization of sociological versus psychological description. In our psychological description we found ourselves concerned with parental figures, with authority, with child-training, mating behavior, and so forth. All of these are concepts frequently referred to by sociologists. On the other hand, we had to stress the fact that the psychological, and in particular the psychoanalytic, approach enables us to catch certain subtle aspects of human behavior which are usually bypassed in purely sociological descriptions. For example, such a formal principle as that of the closeness of opposites, first observed by Freud (1915a) in discussing the vicissitudes of instincts, has been shown to be a much more general characteristic of individual behavior than was originally anticipated; it is probably applicable to societies as well. Depth psychology has challenged the dominance of the phenotype in psychological thinking and has sharpened our eyes to the underlying dynamic patterns.

Thus we found in our ethnocentric men that stress on virility goes hand in hand with an underlying passivity and receptivity which leads to the wish to follow a strong leader and to be his lieutenant. A person of this kind demands approval of, and submission to, parents, teachers, and authority in general; at the same time his underlying resentment and even hatred of such authority is only thinly disguised in his protocols. His explicit emphasis on conventional values is paralleled by a leaning toward destruction and chaos. In fact, there seems to be a vacillation between a total adoption and a total negation of the prevalent values of society; in this sense, lack of distance and too much distance from cultural values seem closely related. The avoidance of ambiguity and the need for absolutes indicate a desperate attempt to counteract internal chaos and the lack of social and personal identity. Ramifications of the pattern can be found in the prevalence of premature reduction of ambiguous perceptual and cognitive patterns to certainty by clinging to the familiar or by superimposing one or many distorting clichés upon stimuli which are not manageable in a simple or stereotyped fashion. The same tendency toward oversimplification often leads to anti-intellectualism and to the feeling that individualism, with its emphasis on uniqueness and on responsibility, is too heavy a burden.

In a society in which alternative ideologies are offered, a prediction from psychological data of such social and political beliefs as liberalism or totalitarianism seems to offer good chances of success. Prediction of the ethnocentrism score on the basis of the clinical interview has been fairly successful in our studies. In addition to the features already mentioned, insight into one's own shortcomings, thinking in social and psychological terms, and equalitarianism in interpersonal relations seemed intimately connected with liberalism, while externalization of one's own problems and their projection into the environment and into the social scene, as well as excessive power orientation, seemed intimately connected with ethnocentrism. Certain personality scales correlate as high as .8 with fascist ideology.

The correlations of authoritarian attitudes with socioeconomic factors as such are much less pronounced. Some relations have been found to occupational categories, as well as to the fact of having a long history of American ancestry. Particularly important in this connection is the concept of social marginality. Since this concept is best defined in terms of the relation between aspired-to and achieved status, it is tied to both sociological and psychological factors; and it has been extended to cover sexual and physical marginality as well. Any of these kinds of marginality will often—but by no means always—lead to overconformity and rigidity in the social, as well as in the cognitive, area.

All this is not to say that the frequency of the authoritarian personality within a given society will primarily determine whether totalitarianism as a political movement will or will not come to the fore in that society at a given time. It is not enough that a few people support such a movement; there must be mass support in the end. In our society the increasing mental standardization accompanying the processes of mass production, the increasing difficulty of genuine identification with society due to the anonymity of the big organizations and the ensuing isolation of the individual, the unintelligibility of political and social forces, the decline of the individual's ability to decide and master his life rationally and autonomously, and, finally, the power of propaganda machinery to manipulate, are among the most potent of the factors which might contribute to such mass support in the foreseeable future. The tradition of having a many-power system and the tradition of democracy, the readiness to criticize governmental as well as parental authorities, the resistance against oversystematization, the increased number of choices offered by technological progress, and the intensified attempt to understand the social and economic processes in their inconsistencies and irrationalities, are among the most potent preventive factors which justify an optimistic outlook.

Since every person possesses features of the authoritarian as well as of the democratic personality, though in varying proportions, such objective factors as economic conditions and such psychological factors as feelings of dissatisfaction, helplessness, and isolation may decide the issue in a particular over-all situation. Otherwise we could not understand the relatively abrupt increase of authoritarianism and ethnocentrism in Nazi Germany. We certainly cannot consider ethnocentrism, fascism, and communism as due solely to shortcomings of backward and immature persons; rather, we must see such mass movements as intrinsic in the totality of social organization. As we have stated before, it is especially the ethnocentric person who seems to be responsive to trends within our society, to the extent that he seems culture-bound. Instead of showing individual faults, he seems to be the prototype of a member of a mass society. He has given up his personal identity and is ready to be moved by propaganda. Even his hate is mobile and can be directed from one object to another. Therefore, we overrate such a person if we assume that his behavior is determined by self-interest, political, economic, or social. In effect, the Nazi elite acted against its own interest and in the direction of self-destruction; in this case, rational self-interest was overlaid by the need for self-glorification and for an overestimation of the self's own strength, as well as by the corresponding need to depreciate the strength of the enemy and—characteristically—to see the enemy as effeminate.

Returning once more to the authoritarian person in our society, we note that—strangely enough—it is this externally overadjusted type who is internally much less adjusted than the democratic-minded person. The relation of the latter to society can best be described as one of medium distance. It is true that the authoritarian character in a certain sense is a mirror of his society. Yet at the same time he oversimplifies and distorts the social and cultural realities which have shaped him, as he distorts the perceptual ones. He reacts to some of the clichés rather than to the underlying complexities of our society. For this reason his adjustments function only under narrowly circumscribed conditions. He is not adapted to change and thus lacks one of the most important requirements in all modern societies.

The person whose relationship to society is more basic and more reliable is at the same time one who can afford to be more critical and who can face more easily the external as well as the internal inconsistencies. So long as these inconsistencies can be faced, splitting of the personality can be avoided and a greater flexibility and integration is possible, even if this integration is achieved by nothing more than an awareness that one has to behave inconsistently. There is no way around the fact that in a democracy each citizen is called upon to accept many-sidedness, conflicts, uncertainties, differences, and complexities. But this necessity is compatible with, and even congenial to, the holding of strong beliefs in intrinsic principles of conduct, so long as these principles are broadly and flexibly conceived and alternative manifestations are permitted. Rigid adherence to an absolute dogma is a poor substitute for such intrinsic, and basically more consistent, principles; it constitutes an inadequate attempt to escape lurking chaos, cynicism, and unbridled relativism. It is for this reason that superpatriots and defenders of a rigid national code may abruptly turn to disbelief and even treachery.

Should the more individualized approach to other people and to themselves and the greater courage to be "different" which are found among democratic-minded persons be interpreted to mean that they are less interwoven with their culture than are ethnocentric persons? We can perhaps say that the former are less rigidly culture-bound; but they are not any less determined by the general institutions of our culture than are the authoritarian personalities. Christian ethics with its emphasis on internalization, the American melting-pot ideal, the democratic tradition with its protective attitude toward the weak, the emphasis on individualism— all of these human institutions must certainly be called upon to help explain the democratic personality. Today as never before we witness a contrasting crystallization of the two patterns, although they may frequently be interwoven. Power orientation, anti-intellectualism, externalization, hostile exclusion, rigid stereotyping, and dogmatism are on the one side; understanding, thoughtfulness, empathy, compassion, insight, flexibility, justice, reason, and scholarship are on the other.

One of the important questions facing us today is just how much ambiguity, uncertainty, and dissolution of traditional values people are able to face without being overcome by anxiety and by a wish to "escape from freedom," to use the term popularized by Fromm. New constructive solutions, free of recourse to oversimplification and dogmatism, will have to be substituted for discarded ones if we are to avoid putting too great a burden upon the individual. Only if we succeed in this effort can we circumvent the tendency of certain persons to compensate for their own personal impotence by erecting the image of an all-powerful leader and by attaching themselves to a doctrine which promises an absolute and all-embracing answer to their confusions.

6

ENVIRONMENTAL CONTROLS AND THE IMPOVERISHMENT OF THOUGHT

THE ROLE OF PSYCHOLOGY IN THE STUDY OF TOTALITARIANISM

It is conceivable that in the study of certain social and political movements, especially the more matter-of-fact or rational ones, psychology will have little to say. Thus psychology may not play an obvious or prominent role in the explanation of the formation and structure of the American Constitution. But in the elucidation of inherently compensatory and distortive social systems such as totalitarianism, the picture could not be made complete without the aid of psychology. To be sure, totalitarianism originates in the structure of society as a whole and this structure is shaped in the ultimate analysis by historical, economic, and political forces. Since all these factors depend on psychological processes for their mediation, it is obvious that psychological dynamics may play into the resulting course of events. Especially as soon as we shift our view from the origin of political institutions to the manner of their functioning, and particularly to the influence they exert upon the cognitive and social behavior of the individuals and groups that make up the concrete instruments of their execution, it becomes clear that totalitarianism, almost by definition, undertakes to permeate and to indoctrinate every area of individual or collective life. An inquiry into the complete cycle must therefore consider both the structure of the social institutions and the differ-

---

Reprinted by permission of the publishers from *Totalitarianism*, ed. C. J. Friedrich. Cambridge, Mass.: Harvard University Press, 1954, pp. 171-202. © 1954 by the President and Fellows of Harvard College.

ent ways in which the political and social organization is experienced by, and incorporated within, the individual.[1]

Although promises concerning economic and social amelioration seem to play an outstanding role in authoritarian systems, there are strong reasons to believe that it is not these promises which exercise the most potent psychological appeal. For those who have fallen within the grasp of totalitarianism, rational argument is overshadowed by the image of an all-powerful, superhuman leader whose aura of strength, superiority, and glory afford surcease from feelings of isolation, frustration, and helplessness, and whose doctrines provide an absolute and all-embracing answer to the conflicts and confusions of life and relief from the burdens of self-determination. These solutions, presented in a dogmatic, apodictic, and often inarticulate and unintelligible way, are formulated for the explicit purpose of bypassing the processes of reasonable consideration and to find their mark in those emotional and instinctual processes which prompt precipitant action. Reason, deliberation, and a many-sided orientation toward objects, situations, or life itself then appear as irrelevant and thus as morbid. Beyond and above material advantages offered, there is provided a style of thought and of life, a systematic outlook, an ideology.

This ideology not only delineates the required political attitudes, but implies by force of psychological necessity the attitudes toward authority in general, and the conceptions of family, of work, of sex roles;[2] upon some scrutiny it seems that hardly a corner of thought or activity remains that completely escapes its reach.

Here again we must call upon historical, economic, and political factors to explain the conditions under which people are rendered helpless and develop a longing for total surrender and a craving for absolute and definite solutions. The same factors may provide an explanation of why certain groups within a population, for instance the lower-middle class in Germany, are especially susceptible to totalitarian ideology. The marginality of this group and the discrepancy between its social aspirations and its actual socioeconomic position have frequently been mentioned in this context. But look-

[1] For the function of psychology in the study of political and social movements, see also this volume, Chapter 5.
[2] The function of ideology in totalitarian systems has been emphasized by most students of totalitarianism. See especially Fromm (1941) and Mannheim (1936).

ing beyond the socioeconomic factors concerned, it is psychology which is instrumental in discerning the particular psychic needs to which totalitarian ideology appeals, and in identifying the strong emotive reactions which lead to a partially voluntary renunciation not only of critical faculties but in the end of self-interest as well, and to a readiness for self-sacrifice or even self-destruction.

Although the ideology as such must also be conceived as originating in the total structure and history of a given society, it is its psychological function which provides an explanation of why dictators are able to elicit spontaneous and genuine followings over and above the adherence they ever could achieve by compulsion, and why those who follow do not become disillusioned in the face of material promises which are never fulfilled. We may perhaps expand psychologically upon the frequently used phrase that the function of totalitarianism is comparable to that of a religion (see especially Neumann, 1942). Totalitarianism seems to create the illusion that merely embracing its ideology confers a kind of magical participation in the source of all power and thus provides absolute salvation and protection.[3] The analysis of magical thinking with its characteristic confusions of subject and reality and of reality and symbol has been one of the prime concerns of recent psychology, especially in areas bordering on anthropological and evolutionary or developmental considerations (Werner, 1940). Only by recourse to magical involvement can we hope to account for the fact that individual freedom is cheerfully relinquished by many and that the most contradictory statements—such as the Nazis' promise of socialism to the masses and their promise to industry that capitalism would be saved—are taken in stride. The function of the ideology more than compensates for the lack of a realistic program. This is one of the reasons why fascistic movements must depend as much as they do on elaborate ideologies.

This system of ideas as expressed in an ideology is not, as Marx would have it, merely a superstructure or an epiphenomenon; it is the formative force which molds and shapes into total subjection those whom it touches. These ideologies not only appeal skillfully to the so-called higher moral forces by their reference to glory,

---

[3]The propensity toward magical thinking and superstition in persons susceptible to totalitarianism has been empirically demonstrated: see Adorno et al. (1950) and Frenkel-Brunswik (1948c).

superiority, honor, and other virtues: they also provide outlets and give permission for the release of "lower" needs, especially aggression, under the pretext of subordinating these needs to the exercise of moral indignation. Though it is of course beyond doubt that opportunistic reasons are of considerable significance in the totalitarian appeal, especially as far as adequate instrumentality and adequate means-end relationships are concerned, much of the behavior, especially on the part of the genuinely enthusiastic branch of the followership, must be viewed as irrational.[4] In the face of the concrete psychological evidence which is continually accumulating, and some of which is to be surveyed below, it would be extremely difficult to shut one's eyes to the fact that irrationality, distortion of perception, and the projections of hostility and of other thwarted tendencies enter the social and political scene as a major component. In turn, this irrationality, although more prominent under certain specified historical and socioeconomic conditions, cannot be explained within the framework of these conditions alone but must be viewed, in addition, from a psychological point of view.

In the present paper an attempt is made to throw light on the psychological mechanisms by which the totalitarian outlook is transmitted and on the role it plays in the adjustment balance of the individual. Our findings show a parallelism between the social and political organization of totalitarianism and the structure and functioning of persons who are susceptible to this ideology. Thus we will find in statistical samples of such persons a more or less pronounced preponderance of mechanization, standardization, stereotypy, dehumanization of social contacts, piecemeal functioning, rigidity, intolerance of ambiguity and a need for absolutes, lack of individuation and spontaneity, a self-deceptive profession of exalted ideals, and a combination of overrealism with bizarre and magic thinking as well as "irrationality with manipulative opportunism" (see this volume, Chapter 5, p. 234). All these are features inherent in the system of totalitarian ideologies. Not only do we find statistically significant relationships between political attitudes and personality make-up, but our understanding of social and political beliefs and of religious and ethical

[4]The quality of irrationality has been stressed by many investigators of totalitarianism. See especially Fromm (1941) and Mannheim (1936).

ideologies is deepened when these factors are woven into the matrix of the total person. That these attitudes are also woven into the pattern of society is more widely stressed and more generally accepted than are the relationships of these attitudes to the seemingly more remote intimate aspects of our lives.[5] The time seems to have come to establish a proper balance by stressing personality structure along with social behavior as an important link in the societal network. An analysis of the psychological processes involved will increase our understanding and possible control of totalitarianism, as long as we remain aware that this avenue of approach is by no means the only one and that totalitarianism, like every social movement, is multidetermined. This fact, however, does not require that every single investigator deal with and control all the factors involved. Such a quest for completeness would be but an invitation to dilettantism.

Since the eradication of independent and critical judgment lies at the very core of totalitarianism, we shall concentrate on this theme. But we hope at the same time to throw light on other psychological aspects of totalitarianism. We shall draw on the resources of academic psychology, with its emphasis on perception and cognition and the adaptive processes in general, as well as on those of social psychology, with its emphasis on social attitudes and their relationship to social institutions, and last but not least on those of depth psychology, which has sharpened our eyes to the underlying pattern of the emotive and instinctual life and has helped us to differentiate the "official" façade from the "dynamic" realities of social behavior.

In order to expand our knowledge concerning distortive interference with thought processes, our group at the University of California undertook to study the cognitive approach of a sample of children and adolescents (age 10 and older) growing up in American homes.[6] We proceeded through direct observation and

---

[5] Harold D. Lasswell's *Psychopathology and Politics* (1930) should be singled out as a pioneer study in relating political attitudes to personal life histories.

[6] For brief surveys of the plan and of some of the major results of the project involved, the California Study of Social Discrimination in Youth, see Frenkel-Brunswik (1948c, 1951a). This project was part of the activities of the Institute of Child Welfare of the University of California. The separate project on the authoritarian personality, cited above (Adorno et al., 1950), dealt with adult subjects only and did not involve a study of the conception of social roles at the ideological level or of purely cognitive processes, nor did it involve a direct observation of the subjects' families. The present paper concentrates on the aspects just listed.

by experiment, using as our subjects those who had previously been found to have either a relatively extreme democratic or a relatively extreme totalitarian outlook. The susceptibility to totalitarian ideas turned out to be correlated with the outlook of, and the home regime exercised by, the parents, who had been interviewed separately from the children. These data were collected during and shortly after the last war. Many of the parents selected on the basis of their susceptibility to totalitarian ideas expressed more or less veiled sympathies for the existing dictatorships in Germany or Italy, or at least they made some attempts to vindicate these regimes.

Choice of the approach via personality is especially called for when objective social structure is taken for granted as a common background for an investigation aiming primarily at the finding of differences in the appeal that various aspects of one and the same civilization—here the American—exert upon varying personalities. In a society as complex as ours, we find contradictory social institutions and political currents. Psychological factors must be called in to help explain selectivity and choice between alternative ideologies. Although our studies are concerned with American samples, the universality of the authoritarian personality type will emerge by the comparison of our findings with the views of the leading Nazi psychologist, E. R. Jaensch, who explicitly extolled rigidity, lack of adaptability, and anti-intellectualism—all features which develop in the wake of totalitarianism and which we too found prominently displayed in persons in this country who are susceptible to totalitarian ideas.

For a number of years my students and I collected materials on perception, reasoning, and imagination and related them to the types of upbringing to which our subjects were exposed. The intimidating, punitive, and paralyzing influence of an over-disciplined, totalitarian home atmosphere seems to have effects upon the thinking and creativity of the growing child analogous to those which are apparent under totalitarian social and political regimes. We came to realize that situations encountered within the family unit and the special destinies of early experiences stemming from these situations contribute in large measure to the way social institutions are experienced, integrated, and selectively responded to. This may be especially true in countries where such choices are actually open to the individual. A consideration of the responses to threats in childhood seems to reveal much about the ways in which people react to threats in adult life, though such intensive experiences in later life are undoubtedly in themselves capable of superseding both earlier influences and individual predispositions to a certain extent. It seems that external pressures of a traumatic character, be they past or be they currently imposed, are likely not only to bring authoritarian personalities to the fore but to reinforce authoritarian trends in persons who would otherwise remain democratic-minded.

Our finding that harsh discipline at home inhibits and paralyzes the thought processes of growing children does not necessarily imply a direct or exclusive causal relationship between family structure and the rise of totalitarianism. Although in Germany a long history of authoritarian regimes is mirrored in, and undoubtedly reinforced by, authoritarian family and school structures, totalitarianism may well arise in countries with more permissive family atmospheres. Anxiety-inducing social and political situations such as economic depression or war can bring to the fore irrational elements and feelings of helplessness, and thus create susceptibility to totalitarianism regardless of how democratic the family situation might have been. What we mainly want to achieve by reference to the family atmosphere of our authoritarian subjects is to demonstrate in slow motion the effects of threats upon thinking and thus to understand better the analogous processes in the social and political area.

SUBMISSION TO AUTHORITY, DOGMA, AND CONVENTION

Before we proceed to a more detailed discussion of the thought patterns, in the cognitive area proper, of the persons susceptible to totalitarian ideas, let us sketch briefly the way in which preconceived and stereotypic categorizations determined by authority, dogma, and convention permeate their general social outlook. The materials reveal a hierarchical rather than equalitarian conception of human relationships, characterized primarily by admiration for the strong and contempt for the weak. There is a tendency for total, unquestioning, albeit ambivalent, surrender to every manner of authority—be it a political leader, a superior in business or army, a teacher, a parent, or, as we will see, even a perceptual stimulus. The same rigid and compulsive conformity is exercised toward socially accepted standards of behavior—even though the standards may sometimes be unwritten and those of a small "ingroup"—and this conformity is accompanied by an unrealistic and punitive condemnation of those who deviate from such norms.

This compulsive conformity, with its all-or-none character, differs in several ways from genuine and constructive conformity. First, it is excessive since it compensates for feelings of marginality and the attendant fear of becoming an outcast, and since it often serves the function of covering up resentment—unconscious as this resentment may be—toward the social system as a whole. The lack of a genuine incorporation of the values of society accounts for the rigidity of the conformity; at the same time it accounts for a certain unreliability, a readiness to shift allegiance altogether to other authorities and other standards. The adherence to the letter rather than to the spirit of the social institutions, which further characterizes the compulsive conformist, issues from his distortion and simplification of the system of norms and commands in the direction of what one may call unidimensional interpretation.

Along the lines just listed the ingroup is glorified while the outgroup is rejected *in toto*. External criteria rather than intrinsic values are prevalent in these dichotomies. In order to be able to maintain the image of oneself and of one's ingroup as strong and at the same time virtuous, fear, weakness, passivity, and aggressive feelings against authoritative ingroup figures are repressed. Lack of insight and differentiation in the emotional area result in the impoverishment of interpersonal relations and to projection of the unaccepted tendencies into the environment. Thus the other ones—and especially outgroups—are apt to be seen not only as basically weak and impotent but also as immoral, hostile, and depraved, and as imbued, therefore, with all the secondary power and strength such forces of darkness may be able to impart. In the wake of this there follows an attempt to compensate for the ensuing general distrust of people and pervasive cynicism by an overcredulity toward a few chosen leaders.

In the evaluation of the self[7] the authoritarian person is prone to emphasize such morally overpitched traits as "will power" and an iron determination in overcoming the handicaps and vicissitudes of a struggle for existence, the hardships of which are perceived in the image of unmitigated brutality. Energy, decisiveness, "ruggedness," and "toughness" tend to be particularly prominent in the ego ideal of the men in this group. There is evidence in our material that the display of a rough masculine façade serves to a considerable extent as a compensation for a basic self-contempt and intimidatedness and for the ensuing tendency toward passivity and dependence.

The ostentatious stress which, according to the findings in *The Authoritarian Personality* (Adorno et al., 1950), is placed by the ethnocentric person upon sincerity, honesty, courage, and self-control, along with his tendency toward self-glorification, must be evaluated in the light of certain earlier results based on a comparison of verbally espoused ideals with actual behavior (see also Frenkel-Brunswik, 1939). It was found that emphasis on favorable traits, of the type just mentioned, in one's "official" self-image or self-ideal tends to go with objective weakness rather than strength in the particular area concerned. One of the most significant findings concerning the authoritarian personality is the fact that the explicit self-image is in exactly the same contradiction to the one revealed in a more objective evaluation by the expert as had been found in the earlier study just referred to.

In line with repressions and the lack of insight, we also find in authoritarian persons a break in the experienced continuity between childhood self and present self. Subjects in this group tend to display a reluctance to make spontaneous reference to their lives as developmental units. They also tend to refrain from going into judicious sociopsychological explanations of the self as well as of others or of society in general.

The stereotypical approach to social and ethical challenges with all its inherent inhibitions carries over into such related, more specific areas as the conception of sex roles, parental roles, and so forth. At least on the surface there is an emphasis on aggression

---

[7]For more extensive discussion of the attitude toward the self, toward sex roles, and toward parents and other figures of authority, see the present writer's Chapters 10, 11, and 12 in *The Authoritarian Personality* (Adorno et al., 1950), and the material on adolescents in (1948c, 1951a).

and "toughness" and a disparagement of tenderness and softness ("sissiness") in the masculine ideal, and an emphasis on submissiveness, docility, and "sweetness" in the feminine ideal professed by the authoritarian of either sex. The possibility of trespassing from one syndrome to the other is explicitly excluded. Rigid defenses are erected against cross-sexual tendencies, leading to a "rigid and exaggerated conception of masculinity and femininity"[8] at the ideological level, albeit with frequent breakthroughs of these repressed tendencies on the action level.

There is rigid categorization in terms of clearly delineated norms, even if this should imply the acceptance of restrictions and disadvantages for one's own sex group.

Aside from strength versus weakness, virtue versus vice, badness versus goodness, masculinity versus femininity, such dichotomies involve cleanliness versus dirtiness and a host of other pairs of opposites vaguely related to the basic juxtapositions. In each case the cleavage between the opposite attributes tends to be considered mutually exclusive, absolute, natural, and eternal. In this manner, there is a general tendency toward prejudgments on the basis of rigid set or dogma. Such an approach does not provide sufficient space for an independent variability or evaluation of facts nor for learning to use one's own experiences. It is in this manner that human relations become shallow and externalized.

In the individual children whom we have studied the total outlook, just described, seems to a very appreciable extent to have its root in the home. However, as mentioned above, we do not imply that this is the only or the decisive source of such attitudes; it is necessary to keep in mind that social conditions and institutions have a direct bearing on the family structure. Second, political institutions influence personality formation directly, especially if they are forcefully imposed with the help of all-inclusive ideologies as is the case in totalitarian regimes. In this context we must not forget that although at the action level Hitler may have contributed to the weakening of the family by placing loyalty to the state over loyalty to the family, at the ideological level he made use of the family as a potential instrument in the execution of to-

---

[8]See Frenkel-Brunswik (1948c, p. 299) for verbatim passages from the protocols of authoritarian and democratic-minded adolescents concerning their notions of masculine and feminine ideals.

talitarianism by advocating as a model of a man one who is a good soldier-father and as an ideal woman one who fulfills her child-rearing functions.

It is primarily the fact that the home discipline in authoritarian homes is experienced as overwhelming, unintelligible, and arbitrary, demanding at the same time total surrender, which makes for a parallelism with totalitarian political and social organizations. The parallel becomes even more evident if we consider that the child, by virtue of his objective weakness and dependence, is entirely at the mercy of the parental authorities and must find some way to cope with this situation. In our study we found that parents in the authoritarian group frequently feel threatened in their social and economic status, and that they try to counteract their feelings of marginality by an archaic and frequently unverbalized need for importance. It is noteworthy that what seems to matter is not so much the actual status on the socioeconomic ladder, nor the objective marginality within a certain class, but rather the subjective way these conditions are experienced and allowed to build up to certain vaguely conceived aspirations. Recent data further suggest that the concern with status of persons susceptible to totalitarianism is quite different from a realistic attempt to improve their position by concerted effort and adequate means-goal instrumentality. More often, we find their aspirations to take the form of an unspecific expectation of being helped by sudden changes in the external situation or by an imaginary person who is strong and powerful.

Authoritarian disciplinary rules seem to have their chief origin in this vaguely anticipatory yet inefficient state of social unrest on the part of the parents rather than in the developmental needs of the child. The parents expect the child to learn quickly certain external, rigid, and superficial rules and social taboos. At the same time they are impatient, demanding a quick execution of commands which leaves no time for finer discriminations and in the end creates an atmosphere comparable to acute physical danger. The rules to be enforced are largely nonfunctional caricatures of our social institutions based on a misunderstanding of their ultimate intent; in many ways one may even speak of a defiance of culture by external conformity. In any case, the rules are bound to be beyond the scope and understanding of the child. Compelling the child to obey the rules which he is thus unable to internalize may be considered as one of the major interferences with the development of a clear-cut personal identity. The authoritarian form of discipline is thus "ego destructive" in that it prevents the development of self-reliance and independence. The child, being stripped of his individuality, is made to feel weak, helpless, worthless, or even depraved.

Parents and parental figures, such as teachers or other authorities, acquire a threatening, distant, and forbidding quality. Disciplining, controlling, and keeping one in line is considered to be their major role. A systematic inquiry into the children's conceptions of ideal parents has shown that authoritarian children tend to consider strictness and harshness as some of the prime attributes of ideal parents. Next to this, another desirable quality of the ideal parent stressed by children in this group is that of delivering material goods. In contrast, the more democratic-minded children are given to stressing primarily companionship, understanding, and demonstration of love as the function of ideal parents.

It seems to be largely fear and dependency which discourage the child in the authoritarian home from conscious criticism and which lead to an unquestioning acceptance of punishment and to an identification with the punishing authority. This identification often goes as far as an ostentatious glorification of the parents. As we have learned from psychoanalysis, however, repressions of hostility cannot be achieved without at least creating emotional ambivalence. Thus the same children who seem most unquestionably to accept parental authority have frequently been found to harbor an underlying resentment and to feel victimized without being fully aware of this fact. The existing surface conformity without genuine integration expresses itself in a stereotypical approach devoid of genuine affect. The description of the parents elicited by interview questions is characterized by the use of exaggerated clichés rather than by expressions of genuine feelings. The range of responses is rather narrow and without the variations commonly found in descriptions of real people. Only the more palpable, crude, and concrete aspects are mentioned.

The rigidification of the child's personality originally induced by the stress on self-negating submission and on the repression of nonacceptable tendencies not only leads to stereotypy; eventually the inherent pattern of conflict may result in a more or less open break between the different layers of personality, and in a loss of control of instinctual tendencies by the individual. This contrasts rather sharply with the greater fluidity of transition and intercommunication between the different personality strata which is typical of the child in the more permissive home. This is not to say that we necessarily find a minimum of guidance and direction in the homes of those of our children and adolescents who show liberalism of personality structure and social outlook most markedly. On the contrary, guidance is essential, especially when it is combined with acceptance and understanding and thus strengthens the moral functions of the children and helps them to overcome their impulses toward selfishness and aggression.

PATTERNS OF PERCEPTION AND THOUGHT; INTOLERANCE OF AMBIGUITY

The emotional make-up and the rigidity of defense, lack of insight, and narrowness of the ego of the authoritarian personality as just described carries over even into the purely cognitive domain. Here too, ready-made clichés tend to take the place of realistic spontaneous reactions. This is one of the findings of experiments on perception, memory, and thinking in liberal and authoritarian children (see this volume, Chapter 2) which have been conducted with the purpose of investigating the pervasiveness of ways of functioning within the authoritarian personality. The shift from the social and emotional to the cognitive area has the added advantage of removing us from the controversial social issues under consideration. So long as we remain under the potential spell of certain preconceived notions, the evaluation of what is reality adequate or reality inadequate may be difficult. The fascist may accuse the liberal, and the liberal the fascist, of distorting reality.

In one of the experiments a story—conceived as a clear-cut piece of reality—was presented to children of distinctly authoritarian and of distinctly liberal outlook. The story began with the portrayal of a number of different children and proceeded to a description of their behavior toward a newcomer in terms of aggressiveness versus protectiveness. In retelling the story, authoritarian children tended toward a restriction of scope by concentrating on certain single phrases and details; or else they tended to stray away from the original altogether so that in extreme cases there was almost no relation to the material presented. In other words, there was either a clinging to the original elements with little freedom and distance—a "stimulus boundness" in the sense of the psychiatrist Kurt Goldstein (1943; see also Goldstein and Scheerer, 1941)—or else a far-reaching neglect of the stimulus in favor of purely subjective fantasies. In this manner a rigid, cautious, segmentary approach seems to go well with one that is disintegrated and chaotic. The same child sometimes manifests both patterns in alternation or in all kinds of bizarre combinations. Both of these ways of responding result in an avoidance of uncertainty, one by fixation to, and the other by breaking away from, the given realities.

Another result of this experiment was that the authoritarian children tended to recall a higher ratio of undesirable over desirable features in the characters involved. This result is in line with another of our empirical findings, that is, a general overemphasis on negative, hostile, and catastrophic features in stories given by authoritarian-minded subjects in responses to the Thematic Apperception Test (see Murray, 1938).

In democratic-minded children the average ratio of undesirable to desirable features recalled was closer to the ratio in the original story than was the case in authoritarian children, indicating greater faithfulness to the "reality" presented. In addition, there is some tendency toward remembering the friendly features better than the unfriendly ones. This is in line with other evidence from liberal subjects revealing the operation of a mechanism of "denial" of aggression and violence, that is, a certain naïveté or ostrich policy toward evil.

Some of the trends reported above become especially apparent in an experiment on perception. When presented with pictures of familiar objects and then with similar but ambiguous or unfamiliar stimuli, authoritarian children tended to cling to the name of the original object and in other ways to respond but slowly to the changing of the stimuli. There was a marked reluctance to give up what had seemed certain, and a tendency not to see what did not harmonize with the first set, as well as a shying away from transitional solutions. Once broken, this rigid perseveration was usually followed either by a spell of haphazard, reckless guessing or by a complete blockage. Situations possessing inherent uncertainties or otherwise lacking in firmness thus seem bewildering and disturbing to the authoritarian child even if there is no particular emotional involvement. In most of the other verbal productions there is a similar pattern of either restrictiveness or flow of sterile rumination. Assumptions once made, even though proved faulty and out of keeping with reality, tend to be repeated over and over and not to be corrected in the face of new evidence.

The conclusion suggests itself that all this constitutes an effort to counteract, in the cognitive sphere, the excessive underlying emotional ambivalence induced by environmental overcontrol. The resulting syndrome I have proposed to call "intolerance of ambiguity." A rigid cognitive superstructure in which everything opaque and complex is avoided as much as possible is superimposed upon the conflict-ridden emotional understructure. In effect, this merely duplicates slavery to authority rather than remedying it. Now there is not only slavery to the authority of the other person; there is also slavery to the authority of the stimulus. In other words, the attitude toward a perceptual stimulus or a cognitive task mirrors the attitude toward authority.

The following aspects of intolerance of ambiguity may be specified: tendency toward unqualified black-white and either-or solutions; oversimplified dichotomizing; stereotypy; perseveration and mechanical repetition of sets and of faulty hypotheses; premature "closure" and preference for symmetry, regularity, and definiteness in the sense of "good" (or *prägnant*) form as defined by Gestalt psychology (see Koffka, 1935), achieved either by diffuse globality or by overemphasis on concrete detail; compartmentalization; piecemeal approach; stimulus boundness; quest for unqualified certainty as accomplished by pedantic narrowing of meanings, by stress on familiarity, by inaccessibility to new experience, or by a segmentary randomness and an absolutizing of those aspects of reality which have been preserved; satisfaction with subjective yet unimaginative, overconcrete, or overgeneralized solutions. Totalitarian propaganda takes advantage of this syndrome by the use of vague generalities combined with reference to unessential concrete detail. The opposite attitude, "tolerance of ambiguity," embraces the many-sidedness, complexity, and differentiation which is an essential aspect of the creative process. It has nothing to do with confusion or inarticulate vagueness; in fact, it is in diametrical opposition to these latter features.

The fact that specific manifestations of intolerance of ambiguity tend to recur within a person in contexts seemingly far removed from each other is best brought out by a synoptic analysis of corresponding segments in the protocols of individual cases. Thus, one of the boy subjects in our study showed a great deal of conformity and compliance toward parents and authorities with an occasional breaking through of fits of rage and explosive aggression. This was reflected in the various perceptual and thinking experiments by a generally cautious, restricted, and conservative attitude toward the stimulus with an occasional shift toward disintegrated, random behavior when the strain of coping with the task became too great. Other case studies reveal that some of the authoritarian children perform well on some relatively simple or routine perceptual and cognitive tasks—tasks which do not require imagination or freedom from stimulus boundness—in spite of the fact that there are signs of rigidity in their performance; here we are reminded of the frequently noted technological abilities of the Nazis.

The subtle but profound distortion of reality in the course of the elimination of ambiguities is in the last analysis precipitated by the fact that stereotypical categorizations can never do justice to all the possible aspects of reality. So long as a culture provides socially accepted outlets for suppressed impulses, smooth functioning and fair adjustment can be achieved within the given framework. But the adjustment of the authoritarian-minded person depends on conditions that are comparatively narrowly circumscribed. Whenever differentiation and adaptability to change are required, this adjustment will run the risk of breaking down. Basically, therefore, the various forms of rigidity and of avoidance of ambiguity, directed as they are toward a simplified mastery of the environment, turn out to be maladaptive in the end.

Dramatized, concrete, and at the same time global, diffuse, and undifferentiated types of thinking are, of course, characteristic of certain early developmental stages as such. However, the atmosphere of the home and the more specific expectations of the parents regarding the child's behavior determine whether such primitive reactions become fixated, or whether progress toward higher developmental stages can take place. For the latter course, a reduction of fear, greater relaxation, and acceptance of and tolerance for insecurity and weakness in and by the child are necessary. Realism, originality, and imaginative cognitive penetration presuppose some such advance in general psychological maturity.

Closeness of Opposites as a Principle of Personality Organization

In spite of the rather consistent recurrence of common elements in various areas, there is no obvious or simple "unity of style" in the authoritarian personality. This is due at least in part to the many repressions and to the break between the conscious and unconscious levels as discovered and explored by depth psychology (Freud, 1915a). The authoritarian person has been found to combine within himself rigid perseverative behavior with an overfluid, haphazard, disintegrated, random approach; compulsive overcaution with the tendency toward impulsive shortcuts to action; chaos and confusion with orderly oversimplification in terms of black-white solutions and stereotypy; isolation with fusion; lack of differentiation with the mixing of elements which do not belong together; extreme concreteness with extreme generality; cynicism with gullibility; overrealism with irrationality; self-glorification with self-contempt; submission to powerful authorities with resentment against them; and stress on masculinity with a tendency toward feminine passivity.

The seeming paradox given by these coexistences is resolved when one considers the fact, hinted at previously in this paper, that a personality thrown out of balance in one direction usually requires counterbalancing in the opposite direction. Elsewhere I have spoken of the "closeness of opposites" as an essential feature of authoritarian personality organization. Indeed, the authoritarian personality may be characterized as consistently inconsistent, or as consistently self-conflicting. In elaborating on intolerance of ambiguity it became evident that lack of distance and too much distance to culture, parents, and other stimulus configurations are more closely related to each other than is either of these opposites to what may be termed "medium distance" from these environmental realities. The nonauthoritarian personality avoids undue reduction of existing complexities and retains balance by maintaining a flexible type of conformity and order. A kind of self-reconciled consistency is thus achieved which manages the inconsistencies of reality at the conscious level rather than allowing them to invade the unconscious and to be lived out by devious means of tension reduction and by displacement of aggression upon substitute targets.

Although most of our authoritarian adolescents tend to follow the self-conflicting pattern described above, we are able to distinguish subvarieties in whom one or the other side prevails. In one there is a prevalence of control, rigidity, caution, and order as far as overt behavior is concerned, while the chaotic side becomes manifest only under stress; in the other there is a predominance of chaos, fusion, and impulsive action while the ideal of control and rigid order remains to a large extent confined to the symbolic level of consciously accepted values.

Explicit Espousal of Rigidity in the Nazi Personality Ideal

While to us the authoritarian pattern of personality seemed impoverished and closed to new experiences, many of the features which from the standpoint of adjustment to physical or social realities must be described as negative were listed among the desirable attributes of an ideal type of personality by E. R. Jaensch of Marburg. Jaensch is probably the most articulate and brilliant exponent of the Nazi ideology so far as professional psychological contributions to this field are concerned. He was the Hitler-appointed permanent president of the German Psychological Association until his death in 1940. He formulated a comprehensive valuative personality typology in the thousands of pages he published during the last years of his life. An analysis of his writings reveals some important aspects of the most markedly fascistic version of German thinking. Exposure of his self-contradictions and rectification of his errors is important in view of the fact that his writings carry a great deal of sweep and persuasive power, hardly diminished by the endless repetitions and confusions with which they are encumbered. His misuse and distortion of basic categories and facts, his subtle mixture of insight and confabulation will continue to have a great appeal to a frame of mind by no means dead with the military defeat of Nazism. Jaensch's most comprehensive publications on the subject (1938) bear the following characteristic title, in translation: "The Antitype: Psychological-Anthropological Foundations of German Cultural Philosophy Based on What We Must Overcome." This antitype (*Gegentypus*) is seen as the enemy of the national German movement and the incorporation of all that is evil.

The antitype is characterized primarily by tendencies toward loosening (*Auflockerung*) and dissolving (*Auflösung;* hence also the term "lytic type"). The antitype is also called the S-type since he allegedly often manifests synesthesia, the well-known phenomenon of color-hearing or tone-seeing. Jaensch sees in this latter phenomenon a lack of clear-cut and rigid evaluation of, and submission to, the stimulus on the part of the perceptual response.

Passages from Jaensch's *Der Gegentypus* (1938), presented in my own literal translation, will illustrate his notions of the antitype. It should be stressed at this point that Jaensch is notorious for his neglect of even the most elementary principles of statistical scrutiny. Many of his statements concerning interrelationships of traits are downright incorrect, while others are merely unsubstantiated.

We begin with a quotation referring to perception:

> His spatial percepts are unstable, loosened up, even dissolved. Normally the objects of the external world are given to the psychophysical organism of man in a univocally determined spatial order. (Each object in the external world creates an image on the retina of our eye ... To the points of the retina correspond firmly and univocally determined locations in visual space or, as this is usually expressed, the spatial values of the retina are fixed.) This fixed—more precisely we should say relatively fixed—coordination between its stimulus configuration and perceptual gestalt is disrupted in the case of the S-type [p. 37].

In this quotation, Jaensch considers his ideal German type as giving unambiguous reactions to stimuli, a feature which he confuses with receptiveness and precision. This desideratum of a one-to-one relationship between stimulus and response directly contradicts the findings of modern psychology, especially those of the so-called Gestalt psychology, which experimentally demonstrated the universal multiple determination of our perceptual responses by a variety of factors, some of them constellational and some attitudinal or temporal. It is for the stress on spontaneous perceptual "restructuring" and on its crucial role in problem solving and in scientific or artistic creativity that Jaensch has declared the orientation of Gestalt psychology to be "morbid." Jaensch's glorification of rigid stimulus-response relationships and his assertion of their predominance in the ideal Nazi type fits well with the fact that what we have called intolerance of ambiguity is predominant in our authoritarian children.

Rigid control, perseveration, and avoidance of differences are also an integral part of Jaensch's ideal of discipline. To him, one of the most gratifying experiences is the feeling of "equality of palpable, physical characteristics... [wearing a] uniform, marching in step and column" (p. 337). The antitype is criticized for his aspiration to some measure of being different in developing his individuality.

All this ties in with a questionable notion of masculinity. As we have found in our authoritarian subjects, emphasis on an exaggerated ideal of "toughness" goes with repression and rejection of feminine traits in men, and with contempt for women. There is hardly any mention of women in Jaensch's presentation; when there is, usually some affinity between women and the antitype is construed. According to Jaensch, the struggle between firmness and lack of firmness, between stability and what he calls "lability," is identical with the struggle between the masculine and its opposite, disparagingly labeled the "effeminate."

All-important to Jaensch is the evaluation of the antitype as to his aptitude for military service, considered by him one of the highest values:

> The pronounced lytic type is . . . an "antitype" not only from the standpoint of our German national movement but also from that of military psychology. He is the one of whom the army must beware most, the extremely unsoldierly type. . . . Since he lacks all firmness the lytic type is always more or less unvirile . . . far removed from a heroic conception of life [pp. 38ff.].

The intellect, as such, is considered a nonvirile element in this latter sense. The antitype is said to have an inclination toward the playful, aesthetic, and intellectual. We have actually found this inclination to be present in our liberal-minded subjects but have found little reason for looking askance at it. Again, Jaensch confuses two essentially disparate and incompatible features, the looseness of arbitrary license on the one hand, and the loosening of rigid fixations that defines genuine mastery of the stimulus at the level of essentials on the other. So he comes to think that "liberalism" of any kind—"liberalism of knowledge, of perception, of art, etc." (p. 44)—is identical with a libertine lack of firmness and stability of the personality. And he assumes liberalism—along with "adaptability" in general (see below)—to be degenerative, immoral, and dangerous for society.

Prominent in Jaensch's version of anti-intraceptiveness and anti-intellectualism is his attitude toward scientific theorizing. Jaensch sees theory not in its positive function as a detour to better understanding of reality but rather as a subjectivistic leading away from reality. (It is possible to trace such overemphasis on nearness to reality to an underlying tendency to escape from reality.) Concerning the particular case of relativity theory in physics, Jaensch has this to say:

> The struggle conducted by the physicists Lenard and Stark in an attempt to dislodge the theory of Einstein by establishing a more concretely oriented "German physics" can be understood only from this point of view. It is the struggle for consideration of reality in natural science and against the . . . inclination to dissolve all reality into theory [pp. 46, 49].

It will be remembered that more recently Soviet writers have attacked Einstein from an antitheoretical standpoint very similar to that of the Nazis, accusing him of an "idealistic" orientation in his physics.

Systematic espousal of rigid environmental controls by totalitarian regimes thus seems not only to stifle imagination and to prevent the acquisition of the theoretical skills so necessary for the comprehension of reality, but even to lead to glorification of this defect and to its being turned into a propagandistic weapon. In tricks of this kind lie one of the seeds of self-destruction inherent in totalitarian systems.

The way in which intolerance of ambiguity and anti-intellectualism tie in with racial theory is revealingly illustrated by the following quotation from Jaensch. In the case of racial mixture,

> nature has to leave . . . everything uncertain and in suspense. . . . The individual at birth may be endowed with nothing fixed and certain, just with the uncertainty, indeterminability, and changeability which will enable him to adjust to each of the various conditions of life . . . The opposite is true if an individual possesses only ancestors who from time immemorial have lived in the North German space and within its population . . . The characteristics necessary for this life therefore may be safely placed in his cradle as innate, fixed, and univocally determined features [pp. 230ff.].

Jaensch further states that in the case of blood mixture, which he considers an "abnormal state of affairs," adaptability must be increased since "the entire conduct of life and the total existence is entrusted to intelligence alone"; and he adds condemningly that "among all the higher mental functions intelligence is the most flexible and adaptable." In discussing adaptability, Jaensch further points out that the antitype, when engaged in psychology and anthropology, is prone to think in terms of environment, education, intellectual influences, and reason, whereas his ideal type will refer to such factors as blood, soil, and heredity.

The Jews are considered the purest though by no means the only representatives of the S-type, and this Jaensch attempts to relate to racial mixture:

> According to Hans F. K. Gunther, the Jews do not constitute a primary race but rather a highly complex racial mixture. This may be taken as an explanation for the fact that they tend so much toward the dissolving type, and that they play such an outstanding role in the development of a dissolution culture [p. 22].

Racial pollution is connected in Jaensch's mind with physical pollution by germs: "Already in studying adults we were impressed by the fact that bodily illness, especially tuberculosis, is found most frequently in the group representing the S-type" (p. 22). Fear of germs and of spread of contagious disease has in our California material been found to be a prominent preoccupation of the authoritarian personality syndrome. According to psychoanalytic theory, the idea of pollution and contamination with germs is related to sexual thoughts. And indeed, Jaensch somewhat fantastically proceeds to say:

> Since some kind of connection between tuberculosis and schizophrenia is established on the basis of the development and the symptomatology of the two diseases, and since, on the other hand, the connection between schizophrenia and an affliction of the genital sphere seems highly probable, it seems to follow that we should pay more attention than hitherto to the hidden effects of camouflaged tuberculosis, infections (and mixed infections) in the genital sphere when approaching the problem of schizophrenia [p. 460].

Our above considerations are by no means limited to Jaensch. It is well known that Hitler thought of blood mixture as the sole cause of the decline and death of cultures. Equally well known is the exaggerated fear of syphilis—"syphilidophobia" as labeled in psychiatry—in the writings of the leading Nazis, and the connection they see between this infection and sexual intercourse between what they consider different races. Like Hitler, Jaensch thinks of the Nazi movement as "a biological movement, a recuperative movement, with the purpose of guiding humanity or at least our own people out of the vestibule of the psychiatric clinic" (p. 461).

Jaensch's programmatic quest for firmness, for absence of ambiguity, and for definiteness is in strange contrast with the fact that his own writings are endless, full of needless repetitions, speculative intricacies, and bizarre if sometimes shrewd and subtle observations. It seems that Jaensch is struggling for a way out of his own and his culture's unbearable complexity. Reportedly Jaensch was well aware of the presence of "antitypical" features in himself; apparently it is the projections of these features which he fights in his image of the antitype.

In his conception of mental health as being mainly a matter of vitality and physical vigor Jaensch somewhat resembles Nietzsche, whom he often quotes as his master. It is interesting to note that he joins forces with Nietzsche, another sick man, when he says: "The struggle against the hollowed-out and diseased Christianity [of the antitype] . . . was at the climax of this unfortunate epoch already carried on by Nietzsche . . . Today we shall carry it on by action" (p. 511).

Just as in our empirical findings on authoritarian children, the stimulus boundness ascribed by Jaensch to his ideal German personality type all too soon reveals its affinity to confusion, chaos, and to a missing out on essential aspects of reality adaptation. The Nazi tendencies to expansion were unrealistic, to say the least, and so was their gross distortion of the personality of the enemy, as, for example, their view of the American as unsoldierly and effeminate. In this manner the refusal to face masculinity-femininity conflicts or other alleged or real difficulties or shortcomings in oneself turns out to lead to a personalized, "projective" view of other nationalities and of the outside world, resulting in a general distortion of reality and eventually in self-destruction.

Social and Political Outlook

The political irradiations of the personality pattern as found in the authoritarian person and as idealized by Jaensch are grave. The feeling of unworthiness and the resulting anxiety implanted into the person in an authoritarian atmosphere prevent him from squarely facing his weaknesses, shortcomings, and conflicts, and prompt him to project into his social environment—that is, to "externalize"—what he considers "evil." Evil then is fought outside rather than inside. There is, as we have seen, a striving for compensatory feelings of superiority as afforded by the condemnation of others, especially of outgroups. Images of social groups are thus dramatized and conceived as either altogether good or altogether bad, and social realities appear as oversimplified and excessively clear-cut structures.

Under an authoritarian regime—be this a state or the home—the hostilities against the given authority must be repressed and the helplessness of the individual is exploited. This fact must be considered a strong reinforcing agent for the "antiweakness attitude" which in our material was found to be a further attribute of the authoritarian personality and an accompaniment of his positive if superficial identification with the strong. Sympathy for the weak cannot develop where there is ingrained fear of weakness and where the weak furnish the only practical target of aggression. It is this same fear which makes for a shying away from responsibility and from the facing of one's own guilt, for the rejection of individuals, groups, and nations different from oneself, and for magic expectations of, and magic dependence on, strong leaders and "fate." Blind trust in the potency of fate frequently leads to the development of elaborate systems of superstition. It is primarily the "strength" of the leader and the fact of force in general which reach the authoritarian person. He pays very little attention to the political program as such but follows the lure of a few slogans incorporating the dichotomies discussed above in the context of intolerance of ambiguity. Such persons could not possibly at the same time be accessible to democratic values.

The authoritarian person may sometimes be kept in check by authorities, who take over for them the regulatory functions of conscience and reality testing. This need for permanent reinforcement tends to persist and is likely to become an entrenched state of affairs. The preferred authority is the one who promises most in terms of material goods, who offers an ideology as a means of orientation and self-confidence, and who grants permission for more or less unbridled release of the suppressed hostile tendencies in certain specified directions. It is in this manner that the combination of overrealism and irrationality finds its expression in the political scene.

Since, as we have seen, there is ample underlying resentment against authorities on the part of the authoritarian-minded follower, we find a tendency toward easy exchange of such authorities. The combination of surface conformity with lack of internalization and integration explains the apparently paradoxical fact that we often find the rigid conformist flooded by repressed unsublimated and unmodified tendencies which threaten the brittle and tenuously maintained superstructure. Out of anxiety this person adheres to the familiar and unquestioningly accepts the customs of his society; out of the same anxiety, however, he readily turns against this very society, the values of which he has never espoused with more than a divided heart. This is but one of the vicious circles inherent in a personalization of the social and political scene.

Under an authoritarian regime, the conception of society must become as unpsychological and ahistorical as is that of one's own life. Since continuities can be perceived only when there are no repressive breaks and no taboos on the application of freely searching social or psychological concepts and theories, the authoritarian person tends to explain individual actions or social events in terms of incidental factors or of superstition and magic forces.

The feelings of social and economic marginality which we found to be predominant in the home atmosphere of our authoritarian subjects suggests a further parallel between certain results of our studies and the rise of fascism, especially the rise of Nazism in Germany.

Another comparison may be based on the fact that differentiation, articulation, spontaneity, and autonomy are in an authoritarian home or state taken away not only from the individual; these characteristics are also lost so far as the organization of society as a whole is concerned. Both the individual and the society in which he lives are transformed into an amorphous aggregate with a superimposed strong leadership (Lederer, 1940). In our California studies we have tried to supply details on the impoverishment of the individual personality that forms the counterpart to the impoverishment of the social institutions under authoritarian rule. Under this aspect it is primarily the lack of integration and individuation which compels the authoritarian person to use all kinds of stereotypes, clichés, and ideologies as crutches and substitutes for personal opinion and as an antidote against underlying confusion.

The Role of Reason

In spite of the great hopes that the eighteenth and nineteenth centuries placed upon reason and progress, we are faced today with an eruption of the irrational and with a skepticism concerning reason and science. In part, the abandonment of the critical and independent faculties of man is voluntary. Were the expectations concerning the dynamic force of reason unrealistic? Has the rational approach been overrated and did modern civilization nourish an illusion? Is mankind governed, perhaps, by altogether different forces? I think these questions must partially be answered in the affirmative. It is certainly true that in the era of the Enlightenment an oversimple conception of human motivation was entertained. We have learned from Freud that the unconscious and irrational factors are of great importance in the formation of personality. We know today that they also influence social and political attitudes, at least of some persons. Under irrational factors Freud includes tendencies toward destruction and excessive dependence along with derivatives of infantile sex attitudes, such as Oedipal residues, especially if unconscious and displaced; further included are magic, archaic, and primitive patterns of thought and action. Over and above these irrational factors, which are rooted in the history of the individual, Freud (1921) as well as some sociologists, among them Le Bon (1895) and Mannheim, have stressed the irrational factors which derive from participation in groups. Total identification with the masses and the collective often leads to the renunciation of individual responsibility, a reduction of intellectual ability, an increase of cruelty, and a lack of moderation. Unless some measure of individuation is achieved, there can be no constructive group membership.

Both Durkheim and Weber have emphasized that the foundation of society lies in fundamentally nonrational moral or religious qualities. In contrast with the irrational factors just mentioned, Durkheim (1894) stresses such factors as respect for normative rules and moral obligation. Although Weber (1904-1905) elaborated on the rationalism of Western civilization, he was much concerned with the problem of the nonrational meaning of life; he made the well-known assumption that within Protestantism religious feelings, interests, and experiences have led from the preoccupation with salvation to an ascetic puritanism and the emphasis on exemplary earthly life based on work, self-reliance, rational planning, and virtue. It was also Weber who predicted that there would be a reaction to the rationalism of the nineteenth century. Pareto, Sorel, and Nietzsche thought they had to abandon—with varying degrees of despair—the hope that the masses would be open to reason.

Freud, on the other hand, while far from underestimating the power of irrational tendencies, was not discouraged. He never relented in supporting the struggle for greater awareness and mastery of the unconscious. His famous statement (1927) that the voice of the intellect, though low, does not stop until it is heard, is one of the many expressions of his belief that some day reason would prevail. Further relevant in this context is the realization that for the establishment of genuinely ethical behavior it is not enough to make the instincts conscious and integrated so as to render them modifiable. Ethical behavior can be achieved only if both the so-called id tendencies and the frequently overlooked, likewise unconscious sadistic, primitive, and unadaptable superego tendencies, clothed as they are in moralism and the condemnation and exclusion of others, are replaced by more reasonable moral judgments.

In some respects the authoritarian children of our study were found to display a severity of moral standards reminiscent of the primitive superego tendencies just referred to. Thus, in answering the question of what type of punishment should be imposed for different types of misdemeanor, children in this group tended to demand cruel and extreme retaliation for the slightest infractions. We know today that sheer repression and denial of evil does not assure its being overcome and that such devices are detrimental rather than constructive for genuinely socialized behavior. The avoidance of conscious guilt feelings and of related kinds of suffering is achieved by projection of the unaccepted impulses onto others, especially outgroups, and by unquestioning loyalty to a questionable ideal or leader on whom the moral demands of the conscience are projected and at whose disposal the individual has placed himself. The authoritarian person does not generally succeed in making the maturational step from repressive fear of authority to an internalized social conscience. It is the repressed, latent forces which are most likely to be projected onto the political and social scene. Especially in the authoritarian personality, rational control extends to a relatively small sector of the personality only, and the repressed impulses lurk close to the surface, ready to break through at any appropriate occasion. Totalitarianism and its political and social propaganda machinery attempt to appeal primarily to these impulses, reinforcing them at the same time. In order to counteract effectively the potential chaos resulting from these impulses, such slogans as that of Goebbels, "Cleanliness and orderliness are the foundation of life," were at the same time promoted.

For the clarification of the interplay of impulses and their eventual mastery we owe much to psychoanalysis with its stress on the importance of awareness, integration, rationality, cooperativeness, and maturity. However, psychoanalysis has often been misunderstood; by virtue of such misunderstanding it has contributed, along with other theoretical systems, to a swinging of the pendulum from the traditional blind faith and belief in reason to an overextended relativism and tendency toward unmasking of motives. A number of misunderstandings have arisen through the widespread tacit notion that if something is bad, its opposite must be good. Thus, the idea has been promoted in many homes and in some educational systems and political circles that in order to avoid authoritarianism, all authority must be forsworn. Against this ultramodern view it must be held that total permissiveness would verge upon anarchy. Respect for the authority of outstanding individuals and institutions is an essential aspect of a healthy society. It does not as such lead to total surrender to, nor to an absolutistic glorification of, the given leaders. This is especially true if leadership is limited to specialized fields or to special functions.

We must further stress that rationality does not imply amorality and freedom from obligation. On the contrary, genuine ethical behavior involves a comprehension of the issues involved, a facing of all uncertainties, conflicts, and one's own guilt, and a readiness to accept the anguish involved in such an open confrontation. Irrationality and the tendency toward destruction of self and of others, on the other hand, are often combined with a short-range overrealism and an orientation toward immediate material benefits.

Furthermore, the avoidance of the quest for certainty does not imply cynicism and morbid doubt. On the contrary, in the authoritarian personality the need for absolutes turns out to be combined with basic disbelief and general distrust. In this sense the obvious function of the philosophical outlook which at the present time dominates Germany in general, and her philosophy and psychology in particular, that is, existentialism, is that of emphasizing—to a generation plagued by the deepest doubts about the value of living—the worthwhileness of anything that exists by virtue of the sheer fact of its existence. Nazi rigidity and intolerance of ambiguity have here given way, in a remarkably close succession of opposites, to the extreme relativism which is at the core of existentialism.

Many modern writers seem resigned to the fact that only what is irrational, absolute, and dogmatic can really incite people and motivate them to action, whereas the rational, many-sided approach is seen as inherently inhibitory and as leading to a barren and sterile conception of life. Against this we must hold that virility of a nation does not seem to be grounded in blind fanaticism, militant aggressiveness, and shortcuts to action. The "official" optimism often characteristic of such an outlook disguises only thinly an underlying despair. Our findings show that persons who are more open to reason and facts are in general those who have a more differentiated internal life and deeper and more reliable—though often relatively calm—emotions. They are also those who, although less fanatic and less compulsive, show more consistency, conviction, and dedication in their principles and ideals. But the fact remains that the extreme and obvious positions lend themselves more readily to verbal formulation and thus give the false impression of solving some of the eternal perplexities. Very concrete as well as very general formulations can be put into the service of such definite and unqualified statements. In the task of a positive formation of democratic outlook and values, we must face the difficulties intrinsic in the complexities, ambiguities, flexibilities, and less fetching logicalities of the social realities.

Examples of apodictic and nonrational systems are given by both the race doctrine of Nazi Germany and the dialectical materialism of Soviet Russia. Though the two differ in the particulars of their bizarreness, both offer an essentially unscientific, metaphysical, all-inclusive *Weltanschauung* which has the appearance of definiteness, but is unrelated to fact. There is empirical evidence that persons susceptible to totalitarianism manifest more disturbance in their empirical and rational thinking than they do in the area of pure logic; furthermore, metaphysical systems do not prevent the acquisition of technological skills which constitute a domain by themselves. However, totalitarian states stifle free inquiry not only in the social sciences and in psychology, but even in physics, at least so far as theory construction is concerned. We have witnessed this in the reaction to Einstein on the part of both Nazi Germany and Soviet Russia. An interesting problem is posed by the question of how long a society can exist in which there is a certain mastery of technology but in which the social, political, and human outlook is impoverished to the point of dogmatic and distortive schemes.

Different countries vary to some degree in their readiness to tolerate ambiguity. As we have seen, this readiness not only relates to the structure of social and political institutions, but is also expressed in the philosophical and psychological outlook. For America, a long-range optimism seems justified to this writer. On the one hand, it must be granted that there are probable reinforcers of the authoritarian personality pattern in our culture. Among them we may list the following as the most important: presence of external threats; cultural emphasis on success and power; the necessity of proving oneself, if by no other means than by establishing social distance from those who are allegedly lower on the social scale; increasing standardization; increasing unintelligibility of political and social forces; presence of a powerful propaganda machinery used to manipulate public opinion; increasing difficulties in a genuine identification with society, resulting from the anonymity of big organizations and the ensuing isolation of the individual; some tendency toward a shortcut to action, toward externalization, and toward avoidance of introspection and contemplation. But it seems that these reinforcers of authoritarianism are more than counterbalanced by a long list of powerful reinforcers of tolerance for ambiguity and for liberalism in general: the democratic political tradition with its many-power check-and-balance system; the tradition of a pragmatic philosophy which, in contrast to the German philosophical tradition, is undogmatic and antimetaphysical; the general preference for scientific and rational explanations; the relative weakness of the tendencies toward oversystematization and fanaticism; the American "melting-pot" ideal; the democratic tradition with its protective attitude toward the weak; the emphasis on individualism; the egalitarian relationships between children and parents, and between pupils and teachers; the readiness to criticize governmental as well as parental authorities; the increased choices offered by technological progress; the rising attempts to understand the social and economic processes in their inconsistencies and irrationalities; and the readiness and ability to accept tentativeness, conflict, and suspense.

The struggle between these opposing forces characterizes not only our civilization as a whole, but every single individual. How this struggle will end and which of these opposing trends will be victorious hinges by no means solely on the number of mature and rational individuals, but on the interplay of political, social, and psychological phenomena in their entirety.

7

SOME THEORETICAL AND EMPIRICAL ASPECTS OF THE PROBLEM OF VALUES

Before describing some of the contributions a psychologist may be able to make to the topic of "Value Theory in the Social Sciences," I should like to attempt to differentiate some of the diverse aspects of what is called value theory. The confusion of these aspects has hampered the discussion of values considerably. Thus, for instance, the problem of whether the concern for values belongs outside or inside the social sciences—which has been discussed so arduously for the past years in the social sciences—cannot be answered without introducing and keeping apart a number of basically different approaches.

First, there is the logical analysis of value judgments and ethical terms. Second, there is the problem of valuation and bias as it involves the sciences, especially the social sciences, explicitly or, more often, implicitly. This problem area overlaps what may be called the psychology and sociology of knowledge. Third, there is—and this again is an altogether different task—the empirical study of values, norms, and moral evaluations as they differ to some degree from person to person and from society to society. Finally, there is the important question of what the social sciences can contribute to the choice between alternative values, be these instrumental or ultimate.

Read at Social Science Faculty Colloquium, March 15, 1955, the second in a series of five devoted to the topic of "Value Theory in the Social Sciences."

The editors wish to acknowledge the kind permission of Mrs. Marta Fischler and Mrs. Johanna Urabin to print this hitherto unpublished paper.

The Logical Status of Value Judgments

While these four aspects must be held apart conceptually, they will have to flow together to a certain extent in actual treatment and discussion. Let us begin with the first of our problems, the logical aspects of value judgments. Philosophers speak of value statements when such terms as "ought," "should," "desirable," "good," or "bad" occur. There is a difference between statements describing what people desire and those describing what they find desirable. Philosophers differ widely as to the meaning and justification of moral statements. (We will not deal here with the traditional, theologically or metaphysically oriented moral philosophies which assume that values are objectively existing essences and standards providing an absolute order which is discovered and validated by revelation, a priori intuition, or rational speculation.) For our purpose, the most important distinction is that between the naturalistic and emotive moral theories.

The naturalistic point of view holds that statements about values are not to be considered different from empirical statements but are open to verification in the same manner as other scientific statements. According to this view, moral predicates can be restated in nonmoral predicates, such as saying that "better" conduct is of "greater complexity"; in general, restatement of moral judgments takes place in terms of consequences. (Thus the certainty of moral statements is seen as neither greater nor less than that of scientific statements.) In the opinion of the naturalists, ethics is not autonomous and normative; it becomes a branch or an application of the natural and social sciences.

In criticizing the naturalistic point of view, Schlick, an earlier representative and leader of the so-called Vienna school, states (1939): "A fundamental error lies at the basis of the whole attempt; it consists in seeking value distinctions in the objective facts themselves, without reference to the acts of preference and selection through which alone values come into the world" (p. 104). Charles Stevenson (1945) has elaborated most fully on the distinction between value judgments on the one hand, and scientific or factual judgment on the other. A similar point of view has been taken by most logical positivists. Ethical judgments (that is, statements containing such terms as "good," "desirable," "ought to," etc.) are considered to be emotive expressions in which preferences are stated. Stevenson is especially impressed by the fact that there can be ethical disagreement—"disagreement in attitude"—without a disagreement about facts, that is, without "disagreement in belief." Thus, he points out, two persons can fully accept the same facts and still differ in their attitudes toward the facts. Although our values are often based on facts, neither facts nor scientific methods can be granted a definitive role in a "normative science" such as ethics.

The decisive reason for the separate logical status of value judgments lies in the fact that value judgments are neither true nor false. As far as my own position is concerned, I am inclined to agree with Abraham Kaplan, according to whom both normative judgments and knowledge verifiable by an empirical criterion of meaning are logically necessary conditions for a genuinely ethical statement, whereas Stevenson stresses only the psychological connection between reason and moral judgment. In Kaplan's view the normative aspect remains irreducible to facts. Similar positions have been taken by Kenneth Boulding, who has differentiated between the empirical field factors and the normative welfare functions, and by Clyde Kluckhohn.

It must be added, however, that in many cases an alleged value statement turns out to be fully translatable into a statement about facts. This holds especially for the statements dealing with instrumental values, a case which is one of our more frequent concerns. Recently a psychologist, Masling (1954), raised the objection that in the California studies (Adorno et al., 1950) the authoritarian personality was described in evaluative—and mainly in negative—terms. Masling is certainly right in taking for granted that such terms as prejudice, aggression, and rigidity that our group has employed carry some negative connotations. But in my opinion statements containing these and related terms are by no means necessarily value judgments in the technical, logical sense. The question arises here whether or not as a matter of principle terms with evaluative connotations can or should be avoided in the social sciences. Almost all trait names are evaluative, imbued as they are with instrumental—that is, functional versus nonfunctional or malfunctional—connotations. It would be extremely awkward to list each time a series of sober operational specifications instead of using the emotionally somewhat loaded terms of the vernacular or of current personality psychology. And even so, instead of saying that authoritarians are rigid, we would have to say that they tend to cling to the familiar and definite; that their approach stresses detail and is generally stimulus bound; that they have difficulty in changing their attitude or set; that they are apt to search for absolute solutions; that most of their actions stem from the need to protect themselves rather than being free and spontaneous; and that their feelings and thoughts are highly channelized, making them relatively inaccessible to new experience. Obviously this attempt to eliminate the general term by giving behavioral specifications would not rid us of evaluative involvement.

The reason for the inescapability of valuative entanglement is obvious: there are richer and poorer, more efficient and less efficient orientations or ways of dealing with reality, and as scientists we are not entitled to obscure or to circumvent this fact. Yet it is important to remember that statements asserting the presence of such survival-relevant traits as rigidity, conventionality, superstition, or punitiveness in a person or group can be fully translated into more descriptive statements about ways of dealing with reality, and that such statements do not constitute value judgments in the sense of an expression of preference or rejection on the part of the investigator. The fact that some of these attitudes are in general ill-suited for coping adequately with the complexities of social and cognitive problems, and that they tend to lead to consequences that are ultimately detrimental either to society or to other persons, and often to their holder himself, is no obstacle to the empirical verifiability of such tendencies along with that of any other factual trends.

The situation described is by no means unique to psychology. Medicine and physiology are predicated on the definition and constant consideration of health and adjustment. Even in chemistry such originally emotive terms as "noble" versus "base" have come to be accepted in the purely scientific characterizatiion of certain properties of metals that are relevant to their own "survival."

There is still another reason in favor of not overdrawing the distinction between normative and empirical statements in science. Statements and agreements about facts are not as clear-cut and uncontroversial as meets the eye, largely because of the preconceptions which enter our view of the facts as we approach them. Even in the most "objective" sciences the so-called theoretical structure, although guided by experience, is in the main a product of our imagination. It is connected only loosely, by so-called interpretative links, with the observational data, thus allowing for alternative explanations of the same facts. Einstein has stressed that in physics there is an ever-widening gap between theory and fact. Since theories do not possess as definite a relation to fact as is frequently assumed, a number of other factors, among them social and ethical influences, are permitted to codetermine the choice of theory even in the physical sciences.

The Influence of Values on the Development of Science

This brings us to our second problem, the psychological and sociological influences upon the formation of scientific views. Philipp Frank (1954) has impressively demonstrated the impact of such value systems on the acceptance or rejection of scientific theories. He points out that the Copernican theory was rejected at a time when all scientific data in favor of that theory were assembled. The reasons were extratheoretical, such as the incompatibility of the Copernican system with the traditional interpretation of the Bible, the disagreement between the Copernican system and the prevailing philosophy of that period, and the fact that the asserted mobility of the earth contradicts the commonsense view of nature. Epicurus's view that all bodies in the universe, including earth and stars, consist of the same material was rejected by many social leaders because they feared that a denial of the exceptional status of the celestial bodies in physical science would make it more difficult to teach the belief in the existence of spiritual beings as distinct from material bodies. Since it was their general conviction that belief in spiritual beings is a powerful instrument for bringing about desirable conduct among citizens, a physical theory that supported this belief seemed to be highly desirable.

There is no essential change in this picture as we move on to modern times. In twentieth-century physics, as Frank goes on, we observe that Einstein's theory of relativity has been interpreted as advocating an "idealistic" philosophy, which, in turn, would be useful as a support of moral conduct (similarly, quantum theory is interpreted as supporting a weakening of mechanical determinism and, along with it, the introduction of "indeterminism" into physics). In turn, a great many educators, theologians, and politicians have mistakenly acclaimed this "new physics" as providing support for the freedom of will which they believe to be essential for moral behavior.

In this discussion, Frank takes a point of view similar to that of Durkheim, who has stated that the acceptance and rejection of concepts is not determined merely by their validity but also by their consistency with other prevailing beliefs. All this holds even more for the social sciences. Within the framework of this paper I can refer only briefly to the works of Scheler, Mannheim, Merton, and Bendix concerning the social roots of our cognitive perspectives. All these authors emphasize how cultural values in general, and specific values as they derive from a certain position within the society in particular, codetermine our formulations in the social sciences; without rendering these formulations altogether invalid, each value system represents only one view which cannot be generalized.

Mannheim's (1936) relative confidence in the statements of intellectuals stems from his view of their relative social unattachment and classless position in society. This gives them the opportunity to take into account a wider array of perspectives, rather than being bound to the outlook of one generation, status, or occupational group. By thus coming in contact with different modes of thought, intellectuals should come to doubt the general validity of one over the other form of thought. At the same time Mannheim repudiates the total relativism which sees in intellectual activity no more than personal judgments. (Mannheim was not very clear, nor very consistent, about the objectivity of the social sciences in view of the relevance of values determining their formulation.) Modern philosophy of science, especially in its development during recent years, should have been a comfort to Mannheim. Moving away from a narrow positivism and empiricism and a simple correspondence theory of truth, it stresses the necessity of selection of conceptual schemes which are only partially determined by the data. (The influence of the observer is also stressed with the famous Heisenberg effect.) The validity of a scientific system is not maintained by its reducibility to a rock bottom of sense data which can be demonstrated, but by the explanatory power of certain phenomena to which it is often linked only indirectly. This viewpoint would thus neither absolutize nor deny the validity of a number of complementary perspectives.

Let us take an example from the social sciences in which the occupational values that Mannheim stresses enter the study of social norms and of the individual's relatedness to them. Durkheim (1894), the sociologist with a most outspoken institutional perspective, declares society to be the "highest reality of the intellectual and moral order. Because society is above us, it commands us; and on the other hand, because while superior to us it penetrates us and makes up part of ourselves, it draws us with that special inspiration that moral ends have for us." By virtue of this identification of the moral and social orders, conformity appears desirable to Durkheim.

Freud, on the other hand, with his individualistic perspective, stresses the independence of the ethical and the social to the point of assuming that they are—or may be—contradictory. Whereas Durkheim and Weber (1904-1905) consider the adoption of common norms and values by the individual as a means for the fulfillment of basic moral obligations and even of happiness, Freud not only sees a conflict between civilization and the instinctual tendencies of the individual; he also emphasizes the conflict between individual conscience and group conscience. Freud thinks that a group is the more moral the more it preserves rather than extinguishes the characteristics of the individual.

Social and Psychological Determinants of Values

Sociologists and anthropologists have been able to contribute materially to our understanding of cultural standards and institutional norms; these standards and norms in turn provide the broader matrix from which individuals select what they find desirable, ideal, or good. Psychologists, on the other hand, have thrown light on the way social norms are experienced and incorporated by the individual. However, an integration of the social sciences can be achieved only if the different perspectives, such as the institutional and the individual aspects, are clearly discerned and the areas of their application delimited. Thus the genetic approach of psychoanalysis is a powerful tool in the understanding of the individual, while it may lead to fallacies so far as the treatment of institutions per se is concerned.

Proceeding from the different perspectives of scientists to the problem of value formation in individuals, we enter our third problem. We are just beginning to understand some of the determinants of preferences in individuals within the ethical alternatives offered by our complex society. In a study of adolescents (Frenkel-Brunswik, 1948c) which was a continuation of a study of the adult authoritarian personality, I had occasion to explore the origin of ethical ideologies, conscience, and conformity. In families exercising threatening and traumatic forms of discipline and stressing clearly defined roles of dominance and submission, the children tend to consider the ideal function of figures of authority to be that of controlling and keeping in line. Or they describe the ideal parents in such negative terms as abstaining from severe corporal punishment. Children who come from equalitarian homes, on the other hand, tend to describe the perfect father as companionable and relaxed, and tend to refer to positive values such as a kind, loving, and gentle disposition. Furthermore, children from authoritarian homes are frequently oriented predominantly toward external and conventional values, condemning all who do not conform to the rigid patterns of behavior envisaged, whereas those from equalitarian homes are more concerned with internalized values and with intrinsic ethical standards.

It appears that wherever the parents acquire a threatening quality, no genuine identification with them can be achieved. Since in such circumstances the moral requirements in the home must appear to the child as overwhelming and at the same time inconsistent and unintelligible, and the rewards meager, submission to them must be reinforced by fear and pressure from outside. Real internalization of values and the formation of an adequate superego are likewise in jeopardy. The fearfully conforming child does not make the important developmental step from mere social anxiety to a mature conscience.

The superficial character of the identification with the parents, and the consequent underlying resentment against them, recurs in the attitudes to authority and social institutions in general. (The external authorities who take over the functions of the superego sometimes even usurp those of the ego.) There results a compulsive type of conformity which is characterized by unreliability and by a readiness to shift allegiance and to exchange authorities; it also is characterized by rigid adherence to the letter rather than the spirit of social norms so that their meaning is distorted or oversimplified. In many ways one may even speak of a defiance of an existing culture by external overconformity to its rules, rules which were never espoused with more than a divided heart. The ideal, reliable, and flexible conscience is based on a genuine incorporation of the values of society, with some degree of independence left intact.

Conscience is an old philosophical value problem; it was debated by Plato, Socrates, and others and was given an absolutizing solution by Kant. From a phenomenological point of view, conscience is an experience *sui generis;* this psychological fact underlies many of the metaphysical speculations. We cannot, however, agree with Plato and the rationalists when they assert that the true values can be grasped with absolute certainty. Causally, the content of our conscience can be derived from the cultural and social norms in general, and from our earlier experiences especially in relation to the parents (superego formation) as well as from the values adopted later in life which are called ego ideals. Psychoanalysis has thrown a great deal of light on conscience formation, showing various ways in which it functions. We have just briefly described a form of conscience which is not internalized but oriented toward external authority and based on fear. In an unhomogeneous society such as ours, with its shifting value patterns, an internalized conscience in which the individual is the focus but remains related to social norms is of crucial importance.

Further differentiations which may be derived from psychoanalysis concern an overstrict and primitive superego which leads to excessive guilt feelings or to masochism, which in turn are closely related to punitiveness and sadism. It is one of the greatest and least appreciated contributions of psychoanalysis to have seen that for genuinely ethical behavior not only must the instincts, insofar as antisocial, be made conscious and absorbed by integration, but that the superego as well as the id may be a source of unconscious sadistic and primitive tendencies. The noxious aspects of the superego derive from archaically interpreted or distorted cultural taboos. Unconscious moral tendencies stemming from rigid repressions generally turn out to be unrealistic, unadaptable, infantile, and out of touch with social realities. To use a phrase of Fenichel's, in the superego the ego is confronted with an often "irrational representative of reality." It is for this reason that the resulting prescriptions may come to represent a mere caricature of moral standards which may become extremely destructive of the individual and of his society. Thus arises the seemingly paradoxical picture of a superego which originates outside—being an introjection of parental authorities and of the norms they represent—and which then becomes endowed with all kinds of unsocialized subjective tendencies (such as aggression).

If the neurotic person keeps punishing himself for sins he has never actually committed, say, for mere feelings of aggression, a total relativism concerning real social action may easily develop. Indeed, some psychiatrists are inclined to put the blame for psychopathy, that is, moral blindness and delinquent behavior, not upon an underdevelopment of conscience but upon a desire for punishment due to severe unconscious guilt feelings, and thus upon a punitive and infantile form of conscience.

Freud, in referring to the fact that some aspects of our conscience are repressed, once stated (1923, p. 75), "the normal man is not only far more immoral than he believes but also far more moral than he has any idea of." And he added that "human nature has a far greater capacity, both for good and for evil, than . . . it is aware of through the conscious perceptions of the ego" (p. 76).

Psychoanalysis and psychology help us to understand why some people have needs for absolutes and others subscribe to relativism; why some solve their ethical struggles in one way and some in another; why some believe in determinism and others in indeterminism or freedom of will. Hume and Kant were different personalities; they also espoused different ethical systems.

Studies of individuals in research and therapy and the explorations of ethical theorists further show that the ethical outlook is closely interwoven with cognitive patterns. Thus the rigidly conforming adolescents whose values show prejudgment on the basis of dogma or convention also tend to display perceptual and cognitive intolerance of ambiguity. They exhibit in general a tendency toward black-white, either-or solutions. Their stereotypy, rigidity, inaccessibility to new experience, and enslavement to authorities and social rules tend to go with a similar enslavement to, or else rebellion against, the perceptual stimulus. They do not possess the balance and distance necessary for creative thought and genuine moral behavior. On the other hand, persons who are able to relate themselves to the stimuli in such a way as to utilize them for creative purposes usually also show a medium distance to social norms; they are neither rigidly stimulus bound nor rigidly culture bound. Those who ignore the perceptual and cognitive realities altogether often go off into sterile generalities; an example is the compulsive underconformist who shows a similar pattern to that of the rigid conformist.

The area under discussion may be labeled psychology of knowledge. Previously we called attention to the ways in which social and cultural values at least partially determine scientific perspectives. There is also evidence that differences in values from person to person determine the cognitive approach in science and daily life. On these grounds the Sophists disputed both the objective validity of factual statements based on sense perceptions and the objective validity of value judgments based on feelings. In Plato's theory of ideas, logic and ethics fuse into a unity. The concept is considered an ideal, and a value hierarchy corresponds to the logical heirarchy of concepts.

All this entanglement with values has little to do with the validity of the factual aspect of the systems concerned and vice versa. In the area of some of the concrete research we have mentioned, the independence of factual insight and valuation is well documented by the fact that the prominent Nazi psychologist, Jaensch (1938), explicitly espoused rigidity, perseveration, and uniformity as the characteristics of the ideal German, whereas our California study viewed these same traits as maladaptive. Jaensch even considered the intellect and adaptability as a sign of morbidity and lack of virility. His so-called antitype, the opposite of his ideal German type, is said to have an inclination toward the intellectual, the playful, and the aesthetic. Jaensch's programmatic quest for firmness, for absence of ambiguity, and for definiteness is in strange contrast with the fact that his own writings are endless, full of conflicting statements, needless repetitions, speculative intricacies, and bizarre, if sometimes shrewd and subtle, observations.

It seems that Jaensch was struggling for a way out of his own and his culture's unbearable complexity. Reportedly Jaensch was well aware of the presence of "antitypical" features in himself; apparently it was the projections of these features that he fought in his image of the antitype. In his conceptions of mental health as being mainly a matter of vitality and physical vigor, Jaensch somewhat resembles Nietzsche, whom he often quoted as his master. It is interesting to note that he joins forces with Nietzsche, another sick man, when he says: "The struggle against the hollowed-out and diseased Christianity [of the antitype] ... was ... already carried on by Nietzsche. ... Today we shall carry it on by action" (p. 511).

The fact that Jaensch's ego ideal is so different from himself (he was very "intelligent," if in a distorted way) leads us to an important point, that is, the relation between values or ethical perspectives on the one hand, and behavior on the other. In a study of self-deception (1939) undertaken at the University of Vienna I compared the guiding ethical principles professed by students with their actual behavior as described by close acquaintances. It turned out that more often than not high professed standards go with an actual weakness rather than strength in the corresponding behavior. Thus a subject who stressed that she was guided by sincerity in all circumstances was described as particularly insincere by her classmates. The ultimate function of this inverse signalizing in consciousness is probably an attempt to modify some aspects of one's behavior of which one is not fully aware. Thus sometimes the function of explicitly espoused values or ideals seems to be of a defensive and compensatory nature, protecting the person from a painful truth which he has been unable to face as such. (Similarly Jaensch, who himself was for a while confined in a mental institution, glorifies the Nazi movement as a "biological movement, a recuperative movement, with the purpose of guiding humanity or at least our own people out of the vestibule of the psychiatric clinic" [1938, p. 461].)

In other cases we found a conscious realization of moral shortcomings in oneself which were not perceived by others until later because they were hidden behind a well-functioning façade. In our inquiries into the students' views of how other people ought to behave, we also found projective types of distortion, exemplified by a subject, judged to be very aggressive, who demanded that others be more friendly.

In general, exaggeration in stating one's own ethical principles was found to be particularly symptomatic of the absence of the desired trait. In addition to exaggeration, it was possible to develop a number of other formal criteria which help us to discern whether in a given case the professed values are likely to distort rather than to mirror the actual conduct. Among these formal criteria are absoluteness of emphasis; predominant use of the extreme values of what actually are continua; degree of realism; intolerance of ambiguity; such inconsistencies as are found in the comparisons of general with specific features of behavior or of verbal statements, or in the comparison of responses to direct questions with those to indirect questions; the occasional breaking through of a pattern of denial.

The relationship between form and content may be expected to be of utmost importance in dealing with such questions as, say, what degree of conviction goes with what kind of values. We often find narrow and destructive systems of values going hand in hand with fanatic conviction (e.g., in fascism). A differentiation between rigidity and consistency of belief would also be necessary. Problems of relativism and absolutism must be investigated. An attempt should also be made to explore readiness for activity versus passivity in relation to the content of beliefs. This could help to clarify the problem of whether absolutism possesses a greater affinity to action than the various forms of relativism.

Still another problem to be considered is that of the relation between reason and belief. It also concerns the extent to which the subject considers his convictions to be based on facts and thinking, and the degree of their susceptibility to modification by discussion and increased information.

In all this we must realize that the general concept of "value" involves all the different layers of the personality. The first of these levels is that of explicit verbalization and "official" beliefs. A second level concerns the actual experiential foundation on which concrete moral decisions are based. A third level, finally, may be reached by the use of projective techniques, to be constructed so as to permit the execution of a variety of ethical solutions at the fantasy level.

The fact that psychoanalysis sometimes interprets extreme altruism as a reaction formation to aggression, or the pursuit of the highest intellectual goals as a sublimation of the sex instinct, or sainthood as an expression of masochism, led to the accusation that psychoanalysis is immoral. Arguments of this kind were raised not only by philosophers in search of a system of absolute values, but also by empirically oriented social scientists and psychologists of major stature, among them Max Weber. Weber saw in psychoanalysis an expression of a tendency to loosen our basic ethical principles. In a letter of 1907 Weber accused Freud of proposing a psychiatric or "nerve" ethics characterized by the prevalence of the "hygienic" point of view (see Marianne Weber, 1950, p. 417).

There is no doubt that by virtue of its inherent incompleteness psychoanalysis has not fully avoided the pitfalls of motivational relativism and of a genetic dissolution of values. But at the same time it may be said that with all the reservations that psychoanalysis has voiced against a naïve rational interpretation of ethics, it has turned against merely the assumed major executive principle of the traditional forms of ethics rather than against their basic constructive content. This particular executive principle is the mechanism of repression. Most prepsychoanalytic ethical systems stress such inhibitory devices as the looking away from evil, or its denial, or its mastery through strength of will. From psychoanalysis we have learned about the inefficiency and the dangers of these various forms of repression; from the same source we have learned of the importance of consciousness, integration, and maturity. All qualities that are considered essential ingredients of maturity in psychoanalysis—rationality, the overcoming of aggression, cooperativeness, the ability to love and to work, and the courage to face inside and outside threats that oppose these characteristics—bespeak standards that stand up well among the traditional systems of ethics. At the same time the psychoanalytic outlook is in accordance with Plato's statement that the virtuous man is the one who is also happy. In psychoanalysis every neurosis is in and of itself considered as a failure of moral control. The important historical contribution of traditional systems of ethics is the attempt to strengthen consciousness and conscience against the invasion of the instincts; through psychoanalysis we have become aware that such strengthening can be achieved only by facing and working through, rather than by merely condemning, the forces threatening our conscious personal and social values. From this latter viewpoint the mortal sin is self-deception and lack of insight, rather than a lack of repression.

It may be that the diversion of attention from the functions of reason in psychoanalysis has contributed to the semblance of ethical relativism. Psychoanalysis was so overwhelmed by its epoch-making discovery of the role of irrational forces that the explicit exploration of reasoning processes was temporarily obscured, even though it was reason and not the irrational that held the top spot so far as the evaluative attitude of psychoanalysis was concerned. Genuine ethical behavior involves a comprehension of the issues involved, a facing of all uncertainties, conflicts, and one's own guilt, and a readiness to accept the anguish involved in such an open confrontation. Irrationality and the tendency toward destruction of self and of others, on the other hand, are often combined with a short-range overrealism and an orientation toward immediate material benefits, both of which are essentially unethical.

Furthermore, the avoidance of the quest for certainty does not imply cynicism and morbid doubt. On the contrary, the need for absolutes turns out to be combined with basic disbelief and general distrust. Many modern writers seem resigned to the fact that only what is irrational, absolute, and dogmatic can really incite people and motivate them to action, whereas the rational, many-sided approach is seen as inherently inhibitory and as leading to a barren and sterile conception of life. Against this we must hold that the virility of a nation does not seem to be grounded in blind fanaticism, militant aggressiveness, and shortcuts to action. Upon probing, the "official" optimism often characteristic of such an outlook disguises only thinly an underlying despair. Our findings show that persons who are more open to reason and facts are in general at the same time those who have a more differentiated internal life and deeper and more reliable—though often relatively calm—ethical convictions. They are also those who, although less fanatic and less compulsive, show more consistency and dedication in their principles and ideals. The fact remains, however, that the extreme and obvious positions lend themselves more readily to verbal formulation and thus give the false impression of solving some of the eternal perplexities. Very concrete as well as very general formulations can be put into the service of such definite and unqualified statements. In the task of a positive formation of the outlook and values of our society, we must face the difficulties intrinsic in the complexities, ambiguities, flexibilities, and less fetching logicalities of social reality.

The Contribution of the Social Sciences to Value Choice

I have touched upon a variety of problems so far. But the fourth topic mentioned in the introduction, that of the possible contribution of the social sciences to a choice between competing ideologies, has been with us only by indirection. In turning to this last problem more explicitly, I shall at the same time attempt to conclude by weaving the various threads followed in this paper more closely together.

One may agree with the position which assigns a special logical status to normative statements, at the same time stressing that facts play an important role in the justification of values. Thus the emphasis which the Oxford School places on the process of reasoning in the assertion of values is of significance. Through the reasoning process we can often determine whether or not the value judgment is a disguised factual statement. In their involvement with values the sciences deal mainly with instrumental and not with ultimate values.

On the other hand, it must be stressed that reasoning as an approach to justification may be no more than an illusory rationalization that obscures rather than clarifies the relationships between value and fact. We know that emotionally vested values may remain untouched by fact, reason, or evidence. Not only are value statements often disguised factual statements, but the reverse is also true: biases and emotive preferences are often clothed in pseudofactual statements, as we have seen from our examples from the history of science.

The normative position concerning values has been criticized on the ground that it sees in value statements purely arbitrary expressions of emotions and preferences. One may counter this argument by pointing out that even though ethical norms must be differentiated from facts, facts play a part in all value statements. Furthermore, individuals and cultures do not differ widely with respect to what are considered the ultimate ethical goals. Psychoanalysis has contributed to the emphasis on the universality of human nature whereas behaviorism emphasizes its plasticity. Ruth Benedict, who tended to stress cultural relativity and the fact that every society must be viewed in the framework of its own ethos, was not so reluctant to speak of good and bad cultures in informal conversation, obviously using a universal yardstick. Even Jaensch is found to be in agreement with us on many values, such as the desirability of health.

But what can we do with such deviations in values as Jaensch's glorification of rigidity and externalization, and his rejection of adaptability? Let us take Jaensch's aversion to internalization. Why indeed should awareness be better than unawareness? Is not external projection a good way of getting rid of psychological troubles, especially of guilt, often too great to handle for the person who is wide awake? Is not an oversimplified stereotype or black-white categorization the best way of concretizing a social reality too complex and unintelligible to penetrate? Are not we social scientists just troublemakers who by our very nature disturb simple solutions and complacency?

In an attempt to show in what way reasoning and social science may be able to influence valuation, I shall suggest three criteria. The first criterion rests on an empirical examination of the validity of the facts on which the value judgment is based. For example, do the Germans actually exhibit the syndrome attributed to them by Jaensch as opposed to other nations? Quite often we find the fault right here.

The second criterion is based on the purely formal consistency of the value system. Among Jaensch's many inconsistencies perhaps the following is the most important: His ideal type is considered to have the ability of being a good fellow, friend, and comrade. Thus there is an ideal of love and brotherhood. But together with this we find the assumption that a good portion of the population—all who are not pure Germans and perhaps all who are women—is biologically incapable of participating in this ideal. Love and brotherhood must be considered inclusive ideals. Jaensch's value system is highly exclusive.

The third criterion is the compatibility of a system with some basic values, such as survival. Jaensch's ideal type, in order not to fall back on such allegedly inferior traits as intelligence or adaptability, requires a narrowly specified world, and survival becomes questionable under present-day conditions, which require quick adaptation to major changes. In order to maintain a glorified image of oneself and of the ingroup, certain tendencies (such as fear, weakness, passivity, and aggressive feelings against authoritative figures) must be kept in a repressed or suppressed state. Not facing weakness and aggression in oneself leads to an exaggeration of hostile, threatening, and weak characteristics in others. The readiness to stereotypical categorization commonly found in ideologies such as that of Jaensch thus seems to be unable to do justice to all crucial aspects of reality. Hence the unrealistic tendencies toward expansion and the gross underestimation of the enemy. (It must be someone else, say, the American, who is considered unsoldierlike and effeminate.) Not facing conflicts and shortcomings in oneself thus leads to a personalized view of other people and the outside world, resulting in a distorted view of reality, and eventually leading to doom.

In the cases described, long-range types of adjustments have been sacrificed in favor of short-range adjustments and the elimination of immediate conflicts and anxieties. We have found that this type of policy is one of the main characteristics of the authoritarian personality; it is also generally considered to be an indicator of immaturity.

The emphasis on long-range adjustment can of course in itself be considered a culture-bound ideology in the sense of Mannheim. Here we come once more to the problem of values as determiners of scientific perspectives. We do not agree with Max Weber's assertion that social sciences are value free. Ideally, the only value system that should be involved while one is engaged in scientific work is what Spranger has called "theoretical values." More aptly, it may be characterized as the value system of scientific objectivity. However, as we witness in even the most abstract and logically rigorous theoretical systems in physics or in psychology—say, Hull's postulational theory of learning—science as an actual human undertaking has always been full of subjective preconceptions. These preconceptions are often of an aesthetic or formalistic character. Those who deny the existence of such biases in their own work in most cases turn out not to have made them sufficiently explicit to themselves. In this respect, the social scientist is as much a child of his period, with its varying climates of conceptualization, as are his colleagues in other areas. In addition, there is probably no way for the social scientist fully to escape infiltration of his outlook by the sociopolitical climate of opinion in which he lives, no matter how hard he may try. An analysis of the subtle effects of the attitudes involved would probably be as difficult as an analysis of the fact that, say, psychologists in some countries have tended to become Gestalt psychologists while in others they became behaviorists. It is one of the foremost tasks facing the historian of science and culture, if not the social scientist, to make explicit and to trace the influences of the biases inherent in declared or tacit allegiances to any of these so-called points of view.

In discussing the existential determination of human thought, Mannheim (1936) states: "From Nietzsche the lines of development led to the Freudian and Paretian theories of human impulses and to the methods developed by them for viewing human thought as distortions and as products of instinctive mechanisms." Considerations of this kind should not, in my opinion, inspire a picture of utter chaos. The conscious and unconscious forces, both collective and individual, produce not only errors but also visions and a penetrating versatility in the grasp of relationships. The personal equation yields an additional variable which can be studied and harnessed with the usual techniques of the behavioral sciences. The empirical study of normative values in the scientist and the nonscientist alike should enable us to control this factor to our advantage and to keep within sight the numerous perspectives that must be combined in the edifice of knowledge.

For all these reasons, the knowledge accumulated in the social sciences may help us to make a choice among alternative value systems. In working on the authoritarian personality an attempt was made to establish a network of empirical relationships between the holding of certain social attitudes, such as ethnocentrism, and a host of seemingly more neutral personality traits. Even though statements about personality traits almost always carry a certain evaluative reference as to the immediate or long-range adjustment of the individual or society, they remain in themselves cognitive statements in that they refer to relations between empirical facts. Although the social scientist, as a scientist, cannot make the ultimate choice for mankind, his function is to throw as much light as possible on the implications involved in existing value systems, and to make explicit all the ramifications inherent in the options.

REFERENCES

Adorno, T. W., Frenkel-Brunswik, E., Levinson, D. J., & Sanford, R. N. (1950), *The Authoritarian Personality*. New York: Harper.
Alexander, F., & Healy, W. (1935a), Ein Opfer der Verbrechermoral und eine Nichtentdeckte Diebin. *Imago*, 21:5-43, 158-206.
_____ (1935b), *The Roots of Crime*. New York: Knopf.
Allport, G. W. (1935), Attitudes. In *A Handbook of Social Psychology*, ed. C. Murchison. Worcester, Mass.: Clark University Press, pp. 798-844.
_____ (1937), *Personality*. New York: Holt.
_____ (1942), *The Use of Personal Documents in Psychological Science*. New York: Social Science Research Council.
Barker, R., Dembo, T., & Lewin, K. (1941), Frustration and Regression: An Experiment with Young Children. *University of Iowa Studies in Child Welfare*, 18(No. 1).
Bendix, R. (1951), Social Stratification and Political Power. Paper presented at the Forty-Seventh Annual Meeting of the American Political Science Association, San Francisco.
Benussi, V. (1904), Zur Psychologie des Gestalterfassens. In *Untersuchungen zur Gegenstandstheorie und Psychologie*, ed. A. Meinong. Leipzig: Barth.
Bergmann, G. (1943), Psychoanalysis and Experimental Psychology. *Mind*, 52:122-140.
_____ (1953), Theoretical Psychology. *Ann. Rev. Psychol.*, 4:435-458.
Bernfeld, Siegfried (1931a), Zur Sublimierungstheorie. *Imago*, 17:399-403.
_____ (1931b), Das "Widerstandsargument" der Psychoanalyse. *Nervenarzt*, 4:277-283.
_____ (1944), Freud's Earliest Theories and the School of Helmholtz. *Psychoanal. Quart.*, 13:341-362.
Bernfeld, Suzanne (1951), Freud and Archeology. *Amer. Imago*, 8:107-128.
Betlheim, S., & Hartmann, H. (1924), On Parapraxes in the Korsakow Psychosis. In *Organization and Pathology of Thought*, ed. D. Rapaport. New York: Columbia University Press, 1951, pp. 288-310.
Blake, R. R., & Ramsey, G. V., eds. (1951), *Perception: An Approach to Personality*. New York: Ronald Press.
_____ & Moran, L. J. (1951), Perceptual Processes as Basic to an Understanding of Complex Behavior. In *Perception: An Approach to Personality*, ed. R. R. Blake & G. V. Ramsey. New York: Ronald Press, pp. 3-24.

REFERENCES

Bleuler, E. (1911), *Dementia Praecox or the Group of Schizophrenias*. New York: International Universities Press, 1950.

Blum, G. S. (1949), A Study of the Psychoanalytic Theory of Psychosexual Development. *Genet. Psychot. Monogr.*, 39:3-99.

Boring, E. (1950), *A History of Experimental Psychology*. New York: Appleton-Century-Crofts.

Brenman, M. (1942), Studies of Normal and Hypnotic Recall of Fairy Tales Heard in Childhood. Manuscript.

Bridgman, P. W. (1928), *The Logic of Modern Physics*. New York: Macmillan.

Bronfenbrenner, U. (1951), Toward an Integrated Theory of Personality. In *Perception: An Approach to Personality*, ed. R. R. Blake & G. V. Ramsey. New York: Ronald Press, pp. 206-257.

Bruner, J. (1951), Personality Dynamics and the Process of Perceiving. In *Perception: An Approach to Personality*, ed. R. R. Blake & G. V. Ramsey. New York: Ronald Press, pp. 121-147.

────── & Goodman, C. C. (1947), Value and Need as Organizing Factors in Perception. *J. Abnorm. Soc. Psychol.*, 42:33-44.

Brunswik, E. (1934), *Wahrnehmung und Gegenstandswelt*. Leipzig: Deuticke.

────── (1939a), The Conceptual Focus of Some Psychological Systems. *J. Unified Sci.*, 8:36-49.

────── (1939b), Probability as a Determiner of Rat Behavior. *J. Exp. Psychol.*, 25:175-197.

────── (1943), Organismic Achievement and Environment Probability. *Psychol. Rev.*, 50:255-272.

────── (1947), *Systematic and Representational Design*. Berkeley: University of California Press.

────── (1952), The Conceptual Framework of Psychology. *International Encyclopedia of Unified Science*, 1(No. 10). Chicago: University of Chicago Press.

Bühler, C. (1931), *Kindheit und Jugend*, 3rd ed. Leipzig: Hirzel.

────── (1933), *Der Menschliche Lebenslauf als Psychologisches Problem*. Leipzig: Hirzel.

────── (1935), *From Birth to Maturity*. London: Routledge & Kegan Paul.

Bühler, K. (1927), *Die Krise der Psychologie*. Jena: Fischer.

Cameron, N. (1947), *The Psychology of Behavior Disorders*. Boston: Houghton Mifflin.

────── (1951), Perceptual Organization and Behavior Pathology. In *Perception: An Approach to Personality*, ed. R. R. Blake & G. V. Ramsey. New York: Ronald Press, pp. 283-306.

Carnap, R. (1936), Testability and Meaning. *Phil. Sci.*, 3:420-471.

────── (1937), Testability and Meaning. *Phil. Sci.*, 4.

────── (1938), Logical Foundations of the Unity of Science. *International Encyclopedia of Unified Science*, 1(No. 1):42-62. Chicago: University of Chicago Press.

Cattell, R. B., & Tiner, L. G. (1949), The Varieties of Structural Rigidity. *J. Pers.*, 17:321-341.

Christie, J. R. (1949), The Effects of Frustration upon Rigidity in Problem Solution. Unpublished doctoral dissertation, University of California.

Cole, L. (1939), *General Psychology*. New York: McGraw-Hill.

Dennis, W. (1951), Cultural and Developmental Factors in Perception. In *Perception: An Approach to Personality*, ed. R. R. Blake & G. V. Ramsey. New York: Ronald Press, pp. 148-169.

REFERENCES

Dingle, H. (1949), The Logical Status of Psychoanalysis. *Analysis,* 9:63-66.
Dollard, J., & Miller, N. E. (1950), *Personality and Psychotherapy.* New York: McGraw-Hill.
Durkheim, E. (1894), *The Rules of Sociological Method.* Glencoe, Ill.: Free Press, 1950.
Einstein, A. (1944), Remarks on Bertrand Russell's Theory of Knowledge. In *The Philosophy of Bertrand Russell,* ed. P. A. Schilpp. Evanston, Ill.: Northwestern University Press.
Ellis, A. (1950), An Introduction to the Principles of Scientific Psychoanalysis. *Genet. Psychol. Monogr.,* 41:147-212.
Erikson, E. H. (1945), Childhood and Tradition in Two American Indian Tribes. *The Psychoanalytic Study of the Child,* 1:319-350. New York: International Universities Press.
―――― (1950), *Childhood and Society.* New York: Norton.
Feigl, H. (1949), Some Remarks on the Meaning of Scientific Explanation. In *Readings in Philosophical Analysis,* ed. H. Feigl & W. Sellars. New York: Appleton-Century-Crofts, pp. 510-514.
―――― (1950), Existential Hypotheses. *Phil. Sci.,* 17.
Fenichel, O. (1945), *The Psychoanalytic Theory of Neurosis.* New York: Norton.
Flew, A. (1949), Psychoanalytic Explanation. *Analysis,* 10:8-15.
Frank, L. K. (1939), Projective Methods for the Study of Personality. *J. Psychol.,* 8:389-413.
Frank, P. (1941), *Modern Science and Its Philosophy.* Cambridge: Harvard University Press.
―――― (1954), The Variety of Reasons for the Acceptance of Scientific Theories. *Sci. Monthly,* 79:139-145.
Frenkel, E. (1931a), Atomismus und Mechanismus in der Assoziationspsychologie. *Zeitschr. Psychol.,* 123:193-258.
―――― (1931b), Lebenslauf, Leistung, und Erfolg. *Bericht über den 12. deutschen Psychologenkongress.* Hamburg, pp. 331-335.
―――― (1936), Studies in Biographical Psychology. *Character & Pers.,* 5:1-34.
―――― (1938), Ichideal und Selbstbeurteilung in Objektiver Kontrolle. *Report on 11th International Congress of Psychology,* ed. H. Pieron & J. Meyerson. Paris: Alcan (abstract).
―――― & Weisskopf, E. (1937), Wunsch und Pflicht im Aufbau des Menschlichen Lebens. *Psychol. Forschungen über den Lebenslauf,* Vol. 1, ed. C. Bühler & E. Frenkel. Vienna: Gerold.
Frenkel-Brunswik, E. (1939), Mechanisms of Self-Deception. *J. Soc. Psychol.,* 10:409-420.
―――― (1940), Psychoanalysis and Personality Research. In Symposium on Psychoanalysis as Seen by Analyzed Psychologists, ed. G. W. Allport. *J. Abnorm. Soc. Psychol.,* 35:176-197. [This volume, Chapter 1.]
―――― (1942), Motivation and Behavior. *Genet. Psychol. Monogr.,* 26:121-265.
―――― (1948a), Dynamic and Cognitive Categorization of Qualitative Material. I. General Problems and the Thematic Apperception Test. *J. Psychol.,* 25:253-260.
―――― (1948b), Dynamic and Cognitive Categorization of Qualitative Material. II. Interviews of the Ethnically Prejudiced. *J. Psychol.,* 25:261-277.
―――― (1948c), A Study of Prejudice in Children. *Hum. Relat.,* 1:295-306.
―――― (1948d), Tolerance toward Ambiguity as a Personality Variable. *Amer. Psychol.,* 3:268(abstract).

REFERENCES

———— (1949a), Intolerance of Ambiguity as an Emotional and Perceptual Personality Variable. *J. Pers.*, 18:108-143. [This volume, Chapter 2.]

———— (1949b), Distortion of Reality in Perception and in Social Outlook. *Amer. Psychol.*, 4:253(abstract).

———— (1950), Wishes and Feelings of Duty in the Course of Life. In *Research on Aging*, ed. H. E. Jones. New York: Social Science Research Council, pp. 116-122.

———— (1951a), Patterns of Social and Cognitive Outlook in Children and Parents. *Amer. J. Orthopsychiat.*, 21:543-558.

———— (1951b), Personality Theory and Perception. In *Perception: An Approach to Personality*, ed. R. R. Blake & G. V. Ramsey. New York: Ronald Press, pp. 356-419. [This volume, Chapter 3.]

———— (1952a), Adjustments and Reorientations in the Course of the Life Span. In *Psychological Studies of Human Development*, ed. R. C. Kuhlen & G. H. Thompson. New York: Appleton-Century-Crofts, pp. 94-103.

———— (1952b), Interaction of Psychological and Sociological Factors in Political Behavior. *Amer. Pol. Sci. Rev.*, 46:44-65. [This volume, Chapter 5.]

———— (1954a), Psychoanalysis and the Unity of Science. *Proc. Amer. Acad. Arts. Sci.*, 80:273-347. [This volume, Chapter 4.]

———— (1954b), Further Explorations by a Contributor to *The Authoritarian Personality*. In *Studies in the Scope and Method of "The Authoritarian Personality,"* ed. R. Christie & M. Jahoda. Glencoe, Ill.: Free Press, pp. 226-275.

———— (1954c), Environmental Controls and the Impoverishment of Thought. In *Totalitarianism*, ed. C. J. Friedrich. Cambridge: Harvard University Press, pp. 171-202. [This volume, Chapter 6.]

———— (1954d), Social Research and the Problem of Values: A Reply. *J. Abnorm. Soc. Psychol.*, 49:466-471.

———— (1954e), Tentative Plans for Work at the Center for Advanced Study in the Behavioral Sciences. Manuscript.

———— (1955a), Differential Patterns of Social Outlook and Personality in Family and Children. In *Childhood in Contemporary Cultures*, ed. M. Mead & M. Wolfenstein. Chicago: University of Chicago Press, pp. 369-405.

———— (1955b), Some Theoretical and Empirical Aspects of the Problem of Values. Paper presented at the University of California Social Science Faculty Colloquium on Value Theory in the Social Sciences. [This volume, Chapter 7.]

———— & Havel, J. (1953), Prejudice in the Interviews of Children: I: Attitudes toward Minority Groups. *J. Genet. Psychol.*, 82:91-135.

Freud, A. (1936), *The Ego and the Mechanisms of Defence*. London: Hogarth Press, 1937.

Freud, S. (1908), Character and Anal Erotism. *Collected Papers*, 2:45-50. London: Hogarth Press, 1924.

———— (1911), Formulations regarding the Two Principles in Mental Functioning. *Collected Papers*, 4:13-21. London: Hogarth Press, 1925.

———— (1912), A Note on the Unconscious in Psycho-Analysis. *Collected Papers*, 4:22-29. London: Hogarth Press, 1925.

———— (1913), Totem and Taboo. *The Basic Writings*. New York: Modern Library, 1938, pp. 807-930.

———— (1915a), Instincts and Their Vicissitudes. *Collected Papers*, 4:60-83. London: Hogarth Press, 1925.

———— (1915b), Repression. *Collected Papers*, 4:84-97. London: Hogarth Press, 1925.

———(1915c), The Unconscious. *Collected Papers,* 4:98-136. London: Hogarth Press, 1925.
———(1915d), My Views on the Part Played by Sexuality in the Aetiology of the Neuroses. *Collected Papers,* 4:98-136. London: Hogarth Press, 1925.
———(1920), *Beyond the Pleasure Principle.* London: Hogarth Press, 1942.
———(1921), *Group Psychology and the Analysis of the Ego.* London: Hogarth Press, 1940.
———(1923), *The Ego and the Id.* London: Hogarth Press, 1927.
———(1925), *An Autobiographical Study.* London: Hogarth Press, 1935.
———(1927), *The Future of an Illusion.* London. Hogarth Press, 1928.
———(1930), *Civilization and Its Discontents.* London: Hogarth Press.
———(1933), *New Introductory Lectures on Psycho-Analysis.* New York: Norton.
———(1939), *Moses and Monotheism.* London: Hogarth Press.
———(1940[1938]), *An Outline of Psycho-Analysis.* London: Hogarth Press, 1949.
Fromm, E. (1941), *Escape from Freedom.* New York: Farrar & Rinehart.
Goldstein, K. (1936), The Problem of the Meaning of Words Based upon Observation of Aphasic Patients. *J. Psychol.,* 2:301-316.
———(1943), The Significance of Psychological Research in Schizophrenia. *J. Nerv. Ment. Dis.,* 97:261-280.
———& Scheerer, M. (1941), Abstract and Concrete Behavior; An Experimental Study with Special Tests. *Psychol. Monogr.,* 53(No. 2).
Greenacre, P. (1941), The Predisposition to Anxiety. *Psychoanal. Quart.,* 10:66-95, 610-638.
Hartley, E. L. (1946), *Problems in Prejudice.* New York: King's Crown Press.
Hartmann, H. (1939), *Ego Psychology and the Problem of Adaptation.* New York: International Universities Press, 1958.
Heider, F. (1939), Environmental Determinants in Psychological Theories. *Psychol. Rev.,* 46:383-410.
Hempel, C. G. (1952), Fundamentals of Concept Formation in Empirical Science. *International Encyclopedia of Unified Science,* 2(No. 7). Chicago: University of Chicago Press.
Hilgard, E. R. (1951), The Role of Learning in Perception. In *Perception: An Approach to Personality,* ed. R. R. Blake & G. V. Ramsey. New York: Ronald Press, pp. 95-120.
———(1952), Experimental Approaches to Psychoanalysis. In *Psychoanalysis as Science,* ed. E. Pumpian-Mindlin. Stanford, Cal.: Stanford University Press, pp. 3-45.
Hobbs, N. (1959), Science and Ethical Behavior. *Amer. Psychol.,* 14:217-225.
Hunt, J. McV. (1941), The Effects of Infant Feeding-Frustration upon Adult Hoarding in the Albino Rat. *J. Abnorm. Soc. Psychol.,* 36:338-360.
Jaensch, E. R. (1938), *Der Gegentypus.* Leipzig: Barth.
Jones, H. E. (1935), The Galvanic Skin Reflex as Related to Overt Emotional Expression. *Amer. J. Psychol.,* 47:240-251.
———(1939), The Adolescent Growth Study. *J. Consult. Psychol.,* 3:157-180.
———(1943), *Development in Adolescence: Approaches to the Study of the Individual.* New York: Appleton-Century.
Kardiner, A. (1939), *The Individual and His Society.* New York: Columbia University Press.
Klein, G. S. (1951), The Personal World through Perception. In *Perception: An Approach to Personality,* ed. R. R. Blake & G. V. Ramsey. New York: Ronald Press, pp. 328-355.

────── (1958), Cognitive Control and Motivation. In *Assessment of Human Motives*, ed. G. Lindzey. New York: Rinehart, pp. 87-118.
Kluckhohn, C. (1949), *Mirror for Man.* New York: McGraw-Hill.
Koffka, K. (1935), *Principles of Gestalt Psychology.* New York: Harcourt, Brace.
Krech, D. (1949), Notes toward a Psychological Theory. *J. Pers.*, 18:66-87.
────── & Crutchfield, R. S. (1948), *Theory and Problems of Social Psychology.* New York: McGraw-Hill.
Krechevsky, I. (1937), Brain Mechanisms and Variability. *J. Comp. Psychol.*, 23:121-163, 351-364.
Kretschmer, E. (1936), *Körperbau und Charakter,* 15th ed. Berlin: Springer.
────── (1942), *Körperbau und Charakter,* 16th ed. Berlin: Springer.
Kubie, L. S. (1952), Problems and Techniques of Psychoanalytic Validation and Progress. In *Psychoanalysis as Science,* ed. E. Pumpian-Mindlin. Stanford, Cal.: Stanford University Press, pp. 46-124.
Lasswell, H. D. (1930), *Psychopathology and Politics.* Chicago: University of Chicago Press.
Le Bon, G. (1895), *The Crowd: A Study of the Popular Mind.* London: Unwin, 1920.
Lederer, E. (1940), *State of the Masses.* New York: Norton.
Lerner, D. (1951), Elites: The Psychosocial Elect in Politics. Paper presented at the Forty-Seventh Annual Meeting of the American Political Science Association, San Francisco.
Levinson, D. J. (1949), An Approach to the Theory and Measurement of Ethnocentric Ideology. *J. Psychol.*, 28:19-39.
Lewin, K. (1926), Intention, Will, and Need. In *Organization and Pathology of Thought,* ed. D. Rapaport. New York: Columbia University Press, 1951, pp. 95-153.
────── (1935), *A Dynamic Theory of Personality.* New York: McGraw-Hill.
Linton, R. (1945), *The Cultural Background of Personality.* New York: Appleton-Century.
Luchins, A. S. (1942), Mechanization in Problem Solving—the Effect of *Einstellung. Psychol. Monogr.*, 54(No. 6).
MacCorquodale, K., & Meehl, P. (1948), On a Distinction between Hypothetical Constructs and Intervening Variables. *Psychol. Rev.*, 55:95-107.
Maier, N. R. F. (1949), *Frustration: The Study of Behavior without a Goal.* New York: McGraw-Hill.
Mannheim, K. (1936), *Ideology and Utopia.* New York: Harcourt, Brace.
Masling, J. M. (1954), How Neurotic Is the Authoritarian? *J. Abnorm. Soc. Psychol.*, 49:316-318.
Masserman, J. H. (1943), *Behavior and Neurosis.* Chicago: University of Chicago Press.
Mead, M. (1942), *And Keep Your Powder Dry.* New York: Morrow.
────── (1949), *Male and Female.* New York: Morrow.
Miller, J. G. (1951), Unconscious Processes and Perception. In *Perception: An Approach to Personality,* ed. R. R. Blake & G. V. Ramsey. New York: Ronald Press, pp. 258-282.
Mowrer, O. H. (1950), *Learning Theory and Personality Dynamics.* New York: Ronald Press.
Murphy, G. (1947), *Personality: A Biosocial Approach to Origins and Structure.* New York: Harper.
────── (1949), *Historical Introduction to Modern Psychology.* New York: Harcourt, Brace.

Murray, H. A. (1933), The Effect of Fear upon Estimates of the Maliciousness of Other Personalities. *J. Soc. Psychol.*, 4:310-329.
—— et al. (1938), *Explorations in Personality*. New York: Oxford University Press.
Neumann, S. (1942), *Permanent Revolution: The Total State in a World at War.* New York: Harper.
Neurath, O. (1938), Unified Science as Encyclopedic Integration. *International Encyclopedia of Unified Science*, 1(No. 1):1-27. Chicago: University of Chicago Press.
OSS Assessment Staff (1948), *Assessment of Men.* New York: Rinehart.
Parsons, T. (1948), *Essays in Sociological Theory: Pure and Applied.* Glencoe, Ill.: Free Press.
Piaget, J. (1926), *The Child's Conception of the World.* New York: Harcourt, Brace, 1929.
—— (1932), *The Moral Judgment of the Child.* New York: Harcourt, Brace, 1933.
Postman, L., Bruner, J. S., & McGinnies, E. (1948), Personal Values as Selective Factors in Perception. *J. Abnorm. Soc. Psychol.*, 43:142-154.
Rapaport, D., Schafer, R., & Gill, M. (1946), *Manual of Diagnostic Psychological Testing: Personality and Ideational Content*, Vol. 2. New York: Josiah Macy Jr. Foundation.
Reichard, S. (1947), An Analysis of Rorschach Data of Prejudiced and Unprejudiced Subjects. *J. Orthopsychiat.*, 18:280-286.
—— Livson, F., & Petersen, P. G. (1962), *Aging and Personality.* New York: Wiley.
Reichenbach, H. (1938), *Experience and Prediction.* Chicago: University of Chicago Press.
Reik, T. (1941), *Masochism in Modern Man.* New York: Farrar.
—— (1951), *Dogma and Compulsion.* New York: International Universities Press.
Rogers, C. R. (1931), Measuring Personality Adjustment in Children Nine-Thirteen Years of Age. *Teach. Coll. Contrib. Educ.*, No. 458.
—— (1951), Perceptual Reorganization in Client-Centered Therapy. In *Perception: An Approach to Personality*, ed. R. R. Blake & G. V. Ramsey. New York: Ronald Press, pp. 307-327.
Róheim, G. (1943), The Origin and Function of Culture. *Nerv. Ment. Dis. Monogr.*, No. 69.
Rokeach, M. (1943), Generalized Mental Rigidity as a Factor in Ethnocentrism. *J. Abnorm. Soc. Psychol.*, 48:259-278.
Rorschach, H. (1921), *Psychodiagnostics, a Diagnostic Test Based on Perception.* New York: Grune & Stratton, 1942.
Rosenberg, B. G. (1953), Compulsiveness as a Determinant in Selected Cognitive-Perceptual Performances. *J. Pers.*, 21:506-516.
Rosenzweig, S. (1938), A Dynamic Interpretation of Psychotherapy Oriented towards Research. *Psychiatry*, 1:521-526.
Sanford, R. N. (1937), The Effects of Abstinence from Food upon Imaginal Processes: A Further Experiment. *J. Psychol.*, 3:145-159.
—— et al. (1943), Physique, Personality and Scholarship: A Cooperative Study of School Children. *Monogr. Soc. Res. Child Devel.*, 8(No. 1).
Schafer, R. (1948), *The Clinical Application of Psychological Tests.* New York: International Universities Press.
Scheler, M. (1923), *Wesen und Formen der Sympathie*, 2nd ed. Bonn: F. Cohen.

Schlick, M. (1918), *Allgemeine Erkenntnislehre,* 2nd ed. Berlin: Springer, 1925.
───── (1920), *Space and Time in Contemporary Physics,* 3rd ed. New York: Oxford University Press.
───── (1939), *Problems of Ethics.* New York: Prentice-Hall.
Schrötter, K. (1912), Experimental Dreams. In *Organization and Pathology of Thought,* ed. D. Rapaport. New York: Columbia University Press, 1951, pp. 234-248.
Sears, R. R. (1936), Experimental Studies of Projection: I. Attribution of Traits. *J. Soc. Psychol.,* 7:151-163.
───── (1943), *Survey of Objective Studies of Psychoanalytic Concepts.* New York: Social Science Research Council, Bulletin No. 51.
Sherif, M. (1936), *The Psychology of Social Norms.* New York: Harper.
Shoben, E. J. (1948), A Learning Theory Interpretation of Psychotherapy. *Harvard Educ. Rev.,* 18:129-145.
Skinner, B. F. (1953), *Science and Human Behavior.* New York: Macmillan.
Stagner, R. (1936), Fascist Attitudes: Their Determining Conditions. *J. Soc. Psychol.,* 7:438-454.
───── (1937), *Psychology of Personality.* New York: McGraw-Hill.
Stern, W. (1935), *General Psychology from the Personalistic Standpoint.* New York: Macmillan.
Stevens, S. S. (1939), Psychology and the Science of Science. *Psychol. Bull.,* 36:221-263.
Stevenson, C. L. (1945), *Ethics and Language.* New Haven: Yale University Press.
Symonds, P. M., & Jackson, C. E. (1930), An Adjustment Survey. *J. Educ. Res.,* 21:321-330.
Thurstone, L. L. (1944), *A Factorial Study of Perception.* Chicago: University of Chicago Press.
Tolman, E. C. (1932), *Purposive Behavior in Animals and Men.* New York: Century.
───── (1937), An Operational Analysis of "Demands." *Erkenntnis,* 6:383-392.
───── (1938), Physiology, Psychology, and Sociology. *Psychol. Rev.,* 45:228-241.
───── (1948), Cognitive Maps in Rats and Men. *Psychol. Rev.,* 55:189-208.
Toulmin, S. (1948), The Logical Status of Psychoanalysis. *Analysis,* 9:23-29.
Tryon, C. M. (1939a), Evaluations of Adolescent Personality by Adolescents. *Monogr. Soc. Res. Child Devel.,* 4(No. 4).
───── (1939b), *California Adjustment Inventory.* Berkeley: University of California.
Vernon, P. E. (1938), *The Assessment of Psychological Qualities by Verbal Methods.* London: Medical Research Council.
Weber, Marianne (1950), *Max Weber, Ein Lebensbild.* Heidelberg: Lambert-Schneider.
Weber, Max (1904-1905), *The Protestant Ethic and the Spirit of Capitalism.* New York: Scribner, 1930.
Werner, H. (1940), *Comparative Psychology of Mental Development,* rev. ed. Chicago: Follett, 1948.
───── (1946), The Concept of Rigidity: A Critical Evaluation. *Psychol. Rev.,* 53:43-52.
Wolf, A. (1943), The Dynamics of the Selective Inhibition of Specific Functions in Neurosis: A Preliminary Report. *Psychosom. Med.,* 5:27-38.

ELSE FRENKEL-BRUNSWIK: DESCRIPTIVE BIBLIOGRAPHY

1. (1931), Atomismus und Mechanismus in der Assoziationspsychologie. *Zeit. Psychol.* 123:193-258.

   A logical analysis of the basic principles of association psychology. These are discussed in relation to Gestalt principles and an attempt is made to indicate the similarities as well as the differences between the two schools of thought. (Ph.D. Dissertation, University of Vienna, 1930.)

2. (1931), Lebenslauf, Leistung, und Erfolg. *Bericht über den 12 deutschen Psychologenkongress.* Hamburg, pp. 331-335.

   Part of the developmental studies carried out under Charlotte Bühler, this describes the distribution and quality of productive activity in the life course of the individual. See also No. 4, pp. 20-28.

3. (date unknown), Miscellaneous articles on fairy tales. In *Handwörterbuch des deutschen Märchens,* ed. Mackensen. Berlin: Gruyter, pp. 400, 426-428, 434-436, 565-566.

   Not available.

4. (1936), Studies in Biographical Psychology. *Character & Pers.,* 5:1-34.

   A report based upon Charlotte Bühler's more comprehensive volume, *Der Menschliche Lebenslauf als Psychologisches Problem* (Leipzig, 1933), and upon earlier articles on the biographical studies. The biographies of 400 persons were analyzed in terms of external events, subjective experiences, and actual achievements. Five phases of psychological development are described and related to corresponding biological phases, and a general law of development is formulated. An abbreviated version of this article was published as No. 20.

5. (1937), (with Edith Weisskopf) Wunsch und Pflicht im Aufbau des menschlichen Lebens. Vol. 1 of *Psychol. Forschungen über den Lebenslauf,* ed. C. Bühler & E. Frenkel. Vienna: Gerold.

Sixty-five persons between the ages of 15 and 80 were asked to name their wishes and duties and to explain their meaning. It was found that a shift occurs around age 45, at which time wishes become less important in relation to duties. Deviations from this general developmental law were found only in neurotics. An abbreviated version of this article was published in English as No. 16.

6. (1939), Mechanisms of Self-Deception. *J. Soc. Psychol. (S.P.S.S.I. Bulletin)*, 10:409-420.

A comparison between observations of the actual conduct of a group of university students and various statements made by the students about their own behavior. Discrepancies between the two sets of data are considered as indicators of self-deception. Self-deception is seen as serving a defensive function, and several formal criteria for diagnosing it through self-reports are described.

7. (1940), Psychoanalysis and Personality Research. In Symposium on Psychoanalysis by Analyzed Experimental Psychologists, ed. G. W. Allport. *J. Abnorm. Soc. Psychol.*, 35:176-197.

A discussion of the relationship between fact and theory in psychology and psychoanalysis and the problem of inference from overt behavior to underlying motivation. The second part of the article refers to the development of her own scientific interests and orientation with particular emphasis on her personal experience with psychoanalysis. [This volume, Chapter 1.]

8. (1942), Motivation and Behavior. *Genet. Psychol. Monogr.*, 26:121-265.

A group of 100 subjects in the University of California Adolescent Growth Study were rated on nine motivational variables and the ratings compared with ratings of social behavior and with self-reports. The concept of drive and its alternative manifestations is shown to be helpful in explaining apparent inconsistencies in the latter sets of data and in uncovering relationships in personality.

9. (1945), (with R. N. Sanford) Some Personality Factors in Anti-Semitism. *J. Psychol.*, 20:271-291. Republished in *Anti-Semitism: A Social Disease*, ed. E. Simmel. New York: International Universities Press, 1946; *Yearbook of Psychoanalysis*, Vol. 3, 1947; *Readings in Personal and Social Adjustment*, ed. E. Kube & C. F. J. Lehner. New York: Prentice-Hall, 1954.

An early report on *The Authoritarian Personality* studies (see No. 15). Using data from questionnaires, projective tests, and clinical interviews, the paper describes the personality of college women to whom an anti-Semitic ideology appeals.

10. (1947), (with D. J. Levinson & R. N. Sanford) The Antidemocratic Personality. In *Readings in Social Psychology*, ed. T. M. Newcomb & E. L. Hartley. New York: Holt, pp. 531-541.

Another early report on *The Authoritarian Personality*. The paper describes some of the methods used in this study, focusing on the attitude scales and analysis of the interview material.

11. (1948), Dynamic and Cognitive Categorization of Qualitative Material: I. General Problems and the Thematic Apperception Test. *J. Psychol.*, 25:253-260.

    A discussion of the problem of rating clinical material systematically without losing its conceptual richness. The method described begins with the development of hypotheses from the study of single cases which are then incorporated in the rating schedule. The rating categories, which include attitudinal and motivational variables, defense mechanisms, and characteristics of cognitive and perceptual performance, are global and applicable to a wide variety of materials. Illustrations are taken from analysis of children's TAT stories.

12. (1948), Dynamic and Cognitive Categorization of Qualitative Material: II. Interviews of the Ethnically Prejudiced. *J. Psychol.*, 25:261-277.

    An application of the method described in No. 11 to *The Authoritarian Personality* subjects. The scoring categories used (family, sex, attitude toward others, attitude toward the self, dynamic character structure, and cognitive personality organization), problems of reliability and validity, and limitations of the method are discussed.

13. (1948), A Study of Prejudice in Children. *Hum. Relat.* 1:295-306. Republished in *Race Prejudice and Discrimination,* ed. A. M. Rose. New York: Knopf, 1951; *Selected Studies in Marriage and the Family,* ed. R. F. Winch & R. McGinnis. New York: Holt, 1953 (with alterations); *Readings in Personal and Social Adjustment,* ed. E. Kube & C. F. J. Lehner, New York: Prentice-Hall, 1954.

    A description of the Child Study, including the selection of the subjects and a discussion of the prejudiced and unprejudiced extremes in terms of social attitudes, attitudes toward parents and teachers, conception of sex roles, moralism and conformity, and intolerance of ambiguity.

14. (1949), Intolerance of Ambiguity as an Emotional and Perceptual Personality Variable. In Symposium on Interrelationships between Perception and Personality, Part I. *J. Pers.*, 18:108-143. Republished in *Readings in Personality,* ed. H. Brand. New York: Wiley, 1954.

    A discussion of the concept of intolerance of ambiguity as a basic variable in the emotional and cognitive orientation toward life. Evidence from a variety of cognitive and perceptual experiments and from clinical interviews shows that there is partial generality of this variable, but that there are also compensatory relations that may make for the simultaneous presence of opposite tendencies. [This volume, Chapter 2.]

15. (1950), (with T. W. Adorno, D. J. Levinson, & R. N. Sanford) *The Authoritarian Personality.* New York: Harper.

A report on a four-year study of the personality correlates of attitudes toward minority groups and sociopolitical ideologies. Prejudiced attitudes are described as part of a larger ideology and are shown to be related to distinct patterns of personality organization.

16. (1950), Wishes and Feelings of Duty in the Course of Life. In *Research on Aging*, ed. H. E. Jones. New York: Social Science Research Council, pp. 116-122.

An abbreviated report of the material presented in No. 5.

17. (1951), Patterns of Social and Cognitive Outlook in Children and Family. *Amer. J. Orthopsychiat.*, 21:543-558.

A report on material collected in the Child Study. Clinical case reports of two children, one scoring high on tests of minority group prejudice and one scoring low, are presented in detail. An experiment on memory for stories, which was found to differentiate prejudiced and unprejudiced children, is also described.

18. (1951), Personality Theory and Perception. In *Perception: An Approach to Personality*, ed. R. R. Blake & G. V. Ramsey. New York: Ronald Press, pp. 356-419.

Part of a symposium dealing with the convergence of research in personality and in perception, this paper links developments in psychoanalysis and personality theory to developments in social psychology and to studies of cognition and perception. Problems of making motivational inferences, discrepancies between self-perception and perception by others (including three case reports from the Adolescent Study, previously unpublished), and the relationship between form and content (using case reports and experimental data from the Child Study) are discussed. Data reported originally in Nos. 6 and 8 are also summarized. [This volume, Chapter 3.]

19. (1951), Prejudice in Children. *Idea and Experiment*, 1:7-9.

A popularized account of the Child Study, discussing the personality of the prejudiced and unprejudiced child and the relationships of these personality patterns to perception and thinking and to the nature of family relationships.

20. (1952), Adjustments and Reorientations in the Course of the Life Span. In *Psychological Studies of Human Development*, ed. R. C. Kuhlen & G. H. Thompson. New York: Appleton-Century-Crofts, pp. 94-103.

An adaptation and abridgment of No. 4.

21. (1952), Interaction of Psychological and Sociological Factors in Political Behavior. *Amer. Polit. Sci. Rev.*, 46:44-65. Republished in *Public Opinion and Propaganda*, ed. D. Katz. Society for the Psychological Study of Social Issues, 1954; *American Minorities*, ed. M. L. Barron. New York: Knopf, 1957.

Social behavior and personality structure are presented as important links in the network of societal interaction. The contribution of Freud is discussed at length, as well as his limitations in dealing with social phenomena. Data from *The Authoritarian Personality* are used to illustrate the interaction of psychological and social factors at four levels: overt social behavior, underlying motivation, attitudes toward social institutions and roles, and relations of personality to social and occupational group membership. [This volume, Chapter 5.]

22. (1952), Social Psychology. In *Progress in Clinical Psychology,* ed. D. Brower & L. E. Abt. New York: Grune & Stratton, pp. 508-518.

The convergence of several trends stemming from psychoanalysis, psychology, and the social sciences and the relations between clinical and social data are discussed. Hypothesized relationships between early childhood experiences and personality structure, problems of leadership, and ethnic prejudice in children serve as illustrations.

23. (1953), (with Joan Havel) Prejudice in the Interviews of Children: I: Attitudes toward Minority Groups. *J. Genet. Psychol.,* 82:91-135.

A report on one phase of the Child Study. A group of 81 children, 10 to 15 years of age, were interviewed on their attitudes toward five minority groups. Substantial agreement was found between interview responses and scores on tests of prejudiced attitudes. Components of the attitudes toward each minority group are discussed.

24. (1953), Methods and Concepts in a Study of Old Age. In *Proceedings of the Psychiatric Association Committee on Medical Rehabilitation: Problems of Retirement.* Los Angeles, pp. 39-45.

A preliminary report on a study of aging industrial workers. Data were collected on social-political outlook, attitudes toward aging and retirement, personality structure, using intensive interviews, and perceptual and cognitive performance, using a series of specially designed tests. Hypotheses about the nature of shifts in these variables with age and their social implications are discussed. This study was published as *Aging and Personality* by S. Reichard, F. Livson, & P. Petersen (New York: Wiley, 1962).

25. (1953), Psychodynamics and Cognition. In *Explorations in Psychoanalysis,* ed. R. Lindner. New York: Julian Press, pp. 38-51.

A personality-centered approach to cognition, in which problems are organized around areas of dynamic personality research and then extended to the field of perception and thinking, is discussed. Cognition is seen as adaptive rather than defensive. The psychic mechanisms governing such cognitive processes as the lively imagination of the masochist, the inhibition in experiencing gestalten on the part of the compulsive, and the intolerance of ambiguity in the ethnically prejudiced, are analyzed.

26. (1954), Psychoanalysis and the Unity of Science. *Proc. Amer. Acad. Arts Sci.,* 80:273-347.

An appraisal of the scientific legitimacy and operational status of psychoanalytic concepts (the unconscious and the instincts are used as examples). The broadening of operationism, confirmation of hypotheses and theory construction, relationships between hypothetical constructs and intervening variables, the role of manifest behavior and latent motivation, the explanatory power of psychoanalysis, and problems of verifying psychoanalytic hypotheses are discussed. There is also a brief consideration of psychoanalysis and ethics, covered more fully in No. 28 and in "Some Empirical and Theoretical Aspects of the Problem of Values" (this volume, Chapter 7). [This volume, Chapter 4.]

27. (1954), Further Explorations by a Contributor to *The Authoritarian Personality*. In *Studies in the Scope and Method of "The Authoritarian Personality,"* ed. R. Christie & M. Jahoda. Glencoe, Ill.: Free Press, pp. 226-275.

A discussion of some of the background and the theoretical and experimental implications of *The Authoritarian Personality*. Social and developmental aspects of the "authoritarian personality," based on data from the Child Study, are discussed. Also included are discussions of patterns of emotional and cognitive functioning and unity of style, latent motivation and the manifest person, and the problem of values and bias in social research.

28. (1954), Environmental Controls and the Impoverishment of Thought. In *Totalitarianism*, ed. C. J. Friedrich. Cambridge: Harvard University Press, pp. 171-202.

A discussion of the psychological mechanisms by which a totalitarian outlook is transmitted and the role it plays in the adaptation of the individual. A detailed consideration of the response to threats in childhood, based on empirical data from the Child Study, is seen as having relevance for the ways in which people react to political threats in adult life. [This volume, Chapter 6.]

29. (1954), Social Research and the Problem of Values: A Reply. *J. Abnorm. Soc. Psychol.,* 49:466-471.

Four aspects of the value problem are selected for discussion: the influence of values and preconceptions upon the development of the sciences, the logical status of value judgments, social and psychological determiners of value formation, and the contribution of the social sciences to the choice between alternative systems of values. A later and more detailed discussion of these problems appears in this volume as "Some Empirical and Theoretical Aspects of the Problem of Values" (Chapter 7).

30. (1954), Social Tensions and the Inhibition of Thought. *Soc. Problems,* 2:75-81.

Social forces that make for increasing rigidity in thinking and behavior are contrasted with those that stimulate flexibility and creativity. The governments of Nazi Germany and Russia are discussed briefly and contrasted with the strengths and weaknesses of democratic forms of government.

31. (1954), Meaning of Psychoanalytic Concepts and Confirmation of Psychoanalytic Theories. *Sci. Monthly,* 79:293-300.

A condensation and partial reformulation of No. 26.

32. (1955), Differential Patterns of Social Outlook and Personality in Family and Children. In *Childhood in Contemporary Cultures,* ed. M. Mead & M. Wolfenstein. Chicago: University of Chicago Press, pp. 369-405.

Two subjects from the Child Study, a boy scoring high on tests of ethnic prejudice and a girl scoring low, are discussed in terms of their social beliefs, cognitive organization, personality structure, and family atmosphere.

33. (1957), Perspectives in Psychoanalytic Theory. In *Perspectives in Personality Theory,* ed. H. P. David & H. von Bracken. New York: Basic Books, pp. 159-182.

An expanded version of No. 31. Most of the views expressed here are discussed in greater detail in No. 26.

INDEX

Abasement, 99-100
Achievement, need for, 101
Actones, 38, 39
Adaptation, 24, 25, 31, 61, 246-247, 266, 281, 282, 302, 308, 309
  mechanisms of, 108
Adjustment Inventory, 122-123
Adolescent Study, 16-18, 53-56, 97-102, 118-130, 133, 153, 189
Adorno, T. W., 6, 18, 19, 21, 64, 66, 70, 84, 111, 125, 158, 233, 234, 239, 248, 263, 265, 269, 294
Aggression, 158, 175, 216
  cognition and, 153-157
  manifestations of, 98-99, 101
Aging, 31-32
Alexander, F., 6, 10, 41-43
Allport, G. W., 10, 11, 43, 107, 108, 111, 152, 217
Altruism, 99-100
Ambiguity
  perceptual, 71
  tolerance vs. intolerance of, 23-25, 58, 60, 62, 64-70, 73, 76-82, 84, 85, 89-91, 134-136, 158, 208, 213-214, 217, 245-246, 256, 275-276, 280, 282, 285, 301; case studies of, 138-150; intelligence and, 77; *see also* Adaptation; Rigidity
Ambivalence, 62, 65-66, 90, 91, 134-135
Anal eroticism, 176-177
Anthropology, 110-111
Anti-Semitism, 19, 20; *see also* Authoritarian personality; Ethnocentrism; Nazism; Prejudice, ethnic
Antitype, 279-280, 282, 283, 302-303; *see also* Democratic-minded personality
Anxiety, 107
Authoritarian personality, 13, 18-21, 24, 25, 30-31, 209, 213-215, 234, 235, 239-241, 255-260, 264-270, 283-284, 290, 309, 310
  clinical description of, 241-245
  evaluative description of, 294-295

family structure of, 66-69, 266-267, 271-272
  in America, 291
  perception and thought in, 245-247, 255-257, 273-276, 280
  self-image of, 269
  sociological considerations and, 250-255, 257
  values of, 243, 247-250, 269-270, 280, 284-286, 288, 299-300
  see also Ambiguity; Ethnocentrism; Fascism; Prejudice, ethnic; Rigidity; Totalitarianism
Autism, 88, 112, 211
Barker, R., 204
Behavior
  criteria of, 41, 167-168
  genuineness of, 195, 226-227, 250
  instinct theory and, 226
  meaning of, 29
  motivation and, 17, 94-95, 97-102, 150-151, 188-195, 236-237; *see also* Opposites, closeness of
  psychoanalytic view of, 188-195, 201
  surface, 13, 15, 57
  values and, 303
  see also Personality; Political behavior; Self-deception
Behaviorism, 14, 183-186, 227, 236, 307
Bendix, R., 251, 297
Benedict, R., 307
Benussi, V., 71
Bergmann, G., 182, 191, 199
Bernfeld, Siegfried, 45, 50, 172
Bernfeld, Suzanne, 183
Bertalanffy, L. von, 6
Betlheim, S., 206
Bismarck, O. von, 8
Blake, R. R., 22, 92
Bleuler, E., 210
Blum, G. S., 206
Boas, F., 10
Boring, E. G., 10, 11
Boulding, K., 34, 294
Brenman, M., 206
Bridgman, P. W., 162
Bronfenbrenner, U., 95, 103

327

INDEX

Brown, J. F., 10
Brown, W., 78
Bruckner, A., 8
Brummell, Beau, 8
Bruner, J. S., 59, 79, 92, 95, 111-112, 115, 136
Brunswik, E., 2, 5, 6, 11, 13, 38, 49, 71, 81, 112, 113, 181, 193, 227
Bühler, C., 5, 8, 12, 15, 48, 49, 159
Bühler, K., 5, 7, 12, 48, 49
Burdick, E., 6
Cameron, N., 92, 210
Campbell, D. T., 74
Carnap, R., 12, 25, 48, 167, 195, 197, 225, 228
Carnegie, A., 8
Caruso, E., 8
Casanova, G. G., 8
Catlin, G. E. C., 220
Cattell, J. McK., 10
Cattell, R. B., 135
Child Study, the, 21, 24, 30
Christie, J. R., 68
Closeness of opposites; *see* Opposites, closeness of
Cognition, 92-93, 105-106, 230
　approaches to, 210-218
　concreteness, abstractness, and generalization in, 83-84, 86-88
　ethics and, 301-302
　see also Perception
Cole, L., 14
Compulsive character, 72, 106, 213
Concept formation, 139-140, 144-145
Conformity, 187; *see also* Authoritarian personality; Rigidity
Conscience, 300-301; *see also* Values
Conscious, the *(Cs.)*, 167-169, 171, 172
Consciousness, function of, 207-208
Criminality, psychoanalytic view of, 41-42
Crutchfield, R. S., 6, 60
Cultural relativism, 307
Darwin, C., 182
Death instinct, 175
Defense mechanisms, 104-108, 133-134, 203-205, 207; *see also* Repression; Sublimation
Defenses, perceptual, 23, 79, 136
Dembo, T., 204
Democracy, values of, 235

Democratic-minded personality, 247, 251-255, 258-260, 273-274, 277-278, 281, 299; *see also* Adaptation; Antitype; Liberalism
Denial, 105
Dennis, W., 93
Dingle, H., 193
Dollard, J., 191, 205
Dreams, interpretation of, 173
Drive, 18, 23, 40-43, 101, 129
　conceptions of, 131-132
　see also Instinct; Motivation; Need
Durkheim, E., 187, 220, 221, 287, 297, 298
Ego psychology, 11, 12, 14, 27, 44-45, 57, 102-104, 107-108, 114, 184-185
Einstein, A., 27, 162, 163, 202, 225, 246, 281, 290, 296
Ellis, A., 165, 170
Environment, perception of, 117-118
Epicurus, 296
Erikson, E. H., 8, 29, 111
Eros, 175
Ethics, 218-220, 287-288, 293, 294, 301-302; *see also* Psychoanalysis, ethics and; Values
Ethnocentrism, 149, 240-241, 249-252, 258, 269
　education and, 253
　prediction of, 257
　see also Anti-Semitism; Authoritarian personality; Prejudice, ethnic
Exaggeration; *see* Self-deception
Existentialism, 289
Fascism, 19, 20, 241, 251, 258, 263; *see also* Authoritarian personality; Nazism; Totalitarianism
Feigl, H., 26, 163, 170, 192, 199, 228
Fenichel, O., 72, 105, 106, 108, 175, 206, 213, 222, 230, 242, 301
Ferenczi, S., 10, 213
Fischler, M., 292
Fixation, 203-204
Flew, A., 192, 193
Form and content, censorship of, 151; *see also* Personality; Projective tests
Frank, L. K., 46, 109
Frank, P., 163, 201, 225, 229, 296, 297
Frenkel, E., 5, 7-10, 48, 50

INDEX

Frenkel-Brunswik, E., 1-4, 48, 64, 66, 67, 72, 89, 90, 93, 97, 101, 111, 115, 125, 131, 133, 134, 155, 158, 233, 236, 239-241, 263, 265, 269, 270, 299
 professional biography, 5-35
 psychoanalysis and, 48, 50-52, 55
Freud, A., 11, 40, 45, 95, 102, 104, 105, 182
Freud, S., 10, 27, 45, 46, 50, 96, 103-105, 108-110, 161, 164-180, 182-187, 192, 196, 198, 200-202, 204, 211-213, 215, 218-221, 224-228, 237, 238, 256, 277, 286, 287, 298, 301, 305
Friedrich, C. J., 261
Fromm, E., 29, 67, 111, 233, 260, 262, 264
Frustration, 204-205
Gill, M. M., 81, 159
Goebbels, J. P., 288
Goethe, J. W. von, 8
Goethe, K. E. T. von, 8
Goldstein, K., 60, 76, 78, 82, 83, 85-88, 113, 210, 274
Goodman, C. C., 59, 112
Gordon, L., 74
Greenacre, P., 142
Gunther, H. F. K., 282
Hall, G. S., 10
Hartley, E. L., 111
Hartmann, H., 45, 108, 185, 206
Havel, J., 21
Healy, W., 41-43
Hegel, G. W. F., 8
Heider, F., 38
Heisenberg, W., 297
Helmholtz, H. L. F. von, 172, 194, 226
Hempel, C. G., 163, 164, 197, 228
Herbart, J. F., 167
Hilgard, E. R., 93, 112, 203
Hitler, A., 11, 270, 278, 283
Hobbs, N., 33
Hull, C. L., 181, 186, 192, 228, 309
Hume, D., 301
Hunt, J. McV., 204
Hunter, W. S., 181
Hyman, M., 139
Hypothetical constructs, 27, 195-201, 228
Id, 170

psychology, 43, 102-104, 107; see also Instinct
Ideology; see Totalitarianism
Instinct, psychoanalytic concept of, 173-180, 184, 185, 225, 226; see also Drive; Id
Intellectualization, 108
Intervening variables, 27, 195-201, 228
Intolerance of ambiguity; see Ambiguity
Isolation, 106
Jackson, C. E., 122
Jaensch, E. R., 34, 60-62, 85, 86, 113, 210, 215, 246-247, 266, 278-284, 302, 303, 308, 309
James, W., 4, 10, 26
Jarvik, M. E., 74, 81, 146
Jones, E., 10
Jones, H. E., 5, 16, 64, 89, 97
Jones, M. C., 124
J-type, 61
Jung, C. G., 10
Kant, I., 8, 300, 301
Kaplan, A., 294
Kardiner, A., 111, 233
Klein, G. S., 25
Kluckhohn, C., 6, 34, 111, 233, 294
Koffka, K., 38, 71, 275
Kraepelin, E., 39
Krech, D., 6, 22, 60
Krechevsky, I., 88
Kretschmer, E., 60, 87, 88, 113, 210
Kroeber, A., 6
Kubie, L. S., 202, 206
Landis, C., 10
Lasswell, H. D., 6, 29, 34, 233, 265
Lazarsfeld, P., 6, 7
Learning theory, 186, 191, 205, 230, 309
Le Bon, G., 287
Lederer, E., 286
Leibniz, G. W. von, 8
Lenard, P., 281
Lerner, D., 252
Levinson, D. J., 6, 18, 70, 250
Lewin, K., 11, 95, 204
Liberalism, 60-62, 85, 281; see also Adaptation; Antitype; Democratic-minded personality
Libido, concept of, 196, 200
Lind, J., 8
Linton, R., 111, 233, 247

Liszt, F., 8
Livson, F. B., 6, 79, 139
Livson, N., 79, 139
Logical positivism; *see* Positivism
Luchins, A. S., 143
MacCorquodale, K., 27, 195, 196, 199, 200, 228
MacFarlane, J. W., 5
Magical thinking, 263
Maier, N. R. F., 205
Mannheim, K., 262, 264, 287, 297, 298, 309, 310
Marginality, social, 30, 68, 248-251, 254, 257, 262, 268, 271, 286
Marx, K., 263
Masling, J. M., 294
Masochism, 212
Masserman, J. H., 204
Materialism, dialectical, 290
McDougall, W., 14, 41
McGinnies, E., 79, 112, 136
Mead, M., 111, 233
Meehl, P., 27, 195, 196, 199, 200, 228
Memory, distortion of, 73-76, 153
Merton, R. K., 297
Miller, J. G., 191
Miller, N. E., 205
Moran, L. J., 92
Morrow, W. R., 248
Motivation
  alternative manifestations of, 17, 94-95, 97-102, 182-183, 190, 229, 236-237
  as inferential construct, 101
  cognition and, 59, 63, 230
  experimental approach to, 203-207
  form and content of, 150-151
  in advanced cultures, 151, 236
  perception of, 98, 130-133
  psychoanalytic view of, 94-95, 188-195, 201
  terminology of, 193-195, 230-231
  see also Drive; Id; Instinct; Need; Personality; Self-deception
Mowrer, O. H., 205
Mozart, W. A., 8
Murphy, G., 11, 19, 59, 111, 112
Murray, H. A., 10, 11, 13, 14, 37-41, 47, 52, 55, 57, 59, 98, 111, 132, 160, 194, 216, 274
Naess, A., 34

Nazism, 86, 159, 253, 278-284, 286, 289, 303
  racial theory of, 282-283, 290
  see also Fascism; Jaensch, E. R.; Totalitarianism
Need, 40-43, 182, 183, 194; *see also* Drive; Instinct; Motivation
Neumann, S., 263
Neurath, O., 12, 25, 161, 178
Nietzsche, F. W., 283-284, 287, 303, 310
Operationism, 4, 26-28, 162-163
Opposites, closeness of, 10, 24, 73, 82, 88-91, 96, 151-153, 207, 213, 256, 277-278; *see also* Rigidity; Self-deception
OSS Assessment Staff, 160
Pareto, V., 287
Parsons, T., 233, 247
Passivity, 96
Perception, 22-25, 92-93, 114, 210
  constitution and environment in, 87-88
  ego and, 104
  ethnic prejudice and, 136-150
  functional approach to, 112
  in authoritarian personality; *see* Authoritarian personality
  motivation and, 95, 112, 211
  of environment, 117-118
  pathological, 105-106
  personality and, 58-91
  psychoanalytic theory and, 111
  self-, 114, 125, 269; *see also* Self-deception
  terminology of, 193-194
  see also Ambiguity; Cognition; Memory; Motivation; Stimulus boundness
Personality, 3, 4, 9, 11, 14, 15
  aging and, 31-32
  biographical study of, 8-9, 15, 48-49
  central region of events, 13-16, 37-40, 42-47, 49, 51, 52, 54-57, 102
  distal region of events, 13-15, 38-40, 42-44, 46, 49, 52, 55, 57
  form and content of, 70, 90, 150-160
  interpretations in assessment of, 16, 56-57
  perception and, 22-25, 58-63, 72-73, 114, 159-160, 185, 213-217; *see also* Ambiguity; Authoritarian

INDEX

personality; Memory; Rigidity; Stimulus boundness
peripheral region of events, 13-16, 36-40, 43, 49, 55-57
political attitudes and, 264-266; *see also* Authoritarian personality
proximal region of events, 13-16, 38-39, 43, 49, 55-57
psychoanalytic approach to, 93-94, 185, 188
rational and irrational in, 286-290
society and, 28-31; *see also* Political behavior; Totalitarianism
theory, 92-94, 102, 114, 159-160, 235-238
unity of, 137-138
values and, 304
see also Authoritarian personality; Behavior; Motivation
Petersen, P. G., 6
Physics, 57, 162-164, 166, 167, 180, 202, 225, 281, 290, 296-298; *see also* Science
Piaget, J., 149, 159, 160, 210
Plato, 167, 300, 302, 305
Political behavior, 232-233, 237, 239, 250-251, 255-258, 264-266; *see also* Authoritarian personality
Positivism, logical, 7, 26, 28, 48, 56, 161, 163, 293
Postman, L., 79, 112, 136
Preconscious, the *(Pcs.)*, 168-169
Prejudice, ethnic, 19, 23, 69-70
developmental stages and, 149
perception and, 72-85, 90, 136-150, 155, 158-160, 209
self-perception and, 125
see also Anti-Semitism; Authoritarian personality; Ethnocentrism
Primary process, 172
Projection, 105, 158
Projective tests, 46-47, 81, 109
form and content in, 52-53, 153-159
Psychoanalysis
as a depth psychology, 181
as science, 25-28, 166, 168, 173, 175, 177-178, 180-183, 225-228
attempts to verify, 28, 189-191, 201-207, 209-210, 229-230
authoritarian personality and, 19
biological and social factors in, 109-110, 187-188, 238-239
central region in, 39, 41-46, 51, 52, 57, 181, 182, 227
criticisms of, 107-108, 161-162, 164-165, 173, 179, 181, 182, 184-185, 188, 192-193, 221, 226, 227, 237-239, 305
distal events in, 39, 46, 181, 182, 227
distance from phenotype of, 180-188, 226
economic point of view in, 171-172
ethics and, 218-224, 231, 298, 300, 304-307
Frenkel-Brunswik and, 48, 50-52, 55
hydraulic model in, 196, 200
hypothetical constructs and intervening variables in, 195-201, 228
inferences in, 57, 97, 181, 202-203, 227
motivation and behavior in, 94-95, 188-195
perception and, 71-72, 105-106, 112-113, 211-213
personality theory and, 102, 235-236
polarities in, 96-97
projective tests and, 46-47
psychology and, 3, 10-12, 14, 16, 36, 52-53, 93-95, 108-111
rational and irrational in, 185, 219-221, 223, 231, 286-289, 306
social sciences and, 110-111, 237, 238
topographic systems in, 168-172
see also Defense; Ego psychology; Id; Instinct; Libido; Unconscious
Psychology, 3-4, 10-12, 14, 16, 36, 53, 108-109
association, 7
depth and surface, 15, 43, 49-51, 57, 93-95, 98, 101-103, 110, 114
developmental, 8-9
Gestalt, 60, 72, 279-280
intervening and independent variables in, 143
motivational, 13-15
Nazi, 246-247; *see also* Jaensch, E. R.
physiological explanations in, 191
social, 20, 109-111
sociology and, 29
theory and observation in, 12-13
see also Behaviorism; Learning theory; Personality theory
Ramsey, G. V., 22, 92

Rapaport, D., 81, 159
Rationalism and irrationalism, 220-221, 223; *see also* Psychoanalysis, rational and irrational in; Society, rational and irrational in
Reaction formation, 106-107
Reality
  mastery of, 102-104, 108, 112-113
  omissions and distortions in, 85-86, 105-106
  principle, 104
Regression, 203-204
Reichard, S., 6, 155
Reichenbach, H., 195, 196, 228
Reik, T., 212, 219, 230
Religion, 212, 219-220, 287
Repression, 105, 200, 201, 203-205, 221-223, 305
Rice, P., 32
Rigidity, 65, 68, 77, 78, 80-89, 91, 135-137, 142, 152, 158, 159, 209, 246, 266, 276, 278-284, 302
  Scale, 146-149
  see also Ambiguity; Stimulus boundness
Rockefeller, J. D., 8
Rogers, C. R., 114, 122, 125
Róheim, G., 110
Rokeach, M., 68, 80, 135, 143, 146
Roosevelt, F. D., 111, 239
Rorschach, H., 60, 113; *see also* Projective tests
Rosenberg, B. G., 213
Rosenzweig, S., 68
Rubin, E. J., 71
Sachs, H., 10
Sanford, F., 15
Sanford, R. N., 6, 18, 100, 111
Schafer, R., 81, 159
Scheerer, M., 60, 83, 210, 274
Scheler, M., 93, 297
Schilder, P., 213
Schizophrenia, 86-87
Schlick, M., 12, 25, 48, 161, 163, 293
Schroll, —, 60, 113
Schrötter, K., 206
Science, 1, 3
  Freud and, 166, 168, 175, 177
  levels of explanation in, 192
  psychology and, 4
  theory and observation in, 162-164,
166, 170, 198, 225, 297-298
  unity of, 25-28
  values and, 296-297
  see also Physics; Positivism
Science, social
  psychoanalysis and, 110-111, 237, 238
  values and, 292, 294-295, 297-298, 307-310
Sears, R. R., 10, 132, 133, 176, 203
Secondary process, 172
Self-deception, 9-10, 16, 18, 53-54, 65, 89, 100, 133, 134, 152, 207-209, 229, 303-304
  case studies of, 118-130
  mechanisms of, 115-118
Self-report vs. behavior; *see* Self-deception
Shakespeare, W., 51, 116
Shakow, D., 10
Sherif, M., 59, 112
Shoben, E. J., 186
Skinner, B. F., 185, 186, 188, 227
Social science; *see* Science, social
Society
  industrial, individual and, 234-235, 257
  rational and irrational in, 262-264, 287-290, 306
Sociology, 29, 187, 233
Socrates, 300
Sorel, G., 287
Speech, formal characteristics of, 47, 50
Spranger, E., 309
Stagner, R., 11, 41, 111
Stark, J., 281
Stern, W., 47, 113
Stevens, S. S., 162
Stevenson, C. L., 293, 294
Stimulus boundness, 83, 85, 86, 135, 284; *see also* Rigidity
S-type, 61; *see also* Antitype
Sublimation, 110, 184, 238
Suggestion, posthypnotic, 167, 168
Superego, 186, 222-223, 288, 299-301
Surplus meaning, 196, 228
Symonds, P. M., 10, 122
Thematic Apperception Test, 52, 109, 216-217; *see also* Projective tests
Thurstone, L. L., 60, 70, 113
Tiner, L. G., 135
Titchener, E. B., 10

Tolman, E. C., 5, 43, 79, 136, 181, 182, 192, 227, 228
Tolstoy, L., 8
Totalitarianism, 30, 240, 257
  psychology and, 261-267
  see also Authoritarian personality; Fascism; Nazism
Toulmin, S., 192, 193
Tryon, C. M., 120, 122
Typology, 113
Unconscious, the *(Ucs.)*
  as a quality, 170
  psychoanalytic concept of, 165-173, 178, 179, 192-193, 198, 225
Undoing, 106
Urabin, J., 292
Value judgments, 293-295
Values, 32-35
  democratic, 235
  facts and, 294-296, 302, 307, 308
  social and psychological determinants of, 298-306
  social science and, 292, 294-295, 297-298, 307-310
  theory of, 292-293
  see also Authoritarian personality, values of; Ethics
Verdi, G., 8
Vernon, P. E., 54
Victoria, Queen, 8
Weber, Marianne, 218, 305
Weber, Max, 218-221, 287, 298, 305, 309
Weiss, A. P., 181
Weisskopf, E., 8, 50
Werner, H., 24, 60, 68, 83, 87, 113, 159, 160, 210, 263
Willkie, W., 250
Willoughby, R. R., 10
Wolf, A., 203
Wolf, R. E., 55, 57

ABOUT THE EDITORS

JOAN GRANT received her Ph.D. in psychology from the University of California at Berkeley in 1951. She has been a Research Associate at the Research Center for Human Relations, New York University, at Cornell University Medical College, and at the California Department of Corrections. She is at present a project director with the Social Action Research Center, Berkeley.

NANETTE HEIMAN received her Ph.D. in psychology from the University of California at Berkeley in 1955. She has been Chief Psychologist at the Kaiser Foundation Hospital, San Francisco, and is currently Chief Psychologist in the Department of Psychiatry at the Mount Zion Hospital and Medical Center, San Francisco.